Dachshund Rules

Dachshund Rules

■ WILLOW CREEK PRESS®

Published by Willow Creek Press, Inc.
P.O. Box 147, Minocqua, Wisconsin 54548

Photo Credits:

p2 © La_Corivo/istockphoto.com; p5 © CSP_herreid/agefotostock.com; p8 © Yoshio Tomii/www.kimballstock.com; p11 © RainervonBrandis/istockphoto.com; p12 © Tierfotoagentur/R. Richter./agefotostock.com; p15 © Grzegorz Leraczyk/Lajam/500px; p16 © Anna-av/istockphoto.com; p19 © stanzi11/istockphoto.com; p20 © Mark Raycroft; p24 © Mark Raycroft /Minden Pictures/agefotostock.com; p27 © Anna Oksimowicz/agefotostock.com; p28 © mrPliskin/istockphoto.com; p 31 © TerryJ/istockphoto.com; p32 © J-L. Klein & M-L. Hubert/Naturagency; p35 © H. Schmidt-Roeger/agefotostock.com; p39 © Tierfotoagentur/Pfotenblitzer/agefotostock.com; p40 © Anna-av/istockphoto.com; © p44 Juniors Bildarchiv/agefotostock.com; p47 © J-L. Klein & M-L. Hubert/Naturagency; p48 © Mark Raycroft; p51 © H. Schmidt-Roeger/agefotostock.com; © p52 Roberto della vite/agefotostock.com; p55 © Leung Cho Pan/agefotostock.com; p59 © H. Schmidt-Roeger/agefotostock.com; p60 © ARCO/C. Steimer/agefotostock.com; p63 © J-L. Klein & M-L. Hubert/Naturagency; p64 © J-L. Klein & M-L. Hubert/Naturagency; p67 © Boyle & Boyle/Animals Animals/Earth Scenes; p68 © ARCO/C. Steimer/agefotostock.com; p71 © Gerard Lacz/agefotostock.com; p72 © ArtisticCaptures/istockphoto.com; p75 © Mark Raycroft /Minden Pictures/agefotostock.com; p79 © Mark Raycroft; p80 © Mark Raycroft; p88 © Mark Raycroft /Minden Pictures/agefotostock.com

Printed in China

DETERMiNaTioN

Perseverance, secret of all triumphs.

— *Victor Hugo*

I'm good enough, I'm smart enough,
and doggone it, people like me.

—*Stuart Smalley*

Success seems to be largely
a matter of hanging on
after others have let go.

– William Feather

What counts is not necessarily the size of the dog in the fight—it's the size of the fight in the dog.

—*General Dwight D. Eisenhower*

JoyFUL

All animals, except man, know that the principal business of life is to enjoy it.

—*Samuel Butler*

Contentment is natural wealth.

—*Socrates*

...joy delights in joy.

—*William Shakespeare*

Sometimes your joy is the source of your smile, but sometimes your smile can be the source of your joy.

—*Thich Nhat Hanh*

We know nothing of tomorrow; our business
is to be good and happy today.

—*Sydney Smith*

To get the full value of joy
you must have someone
to divide it with.

—*Mark Twain*

CLOWNISH

Dogs laugh, but they laugh with their tails.

—*Max Forrester Eastman*

The great pleasure of a dog is that you may make a fool of yourself with him and not only will he not scold you, but he will make a fool of himself too.

—*Samuel Butler*

Dogs don't mind being photographed
in compromising situations.

—*Elliott Erwitt*

Be weird. Be random. Be who you are. Because you never know who would love the person you hide.

—*C.S. Lewis*

PATIENT

To know how to wait is the great secret of success.

—*Joseph Marie de Maistre*

Patience is the art of hoping.

—*Luc de Clapiers*

Adopt the pace of nature:
her secret is patience.

—*Ralph Waldo Emerson*

Don't cross the bridge
'til you come to it.

—*Henry Wadsworth Longfellow*

DESIRE

The starting point of all achievement is desire.

—*Napoleon Hill*

The thirst of desire is never filled, nor fully satisfied.

—*Marcus Tullius Cicero*

Is it not strange that desire should so many years out live performance.

—*William Shakespeare*

Obstacles do not block the path,
they are the path.

—*Unknown*

iNTELLiGENT

The dog has an enviable mind. It remembers the nice things in life and quickly blots out the nasty.

—*Barbara Woodhouse*

Intellectuals solve problems. Geniuses prevent them.

—*Albert Einstein*

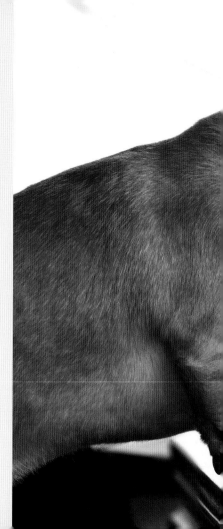

Intelligence is the ability
to adapt to change.

—*Stephen Hawking*

Weak people revenge. Strong people forgive.
Intelligent people ignore.

—Unknown

CURIOUS

A sense of curiosity is nature's
original school of education.

—*Smiley Blanton*

Millions saw the apple fall,
but Newton was the
one who asked why.

—*Bernard Baruch*

I have no special talents. I am
only passionately curious.

—*Albert Einstein*

Curiosity will conquer fear even
more than bravery will.

—*James Stephens*

Curiosity is the engine of achievement.

—*Ken Robinson*

The cure for boredom is curiosity.
There is no cure for curiosity.

—*Dorothy Parker*

HUMBLE

Whoever loves becomes humble.

—*Sigmund Freud*

The higher we are placed, the more humbly we should walk.

—*Marcus Tullius Cicero*

Believe in yourself! Have faith in your abilities! Without a humble but reasonable confidence in your own powers you cannot be successful or happy.

—*Norman Vincent Peale*

The biggest challenge after success
is shutting up about it.

—*Criss Jami*

Loyal

There is no faith which has never yet been broken,
except that of a truly faithful dog.

—Konrad Lorenz

Loyalty means nothing
unless it has at its heart
the absolute principle
of self-sacrifice.

—*Woodrow T. Wilson*

The only people I owe my loyalty to are those who never made me question theirs.

—*Unknown*

Respect is earned. Honesty is appreciated.
Love is gained and loyalty is returned.

—*Criss Jami*

affectionate

Always hold your head up, but be careful to keep your nose at a friendly level.

—*Max L. Forman*

Dogs love company. They place it first on their short list of needs.

—*J.R. Ackerley*

We are shaped and fashioned by what we love.

—*Johann Wolfgang von Goethe*

No act of kindness, no matter how small, is ever wasted.

—*Aesop*

Little friends may prove great friends.

—*Aesop*

Getting There & Away

To get to Piber from Graz, the most convenient option is to catch the **GKB** (www.gkb.at) morning bus at 8am from Graz Griesplatz, arriving in Piber at 9.15am (you have to change to a connecting bus at Voitsberg Hauptplatz). The last bus leaves Piber at 2.45pm. This only works weekdays. Frequent trains also go to Köflach, from where it's a 3.5km walk from Hauptplatz along Piberstrasse (follow the signs).

BÄRNBACH

☎ 03142 / pop 4900

Otherwise unremarkable, Bärnbach is famous for its St Barbara Kirche, a church designed by Friedensreich Hundertwasser. The town is also a centre for exquisite glass-making, and has an interesting factory tour on the theme.

Tourist information is available from the glass-making centre and **Bärnbach Information** (☎ 615 50; tourismus@baernbach.at; ⊙ 8am-noon Mon-Fri & 2-4pm Mon, Tue & Thu) inside the town hall. The church and glass centre are an equal distance west and east respectively from the Hauptplatz.

Sights

Although built after WWII, **St Barbara Kirche** (☎ 625 81; Piberstrasse; admission free, tours adult/child €2/1; ⊙ dawn-dusk) needed renovating in the late 1980s. About 80% of the town population voted to commission the maverick Viennese artist Friedensreich Hundertwasser (p53) to undertake the redesign; work began in 1987 and was completed in 1988. This was a bold move: Hundertwasser was known for his unusual design concepts, particularly his designs based on a spiritual ecology. The gamble paid off; the church is a visual treat. Leave a donation and pick up the explanation card in English, which reveals the symbolic meaning behind the architectural design features. Tours are run by appointment only.

The church is surrounded by 12 gates, each representing a different faith, and all connected by an uneven pathway. By the west façade is a powerful mosaic war memorial by Franz Weiss. The distinctive church steeple is topped by a gold onion dome. Features you wouldn't see in any other church include the bowed roof with green splodges along its flanks, the irregular windows, and the grass growing on the side porch roofs.

The interior mostly retains its original features, although Hundertwasser's 'spiral of life' window (which reflects the afternoon sun onto the font), on the left as you enter, is striking. Also note the glass altar and podium filled with 12 layers of different types of earth representing the 12 tribes of Israel, created by Erwin Talker.

Bärnbach, a glass-making centre for three centuries, is home to the **Stölzle Glas Center** (☎ 629 50; www.stoelzle.com; Hochtregisterstrasse 1; adult/child & concession/family €5.50/3/13; ⊙ 9am-5pm Mon-Fri, to 1pm Sat Mar-Dec), a working glass-blowing factory and museum. Try to get there in the morning, as the entrance fee includes a guided tour (leaving 9am, 10am, 11am and noon Monday to Thursday, 9am, 10am and 11am Friday) of the glass-making facilities and the small museum filled with delicate pieces. In the afternoon the factory is off-limits.

Sleeping & Eating

Bärnbach is an easy day trip from Graz, and not a particularly exciting place at night, so you're better off returning to Graz. If you do stay, the only central hotel is **Gasthof Decelak** (☎ 622 85; Voitsberger Strasse 38; s/d €25/50; **P**). Three kilometres out of town, **Sporthotel Glockenhof** (☎ 623 34; www.glockenhof.at; s €43-53, d €86-106; **P** **⊛**) has full fitness/wellness amenities, including massages and its own tennis courts, but you need your own wheels to get there. For a bite to eat, there are a couple of cheap eateries near the church, including **Pizzera Casa Verona** (☎ 61 5 65; Hauptplatz 1; pizzas €5-10; ⊙ 10am-midnight).

Getting There & Away

Regular trains run from Graz (€6.60, 50 minutes) but the train station is 2km south of the town centre; a bike is useful here. Cross the railway line, follow the road around until you reach the main highway and then take this right. The train station has a toilet and a coin phone if you need a **taxi** (☎ 0664-3402247) to the centre of town (€5). Bundesgestüt Piber (Piber Stud Farm) is close to Bärnbach (€4 by taxi); from the church, head west on Piberstrasse for 2km and after about 30 minutes you'll reach it.

SOUTHERN STYRIA

Southern Styria is known as *Steirische Toskana* (Styrian Tuscany), and for good reason. Not only is this wine country, but the landscape is reminiscent of Chianti; gentle rolling hills cultivated with vineyards or patchwork farmland, and capped by clusters of trees. It's also famous for *Kürbiskernöl*, the rich pumpkin-seed oil generously used in Styrian cooking.

Region Süd und West Steiermark (☎ 03462-43152; www.sws.st, in German; Hauptplatz 34, in Deutschlandsberg) handles telephone, email and postal enquiries for western and southern Styria.

STYRIAN WEINSTRASSEN

Picturesque **Weinstrassen** (wine routes; www .steirischerwein.at) crisscross much of southern Styria, and lead into East Styria. The *Steirische Weinführer* booklet, free from the Graz tourist office (p223), is a comprehensive guide to all eight trails, providing a map and a list of *Buschenschänken* (wine taverns) and vineyards along the way. You'll need your own wheels to explore these properly, though.

The most travelled wine route is the **Schilcher-Wienstrasse**, which runs north–south from Ligist to Eibiswald, passing through the Stainz and Deutschlandsberg. The wine of choice here is Schilcher, a light, dry rosé. Other popular wine roads include the **Klöcher Wienstrasse**, stretching from Fehring to Bad Radkersburg (try the *Gewürztraminer*, a dry white wine typical of the region), the **Südsteirische Wienstrasse**, looping its way from Ehrenhausen to Spielfeld near the Slovenian border, and the **Sausaler Weinstrasse**, which runs west from Leibnitz to Gleinstätten.

DEUTSCHLANDSBERG
☎ 03462 / pop 8000

In the heart of the Schilcher wine region, Deutschlandsberg is a bustling little town dominated by a well-restored castle, some 25 minutes' walk uphill from the town centre. Inside the castle is a **museum** (☎ 56 02; www .burgmuseum.at, in German; Burgplatz 2; adult/student/child €9/8/4; ☾ 10am-7pm Mar–mid-Nov) split into four parts: ancient history, the Celts, historical weapons and antique jewellery. The extensive collection, whose highlights include a delicate gold necklace from the 5th century BC, takes about 1½ hours to see. As with any good castle, there's a torture chamber in the underground vaults.

The **tourist office** (☎ 75 20; www.schilcherheimat .at, in German; Hauptplatz 34; ☾ 9am-noon & 3-6pm Mon-Fri, to noon Sat Mar-Oct, to 3pm Mon-Fri, to 1pm Sat Nov-Jan) is a good source of information on the town and environs.

For sleeping arrangements, look no further than the **Burg Hotel** (☎ 56 56-0; www.burghotel-dl.at, in German; Burgplatz 1; s €47-75, d €94-150, ste €180-310; mains €10-20; P), which is located in the castle. Its crowning glory is the tower suite, with champagne and a fruit basket; rooms are large, quiet and have views of the woods.

If Burg is too pricey then the **HI Hostel** (☎ 22000; deutschlandsberg@jfgh.at; Burg 5; s/d €37/30) is a good option. It's set in a vineyard at the foot of the castle.

Frequent trains connect Graz and Deutschlandsberg (€8.30, one hour).

GROSSKLEIN

Southern Styria was once a stamping ground of the Celts, and this legacy has gradually been unearthed by archaeologists. Some of their finds are housed in the four exhibition rooms of the **Hallstattzeitliches Museum** (Hallstatt Period Museum; ☎ 03456-50 38; www.archaeo-grossklein.com; adult/child & student €4/2; ☾ 10am-noon & 2-5pm Wed-Sun May-Oct) in the small town of Grossklein, 26km southeast of Deutschlandsberg. Most of the exhibits are from the nearby grave mounds and include coins, pottery and tools, and a copy of a bronze mask dating from 600 BC (the original is housed in Schloss Eggenberg in Graz; see p226). The museum has a children's playroom where you can leave the kids. If this fails to get the adrenalin pumping, then a 9km archaeology trail heading northwest from the town towards Kleinklein should – it takes in approximately 700 Celtic grave mounds.

Buses (€3.40, 25 minutes) connect Leibnitz and Grossklein every one to two hours weekdays; a few run on Saturday and virtually none on Sunday. Weekdays, a train-bus connection from Graz via Leibnitz works well (€11.10, 1¼ hours).

EHRENHAUSEN
☎ 03453 / pop 1200

The picturesque town of Ehrenhausen, near the A9 that connects Graz with the Slovenian border, makes a fine base for exploring the vineyards of southern Styria.

The town is little more than one street of pastel-coloured houses dominated by the baroque **Pfarrkirche** (Hauptplatz; admission free; ☾ dawn-dusk). Before setting off for the wine country, follow the path (three minutes' walk) on the right of the Rathaus up to the **mausoleum** (admission free) of Ruprecht von Eggenberg (1546–1611), hero of the Battle

---

HUNDERTWASSER SPA

East Styria is well known throughout Austria for its thermal activity, and in particular the spa centres that have sprung up around its thermal springs. Fans of the architectural style of Friedensreich Hundertwasser won't want to miss the unusual spa **Rogner-Bad Blumau** (☎ 03383-51 00-0; www.blumau.com; s €139-149, d €218-298), near the town of Bad Blumau, 50km east of Graz. The spa has all the characteristics of his art, including uneven floors, grass on the roof, colourful ceramics and golden spires. Overnight accommodation includes entry to the spa.

---

of Sisak against the Turks. Towering above Hauptplatz, this white and yellow building is guarded by two Roman-like bruisers who seem to be suggesting you don't mess with the baroque. And sure enough, the stucco inside is starkly white, with plenty of baroque embellishments clinging to the central dome, and stucco vines swirling around supporting pillars. The mausoleum is normally locked; get the key from the **manse** (Pfarrhof; ☎ 2633) next to the Pfarrkirche. Schloss Ehrenhausen, a little further up the hill from the mausoleum, is closed to the public.

Sleeping & Eating

If you're in town and looking for a private room, the best thing to do is ask around in the shops. **Zur Goldenen Krone** (☎ 26 40; Hauptplatz 24; s/d €45/58; closed Thu; P) is one hotel with doubles that's good value, and **Die Burg zum Goldenen Löwen** (☎ 204 15; Hauptplatz 28; s/d €40/80; mains €7-17; P) is just a few doors along and slightly more upmarket. It also has a popular restaurant with courtyard seating. **Klapotetz Weinlokal** (☎ 2977; Hauptstrasse 51; 2-person apt €60, 4-person apt €80) has a couple of apartments you can rent for one or more nights.

Hauptplatz has a bank and shops for provisions. For wine, head to **Erzherzog Johann Vinothek** (☎ 0699-100 64 654; Hauptstrasse 34; 7.30am-noon & 1.30-5pm Mon-Fri, 11am-6pm Sat, 11am-3pm Sun Apr-Dec).

Getting There & Away

Trains run from Graz to Ehrenhausen every couple of hours (€9.30, 45 minutes). The train station is about four minutes' walk east of Hauptplatz.

RIEGERSBURG

☎ 03153 / pop 2560

Located 50km southeast of Graz at Riegersburg and perched on a 200m-high rocky outcrop, **Schloss Riegersburg** (☎ 821 31; riegersburg.com; adult/child & student/family €9.50/7/25; 10am-5pm Apr & Oct, 9am-5pm May-Sep) is a hugely impressive 13th-century castle built against invading Hungarians and Turks; today it houses a **Hexenmuseum** on witchcraft and the **Burgmuseum** featuring the history of the Liechtenstein family, who acquired it in 1822. A **war memorial** is a reminder of fierce fighting in 1945, when Germans occupying the castle were attacked by Russian troops.

A cable car on the north side whisks you up in 90 seconds (one-way €2).

For more information on the Schloss or activities, contact the **tourist office** (☎ 86 70; tourismus@riegersburg.com; Riegersburg 4).

If you have your own transport, consider stopping in at **Schloss Kapfenstein** (☎ 03157-300 30-0; www.schloss-kapfenstein.at; Kapfenstein 1; s €91-113, d €122-196; mains €13-18; P), a hotel-restaurant 17km south of Riegersburg. Weekdays rooms cost significantly less and can be booked for one night or more, but on weekends only Friday to Sunday packages are possible. The restaurant serves delightful Styrian cuisine in its outer courtyard overlooking the valley; a four-course meal as half-board costs €30.

Getting There & Away

Frequent trains run from Graz to nearby Feldbach and from there five weekday buses head for Riegersburg (€1.70, 20 minutes).

NORTHERN STYRIA

Heading north from Graz the landscape of Styria begins to change; gentle hills and flat pastures are replaced by jagged mountains, virgin forests, deep valleys and cold, clear mountain streams. This is also the region's industrial heartland, home to the *Steirische Eisenstrasse* (Styrian Iron Road), where for centuries iron mining was the backbone of the economy and in places, such as Eisenerz, left the landscape scarred.

Huddled beneath the soaring peaks are the towns of northern Styria, home to impressive churches; the best are the pilgrimage church of Mariazell and the abbey of Admont.

MARIAZELL
☎ 03882 / pop 1720

Situated on the slopes of the lower reaches of the eastern Alps, the pretty town of Mariazell is one of Austria's icons. It offers opportunities for hiking, mountain biking and skiing, but what makes Mariazell so well known is its status as Austria's most important pilgrimage site. Its basilica, founded in 1157, holds a sacred statue of the Virgin, and busloads of Austrians flock to the site on weekends and on 15 August (Assumption) and 8 September (Mary's 'name day').

Orientation

Hauptplatz and the basilica comprise the centre of Mariazell. The train station is in St Sebastian, 1km north of Hauptplatz.

Information

Mariazell's **tourist office** (☎ 23 66; www.mariazell .at; Hauptplatz 13; ⏰ 9am-5.30pm Mon-Fri, to 4pm Sat, to 12.30pm Sun May-Oct, to 5pm Mon-Fri Nov-Apr) has a town map-cum-brochure with walking trails marked; it doesn't book rooms but can help with accommodation listings.

The **post office** (Ludwig Leber Strasse; 7am-6pm Mon-Fri, 8.30-10am Sat) is located just west of Hauptplatz next to the bus station. **Hotel Magnus Klause** (☎ 417 67; Hauptplatz 7) has free internet access if you buy a drink. There are a few ATMs around town.

Sights

Most people come to Mariazell to visit the **Basilika** (☎ 25 95; Kardinal Eugen Tisserant Platz 1; admission free; ⏰ 8am-8pm), the town's most important attraction. Originally Romanesque, the basilica underwent a Gothic conversion in the 14th century and then received a massive baroque facelift in the 17th century. The result from the outside is a strange clash of styles, with the original Gothic steeple bursting like a wayward skeletal limb from between two baroque onion domes. The interior works better, with Gothic ribs on the ceiling combining well with baroque frescoes and lavish stuccowork. Both Johann Bernhard Fischer von Erlach and his son Josef Emmanuel had a hand in the baroque features; the crucifixion group sculpture (1715) on the high altar is by Lorenzo Mattielli.

Unusually, the church is centred on a small but exquisite chapel, known as the **Gnadenkapelle** (Chapel of Grace). This gold and silver edifice houses the Romanesque statue of the Madonna, whose healing powers reputedly helped King Louis of Hungary defeat the Turks in 1377. In the upper galleries, the **Schatzkammer** (treasury; ☎ 25 95; Kardinal Eugen Tisserant Platz 1; adult/student/child €3/1.50/0.50; ⏰ 10am-3pm Tue-Sat, 11am-4pm Sun & holidays May-Oct) contains votive offerings spanning six centuries, mainly naive-style paintings.

Activities

Another aspect to Mariazell is its rolling countryside. **Bürgeralpe** (1270m) is a great starting or finishing point for hiking and mountain biking in the summer months, and also has skiing in winter. The **cable car** (☎ 2508; www .mariazell-buergeralpe.at; adult/child return €10.80/6.80) operates year-round. Another way to get there is by mountain bike along one of the trails. **Dellinger** (☎ 2453; www.sport-dellinger.at; Wiener Strasse 30), alongside the cable car, hires out and services ski equipment in winter, and rents mountain bikes in summer (€15 per day). Pick up the tourist office's good hiking/city map (two major mountain bike trails are marked) and ask Dellinger to point you in the right direction for trail heads leading south or to Bürgeralpe.

Bürgeralpe has an artificial lake that feeds snow canons when snow conditions are poor and is used as a lakeside setting for special events. Also up here are two restaurants and the **Freizeitpark** (Erlebniswelt Holzknechtland; entry & cable car adult/child €13.60/8; ⏰ 9am-5pm May-Oct) – a small museum devoted to wood and all its wonderful uses. During winter, adult daily/weekly ski passes cost around €25/123.

The **Erlaufsee**, a small lake a few kilometres to the northwest of the town, reaches about 22 degrees in summer and, apart from swimming, it offers good opportunities for windsurfing and scuba diving; contact addresses for water sports are listed in the booklet *Mariazellerland von A-Z*, available at the tourist office.

An easy four-hour Rundwanderweg (circuit trail; A) runs past the lake and south through forest back into Mariazell; alternatively, you can take a steam **Museumstramway** (one-way/return €5/8), which runs at weekends and holidays between July and September. It leaves from the Museumstramway Bahnhof.

A cultural centre with a wellness complex, known as the **Europeum** and planned to showcase one EU country and its culture each year, is currently being built off Wiener Strasse.

STYRIA

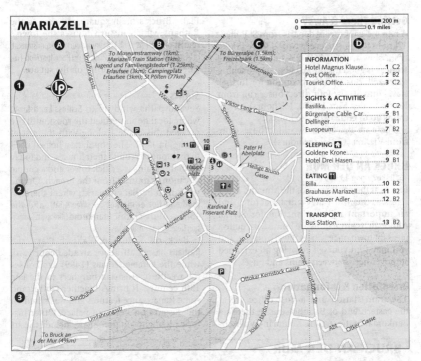

MARIAZELL

INFORMATION
Hotel Magnus Klause............1 C2
Post Office..............................2 B2
Tourist Office.........................3 C2

SIGHTS & ACTIVITIES
Basilika.................................4 C2
Bürgeralpe Cable Car............5 B1
Dellinger...............................6 B1
Europeum..............................7 B2

SLEEPING
Goldene Krone......................8 B2
Hotel Drei Hasen...................9 B1

EATING
Billa....................................10 B2
Brauhaus Mariazell..............11 B2
Schwarzer Adler...................12 B2

TRANSPORT
Bus Station..........................13 B2

Sleeping

The only problem times for finding a room in Mariazell are around the pilgrim days. Aside from hotels and pensions, there is a smattering of private rooms.

Campingplatz Erlaufsee (☎ 49 37; www.st-sebastian .steiermark.at; campsite per adult/tent €4/3; ☼ May–mid-Sep; P) At the southeastern end of Erlaufsee, this small camping ground has a pretty location and is flanked by pine trees.

Jugend und Familiengästedorf (☎ 26 69; stsebas tian@jfgh.at; Erlaufseestrasse 49; s/d €26.50/59; P ⌨) Located halfway between Mariazell and Erlaufsee, this HI hostel is quite new and has loads of facilities, including a café, sauna, solarium, fitness room and sports areas.

Goldene Krone (☎ 2583; www.mariazell.at/krone, in German; Grazer Strasse 1; s €34-68, d €68-76; mains €8-13) Goldene Krone has a homely feel in its big and bright rooms. The ground floor has an excellent restaurant, with traditional Austrian cuisine, toys for the kids and street-side seating.

Hotel Drei Hasen (☎ 2410; www.dreihasen.at; Wiener Strasse 11; s €67, d €108, ste €160; mains €7-14; closed Mar & Nov; P) When the new Europeum is finished a passage will connect this hotel with the wellness facilities, adding another plus to what is currently a very good hotel with a first-class restaurant (specialising in seasonal game dishes).

Eating & Drinking

Among the hotel eating options, Hotel Drei Hasen is the most interesting and varied; there are also plenty of places to eat on and around Hauptplatz.

Schwarzer Adler (☎ 28 63-0; Hauptplatz 1; mains €7-15; ☼ 9am-11pm) With an outside terrace that overlooks the basilica, the Schwarzer Adler serves very decent classics at one of the best locations in the town centre.

Brauhaus Mariazell (☎ 25 23-0; Wiener Strasse 5; r from €57 per person, ste €104 per person, mains €8-15; ☼ 10am-11pm Mon-Wed, to midnight Fri & Sat, lunch Sun) This lovely, rustic microbrewery does one light and one dark beer, both unfiltered (with a shelf life of four weeks); the food is also some of the best Styrian cuisine in these parts and there's a garden out back and a few rooms upstairs.

You'll find a Billa supermarket just north of the tourist office.

STYRIA

Getting There & Away

A narrow-gauge train departs from St Pölten, 77km to the north, every two to three hours. It's a slow trip (€14.50, 2½ hours), but the scenery is good for the last hour approaching Mariazell. Bus is the only option for further travel into Styria; four direct buses run from Bruck an der Mur (€9.50, 1½ hours), where trains go to Graz (€20, 2½ hours).

There are also one to two direct buses daily from Vienna (€18, three hours).

BRUCK AN DER MUR
☎ 03862 / pop 13,430

Bruck, at the confluence of the Mur and Mürz rivers, is the Mur valley's first real town and an important railway junction for Styria. Although its attractions are limited, it's quite a pleasant town once you let it work on you, and you may find yourself enjoying an extended stopover here between trains and buses.

Orientation & Information

The train station and a post office are at the eastern end of Bahnhofstrasse; there's a Bankomat in the station. Koloman-Wallisch-Platz, Bruck's main square, is home to the Rathaus, which in turn houses the town's **tourist office** (☎ 890-121; www.bruckmur-tourismus.at, in German; Koloman-Wallisch-Platz 1; ☼ 9am-4pm Mon-Fri). There's another post office on the square.

Sights

Several paths wind up to **Schloss Landskron**, where local nobility ruled the roost until fire ravaged this castle – along with the rest of town – in 1792. The population helped itself to the stone to rebuild their houses, and today all that remains is a clock tower and a couple of canons captured from the French. On the way, drop by Bauernmarkt, where there's a **food and flower market** (☼ Wed & Sat), and the 15th-century Gothic **Pfarrkirche** (Kirchplatz; admission free; ☼ dawn-dusk).

Back on Koloman-Wallisch-Platz, the **Rathaus** has an attractive arcaded courtyard, while the **Kornmesserhaus** (1499) symbolises the wealth of Austrian burghers in the late 15th century. It brings together Gothic and some Renaissance features and was based on the design of a Venetian palace. Other historic highlights on the square include the **Art**

BRUCK AN DER MUR

0 — 200 m
0 — 0.1 miles

INFORMATION	
Post Office	1 A2
Post Office	(see 12)
Tourist Office	2 A2

SIGHTS & ACTIVITIES	
Art Nouveau Façade	3 A2
Kornmesserhaus	4 A2
Pfarrkirche	5 A1
Rathaus	(see 2)
Schloss Landskron	6 B1
Wrought-Iron Well	7 A2

SLEEPING	
Landskron	8 A2

EATING	
Billa	9 A1
Fleck's Brauhaus	10 B2
Gasthof Zur Post Riegler	11 A2

TRANSPORT	
Postbus Departures	12 C1

STYRIA

Nouveau façade above the ice cream shop at No 10 and the fine Renaissance-style **wrought-iron well** created by Hans Prasser in 1626.

Sleeping & Eating

Jugend und Familiengästedorf (☎ 584 48; www.jfgh .at/bruck.php; Stadtwaldstrasse 1; dm/s/d €27/37/59; P 💻) This family-friendly HI hostel, 10 minutes' walk south of the centre, is in the heart of Weitental, Bruck's woodland playground.

Landskron (☎ 58 458; www.hotel-landskron.at, in German; Am Schiffertor 3; s/d €73/98, ste per person €65; P 💻) Value is best on weekends in this business hotel directly on the Mur River. Here you can loll about in large, tastefully furnished rooms, and in some you can even hear the river gurgling below the window. It has a sauna and good midrange restaurant.

Fleck's Brauhaus (☎ 520 85; Am Grazer Tor; snacks €3-8; 11am-midnight Tue-Sat, to 6pm Sun) This boutique brewery is Bruck's prime spot for a light meal washed down by a local brew. Three house styles are on offer, including a dark wheat beer and a *Rot* (red) with barley.

Gasthof Zur Post Riegler (☎ 549 04; Koloman-Wallisch-Platz 11; mains €7-17; 9am-midnight Tue-Sun) There's something for everyone among the mixed bag of culinary offerings here, not least a well-prepared classic schnitzel.

Billa (Herzog Ernstgasse 6) is the place to stock up on provisions.

Getting There & Away

Bruck is the region's main rail hub; all fast trains to Graz (€11, 45 minutes, hourly) pass through here. Other direct trains go hourly to Klagenfurt (€25, 2¼ hours) and hourly to Vienna's Südbahnhof (€23, two hours).

By road, the main autobahns intersect southeast of town. If you're planning to cycle in the region, the tourist office has useful maps.

Postbus services arrive and depart next to the train station.

LEOBEN

☎ 03842 / pop 25,800

Leoben is another of those unprepossessing towns that reveal a few surprises once you dig down into its modest urban soul. A revamped museum quarter is one very good reason to prolong a flying visit here between trains. Leoben is also a centre for metallurgical industries and home to Gösser beer, and achieved ultimate fame with the peace treaty signed here in 1797 by Napoleon and Emperor Franz II.

Stadt Information Leoben (☎ 440 18; www .leoben.at; Hauptplatz 12; 7am-5pm Mon, 7am-6.30pm Tue-Thu, 7am-1pm & 3-6.30pm Fri, 9am-12.30pm Sat) has a *Gast in Leoben* booklet with useful listings; if you're in town when it's closed, ask at the MuseumsCenter Leoben – they keep a good supply of city material. The city's Leoben map also includes a great environs map with hiking trails.

A second **Tourismusverband Leoben** (☎ 481 48; Peter Tunner-Strasse 2; 9am-5pm Mon-Fri) has information and organises tours for Leoben's Stiftkirche, with a 1000-year-old crypt and paintings in its chapel, and the nearby Göss brewery.

Sights & Activities

Hauptplatz is lined with elegant 17th-century façades, including the baroque **Hacklhaus** (Hauptplatz 9), while Leoben's connection with the iron industry is seen in the curious town motif displayed on the **Altes Rathaus** (Hauptplatz 1) façade, which shows an ostrich eating horseshoes.

Nearby, the dreary exterior of **Pfarrkirche St Xaver** (☎ 432 36; Kirchplatz 1; 8am-7pm) belies an interesting interior of white walls and black-and-gold baroque altars. The church's **Museum Sacrum** (10am-5pm) is linked by a walkway to the **MuseumsCenter Leoben** (☎ 4062-408; Kirchgasse 6; 9am-6pm Tue-Fri) which is the cultural heart of Leoben. This new museum complex has an interesting *Schienen der Vergangenheit* (Tracks of the Past) section telling the history of Leoben and its industries, starting with the present and working back in time, and a large section with changing exhibitions. The standard is very high, so check the town's website for information on current exhibitions.

For tours of the **Stiftskirche** and the **brewery**, ask at the Tourismusverband Leoben.

Sleeping & Eating

Among the hotels in the centre, **Pension Jahrbacher** (☎ 436 00; jahrbacher.gmbh@gmx.at; Kirchgasse 14; s/d €43/85) is one pleasant option. If no one answers the door bell, drop into the adjacent **Cafe am Schwammerlturm** (☎ 43 600; Homanngasse 11; 11am-8pm) and check in there. This tiny café is a visual treat – it has wonderful outdoor seating on top of the circular city tower and breathtaking views over the town and countryside. The stairs are not

STYRIA

for the faint-hearted, but it has a (glass) lift. Spectacular for its arcades, the **Arkadenhof** (☎ 42 074; Hauptplatz; mains €6-17; ☑ 10am-11pm), is a good choice for a full traditional meal.

Getting There & Away

Leoben is 16km west of Bruck (€4.40, 15 minutes) and is on the main rail route from there to Klagenfurt or Linz. The town centre is 10 minutes' walk from Leoben *Hauptbahnhof*: cross the Mur River and bear right.

EISENERZ
☎ 03848 / pop 6430

Eisenerz is one of the important stops along the **Steirische Eisenstrasse** (Styrian Iron Road), and lies at the foot of the extraordinary Erzberg (Iron Mountain), a mine that chomps into the mountains. While the town has certainly seen better days, it's still a fine place to stop by, with narrow, cobblestone streets, solid houses and the gurgle of alpine streams combining to create a relaxed mood.

The **tourist office** (☎ 37 00; www.eisenerz-heute.at, in German; Dr Thedor Körner Platz 1; ☑ 9am-noon & 3-5pm Mon-Fri May-Oct, to noon Sat Jun-Sep, 10am-noon & 3-5pm Mon-Fri Nov-Apr) is in the centre of the town.

Sights

The main reason to come to Eisenerz is **Erzberg** (☎ 32 00; info@abenteuer-erzberg.at; Erzberg 1; separate tour adult/child & student €13/6.50, combined tour adult/student/child €22/19/11; ☑ tours 10am-3pm May-Oct, advance booking required), a peak that has been completely denuded by opencast stope mining and now resembles a step pyramid. The outcome is eerie and surprisingly beautiful, with its orange and purple shades contrasting with the lush greenery and grey crags of surrounding mountains. The ironworks can be seen up-close and personal in two ways; with a 90-minute 'Schaubergwerk' tour which burrows into the mountain to the underground mines, abandoned in 1986, or with a 60-minute 'Hauly Abenteuerfahrt' tour, which explores the surface works aboard an enormous truck, with fine views along the way. Both tours are usually in German, with English-language notes available. The departure point is a 10-minute walk from the centre, following the course of the river.

A walk around the sleepy old town reveals some interesting sgraffito murals, especially around Bergmannsplatz. Also interesting is to stroll up to the **Wehrkirche St Oswald** (☎ 22 67;

Kirchenstiege 4; admission free; ☑ 9am-7pm summer, to 5pm winter), more a fortress than a Gothic church, which gained its heavy walls in 1532 as protection against the Turks. The town is surrounded by **hiking trails**. The tourist office has a free *city & environs* map with trails marked, including to the idyllic **Leopoldsteiner See**, only 3km north on the road towards Admont. This small lake has a wall of granite rising to 1649m as a backdrop; you can hire boats in summer – it's a very chilly swim, though.

Sleeping & Eating

There are several good pensions and hotels in the old town, but fewer good eating options.

Jugend & Familiengästehaus (☎ 605 60; eisenerz@jfgh.at; Ramsau 1; s/d €25.50/51; **P** 💻) This lovely HI hostel is 5km south of Eisenerz; it's situated at an altitude of 1000m and has a sauna, and indoor and outdoor climbing walls. Each room has its own bathroom and there's a restaurant on site.

Gästehaus Tegelhofer (☎ 20 86; www.gaestehaus-tegelhofer.at; Lindmoserstrasse 8; s/d €29/48; **P**) This modern guesthouse is comfortable and offers great value, with spacious and clean rooms spiced with a free sauna and fitness room; there's also an inexpensive apartment for two to six people.

Gästehaus Weninger (☎ 22 580; www.gaestehaus-weninger.at; Krumpentalerstrasse 8; s €33-38, d €54-62; **P**) Another very comfortable guesthouse with fitness room and sauna, Weninger aims at those staying for a few days, but does take guests for one night at very short notice.

Bräustüberl (☎ 23 35; Flutergasse 5; mains €5-12; **P** ; ☑ lunch & dinner Tue-Sat, lunch Sun) Bräustüberl has the local classics and a filling grill platter that's best enjoyed in the beer garden. Rooms are available (single/double €24/32).

If the tourist office is closed when you visit, consider a coffee and cake at **Barbarastub'n** (☎ 51 10; Bergmannplatz 2; €1.50-2.60; ☑ 8.30am-7pm Mon-Sat, 2-6pm Sun), which has some brochures and maps of town.

Getting There & Away

Direct buses run from Leoben to Eisenerz (€6.50, one hour) every two to three hours. Several daily connect Eisenerz and Hieflau (€3.40, 25 minutes), where there are train connections to Selzthal (€7.60, 40 minutes) via Admont and Nationalpark Gesäuse (opposite).

Trains no longer operate to Eisenerz, except for the special Vordernberg–Eisenerz **Nostalgie** (nostalgic train; ☎ 03849-832; www.erzbergbahn.at, in German; adult/child/family €9/4.50/22.50), which runs at 10.30am and 2.30pm Sunday from July to mid-October.

NATIONALPARK GESÄUSE

Only established in 2003, Gesäuse is Austria's newest national park in a pristine region of jagged mountain ridges, rock towers, deep valleys, alpine pastures and dense spruce forests. Unusually for a protected landscape, traditional farming is still allowed on selected meadows.

Dividing the park in two uneven halves is the Enns, a fast-flowing alpine river that eventually spills into the Danube near Mauthausen in Upper Austria. It's a favourite of rafting connoisseurs, and a number of companies offer rafting trips during the summer months. Hiking and mountain climbing, and to a lesser extent mountain biking, also feature among the park's outdoor activities; of the six peaks over 2000m within the park, **Hocktor** (2369m) rises above them all and is the destination of many hikers. The occasional spelunking excursion is also available; around 150 caves burrow under the high limestone mountains, the deepest of which descends 600m below the surface.

More information on activities in the park can be found at the **Nationalpark Gesäuse Information Centre** (☎ 03613-21 000; www.nationalpark .co.at, in German; Weng 2, Weng im Gesäuse; ⏰ 8am-noon & 1-4pm Mon-Fri). The staffed **national park pavilion** (☎ 03611-21101-20; Gstatterboden 25; ⏰ 10am-6pm May-Oct) is a useful source of information, and the park itself is best reached with one to six trains daily to Gstatterboden (€6, 30 minutes) and Johnsbach im Nationalpark (€6, 30 minutes).

ADMONT
☎ 03613 / pop 2770

In a country where the sugary grandeur of baroque abbeys reaches queasy heights, Admont's **Benedictine Abbey** (☎ 23 12-601; www.stiftadmont.at; Admont 1; adult/student & child €9/5; ⏰ 10am-5pm Apr-Oct, by arrangement Nov-Mar) pips St Florian's Augustinian Abbey at the post for the title of Austria's most elegant. It brings together museums, religious art, contemporary art and baroque architecture in a delightful whole – which is why a few years back it won an award for Austria's best museum.

The centrepiece of the abbey is its **Stiftsbibliothek** (abbey library), the largest abbey library in the world. Survivor of a fire in 1865 that severely damaged the rest of the abbey, it displays about 70,000 volumes of the abbey's 200,000 strong collection, and is decorated with heavenly ceiling frescoes by Bartolomeo Altomonte (1694–1783) and statues (in wood, but painted to look like bronze) by Josef Stammel (1695–1765). The restorers have been busily at work on the library lately and in 2008 will complete the work.

The abbey is also home to the **Kunsthistorisches Museum** (Art History Museum), featuring some unusual and rare pieces, such as its tiny portable altar from 1375, made from amethyst quartz and edged with gilt-silver plates, some Gerhard Mercator globes from 1541 and 1551, and a Festival Monstrance from 1747 set with 2175 gems. An innovative **multimedia show** retells the story of St Benedict and the abbey through video, slides and a spacey mirror room whose effect is similar to Dr Who's Tardis.

Another museum, the **Museum für Gegenwartkunst** (Museum for Contemporary Art) contains works by about 100 mainly Austrian artists, and has a section for the vision-impaired, with works you can explore with your hands. The **Naturhistorisches Museum** (Natural History Museum) began in 1674 with a small collection and today includes rooms devoted to flying bugs (one of the largest collections in the world), butterflies, stuffed animals, wax fruits (bizarrely) and reptiles. From the glass stairway and **Herb Garden** there are views to the Gesäuse National Park.

The **tourist office** (☎ 21 160; www.xeis.at, in German; Hauptstrasse 35; ⏰ 8am-6pm Mon-Fri, 10am-4pm Sat & Sun May-Oct, 8am-5pm Mon-Fri Nov-Apr) is opposite the Rathaus and near the abbey church. It doubles as a national park office.

The HI hostel **Admont-Jugendgästehaus** (☎ 2432; admont@jfgh.at; Schulstrasse 446; s €32.50, d €51) is situated on the edge of town, a few minutes' walk from the centre. The stunning **Jugend & Familiengästehaus Schloss Röthelstein** (☎ 26 196; roethelstein@jfgh.at; Aigen 32; s/d €44/64) is where the monks from the abbey used to stay in summer.

Admont has several central guesthouses, some with restaurants. **Hotel Gasthof Traube** (☎ 24 40; www.hotel-traube.info; Hauptstrasse 3; s €38-42, d €62-68; **P**) is a comfortable one with outdoor seating.

Admont is 15km to the east of Selzthal, on the train route to Hieflau; three or more direct trains (€4.40, 15 minutes) run daily.

WEST STYRIA

Like northern Styria, west Styria is a mountainous region divided by jagged ranges and alpine streams which gather speed and volume as they head east. It's an area for enjoying Austria's natural splendour and escaping crowds.

Murau, high up in the Mur valley, is a picturesque town well placed for hikes and cycle trips into the surrounding forests. If you're heading this way from Graz, consider a detour to **Seckau** or **Oberzeiring**. The former is famous for its **Benedictine Abbey** (☎ 03514-52 34; Seckau 1; basilica admission free; tours adult/child/family €4.50/free/10; ☉ 10am-8pm May-Oct, tours 10am & 2pm May-Oct), a stunning Romanesque basilica and mausoleum of Karl II, while the latter is known for its old **silver mine** (☎ 03571-23 87; www.silbergruben.at; adult/child/family €6/3.50/12; ☉ tours 9.45am, 1.45pm & 3pm May-Oct, 4pm Wed Nov-Apr), now resurrected as a small health resort for sufferers of respiratory diseases.

MURAU
☎ 03532 / pop 2330

Murau, in the western reaches of the Mur valley, is an attractive town filled with pastel-coloured houses and surrounded by forested hills and alpine meadows. Its close proximity to Stolzalpe to the north and Metnitzer mountains to the south makes it an excellent base for hiking and cycling during the summer months.

The **tourist office** (☎ 27 20-0; www.stadtmurau.at; Bundesstrasse 13a; ☉ 8.30am-6pm Mon-Fri, telephone information service ☉ 8am-9pm) has loads of brochures on the town and its surrounds, including hiking trails and bicycle ways.

The Liechtenstein family once dominated the region and they built **Schloss Obermurau** (☎ 230 258; Schlossberg 1; tours adult/child €3/2; ☉ 3pm Wed & Fri mid-Jun–mid-Sep) in 1250. Given a Renaissance makeover by the Schwarzenberg family in the 17th century, today it's often used as a film location.

Just below the castle is the restored **Stadtpfarrkirche St Matthäus** (St Matthew's Church; ☎ 24 89, Schlossberg 8; ☉ dawn-dusk), a Gothic church remodelled in baroque style. Both elements work surprisingly well together, especially in the combination of the Gothic crucifixion group (1500) and the baroque high altar (1655). The beautiful frescoes date from the 14th to 16th centuries.

Murau is also famous for its Brauerei Murau, which has a **brewery museum** (☎ 32 66; Raffaltplatz 19-23; adult/child €3/free; ☉ 3-5pm Fri May, Jun & Oct, 3-5.30pm Wed & Fri Jul-Sep). Entry includes a glass of the local brew. The brewery won a pan-European environmental management award in 2005 for its environmental practices.

Bike rental is available from **Intersport Pintar** (☎ 23 97; Bundesstrasse 7a; per day €10), near the tourist office.

Sleeping & Eating

Jugend & Familiengästehaus (☎ 23 95; murau@jfgh .at; St Leonhard Platz 4; dm €17.80, s €22.10, d €44.20) This HI hostel is situated in four historic buildings near the train station and has bike hire, a sauna and a peaceful inner courtyard.

The lovely **Gasthof Ferner** (☎ 23 18; www.hotel -ferner.at; Rosseggerstr 9; s/d €42/76, mains €8-18, ☉ lunch & dinner; P ⬛), on the northern fringe of town, has a restaurant offering trout in summer; the four-star **Hotel Lercher** (☎ 24 31; www.lercher .com; Schwarzenbergstrasse 10; s €61-85, d €92-140; gourmet mains €20-30, Wirsthaus mains €12-16; ☉ gourmet dinner Tue-Sat, Wirsthaus lunch & dinner; P ⬛) has two restaurants: the small and highly rated Panorama (book ahead), and the Wirtshaus for simpler cuisine.

Getting There & Away

If you're coming from Salzburgerland, the most pleasant mode of transport is the **Murtalbahn** (☎ 2231; www.stlb.at, in German; return €16.80), a steam train that chugs its way between Tamsweg and Murau once every Tuesday and Wednesday in July and August, on a private narrow-gauge line.

Fairly frequent direct ÖBB trains connect Murau with Tamsweg (€6.60, one hour) going west. Regular trains to Leoben (€17, 1½ hours) require a change in Unzmarkt.

The Salzkammergut

Sometimes called the 'cradle of Austrian culture', the Salzkammergut is a spectacular region of alpine and sub-alpine lakes, picturesque valleys, rolling hills and rugged, steep mountain ranges. The highest mountains climb to almost 3000m. Not least because of the Salzkammergut's startling beauty, parts of this region – especially those lakes easily reached from Salzburg – can at times be swamped with visitors. But don't despair – much of the region is remote wilderness, and even in those heavily visited parts such as the Wolfgangsee and Mondsee, you'll always find isolated sections where peaceful, glassy waters provide limitless opportunities for boating, swimming, fishing or just sitting on the shore and chucking stones into the water. The popular Hallstätter See is no exception. When the pretty streets in Hallstatt township are full of summer visitors, across the lake a sleepy, swampy Obertraun retains a village atmosphere. Strike out deeper into the region, and you will be rewarded with isolated splendour.

Salt is the 'white gold' of the Salzkammergut, and the mines that made it famous now make for an interesting journey back in time to the settlers of the Iron Age Hallstatt culture, and to the Celts and Romans – all of whom sullied their hands in the mines. Along the western side of the Hallstätter See is a pipeline reputed to be the oldest in the world, used to transport brine. Today, the narrow swathe cut out to build and service the pipeline is a lush hiking trail.

Whatever your reason for coming to the Salzkammergut – swimming, boating, hiking, climbing or exploring cultures – this region rewards the curious and adventurous.

HIGHLIGHTS

- Reeling from views at the surreal **5Fingers platform** (p253) in the Dachstein Mountains
- Hiking around the **Hallstätter See** (p249) from Obertraun to Hallstatt and cooling off in the crystal waters between trails
- Exploring the Wolfgangsee and the remarkable pilgrimage church in **St Wolfgang** (p260), filled with priceless works of art
- Strolling through the **Kaiservilla** (p247), Franz Josef's summer residence, now a handsome museum set in parkland
- Plunging into the chilling depths to masterfully illuminated towers of ice in the **Dachstein Caves** (p252)
- Finding the toilet in Gmunden's **Museum für Historische Sanitärobjeckte** (p257) – a museum dedicated to loos? They must be potty…

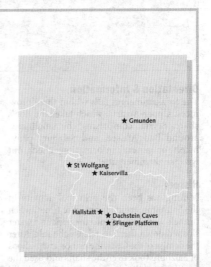
★ Gmunden
★ St Wolfgang
★ Kaiservilla
Hallstatt ★ ★ Dachstein Caves
★ 5Finger Platform

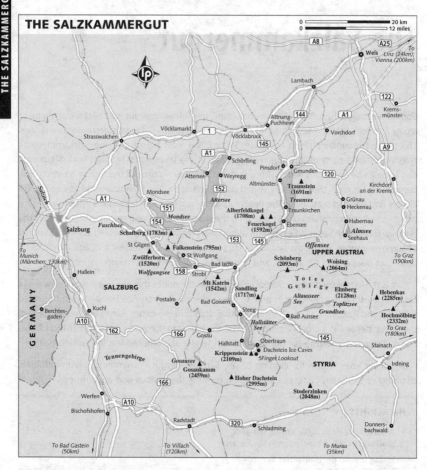

THE SALZKAMMERGUT

Orientation & Information

The Salzkammergut falls within three provinces: Upper Austria, which takes the lion's share; Styria, comprising the small area around Bad Aussee; and Salzburg province. For general information, check out www.salzkammergut.at.

History

Mining has been the principal activity in the Salzkammergut since Celtic times, when tunnels were hacked into the rock and water sloshed down them to release the salt. After the demise of the Celts, the prince-archbishops of Salzburg took over the shafts and used the profits from the dark, dank mines to build their elaborate palaces and pleasure gardens.

Ironically, considering its later popularity as a tourist area, the whole of the Salzkammergut region was banned to visitors until the early 19th century because the Salzburg government, which held a monopoly on salt mining here, wanted to prevent salt from being smuggled out. Later, Emperor Franz Josef's patronage brought central European aristocracy to the region in their droves. They came to promenade around the parks of the elegant spa towns like Bad Ischl, or to tramp through the snowy mountain forests in search of unwary deer.

Climate

Summers down by the Salzkammergut region's lakes tend to be quite warm, with an average temperature of 15°C to 25°C. In spring and autumn especially, beware of the so-called 'string rain' – a soft, yet drenching rain that can soak you through before you've even noticed it. During winter (mid-November to February) the average lies at around -4°C.

Getting There & Away

To reach the Salzkammergut from Salzburg by car or motorcycle, take the A1 to reach the north of the region, or Hwy 158 to Bad Ischl. Travelling north–south, the main road is Hwy 145 (the Salzkammergut Bundesstrasse) which follows the rail line for most of its length. By train, the main rail routes into the province are from Salzburg or Linz, with a change at Attnang-Puchheim onto the regional north–south railway line.

Getting Around

The Salzkammergut is crossed by regional trains on a north–south route, passing through Attnang-Puchheim on the Salzburg–Linz line and Stainach-Irdning on the Bischofshofen–Graz line. The rail line linking these two access points is 108km long, and hourly trains take 2½ hours to complete the journey. Smaller stations on this route are *unbesetzter Bahnhof* (unattended train station); at these you'll have to use a platform ticket machine or pay on the train. Attersee is also accessible by rail.

Regular bus services connect all towns and villages in the area, though less frequently or not at all on weekends. For bus times and prices from Salzburg to the various towns in the region, see p281.

Passenger boats ply the waters of the Attersee, Traunsee, Mondsee, Hallstätter See and Wolfgangsee.

The non-transferable Salzkammergut Erlebnis Card, available from tourist offices and hotels, costs €4.90 and offers significant discounts for 21 days between 1 May and 31 October.

BAD ISCHL

☎ 06132 / pop 14,070

This spa town's reputation snowballed after the Habsburg Princess Sophie took a treatment here to cure her infertility in 1828. Within two years she had given birth to Emperor Franz Josef I; two other sons fol-

lowed and were nicknamed the Salzprinzen (Salt Princes).

Rather in the manner of a salmon returning to its place of birth, Franz Josef made an annual pilgrimage to Bad Ischl, making it his summer home for the next 60 years and hauling much of the European aristocracy in his wake. The fateful letter he signed declaring war on Serbia and sparking off WWI bore a Bad Ischl postmark.

Today's Bad Ischl is a handsome town that makes a handy base for visiting the region's five main lakes.

Orientation & Information

Bad Ischl's town centre is compactly contained within a bend of the Traun River. There are moneychanging facilities at the post office and train station.

Post office (Bahnhofstrasse; ⏲ 8am-6pm Mon-Fri, 9am-noon Sat)

Salzkammergut Info-Center (☎ 240 00-0; www
.salzkammergut.co.at; Gützstrasse 12; ⏲ 9am-8pm) A helpful private regional agency with bike rental (per 24hr €13) and internet (per 10 min €1.10).

Tourist office (☎ 277 57-0; www.badischl.at; Auböckplatz; ⏲ 8am-6pm Mon-Fri, 9am-3pm Sat, 10am-1pm Sun) A telephone service (8am to 8pm) for rooms and information complements this office.

Sights & Activities

KAISERVILLA

Franz Josef's summer residence was the **Kaiservilla** (☎ 232 41; Jainzen 38; www.kaiservilla.com; adult/student/child €9.80/6.50/4.50, grounds only adult/student & child €3.50/2.50; ⏲ 9.30am-4.45pm May-mid-Oct), an Italianate building that was bought by his mother, the Princess Sophie, as an engagement present for her son and Princess Elisabeth of Bavaria. Elisabeth, who loathed the villa and her husband in equal measure, spent little time there, but the emperor came to love it and it became his permanent summer residence for over 60 years. His mistress, Katharina Schratt, lived nearby in a house chosen for her by the empress.

The interior of the villa can only be seen by guided tours (which leave every half-hour in summer), with English information sheets. You'll learn of the emperor's habit of rising at 3.30am each morning to take a bath before beginning his day's work punctually at 4am, and that the only recreation he allowed himself was hunting. The walls of the villa are liberally studded with the fruits of

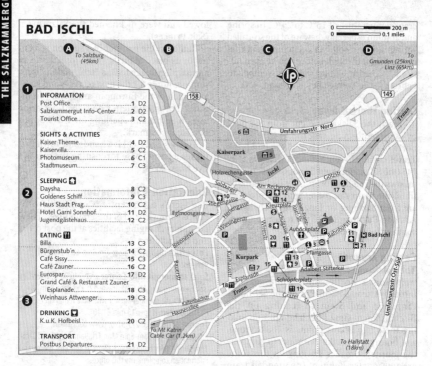

BAD ISCHL

INFORMATION	
Post Office...........................1	D2
Salzkammergut Info-Center....2	D2
Tourist Office......................3	C2

SIGHTS & ACTIVITIES	
Kaiser Therme.....................4	D2
Kaiservilla..........................5	C2
Photomuseum......................6	C1
Stadtmuseum.......................7	C3

SLEEPING	
Daysha...............................8	C2
Goldenes Schiff...................9	C3
Haus Stadt Prag..................10	C2
Hotel Garni Sonnhof............11	D2
Jugendgästehaus..................12	C2

EATING	
Billa..................................13	C3
Bürgerstub'n.......................14	C2
Café Sissy..........................15	C2
Café Zauner.......................16	C2
Eurospar............................17	D2
Grand Café & Restaurant Zauner	
Esplanade.......................18	C3
Weinhaus Attwenger............19	C3

DRINKING	
K.u.K. Hofbeisl...................20	C2

TRANSPORT	
Postbus Departures..............21	D2

his labours, including the stuffed corpse of the 2000th chamois he shot. There are various other exhibits, including a bust of the Empress Elisabeth, made when she was in her mid-40s (a grandmother and still an internationally famous beauty), and a death mask made after she was killed by a knife-wielding madman at the age of 60. The natural-style parkland surrounding the villa contains a small **Photomuseum** (☎ 244 22; adult/child/family €1.50/0.70/3.50; ☉ 9.30am-5pm Apr-Oct).

OTHER SIGHTS

The **Stadtmuseum** (city museum; ☎ 254 76; Esplanade 10; adult/child & student €4.50/2.20; ☉ 10am-5pm Tue & Thu-Sun, 2-7pm Wed Apr-Oct, also Mon Jul & Aug, 10am-5pm Fri-Sun Dec-Mar, closed Nov) is the building where Franz Josef and Elisabeth were engaged (the day after they met at a ball). Today it showcases the history of Bad Ischl and stages changing exhibitions.

The local peak here is **Mt Katrin** (1542m), with walking trails and limited skiing in winter. A **cable car** (☎ 237 88; www.katrinseilbahn .com; return ticket adult/child €13.50/12, ☉ mid-May–Oct, mid-Dec–Mar) glides up there. If you'd like to fol-

low in Princess Sophie's footsteps, check out spa treatments at the **Kaiser Therme** (☎ 204-0; www.kaisertherme.co.at; Bahnhofstrasse 1; adult/child €11.50/6.90; ☉ 9am-10pm).

Festivals & Events

Daily free *Kurkonzerte* (spa concerts) take place in an open-air pavilion in the Kurpark or inside the nearby Congresshaus. Bad Ischl was the home of operetta composer Franz Lehár, and the **Lehár Festival** (www.leharfestival.at) takes place every year in July and August, with stagings of his own and other composers' works.

Sleeping

Staff at both the tourist offices can help find rooms.

Jugendgästehaus (☎ 265 77; jgh.badischl@oejhv.or.at; Am Rechensteg 5; dm/s/d €15/29.50/44) The characterless but clean HI guesthouse is in the town centre behind Kreuzplatz.

Haus Stadt Prag (☎ 236 16; stadt-prag@aon.at; Egelmoosgasse 9; s/d €33/66; ☉ closed Nov; P) Rooms are large and comfortable and this private pension has a peaceful, old-world atmosphere, situated just outside the town centre.

Hotel Garni Sonnhof (☎ 230 78; www.sonnhof.at; Bahnhofstrasse 4; s €65, d €90-120; P) Nestled in a leafy glade of maple trees next to the station, this lovely hotel has cosy, traditional décor, a beautiful garden (complete with a pond), a sunny conservatory and large bedrooms with interesting old furniture, rag rugs and wooden floors. There's a billiard room, sauna and a steam bath on site.

Goldenes Schiff (☎ 242 41; www.goldenes-schiff.at; Adalbert Stifterkai 3; s €85-95, d €115-162, apt €162; P ; mains €10-18) Most doubles in this four-star hotel have bath tubs, and the best rooms (junior suites) have large windows and overlook the river. Some rooms can be very plain, though. There's also a wellness centre with solarium and sauna, and a good restaurant serving classic Austrian cuisine.

Daysha (☎ 289 84; www.dayshahotel.com; Schulgasse 9; s/d/ste €95/177/280; P) The latest addition to Bad Ischl's hotel landscape is a stylish and well-thought-out business hotel with pine floors, a refreshingly low-key colour scheme, a rooftop swimming pool and free wireless internet for guests.

Eating & Drinking

Café Sissy (☎ 241 73; Pfarrgasse 2; mains €6-16; 8am-midnight) Sissy was the nickname of the Kaiserin Elisabeth, unhappy wife of Emperor Franz Josef, and her pictures hang on the walls of this popular riverside bar/café. You can breakfast here, lunch or dine on a Wiener schnitzel and other simple fare, or simply nighthawk at the front-room bar till the midnight hour.

Grand Café & Restaurant Zauner Esplanade (☎ 237 22; Hasner Allee 2; pastries €7-14.50 10am-9pm May-Oct, 10am-8pm Wed-Sun Dec-mid-Apr) This offshoot of Café Zauner, the famous pastry shop at Pfarrgasse 7, serves quite decent Austrian staples, some using organic local meats, in a pleasant location beside the river. The Pfarrgasse pastry shop (open 8.30am to 6pm) takes you back in time: founded in 1832, this was where Franz Josef's mistress ordered pastries for their breakfast every morning when the emperor was in residence.

Bürgerstub'n (☎ 235 68; Kreuzplatz 7; 2-course menu €9; lunch Thu-Tue, dinner Thu & Fri) Back from the street in a courtyard, this cheap and cheerful place has lots of plants studding its outside terrace and serves filling classics.

Weinhaus Attwenger (☎ 233 27; Lehárkai 12; mains €10.50-21.50; lunch & dinner, closed Mon) This quaint chalet with a garden next to the river

serves prime-quality Austrian cuisine from a seasonal menu, with wines to match. It also has a couple of set menus (three/four courses €26/€30).

K.u.K. Hofbeisl (☎ 272 71; Wirerstrasse 4; 8am-4am; food €5-20) This *Beisl* is the scene of some of the liveliest late-night partying in Bad Ischl, but it also does a delicious plate of food. It has two separate drinking areas to choose from, DJs get the floors writhing regularly during events, and the drinks list would do a Russian novelist proud – about 150 cocktails in all.

Supermarkets include Billa on Pfarrgasse and Eurospar on Götzstrasse.

Getting There & Away

Postbus services depart from outside the train station, with hourly buses to Salzburg (€8.70, 1½ hours) via St Gilgen (€4.60, 35 minutes). To St Wolfgang (€6.40, 40 minutes), you often have to change at Strobl (the bus will be waiting and the same ticket is valid).

Hourly trains to Hallstatt (€4.40, 25 minutes) go via Steeg/Hallstätter See, at the northern end of the lake, and continue on the eastern side via Hallstatt station to Obertraun (€6, 30 minutes). A boat from Hallstatt station (€2) takes you to the township. There are also frequent trains to Gmunden (€7.60, 45 minutes), as well as to Salzburg (€19, two hours) via Attnang-Puchheim.

Most major roads in the Salzkammergut go to or near Bad Ischl; Hwy 158 from Salzburg and the north–south Hwy 145 intersect just north of the town centre.

SOUTHERN SALZKAMMERGUT

The Dachstein mountain range provides a stunning 3000m backdrop to the lakes in the south. Transport routes go round rather than over these jagged peaks.

HALLSTÄTTER SEE

The Hallstätter See, set among sharply rising mountains at an altitude of 508m in the Southern Salzkammergut, is one of the prettiest and most accessible lakes in the region. It offers some of the best hiking and

WATER, WILD MOUNTAINS, WONDERFUL VIEWS & 5FINGERS

- **Rock swimming & kayaking** With its crystal clear waters, the Hallstätter See makes for good summer splashing. Rent a kayak or boat for the day from Hallstatt (opposite), paddle over to Obertraun and moor offshore north of the settlement for some swimming off the rocks. The FKK (naturist) beach in Steeg has a lovely, reedy swim as an alternative.

- **Walking above the waters** The eastern shore of the lake is a breeze: flat in most places, and large stretches are even possible for cyclists. The western shore trail, though, is where the walking gets spectacular. Stunning views of the lake open up between lush deciduous forest, and a gruelling climb up steps beyond the waterfall may prompt cries for last-minute mercy.

- **A cool drink and a view** Mercy comes in the form of one of the nicest places to eat or drink outdoors in the Salzkammergut. The restaurant at Rudolfsturm (opposite) – inside a former fortress – does a fine dish, but the killer-bee experience is sitting outdoors and enjoying the cool, mountain breeze on your face, sipping a beer or glass of wine, and watching the boats ripple the lake almost 800m below.

- **When the water washes down** A late afternoon or early evening shower is common in the Salzkammergut, and one of the more enjoyable places to seek refuge indoors in Obertraun is at Restaurant-Pizzeria Simmer (p253). This friendly, family owned and run respite does delicious pizza; and if the rain sets in, two Kegelbahnen (bowling alleys) out the back help kill time. Once the shower passes, you can move back onto the cosy terrace.

- **5Fingers for the sure-footed** In a region where panoramas are plentiful, the 5Fingers viewing platform (p253) offers one of the most interesting. It's at Krippenstein, above the ice caves, and consists of five steely 'fingers' extending from a sheer 400m precipice. Each finger has a different character. One has a symbolic springboard, and the fifth has a transparent floor. The view from the platform over the lake is dazzling.

That's our take, give yours by going to www.lonelyplanet.com and creating your own Bluelist on Austria.

(blu,list) v. to recommend a travel experience. www.lonelyplanet.com/bluelist

BLUELIST.

swimming in summer, good skiing in winter, and a fascinating insight into the cultural history of the region any time of year. Just 5km round the lake lies Obertraun, the closest resort to the Dachstein ice caves; the whole Hallstatt-Dachstein region became a Unesco World Heritage site in 1997.

As well as excursions, **Hemetsberger** (☎ 6134-8228; Am Hof 126; 90min excursions €9; Jul–mid-Sep, weather depending) does a scheduled run between Obertraun and Hallstatt-Markt (€4.50, 25 minutes, three or four times daily from June to September) and the all-important year-round service between Hallstatt-Markt and Hallstatt train station (€2, 10 minutes, five to 12 times daily). This connects with trains in both directions on the main railway line here (see their pamphlet). If you're staying in Obertraun or Bad Aussee, your last boat leaves Hallstatt-Markt at 6.15pm. Going to Bad Ischl, 5.50pm is your last boat-train connection.

HALLSTATT
☎ 06134 / pop 950

With pastel-coloured houses casting shimmering reflections onto the glassy waters of the lake and towering mountains on all sides, Hallstatt's beauty alone would be enough to guarantee it fame. Boats chug tranquilly across the lake from the train station to the village, situated precariously on a narrow slate of land between mountain and shore. So small is the patch of land occupied by the village that its annual Corpus Christi procession takes place largely in small boats on the lake.

Salt in the hills above the town made it a centre of salt mining. The Hallstatt Period (800 to 400 BC) refers to the early Iron Age in Europe, named after the village and the Iron Age settlers and Celts who worked the salt mines here. Today the sheer volume of visitors can not only get annoying at times, but make finding a hotel room difficult in mid-summer.

Consider staying in Obertraun, which retains its village feel.

Orientation & Information

The train station is across the lake from Hallstatt – to get into town you have to take the ferry. Seestrasse is the main street in Hallstatt; some other streets are mere pedestrian paths.

Internet access (Seestrasse 145; ☼ 9.30am-10pm; per 15 min €1; ☼ May–mid-Oct) A small 'umbrella bar'.

Post office (☼ 8am-noon & 2.30-5.30pm) Near the tourist office.

Sparkasse Bad Ischl (Marktplatz 58; ☼ 8am-noon & 2-5pm Mon, Tue, Thu & Fri, 8am-noon Wed) Bank with ATM.

Tourist office (☎ 8208; www.hallstatt.at; Seestrasse 169; ☼ 9am-noon & 2-5pm Mon-Fri Sep-Jun, 9am-5pm Mon-Fri, 10am-2pm Sat Jul & Aug) Turn left from the ferry to reach the office. It has a free *Hiking Friends* brochure with walks in the region.

Sights & Activities

BEINHAUS

Make sure you don't miss the macabre yet beautiful **Beinhaus** (Bone House; ☎ 8279; Kirchenweg 40; admission €1; ☼ 10am-6pm 1 May-27 Oct) behind the church. This small charnel house contains rows of neatly stacked skulls, painted with flowery designs and the names of their former owners. Bones have been exhumed from the overcrowded graveyard since 1600 and the last skull in the collection was added in 1995. The Beinhaus stands in the grounds of the 15th-century Catholic **Pfarrkirche** (parish church; ☎ 8279; Kirchenweg 40) and has Gothic frescoes and three winged altars; arguably the best one, on the right, dates from 1510 and shows saints Barbara and Katharina, with Mary in the middle.

STADTMUSEUM

The revamped, high-tech **Stadtmuseum** (city museum; ☎ 8206; www.museum-hallstatt.at; Seestrasse 56; adult/child/family €7.50/4/19; ☼ 10am-6pm May-Sep, 11am-3pm Wed-Sun Jan-Mar, Nov & Dec, 10am-4pm Apr & Oct) covers the region's history of Iron Age/Celtic occupation and salt mining. All explanations are in German, but pick up the *Museum Hallstatt* booklet (€2; in English) which explains the exhibits. Not to be missed is the room re-enacting the fatal rockslides that may have led to the area being abandoned.

Celtic and Roman excavations can be seen downstairs in **Dachsteinsport Janu** (☎ 8298; Seestrasse 50; admission free; ☼ 8am-6pm), a shop opposite the tourist office, or near the Salzbergwerk (below), where excavation continues.

SALZBERGWERK

Situated high above Hallstatt on Salzberg (Salt Mountain) is another major cultural attraction, the fascinating **Salzbergwerk** (Salt Mine; ☎ 06132-200 24 00; adult/child & concession/family €21/12.60/44.10; ☼ 9.30am-4.30pm May-mid-Sep, to 3.30pm mid-Sep-30 Sep, to 3pm 1 Oct-mid-Oct, closed mid–Oct-Apr). In 1734 the fully preserved body of a prehistoric miner was found and today he is known as the 'Man in Salt'. The standard tour revolves around his fate, with visitors travelling down an underground railway and miner's slides (a photo is taken of you while sliding) to an illuminated subterranean salt lake. Closing times given are admission for the last tour.

There are several ways of getting there – all of them enjoyable. The easiest is with a **funicular railway** (one-way adult/child/family €5.10/3.10/10.80) to the mountain station, from where the mine is 15 minutes' walk past Hallstatt's best lookout restaurant, **Rudolfsturm** (Rudolf's Tower; p102), and an archaeological dig. Alternatively, a switchback trail (about 40 minutes up) starts from the foot of the funicular. If you are feeling fit (and the weather is dry), you might climb the stairs behind the Beinhaus: take the trail until it joins the picturesque **Soleleitungsweg**, go left and follow the very steep trail past the **waterfall** and up steps. It's a tough climb, and not really for children. Last but certainly not least, masochists can walk 18km anticlockwise around the lake (see p99). Leave very early so you reach your sticky end in time for the last tour.

You can hire **boats and kayaks** (per hr from €9) on the lake, or scuba dive in it with the **Dachstein Tauchclub** (☎ 8286); see p100 for nice swimming spots.

Sleeping

Rooms fill quickly in summer, so book ahead or arrive early. If you haven't already booked, go straight for the tourist office and they'll help you find something, either in Hallstatt or Lahn (the southern part of the village). All of the following places provide free parking for guests within the town limits.

Campingplatz Klausner-Höll (☎ 8322; www.camping .hallstatt.net; Lahnstrasse 7; campsite per adult/child/tent/ car €6.50/3.50/3.70/2.90; ☼ 15 Apr-15 Oct; P) This campsite is conveniently located south of the centre.

Gasthaus Mühle (☎ 8318; toeroe@magnet.at; Kirchenweg 36; dm €13; ⏰ closed Tue & November) This youth hostel is part of the restaurant of the same name. It's handily situated on the way up to the church, and the dorms are quite decent.

Jugendherberge (☎ 8212; biene1005@aon.at; Lahn 50; dm €16; ⏰ May-Sep) Only dorms are available here, and some can be cramped. Phone if reception is unattended. It's usually full with groups in July and August, and opening can change according to the weather.

Pension Hallberg (☎ 8709; www.pension-hallberg .at.tf; Seestrasse 113; s €60-80, d €70-130; **P**) Book early in summer for Hallberg. Interesting artefacts rescued from the lake line the staircase leading up to the rooms, the best of which are light and airy, furnished with pale wood and have superb views over the lake.

Gasthof Zauner (☎ 8246; www.zauner.hallstatt.net; Marktplatz 51; s/d €48/96; ⏰ closed mid-Nov–mid-Dec; **P**) Gasthof Zauner is a quaint, ivy-covered guesthouse on the nearest square to the ferry terminal. It has very tasteful, pine-embellished rooms, some with a balcony and a view of the lake. The restaurant (mains €13 to €18) has some of the best food (especially fish) and wines in town.

our pick **Seehotel Grüner Baum** (☎ 8263; Marktplatz 104; r per person €65-100; 🖳) Officially, the Grüner Baum is three-star, but the quality of rooms and service is much more than its rating suggests. These are tastefully furnished without going overboard on décor to impress; three suites have enormous patios to the lake, and doubles have smaller balconies large enough for seating. A complimentary bottle of mineral water arrives each day, and staff will deliver breakfast to your bedside replete with those sweeping views of the lake, making this the ideal place for romantic lakeside sojourns.

Eating

Gasthaus Zur Mühle (☎ 8318; Kirchenweg 36; mains €6.70-8.80; ⏰ lunch & dinner Wed-Mon May-Sep, 4-11pm Oct & Dec-Apr, closed Nov) In the same building as the hostel, this restaurant is a nice place to hang out and chomp on salad, pizza or an inexpensive meat dish.

Restaurant zum Salzbaron (☎ 8263; Marktplatz 104; mains €10-22; ⏰ lunch & dinner, closed Nov) By a long shot the classiest gourmet act in town, the Salzbaron is perched delicately alongside the lake inside the Seehotel Grüner Baum and serves from a seasonal menu; local trout

features strongly in summer on a menu with a pan-European angle.

Bräugasthof Restaurant (☎ 8221; Seestrasse 120; mains €14-19; ⏰ lunch & dinner May-Oct) Beef fillet in port is one excellent choice here, but you can also enjoy a few salads, trout, and other local specialities in this restaurant with a lovely lakeside terrace.

To stock up on provisions for a hike, you'll find a **Konsum** (Kernmagazinplatz 23) between Hallstatt and Lahn.

Getting There & Away

About five buses a day connect Hallstatt town with Obertraun (€1.70, 10 minutes) and Bad Ischl (€4, 50 minutes) until the late afternoon. Get off the Postbus at the Parkterrasse stop for the centre and the tourist office, or at Lahn (at the southern end of the road tunnel) for the Jugendherberge.

Hallstatt train station is across the lake. The boat service from there to the village coincides with train arrivals. The last ferry connection leaves Hallstatt train station at 6.29pm (€1.70, 10 to 45 minutes). Car access into the village is restricted from early May to late October: electronic gates are activated during the day. Staying overnight in town gives free parking and a pass to open the gates.

OBERTRAUN

☎ 06131 / pop 776

Quieter, more low-key than Hallstatt, this village offers access to the caves and is a good starting point for hikes around the lake or more strenuous ones up to the caves themselves.

Orientation & Information

The cable-car station for the ice caves is a 20-minute walk uphill through the woods from the village – turn right along the main road and follow the signposts. The trail (No 16) to the caves is a stiff 2½-hour hike from the valley station.

Tourist office (☎ 351; www.inneres-salzkammergut .at; ⏰ 8am-noon & 2-5pm Mon-Fri Oct-Jun, 8am-noon & 2-6pm Mon-Fri, 9am-noon Sat Jul-Sep) On the way to the Dachstein cable car from the train station (ATM next door).

Sights & Activities

Climb to the Dachstein caves and you'll find yourself in a strange world of ice and subterranean hollows extending 80km in places. The ice in the Giant Ice Cave is no more than 500 years old, forming an 'ice mountain' 8m high – twice as high now as it was when the caves were first explored in 1910.

Both **caves** (☎ 5310; www.dachsteinwelterbe.at; cable car return plus one cave adult/child €23.70/13.80; cable car plus both caves adult/child €28.60/16.30; caves only adult/child €9.30/5.50) are 15 minutes' steep walking from the first stage of the Dachstein cable car at 1350m, and each cave tour lasts an hour. To make sure you see both caves, take the cable car up by 1pm and do the Mammoth Cave first, allowing 30 to 45 minutes to reach the Giant Ice Cave from the Mammoth Cave.

The best of the caves is the **Rieseneishöhle** (Giant Ice Cave; ☉ core tour 9.20am-4pm May–mid-Sep). The enormous ice formations here are illuminated with coloured light and the shapes they take are eerie and surreal. The cave can only be seen on a guided tour, and if you let the tour guide know, they will do the tour with English as well as German commentaries.

The **Mammuthöhle** (Mammoth Cave; ☉ core tour 10.15am-2.30pm mid-May–mid-Sep) is among the 30 or so deepest and longest caves in the world and is without ice formations. Tours give insight into the formation of the cave, which like the Rieseneishöhle, has installations and works of art based on light and shadow to heighten the experience.

The **Koppenbrüllerhöhlen** (guided tour adult/child €7.70/4.50; ☉ May-Oct) are water-filled caves and part of the same Dachstein cave system. They're down the valley towards Bad Aussee.

The **cable car** runs about every 15 minutes. After the middle station **Schönbergalm** (return adult/child €14.40/8.30; ☉ May-mid-Sep), it continues to the highest point (2109m) of **Krippenstein** (return adult/child €20.60/12.80; ☉ late-Jul–mid-Sep), with an eerie **5Fingers viewing platform** dangling over the precipice and walking trails, and beyond that to the Gjaidalm station. In winter Krippenstein is also a ski and snowboard free-riding area (€29.20 for a day pass).

Obertraun has a grassy **beach area** (admission free) with changing huts, a small waterslide, a children's play area and boat rental.

Sleeping & Eating

Obertraun has many private rooms (from €19) and holiday apartments, plus several hotels.

Campingplatz Hinterer (☎ 265; camping.am.see@chello.at; Winkl 77; campsite per adult/child/tent/car €8.40/4.80/5.20/2.80; ☉ May-Oct) This informal,

grassy campsite is by the lake south of the river.

Jugendherberge (☎ 360; www.jutel.at/obertraun, in German; Winkl 26; dm €20, s/d €20/40; ☉ check-in 5-7pm) This HI hostel is 15 minutes' walk from the train station: cross the river and take the first street on the left. Doors are locked during the day.

Gasthof/Pension Dachsteinhof (☎ 393; dachsteinhof@inode.at; Winkl 22; s/d €35/70; **P**) This simple, traditional pension has an idyllic setting by the river on the way to the ice caves. The good-sized rooms are clean and functional, with the sound of rushing water to lull you to sleep at night. There's also a midrange restaurant here serving classics like schnitzel and steak, but also local trout.

Hotel Haus am See (☎ 26777; www.hotel-hausamsee.at; Obertraun 169; s/d €42/86; mains €8.50-19; **P**) Situated conveniently alongside the boat station and swimming area, this comfortable hotel has rooms with views over the lake. While they lack frills, these are very clean and comfortable, and you can throw open the balcony door at night and sleep with a lakeside breeze.

Seehotel Wenk (☎ 462; www.wenk.at; Seestrasse 152; s/d €50/88; **P** 🛋) This large hotel is another comfortable option near the lake, especially to escape Hallstatt crowds. Its large garden area out front and around the pool makes it ideal for families.

Restaurant-Pizzeria Simmer (☎ 335; Seestrasse 178; mains €7-11, pizza €4.80-6.50; 10am-midnight Tue-Sun Nov-Apr & Jun-Sep, closed Oct & closed lunch Tue & Thu May) One time we had the good fortune to get caught in this gem during a tremendous hailstorm fresh from a lake hike. The staff is friendly, the pizza is great, and we found it a cosy respite while the heavens opened up. There's ten-pin bowling out back.

The **Konsum** supermarket near the tourist office is convenient for hiking supplies.

Getting There & Away

See opposite for transport connections.

Obertraun-Dachsteinhöhlen is the train station for Obertraun village. Obertraun-Koppenbrüllerhöhle is the station for the water caves (€1.70, four minutes); trains only stop here in summer when the caves are open. There are frequent trains to Bad Ischl (€6, 30 minutes) via Hallstatt (€2.90, three minutes).

For taxis to the ice caves, call ☎ 542.

GOSAUSEE

☎ 06136 / elevation 923m

This small lake is flanked by the impressively precipitous peaks of the **Gosaukamm range** (2459m). The view is good from the shores, and it takes a little over an hour to walk around the entire lake. The Gosaukammbahn cable car goes up to 1475m (return adult/child €10.70/6.70), where there are spectacular views and walking trails. Before reaching the lake you pass through the village of **Gosau**, which has its own **tourist office** (☎ 8295; www.oberoesterreich.at/gosau; ⏰ 8am-noon & 1-5pm Mon-Fri Sep-Apr, 8am-noon & 1-5pm Mon-Fri, 9am-noon Sat May-Aug), with an accommodation board situated outside.

Getting There & Away

Gosau is at the junction of the only road to the lake and can be reached by Hwy 166 from Hallstätter See. One- to two-hourly Postbus services run to the lake from Bad Ischl (€5.70, one hour) via Steeg.

BAD AUSSEE

☎ 03622 / pop 5080

Quiet, staid Bad Aussee is the largest Styrian town in the southern Salzkammergut. It is close to two lakes and convenient by rail and a walking trail to a third – the Hallstätter See. If it's nightlife you're after, look further – such as Bad Ischl – this is not a high-kicking sort of place, and a stroll in the pretty Kurpark must suffice.

Orientation & Information

The train station is 1.5km south of the town centre. After getting off the train, dash to the bus stop out front to raise your chances of jagging one of the one- to two-hourly buses. The taxi trip is €6 (see p256).

Harreiter Online und Datenverarbeitung (☎ 53250; Bahnhofstrasse 115; per 30 min €1.50; ⏰ 4-11pm Mon-Sat)

Post office (Ischlerstrasse 94; ⏰ 8am-noon & 2-5.30pm Mon-Fri) Doubles as a bus stop with timetable information.

Tourist office (☎ 523 23; www.ausseerland.at, in German; Bahnhofstrasse 132; ⏰ 9am-7pm Mon-Fri, 9am-4pm Sat Apr-Oct, 9am-noon & 1-6pm Mon-Fri, 9am-noon Sat Nov-Mar) The entrance is on Pratergasse, the geographical centre of Austria. Pick up the town map, with hiking trails marked for the region.

Sights & Activities

The **Altaussee Salzbergwerk** (☎ 6132 200 2490; tours adult/concession €11.50/6.90; ⏰ tours hourly 10am-4pm) is still a working salt mine and was the secret hiding place of art treasures stolen by the Nazis during WWII. Tours include the treasure chambers, an underground lake and a chapel made of blocks of salt and dedicated to St Barbara, the patron saint of miners. Guided tours in English are available.

Kammerhof Museum (☎ 525 11-20; www.badaussee.at/kammerhofmuseum; Chlumeckyplatz 1; adult/child €3/1.50; ⏰ 4-6pm Tue & Sat, 10am-noon Fri & Sun Apr–mid-Jun & Oct, 10am-noon & 3-6pm mid-Jun–Sep), housed in a beautiful 17th-century building, covers local history and salt production. There are also some portraits of Anna Plöchl, the local postmaster's daughter who scandalously married a Habsburg prince. All explanations are in German but there's an English sheet available.

There are great views across the town and the mountains beyond it from **Ausseer Lebkuchen** (Gingerbread Bakery; ☎ 52 943; www.lebkuchen.at, in German; Pötschenstrasse 146; admission free; ⏰ 8am-noon & 1-6pm Tue-Sat, 1-6pm Sun), a working gingerbread bakery that offers tours. Buy some gingerbread to take home, or eat it on the spot in the pleasant **café** (⏰ 9am-10pm Wed-Mon).

Five kilometres northeast of Bad Aussee, **Grundlsee** is a longer, thinner lake, with a good viewpoint at its western end as well as walking trails and water sports (including a sailing school). Extending from the eastern tip of the lake are two smaller lakes, **Toplitzsee** (see boxed text, p256) and **Kammersee**. Between May and October, **boat tours** (☎ 03622 8613; www.3-seen-tour.at, in German; full tour adult/child €15/7.50) are available.

A scenic road, the **Panoramastrasse**, climbs most of the way up **Loser** (1838m), the main peak overlooking the Altausser See. The toll for the return trip is €15, regardless of how many passengers there are. You'll need snow chains in winter.

A new 10-km hiking trail, the **Koppentalweg**, runs west through the lush Traun River valley, connecting with the Ostuferwanderweg running along the Hallstätter See (see p99). The trail begins at the train station.

Sleeping

The staff at the tourist office is very helpful and knowledgeable; there's a 24-hour information touch screen and free phone to hotels outside the office. Pick up the Bad Aussee brochure available from the tourist office for listings.

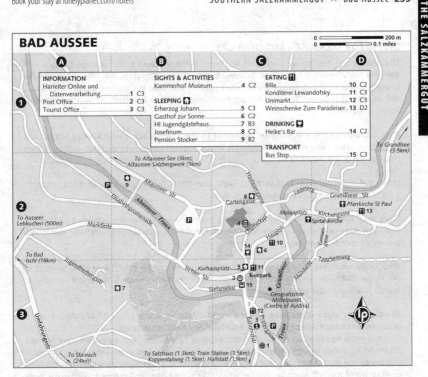

BAD AUSSEE

INFORMATION		
Harreiter Online und		
Datenverarbeitung	1	C3
Post Office	2	C3
Tourist Office	3	C3

SIGHTS & ACTIVITIES		
Kammerhof Museum	4	C2

SLEEPING		
Erherzog Johann	5	C3
Gasthof zur Sonne	6	C2
HI Jugendgästehaus	7	B3
Josefinum	8	C2
Pension Stocker	9	B2

EATING		
Billa	10	C2
Konditerei Lewandofsky	11	C3
Unimarkt	12	C3
Weinschenke Zum Paradeiser	13	D2

DRINKING		
Heike's Bar	14	C2

TRANSPORT		
Bus Stop	15	C3

HI Jugendgästehaus (☎ 522 38; www.jfgh.at/bad-aussee.php; Jugendherbergsstrasse 148; dm €20-23; P) This modern building is on the town's hill. It's 15 minutes' walk by road, but there are shorter (unlit) footpaths.

Pension Stocker (☎ 524 84; www.zimmer-ausseerland.at/stocker; Altausseer Strasse 245; s/d €25/50; P) Located 500m northwest of Kurhausplatz, this is a very pretty pension with wooden balconies and flower-filled window boxes. It has clean rooms and a large garden that overlooks tennis courts.

Josefinum (☎ 521 24; www.tiscover.at/josefinum; Gartengasse 13; s/d €27/54; P) This peaceful retreat has lovely bright rooms with good views of the mountains. It's run by nuns so be on your best behaviour. Telephone ahead for evening arrival.

Gasthof zur Sonne (☎ 522 06; www.gasthofsonne.at; Hauptstrasse 150; s/d €42/84) Although this guesthouse is simple and short on frills, you'll find the rooms comfortable, and the hotel itself is very centrally located.

Erherzog Johann (☎ 525 07; www.erzherzogjohann.at; Kurhausplatz 62; s €86-118, d €142-208; P 💻 😉) Bad Aussee's four-star hotel has rooms with comforts, but the facilities are what really catapult you into seventh heaven: a wonderfully large inhouse sauna and wellness area, a 30m saltwater swimming pool (public, with direct access for guests) and excellent bikes free for guests; they even lend out a GPS so you can get back in time for dinner. The restaurant (mains €16 to €20) is quite good, though quality can be uneven. Steak can be a bit average, but a chicken with herbs washed down with wine does the trick admirably.

Eating & Drinking

Bad Aussee is no great shakes when it comes to eating and drinking, so you're better off splurging elsewhere. The restaurant of Erzherhog Johann (left), however, has a very strong wine list, some good dishes and service with character.

Konditerei Lewandofsky (☎ 532 05; Kurhausplatz 144; Haustorte (house cake) per slice €2.30; 🕙 8am-8pm Mon-Sat, 9am-8pm Sun, till 10pm Jul & Aug) The favoured place in town for coffee and cake or a post-work tipple on an outside terrace alongside the Kurpark.

DIVING FOR TREASURE – AND DEAR LIFE

The picturesque Toplitzsee is off-limits to divers. But that hasn't stopped them trying – and dying in the attempt – to explore its oxygen-free depths. Why does this lake, whose fragile ecosystem was all but destroyed during WWII when it was used in experiments with explosives, still attract rogue divers? Bernhard Schragl from Österreichische Bundesforste (Austrian National Forests), explains.

Herr Schragl, why is everyone so interested in the Toplitzsee? It's because of history and the various stories and rumours – above all, about treasure supposedly dumped in it by fleeing Nazis at the end of WWII.

When did these rumours first surface? Right after WWII. They're proving persistent, although a lot of treasure hunters have dived down there.

Have they found anything? Printing presses for producing counterfeit English pound notes. The notes were printed and circulated to destabilize the currency. Counterfeits were also found, but only printed on one side.

Who owns whatever is found in the lake? If an owner can be established, 90% belongs to the owner. The finder gets 10%. If ownership is open, the finder keeps half and the Republic of Austria holds onto the other half.

Are there any signs of treasure down there? Nothing concrete, just a lot of rumours about gold and Swiss bank accounts. These are without any basis whatsoever.

A few years ago Austrian National Forests began a cooperation with treasure hunter Norman Scott and his company Global Explorations. Bundesforste signed an agreement, but for personal reasons on the part of Mr Scott no diving was conducted. If we do sign a new agreement, a fixed component of this will again be that the whole lake is measured and mapped. We'll make these measurements and maps available to the public.

What does Austrian National Forests hope to get out of any agreement? We want to bring an end to all this talk about secrets, and an end to the disturbance this is causing the lake. A lot of illegal divers try their luck at finding treasure. This threatens the lake's ecology because they don't care about the fish and they leave a trail of pollution. We want the whole lake to be measured, mapped and researched so it can be left in peace at last and there are no secrets anymore.

Weinschenke Zum Paradeiser (☎ 2135 038; Kirchengasse 28; mains €5.50-12; ⏲ 5pm-late Mon-Sat) This cosy and appealing *Heuriger* (wine tavern) with a red-brick floor and calico draped on the ceiling specialises in smoked trout.

Heike's Bar (☎ 548 02; Hauptstrasse 54a; ⏲ 8pm-late) The most popular watering hole in the centre.

Salzhaus (☎ 536 53; www.salzhaus.com; Siessreithstrasse 165; disco €2; ⏲ 5pm-late Wed-Sat) Always worth a shot on a good night – there's a pizzeria and lounge to complement its disco events, a stone's throw from the train station.

There's a Unimarkt supermarket on Bahnhofstrasse, by the tourist office, and a Billa on Hauptstrasse.

Getting There & Around

Bad Aussee is on the rail route between Bad Ischl (€6.60, 35 minutes) and Stainach-Irdning (€6, 35 minutes), with trains running hourly in both directions.

Buses run every one to two hours from the train station to both lakes (€1.70, 15 minutes). **Taxis** (☎ 540 08, 521 75) can be useful here.

NORTHERN SALZKAMMERGUT

The two most popular of the northern lakes are Traunsee – with the three resorts of Gmunden, Traunkirchen and Ebensee on its shores – and Wolfgangsee, home to the villages of St Wolfgang and St Gilgen (the latter provides access to Schafberg mountain; 1783m).

TRAUNSEE

Traunsee is the deepest lake in Austria, going down a cool 192m. The eastern flank is dominated by rocky crags, the tallest of which is the imposing **Traunstein** (1691m). The resorts are strung along the western shore and are connected by rail.

Hourly trains run between Gmunden, Traunkirchen (€2.90, 10 minutes) and Ebensee (€4.40, 20 minutes), continuing to Bad Ischl (€7.60, 40 minutes). Boats operated by **Traunsee Schiffahrt** (☎ 07612-667 00; www.traunsee schiffahrt.at; Rathausplatz, Gmunden) tour the shoreline from Gmunden to Ebensee between late April and mid-October. The one-way trip between Gmunden and Ebensee costs €7.50/6 per adult/child. The paddle steamer *Gisela* takes to the waves on weekends and holidays in July and August (a €2.50 surcharge applies).

GMUNDEN

☎ 07612 / pop 15,075

With its yacht marina, lakeside square and promenades, Gmunden exudes a breezy, Riviera feel. It was formerly known for its castles and ceramics, and it also doubled as an administration centre for both the Habsburgs and the salt trade. Today it makes for an attractive stopover in the lakes region.

Orientation & Information

The town centre is on the western bank of the Traun River, with Rathausplatz at its heart.
Bürgerespresso + Internetcafe (☎ 777 44; Am Graben 2a; per hr €3.60; 🕑 9am-8pm Mon-Sat) Self-service internet café.
Gästezentrum Ferienregion Traunsee (☎ 643 05; www.traunsee.at; Toscanapark 1; 🕑 8am-6pm Mon-Fri, 10am-4pm Sat & Sun May-Jun & Sep-Oct, 8am-8pm Mon-Fri, 10am-7pm Sat & Sun Jul & Aug, 9am-5pm Mon-Fri, 9am-1pm Sat Nov-Apr) Regional tourist office for the lake, with accommodation booking service.
Post office (☎ 0577 677-4810; Johann-Evangelist-Habert-Strasse 1; 🕑 8am-noon & 2-5.30pm Mon-Thu, 8am-5.30 Fri) Up the hill 200m.
Tourist office (☎ 657 520; gmunden@traunsee.at; Rathausplatz 1; 🕑 9am-3pm Mon-Fri May, Jun, Sep & Oct, 9am-6pm Mon-Fri, 10am-4pm Sat Jul & Aug, 9am-3pm Mon-Fri Nov-Apr) The city tourist office for Gmunden, with information and maps of town and the lake. Helps with accommodation bookings.

Sights & Activities

Once a famous centre for ceramics, Gmunden is now blessed with one of Austria's most unusual museums. The **Museum für Historische Sanitärobjeckte** (Klo & So Museum, Museum for Historical Sanitary Objects; ☎ 794 293; Kammerhofgasse 8; adult/child €4.20/1 🕑 10am-noon & 2-5pm Tue-Sat, 10am-noon Sun May-Oct) is basically a monumental collection of toilets. Here you can discover the difference between 'wash-down' and 'wash-out' models, and if you thought the latter with its flat poop deck and horizontal splash is just an anally obsessive Central European quirk, this museum vividly explodes the myth. The British were perching on these in the 19th century. About 80 toilets are on display, including one used by the royal *Po* (bottom) of Kaiser Franz Josef in his hunting lodge near Ebensee.

By May 2008 the Museum for Historical Sanitary Objects will be housed in the same building as the **Stadtmuseum Gmunden** (☎ 794-420; www.museen.gmunden.at; Kammerhofgasse 8); the museum is closed for renovation until then. Once it opens you can expect displays on the history of Gmunden and the salt trade, as well as a gallery. North of the Rathausplatz is the 12th-century **Pfarrkirche** (parish church; ☎ 642 17; Kirchplatz), a Gothic building later remodelled as baroque and sporting an altar (dating from 1678) by the baroque sculptor Thomas Schwanthaler (1634–1707).

Flanking the lake on the eastern side, the Renaissance castle **Schloss Weyer** (☎ 650 18; Freygasse 27; admission €7.50; 🕑 10am-noon & 2-5.30pm Tue-Fri, 10am-1pm Sat May-Sep) has a sizeable collection of porcelain, silver and jewellery. Also out here is the **Grünberg lookout** (984m). A **cable car** (adult/child return €11.50/6.80) takes you up, but it's also easy to walk.

On the western shore, a pretty nature reserve known as **Toscana Park** forms a backdrop to **Seeschloss Ort**. This castle on the lake is believed to have been built on the ruins of a Roman fortress. It dates from 909 or earlier (rebuilt in the 17th century after a fire) and has a picturesque courtyard, a late-Gothic external staircase and sgraffito from 1578.

Sleeping & Eating

Private rooms are the best deal for budget travellers – ask the tourist office to help you find one.

Haus Reiser (☎ 724 25; pension.reiser@aon.at; Freygasse 20; s/d €29/58) This good-value, private pension has a TV room and garden. There are seven bright, fresh rooms with radios, and all but two have their own bathroom.

Hotel-Gasthof Steinmaurer (☎ 704 88; www .steinmaurer.at; Traunsteinstrasse 23; s €53, d €84-92; P) This hotel is by the Grünberg cable car and across the road from a public beach. Rooms are modern, clean and – for the most part – large, and many doubles have a balcony or terrace. The busy restaurant (mains €7 to €15, open breakfast, lunch and dinner) serves the likes of vegetable cakes with to-mato ragout, and smoked-trout-and-prawn salad at outdoor tables overlooking the yacht marina.

Keramikhotel Goldener Brunnen (☎ 644 310; www. goldenerbrunnen.at; Traungasse 10; s/d €58/90; P 🖳) This excellent boutique hotel in the centre has recently been renovated and upgraded with sauna and wellness facilities. Rooms are very tastefully appointed with modern fit-tings, ceramic art adds a decorative touch, and a plus is its midrange restaurant (lunch menu €6.80, open lunch and dinner) with Austrian dishes such as Styrian chicken and some international favourites.

Seehotel Schwan (☎ 633 91; www.seehotel-schwan .at; Rathausplatz 8; s €70, d €110-130; P 🖳) This up-market hotel is right in the middle of town and has lake views from all rooms. These are large, with modern furniture and balcony, but the corridors are a bit gloomy. There's a

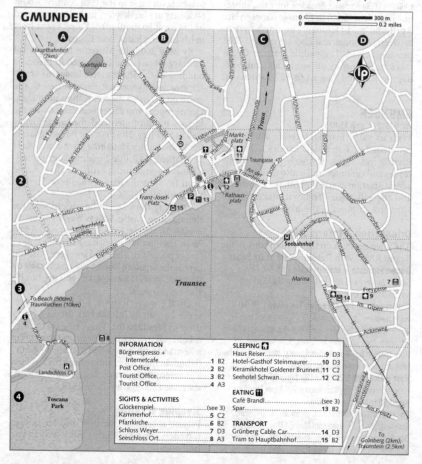

GMUNDEN

0 — 300 m
0 — 0.2 miles

INFORMATION	
Bürgerespresso + Internetcafe	1 B2
Post Office	2 B2
Tourist Office	3 B2
Tourist Office	4 A3

SIGHTS & ACTIVITIES	
Glockenspiel	(see 3)
Kammerhof	5 C2
Pfarrkirche	6 B2
Schloss Weyer	7 D3
Seeschloss Ort	8 A3

SLEEPING 🏠	
Haus Reiser	9 D3
Hotel-Gasthof Steinmaurer	10 D3
Keramikhotel Goldener Brunnen	11 C2
Seehotel Schwan	12 C2

EATING 🍴	
Café Brandl	(see 3)
Spar	13 B2

TRANSPORT	
Grünberg Cable Car	14 D3
Tram to Hauptbahnhof	15 B2

smart restaurant (mains €14.50 to €24, open lunch and dinner) downstairs, serving fresh lake fish on a daily changing menu.

Café Brandl (☎ 641 85; Rathausplatz 1; lunch €2-5; ☻ breakfast, lunch & dinner) This smart café/bar has bright yellow walls, black leather sofas and cubist artworks spiking its interior. It serves breakfast, cakes and light meals during the day and turns into a drinking venue (with snacks) at night.

A Spar supermarket awaits self-caterers at Kursaalgasse 5.

Getting There & Away

The Gmunden *Hauptbahnhof* on the Salzkammergut Attnang-Puchheim to Stainach-Irdning line is the main train station for the town. The Bad Ischl–Gmunden train fare (€7.60, 45 minutes, hourly) also includes the connecting tram to the centre. The Seebahnhof, near the marina, services the slow, private train line from Vorchdorf-Eggenburg.

Getting Around

The *Hauptbahnhof* is 2km northwest of the town centre: tram G (€1.60) departs from outside it to Franz Josef Platz after every train arrival. Bus rides in town cost €1.60. The Bummelzug (an electric train on wheels) takes you to Seeschloss Ort from the Rathausplatz for €2.50/1.50 per adult/child every 30 minutes from 9am to 7pm.

TRAUNKIRCHEN

☎ 07617 / pop 1775

The attractive hamlet of Traunkirchen sits on a spit of land about halfway along the western shore of the Traunsee. It's chiefly famous for the wooden **Fischerkanzel** (Fisherman's Pulpit; ☎ 2214; Klosterplatz 1; ☻ 8am-5pm or 6pm) in the Pfarrkirche. This was carved in 1753 and depicts the miracle of the fishes, with the apostles standing in a tub-shaped boat and hauling in fish-laden nets. The composition, colours (mostly silver and gold) and detail (even down to wriggling, bug-eyed fish) create a vivid impression.

For information on accommodation, contact the **tourist office** (☎ 2234; www.traunsee .at; Ortsplatz 1; ☻ 8am-6pm Mon-Fri, 9am-noon & 2-5pm Sat Jul & Aug, 8am-noon & 1-5pm Mon-Fri Sep-Jun).

Hourly trains from Gmunden go to Traunkirchen (€2.90, 10 minutes, hourly).

EBENSEE

☎ 06133 / pop 8700

In 2006 Ebensee achieved renown as the setting for the Salzkammergut's unusual teenage splatter film, *In 3 Tagen bist du Tod* (In Three Days You're Dead). It lies on the southern shore of the Traunsee and a favoured pastime here is to take the cable car (adult/child €16/€9.30 hourly) up to **Feuerkogel** (1592m), where you can find walking trails leading across a flattish plateau. Within an hour's walk is **Alberfeldkogel** (1708m), with an excellent view over the two Langbath lakes. Feuerkogel also provides access to winter **skiing** (day pass €30) with easy to medium slopes.

In early January every year, the men of Ebensee don giant illuminated head-dresses made of tissue paper in a bizarre ritual known as the Glöcklerlauf.

For details on accommodation and especially for activities like hiking and mountain-bike hire and trails, the local **tourist office** (☎ 8016; www.ebensee.com; Hauptstrasse 34; ☻ 8am-6pm Mon-Fri, 9am-noon & 2-6pm Sat Jul & Aug, 8am-noon & 1-5pm Mon-Fri Sep-Oct & May-Jun, 8am-noon & 1-4pm Mon-Fri Nov-Apr) by the Landungsplatz train station is very knowledgeable.

The train station for the centre and the boat landing stage is Ebensee-Landungsplatz, rather than the larger Ebensee station.

GRÜNAU

☎ 07616 / pop 2100

If you want to get off the beaten track, consider going to Grünau, east of Traunsee. Frequent trains run there from Wels (€9.30, one hour) and frequent buses run from Gmunden (€4, one hour).

The small, friendly **Tree House Backpacker Hotel** (☎ 8499; www.treehousehotel.net; Schindlbach 16; dm/d/tr €19/24/69) offers bike hire, horse riding, canyoning, rafting, skiing and snowboarding, among many other activities. Meals are available, there are bars for partying, and if you call ahead from Grünau station they'll pick you up.

ATTERSEE

☎ 07666 / pop 1500

The largest lake in the Salzkammergut is flanked mostly by hills, with mountains in the south. It's one of the less scenic and less visited of the Salzkammergut's lakes, but a few resorts cling to the shoreline, offering the usual water-leisure activities. The main resort is **Attersee**, which has a museum and a couple of churches. Its **tourist office** (☎ 7719; www.attersee.at; Nussdorferstrasse 15; ☺ 9am-6pm Mon-Fri, 9am-noon Sat, 9-11am Sun Jul & Aug, 9am-noon & 2-5pm Mon-Fri, 9am-noon Sat May, Jun & Sep, 9am-noon & 2-5pm Mon-Fri Oct-Apr) can help with accommodation.

Attersee-Schifffahrt (☎ 7806; www.atterseeschifffahrt.at) does mostly alternating boat circuits of the north (€7.50, 1¼ hours) and south (€13, 2¼ hours) regions of the lake several times most days from early May to late September, and a daily full circuit (€16, 3¾ hours) in July and August.

Getting There & Away

Two lakeside towns, Attersee and Schörfling, are connected to the rail network, each by a line branching from the main Linz–Salzburg route (though only regional trains stop): for Kammer-Schörfling change at Vöcklabruck, and for Attersee town change at Vöcklamarkt.

WOLFGANGSEE

Named after a local saint, this lake has two very popular resorts, St Wolfgang and St Gilgen, of which St Wolfgang is the most appealing. The third town on the lake, **Strobl** (population 2750), is a less remarkable but pleasant place at the start of a scenic toll road (€3 per car and per person) to Postalm (1400m).

A **ferry service** (☎ 06138 22 32-0; www.wolfgangseeschifffahrt.at) operates May to October from Strobl to St Gilgen (€6.40, 75 minutes), stopping at points en route. Services are most frequent from June to early September. Boats run from St Wolfgang to St Gilgen almost hourly during the day (€5.40, 35 minutes); the free *Eintauchen & Aufsteigen* timetable from local tourist offices gives exact times that will help with planning day trips and connecting with buses or the Schafbergbahn.

Schafberg

The Wolfgangsee is dominated by the 1783m **Schafberg** mountain on its northern shore. At the summit you'll find a hotel, a restaurant and phenomenal views over mountains and lakes (especially Mondsee, Attersee and, of course, Wolfgangsee). If you don't fancy the three-to four-hour walk from St Wolfgang (early tourists were carried up in sedan chairs), ride the **Schafbergbahn** (cogwheel railway; ☎ 06138 22 32-0; one-way/return €14/24; 40 min), which runs from May to October. Departures are approximately

hourly between 8.25am and 6pm, but the trip is so popular that you probably won't be able to get on the next train. Queue early, purchase a ticket for a specific train and then go for a wander along the lake or around St Wolfgang until your time comes to depart.

ST WOLFGANG
☎ 06138 / pop 3000

St Wolfgang is a charming town situated on the steep banks of the Wolfgangsee. Although its streets can get clogged with visitors during the day, things usually settle down early evening, which is the best time for a tranquil stroll along the forested lakeshore past the gently creaking wooden boathouses.

The village's main fame came as a place of pilgrimage (see the boxed text, p101) and today's visitors still come to see the 14th-century pilgrimage church, packed with art treasures.

Orientation & Information

The main streets of Pilgerstrasse and Michael Pacher Strasse join at the pilgrimage church. A road tunnel bypasses the town centre, and there are car parks at either end of it.

Tourist office (☎ 8003; www.wolfgangsee.at; Au 140; ☺ 9am-6pm Mon-Fri, 9am-noon Sat May, 9am-7pm Mon-Fri, 9am-noon & 2-6pm Sat Jun & Sep, 9am-8pm Mon-Fri, 9am-noon & 2-6pm Sat, 2-6pm Sun Jul & Aug, 9am-5pm Mon-Fri, 9am-noon Sat Oct-Apr) At the eastern tunnel entrance.

Pilgerstrasse branch (Michael-Pacher-Haus, Pilgerstrasse; ☺ 9am-noon & 2-5pm Mon-Fri Jun-Sep) At the other end of town, near the road tunnel.

Sights & Activities

St Wolfgang's impressive **Wallfahrtskirche** (☎ 2321; donation €0.80; ☺ 9am-6pm) was built in the 14th and 15th centuries and is virtually a spectacular gallery of religious art, with several altars (from Gothic to baroque), an extravagant pulpit, a fine organ and countless statues and paintings. The most impressive piece is the winged high altar, created by celebrated religious artist Michael Pacher between 1471 and 1481 – it's a perfect example of the German Gothic style, enhanced with the technical achievements of Renaissance Italy. The luminous colours of the paintings on the wings are as fascinating as the gilded figures in the centre, and the detail is startling, right down to the notes of music played by the hovering angels. So important was the altar that the wings were traditionally kept closed except for important festivals. Now they are always open, except for the eight weeks before Easter.

Another altar, made 200 years later, stands over the spot where St Wolfgang's axe is supposed to have landed (see the boxed text, p101).

A tourist-office booklet details the many **water sports** on offer. A few minutes' walk anti-clockwise round the lake is the start of the Schafberg railway.

Sleeping

St Wolfgang has some good private rooms in village homes or in farmhouses in the surrounding hills. Lists are available from the tourist office, which will phone places on your behalf.

Camping Appesbach (☎ 2206; Au 99; campsite per adult/child/tent €6.10/3.55/9; ☽ Easter-Sep) This campsite is on the lakeside 1km from St Wolfgang in the direction of Strobl.

Haus am See (☎ 2224; Michael Pacher Strasse 98; s/d without bathroom €20/50; ℗) This is a remarkable pension with features ripe for a Wolfgangsee mystery novel: it's run by a retired professor and his wife, evokes earlier decades, and the owner-couple also rent out four rooms in their boatshed down on the water (same price). Guests get free use of a boat and bike. It's conveniently opposite the Au bus stop.

Gästehaus Raudaschl (☎ 2561; www.haus-raudaschl.at; Au 41; s/d €23/46) Set back from the lake but with fine views over the rooftops to it, this pension run by a lovely old couple has a very homely feel and the advantage of being away from the tourist excesses in town.

Hotel Peter (☎ 2304; www.tiscover.at/hotel-peter; s €56-58, d €112-116; ℗ ▣) The generous-sized rooms at this four-star hotel have balconies looking onto the lake, large bathrooms and tasteful décor. The restaurant (mains €8.80 to €31.90, most under €15) also has a terrace overlooking the lake, with pasta and a good fish platter filled with poached, fried and baked local fish.

Im Weissen Rössl (☎ 2306-0; www.weissesroessl.at; Im Stöckl 74; s €124-140, d €170-248, ste per person €170; ℗ ▣ ☲) St Wolfgang's most famous hotel was the setting for Ralph Benatzky's operetta *The White Horse*, and a bed from the operetta today takes pride of place on one floor. Rooms are individually styled and somewhat idiosyncratic, but the more expensive ones

have a balcony and view over the lake. There's a large wellness area, and two pools – one pool literally floats on the lake (heated to 30°C), and another is indoors. It also has several good junior suites.

Eating & Drinking

There are dozens of hotels and cafés in St Wolfgang's compact town centre; stroll around and make your choice.

Kraftstoff-Bar (☎ 2491; Markt 128; mains €8-19; ☽ lunch & dinner) Decked out like a petrol station, this chilled-out bar and restaurant is an unusual place to curl your fingers around a drink, accompanied by wings and potato wedges, pasta, salads or grills; check out the charming balcony.

Im Weissen Rössl (☎ 2306-0; Im Stöckl 74; mains €12.50-32; ☽ lunch & dinner) There are two restaurants and a lovely wine cellar in this highly respected hotel. The Seerestaurant (kitchen open all day) tempts with regional and international dishes like organic local lamb in a liquorish-root sauce with sage polenta.

There's a Konsum supermarket 200m from the Schafbergbahn.

Getting There & Away

The only road to St Wolfgang approaches from Strobl in the east. For ferries, see opposite. A Postbus service from St Wolfgang via Strobl to St Gilgen (€5.20, 35 to 50 minutes) is frequent out of season, but tails off somewhat in summer when the ships run. For Salzburg (€7.90, 1¾ hours) you need to connect in St Gilgen or Strobl (€1.90, 11 minutes). Wolfgangsee ferries stop at the village centre (Markt stop) and at the Schafberg railway.

ST GILGEN
☎ 06227 / pop 3700

The ease of access to St Gilgen, 29km from Salzburg, is one reason why this town is so popular. It has boomed in the last decade or so, not least because of its very scenic setting. This, along with quieter Strobl, is quite a good base for lake water sports, and it is not quite as crowded as St Wolfgang.

Information

Café Dallman (☎ 2208; Mozartplatz 2a; per min €0.20; ☽ 11am-7pm Jun-Sep) Slow internet access, near the Rathaus.

Tourist office (☎ 2348; www.wolfgangsee.at; Mondsee Bundesstrasse 1a; ☽ 9am-noon & 2-6pm Mon-Fri,

9am-noon Sat May, Jun & Sep, 9am-8pm Mon-Fri, 9am-6pm Sat, 10am-5pm Sun Jul & Aug, 9am-noon & 2-5pm Mon-Fri, 9am-noon Sat Oct, 9am-noon & 2-5pm Mon-Fri Nov-Apr) Helps find rooms. Brochures are also inside the Rathaus on Mozartplatz.

Sights & Activities

The cosy little **Muzikinstumente-Museum der Völker** (Folk Music Instrument Museum; ☎ 8235; Aberseestrasse 11; admission €4; ☗ 9-11am & 3-7pm Tue-Sun Jun-mid-Oct, 9-11am & 2-5pm Mon-Fri mid-Oct–Jan, 9-11am & 2-5pm Mon-Thu, 9-11am Fri, 3-6pm Sun Jan-May) is home to 1500 musical instruments from all over the world, all of them collected by one family of music teachers. The son of the family, Askold zum Eck, can play them all and will happily demonstrate for hours. Visitors are welcome to have a go at anything from an African drum to an Indian sitar. There are some truly beautiful objects here and the family's enthusiasm is infectious.

The **Heimatkundliches Museum** (☎ 2642; Pichlerplatz 6; adult/child €3.50/2; ☗ 10am-noon & 3-6pm Tue-Sun Jun-Sep) won an award a few years back for its eclectic collection ranging from embroidery (originally manufactured in the building) to 4700 animals and religious objects.

Water sports such as windsurfing, waterskiing and sailing are popular here. There's a town swimming pool and a small, free beach with a grassy area beyond the yacht marina.

The mountain rising over the resort is **Zwölferhorn** (1520m); a cable car (€18 return) will whisk you to the top where there are good views and two trails (2 to 2½ hours) leading back to St Gilgen. Skiers ascend in winter.

Sleeping & Eating

Jugendgästehaus Schafbergblick (☎ 2365; jgh .stgilgen@oejhv.or.at; Mondseer Strasse 7; dm €17.50-19.50, s €19.50-29.50, d €35-44; ☗ reception 8am-1pm & 5-7pm Mon-Fri, 5-7pm Sat & Sun; P) This upmarket youth hostel has a good location near the town beach. Night keys are available.

Gasthof Rosam (☎ 2591; www.tiscover.at/rosam; Frontfestgasse 2-4; s €34, d €50-70; ☗ Easter–mid-Oct; P) Situated down near the lake, this family-run pension is well managed and refreshing, with clean rooms that are very good value for the location.

Pension Falkensteiner (☎ 2395; www.pension -falkensteiner.at; Salzburgerstrasse 13; s/d €40/56; P ☐) Some of the rooms have balconies and all are large in this no-frills but spotless pension with helpful management.

Gasthof Zur Post (☎ 2157; www.gasthofzurpost.at; Mozartplatz 8; s €82, d €116-148; P ☐) The 'Post-Geschichten' rooms at this old inn are beautifully designed in a cosily rustic style with shades of minimalism. There are heavy wooden beds, interesting colour schemes and wooden floors. The restaurant (mains €8 to €19, open lunch and dinner) serves national and regional specialities in a low-ceilinged, whitewashed dining room or outside on the elegant terrace. Try the game ragout.

San Giorgio (☎ 2605; Ischler Strasse 18; pizza €6-9; ☗ lunch & dinner Wed-Sun Feb-Apr, Nov & Dec, lunch & dinner Wed-Mon May-Oct, closed most of Jan) This Italian restaurant by the lake has eat-in (inside or in the garden) and take-away food. There's a bar/disco downstairs, the Zwolfer Alm Bar (open from 9pm), claiming to be the oldest nightclub in Austria (it was founded in 1930).

Fischer-Wirt Restaurant (☎ 2304; Ischlerstrasse 21; mains €7-17.50; ☗ lunch & dinner Jul & Aug, lunch & dinner Tue-Sun Sep-early Jan & Apr-Jun, lunch & dinner Thu-Sun Mar, closed early Jan & Feb) Situated on the water's edge, this popular seafood restaurant does a fish platter for two people for €35; some meat dishes also feature on the menu.

Restaurant Timbale (☎ 7587; Salzburger Strasse 2; mains €20-24, 6-course menu €62; ☗ lunch & dinner Sat-Wed, dinner Fri Sep-Jul, lunch & dinner Aug) Reserve ahead for a table in what is considered to be one of the finest restaurants on the Wolfgangsee. The atmosphere is informal and it specialises in seasonal regional dishes.

Getting There & Away

St Gilgen is 50 minutes from Salzburg by Postbus (€5.40), with hourly departures until early evening; some buses continue on to Stobl and Bad Ischl (€4.40, 34 minutes). The bus station is near the base station of the cable car. Highway 154 provides a scenic route north to Mondsee. For details on the ferry service to/from St Wolfgang, see p260.

MONDSEE

☎ 06232 / pop 3200

The town of Mondsee extends along the northern tip of this crescent-shaped lake noted for its warm water; coupled with its closeness to Salzburg (30km away), this makes it a highly developed, popular lake for weekending Salzburgers.

The **tourist office** (☎ 2270; www.mondsee.at; Dr Franz Müller Strasse 3; ☗ 8am-6pm Mon-Fri Apr & May, 8am-6pm Mon-Fri, 9am-6pm Sat Jun & Sep, 8am-7pm Mon-Fri, 9am-

7pm Sat & Sun Jul & Aug, 8am-noon & 1-5pm Mon-Fri Oct-Mar) is between the church and the lake.

Sights & Activities

If you're allergic to the film *The Sound of Music*, there's just one piece of advice: blow town. Even the lemon-yellow baroque façade (added in 1740, incidentally) of the 15th-century **parish church** (☉ 8am-7pm) achieved notoriety by featuring in those highly emotional Von Trapp wedding scenes in the film.

After that, make a beeline for the **Museum Mondseeland und Pfahlbaumuseum** (Wrede Platz; adult/child & student €3/1.50; ☉ 10am-5pm Tue-Sun May-Sep) next door, with displays on Stone Age finds and the monastic culture of the region (Mondsee is a very old monastery site).

The **Segelschule Mondsee** (☎ 3548-200; www.segel schule-mondsee.at, in German; Robert Baum Promenade 3) is the largest sailing school in Austria and offers sailing (five days €214) and windsurfing (two days €99) courses.

Sleeping

For lists of hotels and restaurants, ask at the tourist office.

Jugendgästehaus (☎ 2418; jgh.mondsee@oejhv.or.at; Krankenhausstrasse 9; dm/s/d €19.50/29.50/44; Ⓟ) This HI hostel is a few minutes' walk from the centre of town.

Gasthof Grüner Baum (☎ 2314; www.gruenerbaum .mondsee.at; Herzog Odilo Strasse 39; s/d with breakfast €47/76) Rooms in this small and no-frills pen-sion have been renovated recently, but ask for one away from the busy street.

Leitnerbräu (☎ 6500; www.leitnerbraeu.at; Steiner-bachstrasse 6; s €76-115, d €126-159; Ⓟ 💻) This four-star hotel faces the Marktplatz. Some of the light and airy rooms have a view of the square and the church – ask when booking. There's a sauna, steam bath and small gym on site.

Eating

Gasthof Blaue Traube (☎ 2237; Marktplatz 1; mains €8-15; ☉ lunch & dinner Thu-Tue) The 'Blue Grape', opposite the church, serves a good schnitzel and other classics for eating in or usefully as take away; check out its ice cream.

Mayrhofer's (☎ 36607; Marktplatz 4; mains €9-12.50; ☉ 9am-midnight Wed-Mon) If you feel like a light salad with prawns, Mayrhofer's is where it's done well. This restaurant and bar also stays open long after the tour buses have left town.

Restorante da Michele (Marktplatz 9; mains €10.50-15.50; ☉ lunch & dinner Tue-Sun). The homemade pasta and bread is especially popular at this delightful Italian restaurant in the centre of town.

For self-caterers, there's a Spar supermarket at Rainerstrasse 5.

Getting There & Away

Hourly Postbus services connect Mondsee with Salzburg (€5.40, 50 minutes), but only three direct buses a day go to St Gilgen (€3.70, 20 minutes). Expect to pay €24 for a ride to St Gilgen by **taxi** (☎ 0664-22000 22).

Salzburg & Salzburger Land

Close your eyes, picture Austria and nine times out of 10 it will be the Salzburger Land of childhood that pops to mind. Before most people have set eyes on Salzburg, their heads spin with the sound of Maria belting her heart out as she skips down the Alps, or Mozart's enchanting *Eine kleine Nachtmusik*. Little wonder, then, that this chocolate-box land of edelweiss-clad slopes, towering peaks and medieval fortresses comes back to spark the imagination years later – inviting exploration.

Let's start at the very beginning. Salzburg, to the north of the province, is a mere snow-ball throw from Germany. Built high on the riches of salt, today its Unesco World Heritage centre blends glorious baroque architecture with modern art galleries and musical prowess. Scratch beneath the surface and you'll discover the city's youthful streak: retro cafés with not a strudel in sight and riverside bars oozing urban cool offer a taste of a 21st-century city in the making.

Trace the Salzach River south and the vista shifts from gently undulating alpine pastures to brooding limestone turrets. The chiselled pinnacles of the Tennengebirge are the place to work up a sweat hiking – cliffhanger-style – before shivering in subzero temperatures within the world's biggest accessible ice caves in Werfen. Most travellers don't venture further, but dig a little deeper and you'll unearth offbeat treasures: from the yawning Liechtensteinklamm (Liechtenstein Gorge) to the high moors surrounding Mauterndorf, where the music is the sound of silent hills.

HIGHLIGHTS

- Roaming the clifftop ramparts of **Festung Hohensalzburg** (p271) to see Salzburg spread out beneath you
- Getting drenched by the trick fountains at **Schloss Hellbrunn** (p283), a palace fit for mischievous bishops
- Donning a boiler suit to venture to the bowels of the earth at Hallein's salt mine, **Salzwelten** (p284)
- Gawping at the sheer scale of the 300m-high chasm, **Liechtensteinklamm** (p286)
- Standing in awe of sparkling ice sculptures in the teeth-chattering confines of **Eisriesenwelt** (p285) ice caves in Werfen

Festung Hohensakburg
Schloss Hellbrunn ★
★ Hallein-Salzwelten

★ Werfen
★ Liechtensteinklamm

- POPULATION: 529,000   ■ AREA: 7154 SQ KM   ■ HIGHEST ELEVATION: GROSSVENEDIGER 3674M

History

Salzburg has had a tight grip on the region as far back as Roman times, when the town Juvavum stood on the site of the present-day city. This Roman stronghold came under constant attack from warlike Celtic tribes and was ultimately destroyed by them or abandoned due to disease.

St Rupert established the first Christian kingdom in this part of Austria in about 696. As centuries passed, the successive archbishops of Salzburg gradually increased their power and eventually were given the grandiose titles of princes of the Holy Roman Empire.

Wolf Dietrich von Raitenau (1587–1612), one of Salzburg's most influential archbishops, instigated the baroque reconstruction of the city, commissioning many of its most beautiful buildings. He fell from power after losing a dispute over salt with the powerful rulers of Bavaria and died a prisoner.

Another of the city's archbishops, Paris Lodron (1619–53), managed to keep the principality out of the Europe-wide Thirty Years' War. Salzburg also remained neutral during the War of the Austrian Succession a century later, but bit by bit the province's power gradually waned; during the Napoleonic Wars Salzburg came under the thumb of France and Bavaria. It became part of Austria in 1816.

Climate

Average temperatures in Salzburg range from 23°C in July and August to -1°C in January. In

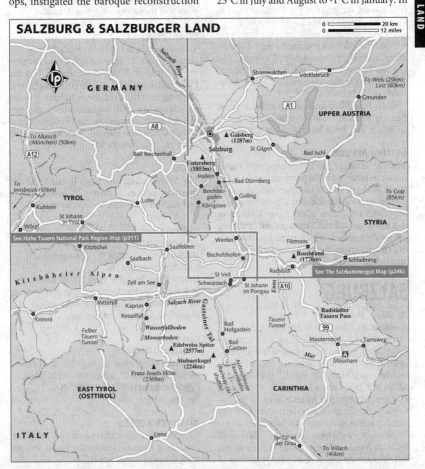

the mountains winter brings heavy snowfalls and much lower temperatures, with cooler but sunny days in summer. Spring is the wettest time, with an average of 13 rainy days per month.

National Parks

A large part of the high-altitude Hohe Tauern National Park lies within Salzburg province. This area is covered separately (p310).

Getting There & Away

Salzburg is well connected to the rest of Austria by public transport, with excellent rail and road connections to neighbouring Salzkammergut and down into Hohe Tauern National Park. Salzburg's *Hauptbahnhof* (main train station) has good connections to Germany, Italy and the Czech Republic.

By road, the main routes into the region are the A8 from Munich and the A1 from Linz. To enter Salzburg Province from Carinthia and the south, you can use the A10 from Spittal an der Drau or the Autoschleuse Tauernbahn south of Bad Gastein.

Both scheduled and no-frills flights from Europe and the USA serve Salzburg airport (p395), a half-hour bus ride from the city.

Getting Around

Salzburg's efficient bus and train network makes it easy to reach even the province's smaller villages. Salzburg itself is compact enough to negotiate on foot but also has a network of city buses and trains (see p282). Tourist offices in the province sell the **Salzburgerland Card** (www .salzburgerlandcard.com), which provides discounts on attractions in the province (six-day card adult/child €39/19.50).

SALZBURG

☎ 0662 / pop 145,800

A shrine to Mozart's melodies? A *Sound of Music* stage? A Disneyfied city with scrumptious cakes, sugar-coated mountains and one helluva fortress? Yep, Salzburg is undeniably touristy and theatrical, yet still it's a composition that takes some beating: from Festung Hohensalzburg atop Mönchsberg to the baroque splendour of Residenzplatz and the slender spires that crowd the skyline.

This is a city where kitsch and class walk hand in hand. If Maria is just itching to get out, take her on a warble-as-you-pedal tour of the sights; if Wolfgang is more your cup of tea, join the well-heeled crowd at Schloss Mirabell to hear the maestro's symphonies. Whether it's to be a shopping spree on Getreidegasse to find lederhosen that fit, or a horse-drawn carriage ride through the cobbled centre, in Salzburg embracing the clichés is positively encouraged. And why not? It's fun.

When the overload of Mozart and Miss Andrews gets too much to handle, Salzburg's lesser-known corners offer blissful respite. The contemporary contours of Museum der Moderne, the chilled bars lining the right bank and the solitude of Kapuzinerberg are the perfect remedy for an overkill of the obvious. Sitting on the banks of the fast-flowing Salzach as the sun sinks over the city, it becomes clear that this place still rocks. Even without Amadeus.

Orientation

Salzburg is split in two by the Salzach River. The compact, pedestrianised *Altstadt* (old town) is on the left bank. Rising above the city, Festung Hohensalzburg clings to cliffs of Mönchsberg. Stepping over the river, the right bank is home to Schloss Mirabell, Kapuzinerberg, and numerous entertainment venues, hotels and restaurants. About 10 minutes' walk further north is the *Hauptbahnhof* and bus station.

MAPS

The tourist office and most hotels hand out free maps of the city centre. Many bookshops and souvenir kiosks also sell city maps.

Information

BOOKSHOPS

Motzko (Map p269; ☎ 88 33 11; Elisabethstrasse 1) Stocks English-language books.
Motzko Reise (Map p269; ☎ 88 33 11-55; Rainerstrasse 24) Across the road from Motzko; sells maps and guidebooks.
News & Books (Map p269; *Hauptbahnhof* platform 2a) International newspapers and magazines.

EMERGENCY

Ambulance (☎ 144)
Hospital (Landeskrankenhaus; Map p267; ☎ 44 82; Müllner Hauptstrasse 48) Just north of the Mönchsberg.
Police headquarters (Map p269; ☎ 63 83; Alpenstrasse 90)

INTERNET ACCESS

Internet cafés are scattered all over Salzburg; those near the train station are much cheaper than those in the *Altstadt*.

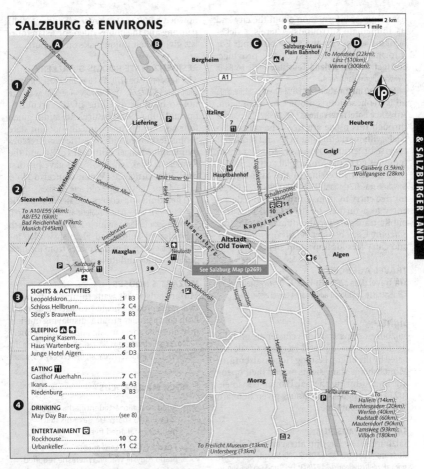

SALZBURG & ENVIRONS

International Telephone Discount (Map p269; ☎ 88 31 99; Kaiserschützenstrasse 8; per hr €2; ⏰ 8.30am–10pm Mon–Sat) Also has cheap international telephone calls.

Salzburg Internet Café (Map p270; ☎ 84 20 63-0; Gstättengasse 3; per hr €2; ⏰ 10am–10pm) Skype and discount international calls available.

LAUNDRY
Norge Exquisit (Map p270; ☎ 87 63 81; Paris-Lodron-Strasse 16; self-service wash €10; ⏰ 7.30am–6pm Mon–Fri, 8am–noon Sat).

MONEY
Bankomaten (ATMs) are all over the place.

Amex (Map p270; ☎ 84 38 400; Mozartplatz 5; ⏰ 9am–5.30pm Mon–Fri, 9am–noon Sat & Sun) Next to the tourist office. Amex travellers cheques are cashed free of charge.

Western Union (Map p269; ☎ 93 00 03-162; ⏰ 8.30am–7pm Mon–Fri, 8.30am–4.30pm Sat) Changes money at its branch in the *Hauptbahnhof*. Exchange booths are open all day every day at the airport. There are also plenty of exchange offices downtown, but beware of high commission rates.

POST
Main post office (Map p270; Residenzplatz 9; ⏰ 7am–6.30pm Mon–Fri, 8–10am Sat)

Station post office (Map p269; Südtiroler Platz 1; ⏰ 8am–6pm Mon–Fri)

TOURIST INFORMATION
The main **tourist office** (Map p270; ☎ 889 87-330; www.salzburg.info; Mozartplatz 5; ⏰ 9am–6pm Mon–Sat Jan–Apr & mid-Oct–Nov, 9am–7pm May–mid-Oct & Dec)

has plenty of information about the city and its immediate surrounds. There's a ticket booking agency in the same building. For information on the rest of the province, contact **Salzburgerland Tourismus** (☎ 66 88-0; www.salzburg erland.com).

Salzburg Information (☎ 88 98 70; www.salzburginfo .at) is the head tourism office for the region. Advance **hotel reservations** (☎ 88 98 73 14) placed through this office are free. The office also deals with marketing inquiries and sends out tourist brochures; however, for in-person inquiries go to the Mozartplatz office.

It's worth investing in the **Salzburg Card** (low/high season 24hr-card €21/23, 48hr €29/31, 72hr €34/36) for free entry to all major sights and reduced entry to a further 24 attractions, plus free public transport for the duration. The free *Salzburg Card* booklet details opening hours and entry fees for important sights.

TRAVEL AGENCIES
STA Travel (Map p269; ☎ 45 87 33-0; www.statravel.at; Rainerstrasse 2) Student and budget travel agency.

Sights
Salzburg's star attractions cluster around the *Altstadt*, a Unesco World Heritage site dominated by the hilltop Festung Hohensalzburg on Mönchsberg. Many sights extend their opening hours during the Salzburger Festspiele (p274) in August. The hours given here are for non-festival times.

SALZBURG MUSEUM
Salzburg's new flagship attraction is **Salzburg Museum** (Map p270; ☎ 62 08 08-700; Mozartplatz 1; www .smca.at; adult/student/child €7/6/3; ☿ 9am-5pm Tue-Sun, to 8pm Thu). Housed in the sublime Neue Residenz palace, the museum sheds light on Salzburg's rich heritage with its hands-on exhibits. A visit starts beneath the cobbled courtyard in the impressively illuminated **Kunsthalle**, which presents rotating exhibitions of contemporary art. On the 1st floor, **Salzburg Persönlich** offers fascinating insight into the characters that have shaped the city's history, including the alchemist Paracelsus and performer Richard Mayr; kids love to watch the birdie-style camera that takes nostalgic portrait shots you can send home by email. Upstairs, prince-archbishops glower down from the walls at **Mythos Salzburg**, which celebrates the city as a source of artistic and poetic inspiration over the ages. Be sure to glimpse Carl Spitzweg's re-

nowned *Sonntagsspaziergang* (Sunday Stroll) painting and the home-videos of Asian tourists giving their unique take on Salzburg.

RESIDENZ STATE ROOMS & GALLERY
The **Residenz** (Map p270; ☎ 80 42-26 90; Residenzplatz 1; adult/child €8.20/2.60; ☿ 10am-5pm Tue-Sun) was the not-so-humble dwelling of the archbishops until the 19th century. An audio guide tour takes in the unashamedly opulent state rooms, festooned with tapestries and frescoes by Johann Michael Rottmayr (p52), and the Konferenz Saal, where Mozart gave his first public performance (Violin Concerto No 5 in A Major) at the ripe old age of six.

The admission covers the **Residenz Galerie** (☎ 84 04 51; www.residenzgalerie.at; Residenzplatz 1; ☿ 10am-5pm Tue-Sun), which features a superb collection of Dutch and Flemish works, including a clutch of masterpieces from the likes of Rembrandt and Rubens.

MOZART'S HOUSES
Mozart fans won't want to miss out on the two museums dedicated to the great man. Both cover similar ground, displaying musical instruments, sheet music and memorabilia.

Mozarts Geburtshaus (Mozart's Birthplace; Map p270; ☎ 84 43 13; www.mozarteum.at; Getreidegasse 9; adult/

ROCK ME AMADEUS

- Aged two, Mozart identified a pig's squeal as G sharp. He gave his first public recital aged five.

- Aged 23, Mozart fell in love with the soprano Aloysia Weber. When she rebuffed him, he promptly married her sister.

- When not composing, Mozart enjoyed billiards, heavy drinking sessions and teaching his pet starling to sing operettas.

- A boy once asked Mozart how to write a symphony. He replied that a symphony was too difficult at such a young age. 'You wrote symphonies at my age!' exclaimed the boy. 'But I didn't have to ask how,' replied Mozart.

- Modern psychologists believe that Mozart suffered from Tourette's Syndrome, a disorder leading to uncontrolled outbursts of swearing and obscene behaviour.

SALZBURG & SALZBURGER LAND

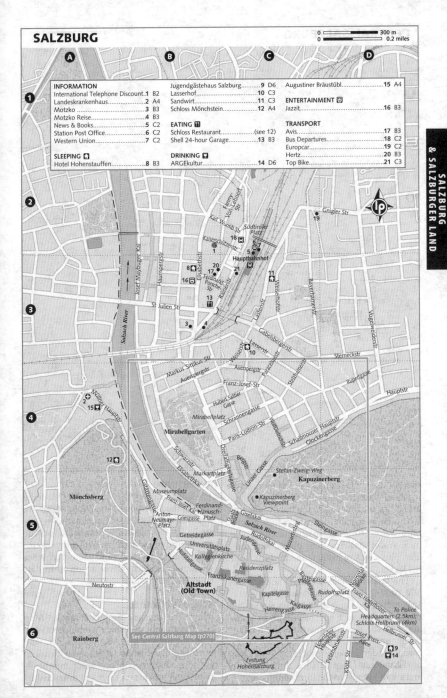

SALZBURG

0 — 300 m
0 — 0.2 miles

INFORMATION
International Telephone Discount....**1** B2
Landeskrankenhaus........................**2** A4
Motzko...**3** B3
Motzko Reise....................................**4** B3
News & Books...................................**5** C2
Station Post Office............................**6** C2
Western Union..................................**7** C2

SLEEPING 🏠
Hotel Hohenstauffen.........................**8** B3

Jugendgästehaus Salzburg...............**9** D6
Lasserhof..**10** C3
Sandwirt...**11** C3
Schloss Mönchstein.........................**12** A4

EATING 🍴
Schloss Restaurant....................(see 12)
Shell 24-hour Garage.....................**13** B3

DRINKING 🍷
ARGEkultur.....................................**14** D6

Augustiner Bräustübl.......................**15** A4

ENTERTAINMENT 🎭
Jazzit...**16** B3

TRANSPORT
Avis...**17** B3
Bus Departures...............................**18** C2
Europcar..**19** C2
Hertz..**20** B3
Top Bike...**21** C3

See Central Salzburg Map (p270)

SALZBURG & SALZBURGER LAND

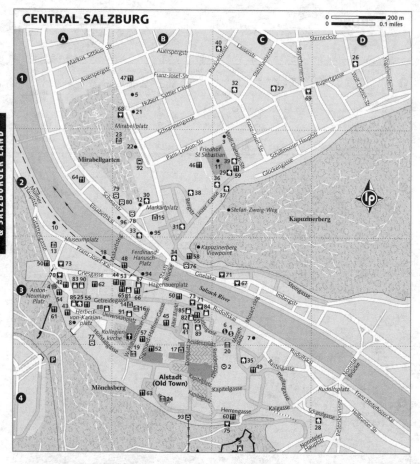

CENTRAL SALZBURG

child €6/1.50; ⏰ 9am-7pm Jul & Aug, 9am-6pm Sep-Jun)
is where Mozart spent the first 17 years of
his life. In the first room, the holy Wolfgang
is shown as a babe beneath a fluorescent
blue halo. Other curiosities include the
mini-violin that Amadeus played as a tod-
dler, plus a lock of his hair and buttons from
his jacket.

The **Mozart-Wohnhaus** (Mozart's Residence; Map
p270; ☎ 87 42 27-40; www.mozarteum.at; Makartplatz 8;
adult/child €6/2; ⏰ 9am-7pm Jul & Aug, 9am-6pm Sep-Jun)
takes a more hi-tech approach, with an audio
guide giving the low-down on the Mozart
family and serenading you with opera ex-
cerpts. Under the same roof is the **Mozart Ton-
und Filmmuseum** (Map p270), a film and music
archive of interest to the ultra-enthusiast.

RUPERTINUM
The sister gallery of the Museum der Moderne
(p272), the **Rupertinum** (Map p270; ☎ 84 22 20-451;
Wiener-Philharmoniker-Gasse 9; adult/child €6/4; ⏰ 10am-
6pm Tue-Sun, 10am-9pm Wed) is devoted to rotating
exhibitions of modern art, with a strong emphasis on graphic works and photography. See
www.museumdermoderne.at for up-to-date
listings of exhibitions.

SCHLOSS MIRABELL
The 17th-century **Schloss Mirabell** (Map
p270) was built by Prince-Archbishop Wolf
Dietrich for his mistress Salome Alt, who
bore the archbishop at least 10 children
(sources disagree on the exact number –
poor Wolf was presumably too distracted by

SALZBURG & SALZBURGER LAND

spiritual matters to keep count himself). The best way to experience the Mirabell magic is to attend a lunchtime or evening concert (see p279) in the palace's magnificent Marble Hall, which boasts chandeliers and wall reliefs.

If you fancy skipping through gardens von Trapp–style, there's no better place to act out those fantasies than the manicured **Mirabellgarten**, where the young scallywags practised singing *Do-Re-Mi* around the Pegasus statue. The neat lawns, rose gardens and tree-fringed avenues are less overrun first thing in the morning and early evening. The Tanzerin sculpture is a great spot to photograph the gardens with the fortress as a backdrop.

FESTUNG HOHENSALZBURG

Rising like a vision above Salzburg, this mighty 900-year-old **fortress** (Map p270; ☎ 84 24 30-11; Mönchsberg; adult/child €10/5.70; ☼ 9.30am-5pm Jan-Apr & Oct-Dec, 9am-6pm May-Jun & Sep, 9am-7pm Jul-Aug) is one of the biggest and best-preserved in Europe. It's easy to spend a half a day up here, roaming the ramparts for far-reaching views over the city's spires, the Salzach and surrounding Alps. The fortress is a steep 15-minute jaunt from the centre, or a speedy ride in the glass **Festungsbahn funicular** (included in the ticket price).

The imposing fortress bears witness to the power of the prince-archbishops. As you stroll around, keep your eyes peeled for **turnips** (there are 58 in total). Rumour has it that Leonard von Keutschach, archbishop of Salzburg from 1495 to 1519, used to squander money, so his uncle flung a turnip at his head to (literally) knock some sense into him. Ironically, the turnip became a symbol for Leonard's new-found wisdom. Other highlights include the **Golden Hall** with its gold-studded ceiling imitating a starry night sky; the **Eiserner Wehrmann** soldier encrusted with 328,000 iron nails (a creative means of raising money for war victims); and the spine-tingling **torture chamber**.

FAR FROM THE MADDING CROWD

The crowds on Getreidegasse and the zillionth souvenir shop selling Mozart paraphernalia are part and parcel of Salzburg. Yet this city has plenty of lesser-known, quiet nooks off the well-trodden tourist track. Here is a rundown of peaceful retreats to help you keep your cool:

- The narrow, cobblestoned **Steingasse** was first a Roman road, then home to tanners and potters during the Middle Ages. It's particularly beautiful in the late morning sun when diffused light casts soft shadows across its medieval façades.
- Take a breather by kicking back with a picnic or beer on the banks of the meandering **Salzach River**. Grab a spot to admire the city's skyline from a different angle on tree-lined promenades such as Elisabethkai and Josef-Mayburger-Kai.
- Festung Hohensalzburg is not the only highlight on **Mönchsberg**; wander a little further at the top to find crumbling, overgrown fortifications and snatch glimpses of Salzburg's rooftops through the trees.
- A few paces from the hubbub of Linzer Gasse, the cloisters of **Friedhof St Sebastian** (Map p270) are an oasis of calm. Amid the sea of iron and stone crosses, pick out the graves of Mozart's wife (Constanze) and father (Leopold). At the centre of the cemetery stands Gabrielskapelle, Archbishop Wolf Dietrich von Raitenau's elaborate mausoleum.
- Stefan-Zweig-Weg climbs up towards the peace of **Kapuzinerberg**, passing through shady beech forest and emerging at a viewpoint with wide-screen views of Salzburg. It's a great vantage point to take photos of the dramatic fortress, Hohensalzburg.

MUSEUM DER MODERNE

Perched atop Mönchsberg, this white-marble, oblong-shaped **museum** (Map p270; ☎ 84 22 20-403; adult/child €8/6; ⊙ 10am-6pm Tue-Sun, 10am-9pm Wed) stands in stark contrast to the fortress. The futuristic glass-and-concrete reels in art aficionados with its rotating exhibitions of 20th- and 21st-century works. While you're up here, enjoy an espresso and fabulous views on the panoramic terrace of **M32** (⊙ 9am-1am Tue-Sat, 9am-6pm Sun), or nip into James Turrell's cylindrical **Sky Space** to while away the hours gazing up at the sky.

STIEGL'S BRAUWELT

Beer lovers should check out Austria's largest private **brewery** (Map p267; ☎ 83 87-14 92; Bräuhausstrasse 9; adult/child €9/4; ⊙ 10am-5pm Wed-Sun Jun-Sep), where a tour runs through the different stages of the brewing process and includes a peek at the world's tallest beer tower. For those who would rather quaff brews than learn about them, a free Stiegl beer and pretzel are thrown in for the price of a ticket. Take bus 1 or 2 to Bräuhausstrasse.

Activities

The old town is squeezed between Kapuzinerberg and Mönchsberg, both of which are crisscrossed with excellent **walking** trails. There is a

viewpoint (Map p270) at the western end of the Kapuzinerberg, with ramparts built during the Thirty Years' War; the climb up from Linzer Gasse takes 10 minutes. On Mönchsberg, the stroll from Festung Hohensalzburg to Augustiner Bräustübl (p279) is scenic. There is also a great network of **cycling routes**; bikes are available for hire in various places in Salzburg (see p282).

The incredibly popular **River Cruises** (Map p270; ☎ 82 58 58; www.salzburgschifffahrt.at; adult/child €12/7, to Schloss Hellbrunn €15/10; ⊙ Apr-Oct) are a leisurely way to see the sights. Cruises depart from Makart bridge and take about an hour, with some of them chugging on to Schloss Hellbrunn (p283; the ticket price does not cover entry to the palace).

Walking Tour

Start this leisurely two- to three-hour walk by absorbing the bustle of **Domplatz (1)** and the adjoining **Kapitelplatz (2)** and **Residenzplatz (3)**. The hubbub from the market stalls lining these broad squares competes with the clip-clop of horses' hooves and the backbeat of buskers. On Residenzplatz, listen out for the chime of the **Glockenspiel (4)** at 7am, 11am and 6pm.

Soaring skywards, the 15th-century **Dom (5;** cathedral; Domplatz) features three bronze doors symbolising – left to right as you face them –

faith, hope and charity. Its striking cupola was rebuilt after being destroyed by a bomb in 1944. Step inside to see the dome and the Romanesque font where Mozart was baptised. The adjacent **Dommuseum** (☎ 84 41 89; adult/child €5/1.50; ☷ 10am-5pm Mon-Sat, 11am-6pm Sun) is a treasure-trove of baroque art, lavish goldwork and tapestries.

Turning left at the first courtyard off Franziskanergasse brings you to the marvellously ornate **Stiftskirche St Peter** (6; St Peter Bezirk). Beneath a green stuccoed ceiling lit by chandeliers, the walls are smothered with religious art and baroque swirls. Look out for the dramatic statue of the archangel Michael shoving a crucifix through the throat of a goaty demon. The graveyard is home to the so-called **catacombs** (7; Katakomben; ☎ 84 45 78-0; adult/child €1/0.60; ☷ 10.30am-5pm daily May-Sep, 10.30am-3.30pm Wed & Thu, 10.30am-4pm Fri-Sun Oct-Apr), cavelike chapels and crypts hewn out of the cliff face.

Back on Franziskanergasse, your gaze is drawn to the slender spires of the **Franziskanerkirche** (8; ☎ 84 36 29-0; Franziskanergasse 5; ☷ daylight), housing a baroque altar surrounded by five pillars.

WALK FACTS

Start Domplatz
Finish Residenzplatz
Distance 1.5km
Duration Two to three hours, including stops

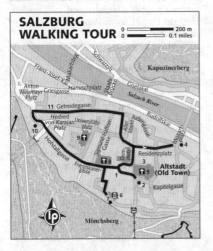

SALZBURG WALKING TOUR

The western end of Franziskanergasse opens into Max-Reinhardt-Platz, where you'll see the back of Fischer von Erlach's baroque **Kollegienkirche** (9; Universitätsplatz; ☷ daylight).

Stroll left to reach Herbert-von-Karajan-Platz and the **Pferdeschwemme** (10; horse trough), a rather elaborate drinking spot for the archbishops' mounts. Created in 1700, this is a horse-lover's delight, with rearing equine pin-ups surrounding Michael Bernhard Mandl's statue of a horse tamer.

Head right around the corner and you'll join the bustling crowds beneath the wrought-iron shop signs along **Getreidegasse** (11). Turning right down Alter Markt brings you back to Residenzplatz.

Salzburg for Children

With marionettes galore, sticky chocolate balls and a *big* fairytale-like fortress, Salzburg is truly a kid-oriented city. If the crowds prove unbearable with tots in tow, take them to let off steam at the city's adventure **playgrounds** (there are 80 to pick from); a great choice is the one on Franz-Josef-Kai (Map p270). In summer, little 'uns love to splash in shallow pools and whiz down the slides at Austria's largest outdoor pool, **Leopoldskron** (Map p267; ☎ 82 92 65; Leopoldskronstrasse 50; adult/child €3.80/1.80; ☷ 7am-7pm May-Sep), just south of the centre.

Salzburg's sights are usually half-price for children and many are free for under-six-year-olds. Plenty of galleries, museums and theatres also have dedicated programmes for kids and families. These include the **Museum der Moderne** (opposite), which has Saturday art workshops for over-fives and guided tours for over-10s (€2), and the matinée performances at the enchanting **Salzburger Marionettentheater** (p280). The **Salzburg Museum** (p268) has plenty of hands-on displays, from coin rubbings and puzzles to a practice bar for budding ballerinas.

Aside from the above, the **Haus der Natur** (Map p270; ☎ 84 26 53; www.hausdernatur.at; Museumsplatz 5; adult/child €5/3; ☷ 9am-5pm) has a massive aquarium with Nemo-style clown-fish and coral reefs, and a reptile enclosure teeming with snakes and crocs. Shark feeding time is 10.30am on Mondays. Near Untersberg, the open-air **Freilicht Museum** (Map p267; ☎ 85 00 11; Hasenweg; adult/child €7/3.50; ☷ 9am-6pm Tue-Sun Mar-Nov) steps back in time and back to nature. There are 60 traditional Austrian farmhouses to explore, tractors to clamber over, goats to feed and a huge adventure playground to run around in.

SALZBURG & SALZBURGER LAND

Tours

The following companies offer broadly the same *Sound of Music* tour; all last from three to four hours and cost around €40. They take in major landmarks featured in the film and include a visit out into the Salzkammergut countryside for more movie locations. You'll see the Nonnberg Abbey, the church in Mondsee used for the wedding scenes, and Liesl's gazebo, now relocated to the gardens of Schloss Hellbrunn (p283). The soundtrack to the film is played in the buses as they bowl merrily along. It can be a real scream if you're with a lively crowd who are prepared to get into the whole thing by singing along and acting out scenes from the film.

Bob's Special Tours (Map p270; ☎ 84 95 11; www .bobstours.com; Rudolfskai 38) Also offers a *Sound of Music* tour in a light aircraft.

Salzburg Panorama Tours (Map p270; ☎ 87 40 29; www.panoramatours.com; Mirabellplatz) Boasts the 'original *Sound of Music* Tour' with letters from Maria von Trapp to prove it. Tours booked through YOHO youth hostel are 10% cheaper.

Salzburg Sightseeing Tours (Map p270; ☎ 88 16 16; www.salzburg-sightseeingtours.at; Mirabellplatz 2) This company claims one of their buses was used in the film.

If you'd rather pedal around town warbling songs from the film, opt for **Fräulein Maria's Cycling Tours** (Map p270; ☎ 342 62 97; incl bike hire €22; ☻ 9.30am May-Sep). These freewheeling tours last a leisurely three hours and take in the main film locations along the route. No advance booking is necessary, so you can just turn up at the meeting point at the entrance to Mirabellgarten.

Festivals & Events

The **Salzburger Festspiele** (Salzburg Festival) is the annual summer bash, which brings world-class opera, classical music and drama to stages across the city from late July to August. This is the zenith of Salzburg's cultural calendar, a time when the city takes on a new vitality, and a few thousand extra tourists, too.

Prices stretch from €5 to €250; the cheapest prices are for standing-room tickets. Under-26 year olds are eligible for reduced-price deals for two or more events (€15 to €22). Most tickets sell out months in advance but try checking for cancellations – inquire at the **ticket office** (Map p270; ☎ 80 45-500; info@salzburgfestival.at; Herbert-von-Karajan-Platz 11; ☻ 9am-start of last performance of the day). You can see the programme as early as the pre-

vious November on the festival's website, www.salzburg festival.at.

Held in late January, the **Mozartwoche** (Mozart Week; www.mozarteum.at) is a nod to Salzburg's most famous son, while Easter is yet another excuse for a mammoth music festival, the **Osterfestspiele** (www.osterfestspiele-salzburg.at). Salzburg leaps back into the 21st century at the **Sommerszene** (www.sommerszene.at), hosting cutting-edge dance, theatre and music performances from mid-June to mid-July. In the city where *Silent Night* was composed, it's little wonder that Advent is a big deal; the **Christmas Market** on Domplatz is a festive highlight, with carol singers and the obligatory stalls offering gingerbread and mulled wine.

Sleeping

Salzburg has long been known for its pricey accommodation, but that's starting to change. Spearheading the city's style revolution, sleeping spots are revamping the old and ringing in the new: from boutique hotels with baroque finery to funky backpacker digs. If you're on a budget, the right bank is probably your best bet. Prices skyrocket during the Festspiele, when you'll need to book well ahead. For a list of private rooms, check www.salzburg.info or inquire at the tourist office.

BUDGET

Camping Kasern (Map p267; ☎ 45 05 76; www.camping -kasern-salzburg.com; Carl-Zuckmayer-Strasse 26; campsites per adult/child/tent €6/3.50/3; Ⓟ ⌨) Just north of the A1 Nord exit, this tree-shaded campsite offers internet access, a laundry and minimarket. Hop on bus 21 from Paris-Lodron-Strasse to Jagerwirt.

YOHO Salzburg (Map p269; ☎ 87 96 49; www.yoho .at; Paracelsusstrasse 9; 8-/6-bed dm €17/18, per person s/d/tr/q €29/22/20/19; ☻ reception 24hr; ⌨) If you just wanna have fun, this hip hostel is the place to meet like-minded backpackers. There's a daily happy hour at the bar and *The Sound of Music* is blasted out at 10.30am (bring your earplugs or join in the singsong). Other perks include free wi-fi and lockers, plus a 10% discount on Panorama tours. You can book adventure sports here such as rafting (€40) and canyoning (€49).

Junge Hotel Aigen (Map p267; ☎ 62 32 48; www.lbsh -aigen.at; Aignerstrasse 34; per person dm/s/d/q €15/31/23/19; Ⓟ) Set in parkland, this HI hostel south of Kapuzinerberg in Aigen offers excellent facilities including a common room, table tennis and dining hall. Family rooms are also available. It's 15 minutes' walk from the old town or take bus 49.

Jugendgästehaus Salzburg (Map p269; ☎ 84 26 70; www.jgh.at; Josef-Preis-Allee 18; per person dm/q/d €15.50/20/37.50; P ⏚) Head to this popular hostel for prime views of the fortress, bike rental and discounts on Salzburg Sightseeing Tours. Half and full board are also available.

Institut St Sebastian (Map p270; ☎ 87 13 86; Linzer Gasse 41; www.st-sebastian-salzburg.at; dm/s/d €19/38/62) Tucked behind Sebastianskirche, this peaceful hostel oozes monastic charm with its high vaults, polished stone floors and roof terrace. The dorms are clean and well kept. Ring the bell if reception is unstaffed.

Sandwirt (Map p269; ☎ 87 43 51; Lastenstrasse 6a; s/d/tr €23/44/57; P) Facing the train tracks, the location of this guesthouse is hardly picturesque, but it's handy if you need to be near the station and like gnomes – the garden is full of 'em! Rooms are crying out for a lick of paint, but still offer good value. The chirpy landlady will let you use her washing machine and kitchen.

Junger Fuchs (Map p270; ☎ 87 54 96; Linzer Gasse 54; s/d/tr without bathroom €28/44/55) Despite being above a kebab shop (handy for late-night munchies), the wood-floored rooms in this conveniently located pension on the right bank are clean and spacious.

Hinterbrühl (Map p270; ☎ 84 67 98; hinterbruehl@aon.at; Schanzlgasse 12; s/d without bathroom €42/54) Part of the original city walls, this 14th-century guesthouse is a bargain given its old-town location. The '70s-style rooms are basic but clean. Try to get room 14 – it's the biggest and has a balcony, private bathroom and lounge area.

MIDRANGE

Trumer Stube (Map p270; ☎ 87 47 76; www.trumer-stube .at; Bergstrasse 6; s €56-89, d €89-103; ⏚) Silvia and Giovanni will make you feel at home at this pretty little pension. Its rooms have an old-world feel – think pastel shades, squishy beds and flouncy fabrics.

Bergland Hotel (Map p269; ☎ 87 23 18; www.berg landhotel.at; Rupertgasse 15; s/d/ste €63/93/135; P ⏚) This peach-fronted hotel attracts creative souls who appreciate Mr Kuhn's brushwork – his fabulous paintings are hung all over the walls. The homy rooms in warm hues display – you guessed it – more art, while the suite is festooned with Austrian straw bonnets. Other

pluses include free parking and wi-fi. Bike hire costs €6 per day.

Lasserhof (Map p269; ☎ 87 33 88; www.lasserhof.com; Lasserstrasse 47; s/d €69/109; P) Smack between Mirabellgarten and the station, this family-run hotel is not a bad deal, but choose your room wisely. The nicer ones have Venetian chandeliers and ceramic stoves, but others are plain and on the poky side.

Hotel Hohenstauffen (Map p269; ☎ 87 21 93; www .hotel-hohenstauffen.at; Elisabethstrasse 19; s/d €80/109; P ⏚) It may not be in the swishest part of town, but this friendly hotel near the station is well set up for cyclists with a garage for repairing punctures – ring the bicycle bell at reception for service. The rooms are a tad dated, but comfy and quiet.

Hotel Wolf (Map p270; ☎ 84 34 53-0; www.hotelwolf .com; Kaigasse 9; s/d €80/110; ⏚) Pass through a Hobbit-like door into this lovingly converted town house in a quiet corner of the old town. The 15th-century hotel exudes an historic feel with its uneven stone staircases and antique furnishings. The light, parquet-floored rooms range from modern to rustic.

Hotel Mozart (Map p269; ☎ 87 22 74; www.hotel -mozart.at; Franz-Josef-Strasse 27; s/d €90/110; P ⏚) Just like Amadeus, this central hotel rocks. The antique-filled lobby gives way to tidy rooms with mod cons such as wi-fi, gleaming bathrooms, and plump beds that will have you creating a snoring symphony. If you want breakfast, though, you'll have to shell out an extra €10.

our pick **Haus Wartenberg** (Map p267; ☎ 84 84 00; www.hauswartenberg.com; Riedenburgerstrasse 2; s/d €55/128; P ⏚) Hemmed in by trees, this gorgeous 400-year-old country cottage just minutes from the old town is a real find. Bedecked with geranium-filled flowerboxes and family heirlooms, the green-shuttered cottage borders a shady garden. Smooth stone steps lead up to light-flooded rooms, which are befitting of this rustic hideaway with their chunky pinewood furniture, floral curtains and stripy bedspreads.

Zur Goldenen Ente (Map p270; ☎ 84 56 22; www.ente .at; Goldgasse 10; s €75-82, d €125-150) Bang in the heart of the *Altstadt*, this 700-year-old town house has oodles of charm – some rooms have four-poster beds, while Emperor Franz Josef guards over others. The sunny terrace overlooks the rooftops of the old town.

Wolf Dietrich (Map p270; ☎ 87 12 75; www.salzburg -hotel.at; Wolf-Dietrich-Strasse 7; s/d €81/129; ⏚ 🐾) Central and friendly, this hotel's fabulous facilities include a pool, sauna and solarium. The swanky rooms are heavy on the floral fabrics and chandeliers and the breakfast buffet is 100% organic. There's also a fabulously over-the-top suite based on Mozart's *Magic Flute*, featuring a star-studded ceiling and freestanding bathtub.

Hotel Amadeus (Map p270; ☎ 87 14 01; www.hotel amadeus.at; Linzer Gasse 43-45; s/d €88/170; ☑) Situated on the right bank, this three-star hotel has a boutiquey feel, with personal touches such as free afternoon tea. The airy rooms are decorated in vibrant colours; some are kitted out with wrought-iron four-poster beds and chandeliers.

TOP END

Arthotel Blaue Gans (Map p270; ☎ 84 24 91-50; www .blauegans.at; Getreidegasse 43; s €99-119, d €135-185; ☑) An extreme face-lift has propelled this 650-year-old hotel into the 21st century. The revamped inn now brims with abstract artworks and modernist furnishings. Clean lines, wooden floors and flat-screen TVs spruce up the whiter-than-white rooms. The centuries-old vaults harbour the excellent Blaue Gans Restaurant (p278).

Hotel Stein (Map p270; ☎ 87 43 46-0; www.hotelstein .at; Giselakai 3-5; s €99-125, d €140-165, ste €220-275; ☑ ☑) This funky design hotel on the banks of the Salzach is no wallflower. The rooms are jazzed up with splashes of purple or ruby red, black leather chairs and zebra-print bedspreads; many also feature marble bathrooms.

Das Auersperg (Map p269; ☎ 88 94 40; www.auers perg.at; Auerspergstrasse 61; s €95-105, d €145-185, ste 205; ☑ ☑ ☑) This charismatic villa fuses late-19th-century elegance with contemporary design. The modern rooms have free wi-fi and guests can kick back in the serene garden, centred on a lily pond, or in the rooftop sauna. Free bike hire is an added bonus.

Hotel Gablerbräu (Map p270; ☎ 889 65; www.gabler brau.com; Linzer Gasse 9; s/d €102/148; ☑) This swish hotel has been around since 1429. Expect contemporary, high-ceilinged rooms with parquet floors, comfy beds and spotless bathrooms. The vaulted restaurant (mains €8 to €15) has a seasonal menu with vegetarian options.

Hotel Sacher (Map p270; ☎ 88 97 70; www.sacher .com; Schwarzstrasse 5-7; s €149-265, d €220-390; ☑ ☑) Down by the river, this turn-of-the-century hotel is pure class with its glittering chandeliers and posh piano bar. The opulent rooms feature antiques, oil paintings and shiny mar-

ble bathrooms. Tom Hanks, the Dalai Lama and Maria herself (Julie Andrews) have all snoozed here.

Goldener Hirsch (Map p270; ☎ 80 84-0; Getreidegasse 37; s €204-376, d €274-538; ☑) A skylight illuminates the arcaded inner courtyard of this 600-year-old hotel in the *Altstadt*. The rustic, low-ceilinged rooms are pretty plush with lots of polished wood and sparkly pink-marble bathrooms. Queen Elizabeth and Pavarotti top the list of famous guests. Downstairs are two award-winning restaurants: S'Herzl (opposite) and Restaurant Goldener Hirsch (p278).

Hotel Bristol (Map p270; ☎ 87 35 57; www.bristol -salzburg.at; Makartplatz 4; s/d/ste €289/340/581; ☑ ☑) Emperor Franz Josef and Sigmund Freud felt at home in this elegant hotel on the square, just around the corner from Mirabellgarten. The plush pad has palatial rooms with five-star luxuries that come with their hefty price tag.

Schloss Mönchstein (Map p269; ☎ 84 85 55-0; www .monchstein.at; Mönchsberg Park 26; d €335-445, ste €475-1195; ☑ ☑) Nestled in acres of grounds, this gabled medieval castle on Mönchsberg is fairy-tale stuff. The sumptuous rooms have all the trimmings: Persian rugs, antiques, oil paintings and Calcutta-marble bathrooms are standard. If you have money to burn, you can even rent the whole castle.

Eating

Schnitzel with noodles and crisp apple strudel may have been Maria's favourites, but there's a whole lot more to Salzburg's gastro scene, ranging from African restaurants with attitude to nice-and-spicy vegetarian places. If you're seeking classics – and let's face it, they taste pretty good – the wall-to-wall *Gasthöfe* (inns) in the old town won't disappoint.

RESTAURANTS
Budget

Mensa Toscana (Map p270; ☎ 80 44 69 09; Sigmund-Haffner-Gasse 11; lunch €4-4.70; ☽ lunch Mon-Fri) With its old town location, sunny terrace and (surprisingly) good food, the Toscana is no cookie-cutter *Mensa* (university restaurant).

Fisch-Krieg (Map p270; ☎ 84 37 32; Ferdinand-Hanusch-Platz 4; mains €4-7; ☽ 8.30am-6.30pm Mon-Fri, 8.30am-1pm Sat) The fish that lands on your plate at this cheap-and-cheerful place is as fresh as it comes. Take a seat on the riverside terrace to chomp on fish kebabs, octopus and paella.

Il Sole (Map p270; ☎ 84 32 84; Gstättengasse 15; mains €5.50-8.50; ☽ lunch & dinner) The wood-fired pizza at this authentic trattoria is delicious. The smiley Italian owner starred on the German TV series *Das Traumschiff* (Love Boat), and the evidence is plastered all over the walls in the entrance.

SKS Spicy Spices (Map p270; ☎ 87 07 12; Wolf-Dietrich-Strasse 1; mains €6; ☺ lunch & dinner) 'Healthy heart, lovely soul' is the philosophy of this Indian vegetarian restaurant with an ethnic atmosphere and cheerful staff. A few euro buys you a slap-up samosa feast or fiery curry. The organic juices and lassis pack a vitamin punch.

Wilder Mann (Map p270; ☎ 84 17 87; Getreidegasse 20; mains €6.50-8.50; ☺ lunch & dinner Mon-Sat) Creaking with age, this cosy Austrian tavern in the *Altstadt* dishes up dumplings, fried sausages and other light and airy fare at rock-bottom prices.

Stadtalm (Map p270; ☎ 84 17 29; Mönchsberg 19; mains €7-12.50; ☺ lunch & dinner mid-May–mid-Sep) Affording sweeping views over Salzburg, the cosy Stadtalm on Mönchsberg has a hearty menu with lashings of goulash and *Tafelspitz* (boiled beef with apple and horseradish sauce).

St Paul's Stub'n (Map p270; ☎ 84 32 20; Herrengasse 16; mains €7-14; ☺ 5pm-1am Mon-Sat) Set in a quiet corner of town, this small, wood-panelled restaurant has a good-value menu stretching from *risotto nero* (risotto made with cuttlefish ink) to roast suckling pig. There's a lovely garden for warm evenings.

Shrimps Bar (Map p270; ☎ 87 44 84; Steingasse 5; mains €7-18; ☺ dinner) Luminous butterflies, tangerine walls and modern art give this bar a funky twist. The shrimps baguette slathered in cocktail sauce is a lip-smacking speciality (both hands required), but you can also sink your jaws into a shark steak.

Sternbräu (Map p270; ☎ 84 21 40; Griesgasse 23; mains €8-16, set menu €16.50-18.50; ☺ lunch & dinner) The tree-shaded courtyard is the big draw at this rustic restaurant. House specials such as venison stew and trout are accompanied by copious amounts of Sternbräu beer. *The Sound of Music* dinner show takes place here (see p279).

Saran Essbar (Map p270; ☎ 84 66 28; Judengasse 10; mains €9-13; ☺ lunch & dinner) Superfriendly Mr Saran uses the freshest ingredients in his tasty Indian dishes. Savour a Bengali fish curry or wok-fried vegetables beneath medieval vaults or on the pavement terrace. If you've room, finish off with a slice of Zaga's homemade strudel.

Midrange

Nagano (Map p270; ☎ 84 94 88; Griesgasse 19; mains €10-18; ☺ lunch & dinner) Hidden in the cobbled Artis Hof courtyard, this unassuming Japanese restaurant pushes the right buttons with fresh sushi, tempura and sashimi.

ourpick Afro Café (Map p270; ☎ 84 48 88; Bürgerspitalplatz 5; mains €10-20; ☺ 9am-midnight Mon-Sat) This eye-catching African café ventures into Salzburg's wackier waters. The retro design is pure genius: a blend of hot-pink walls, butterfly-shaped chairs, plastic palms and artworks sculpted from junk gathered on the beach. The menu takes some beating too – try the sticky ostrich kebabs or coconutty Zanzibar salad with Algiers ginger punch.

Alt Salzburg (Map p270; ☎ 84 14 76; Bürgerspitalgasse 2; mains €10.20-25.80; ☺ lunch & dinner Tue-Sat, dinner Mon) Tucked into a cobblestone courtyard at the base of the Mönchsberg, this cosy restaurant has prim-and-proper service and a meaty menu featuring specials such as venison and veal knuckle.

S'Herzl (Map p270; ☎ 80 84-0; Getreidegasse 37; mains €11-19; ☺ lunch & dinner) Dark wood beams, arched windows and low lighting create a cosy feel in this tavern, housed in the Goldener Hirsch (opposite). It's a fine place to snuggle up in winter over calorie-rich treats such as sausages and sauerkraut or scrumptious puddings.

Stiftskeller St Peter (Map p270; ☎ 84 12 68-0; St Peter's Bezirk 1-4; mains €11-21.50; ☺ lunch & dinner) Set around a vine-clad courtyard by Stiftskirche St Peter, this restaurant comprises a string of wood-panelled rooms that roll out Austrian fare such as wild boar and roast pork with sauerkraut. It's well known for its Mozart dinner concerts (see p279).

Zum Eulenspiegel (Map p270; ☎ 84 31 80; Hagenauerplatz 2; mains €11-23; ☺ lunch & dinner) There's a gingerbready feel about this restaurant, with its fairy lights, wonky walls and low beams. Stone steps twist up to intimate cubbyholes (some just big enough for four people), where you can savour 650 years of history, prime views of the square and flavours such as stroganoff and sander fillet.

Gasthof Auerhahn (Map p267; ☎ 45 10 52; Bahnhofstrasse 15; mains €13-22; ☺ lunch & dinner Tue-Sat, lunch Sun) It's off the beaten track, but that doesn't stop foodies from making the pilgrimage to Auerhahn. This award-winning restaurant serves specialities such as clams in lime froth and fluffy *Topfenknöedel* (sweet dumplings). The chestnut-tree-shaded garden is popular when the sun's out.

Pan e Vin (Map p270; ☎ 844 666; Gstättengasse 1; mains €15-30; ⏰ lunch & dinner Mon-Sat, trattoria closed Mon) This cheery place comprises a smart trattoria and Mediterranean restaurant. As well as antipasti and pasta just like *mamma* used to make, the chef excels in the art of preparing shellfish.

Blaue Gans Restaurant (Map p270; ☎ 84 13 17-54; www.blauegans.at; Getreidegasse 43; mains €16-20; ⏰ lunch & dinner Wed-Mon) In the historic vaults of Arthotel Blaue Gans (p276), this smart restaurant is prized for fresh, locally sourced fare like tender Pinzgauer lamb. Dwarfed by the cliffs of Mönchsberg, the palm-shaded terrace is wonderful when the sun's out.

Top End

Schloss Restaurant (Map p269; ☎ 84 85 55-0; Mönchsberg Park 26; mains €20-30; ⏰ lunch & dinner) This grand restaurant in Schloss Mönchstein dishes up a right royal feast, from tender loin of lamb to herb-crusted sole. Service is (as befits a castle) impeccable.

Restaurant Goldener Hirsch (Map p270; ☎ 80 84-0; Getreidegasse 37; mains €21-27; ⏰ lunch & dinner, closed Sun in winter) Vaulting and polished wood set the scene for gourmet flavours at this well-heeled restaurant in the Goldener Hirsch (p276). The chef has won awards for signature dishes such as venison saddle with cabbage and dumplings.

Riedenburg (Map p267; ☎ 83 08 15; www.riedenburg .at; Neutorstrasse 31; lunch €18, mains €26-35; ⏰ lunch & dinner Tue-Sat) Pop art adds a splash of colour to this sleek Michelin-starred restaurant. The chef presents delicacies such as crayfish on Riesling risotto, with a razor-sharp eye for detail. The pavilion in the garden is a romantic hideaway in summer.

Hangar-7, the spacey complex at Salzburg airport, shelters the exclusive **Ikarus** (Map p267; ☎ 21 97-77; www.hangar-7.com; set menu €85-110; ⏰ lunch & dinner) restaurant, where each month different celebrity chefs are invited to put their creative stamp on the menu. Be sure to head for some after-dinner drinks in the Hangar-7's hi-tech May Day Bar (opposite).

QUICK EATS

Icezeit (Map p270; ☎ 84 33 73; www.icezeit.at; Chiemseegasse 1; scoop €1-1.30; ⏰ 11am-9pm) The snaking queue speaks for the quality of the homemade ice cream at this hole-in-the-wall

gelateria. Refresh with zingy varieties such as choco-chilli, ginger and lemon-pepper.

Indigo (Map p269; ☎ 87 08 62; Auerspergstrasse 10; light meals €2.50-6; ⏰ 10am-10pm Mon-Fri, 10am-6pm Sat) Salads by the scoopful, sushi and vegetarian curries feature on the healthy menu at this gallery-style café, decked out with wicker chairs and vibrant art.

Capp&ccino (Map p270; ☎ 87 55 45; Linzer Gasse 39; snacks €3-9, lunch €6.90; ⏰ 8am-11pm) Capp&ccino is the right bank's coolest café with its high ceilings, laid-back terrace and lounge music. The moreish *tramezzini* (small Italian tea sandwiches) and free wi-fi access add to its popularity.

Coffee Shop (Map p269; ☎ 89 07 73; Franz-Josef-Strasse 3; bagels €3; ⏰ breakfast, lunch & dinner) Based on Ayurvedic principles, this Zen-like café is a temple of calm and healthy living. The all-vegetarian menu includes a superb selection of bagels, salads and freshly squeezed juices.

Café Tomaselli (Map p270; ☎ 84 44 88; Alter Markt 9; pastries €4; ⏰ breakfast & lunch) If you like your service with a dollop of Viennese grumpiness and strudel with a dollop of cream, this grand, wood-panelled coffee house in the centre is just the ticket.

Scio's Specereyen (Map p270; ☎ 84 16 38; Sigmund-Haffner-Gasse 16; mains €5.50-11, snacks €2.20-4.90; ⏰ 10am-8pm) Breathe in as you enter this pint-sized bistro, which bursts at the seams at weekends. No wonder, with a menu starring tasty morsels such as blinis with trout caviar. Don't leave without sampling the divine chestnut-and-nougat *Venusbrüstchen* (Venus breasts).

Vegy Vollwertimbiss (Map p270; ☎ 87 57 46; Schwarzstrasse 21; lunch €8; ⏰ lunch Mon-Fri) Helga has been dishing up wholesome vegetarian food to Salzburg for more than 25 years. Try the tasty soups and honey-sweetened cake.

SELF-CATERING

If a picnic on the banks of the Salzach appeals, stock up on cheese, bread and honey at the market (Map p270) on Universitätsplatz.

There are several supermarkets for self-caterers, including **Billa** (Map p270; Griesgasse 19). The **Shell** (Map p269; St Julien Strasse 33) garage has a shop open 24 hours, with snacks, provisions and alcohol.

Drinking

Salzburg is starting to shake off its purely traditional image with some trendy bars sprouting up by the Salzach. You'll still find the beer-and-pretzel type places that have been around for donkey's years, but they are making space for a new generation of lounge bars and clubs that keep party-goers on their toes till the sun rises.

Humboldt Stub'n (Map p270; ☎ 84 31 71; Gstättengasse 4-6; ☻ noon-4am) This bar has an upbeat, pre-clubbing vibe. Cartoons deck the walls and a nail-studded Mozart punk guards the bar. Speaking of Mozart, there's even a cocktail dedicated to the virtuoso here (a sickly sweet composition of liqueur, cherry juice, cream and chocolate). Wednesday is student night, with beers a snip at €2.50.

Republic (Map p270; ☎ 84 16 13; Anton-Neumayr-Platz 2; ☻ 8am-1am Sun-Thu, 8am-3am Fri & Sat) Opposite Humboldt Stub'n, this café is defined by high ceilings and neon lighting. By night it morphs into one of the city's trendiest haunts when DJs spinning house, salsa and electro attract a 20-something, daiquiri-sipping crowd.

Die Weisse (Map p269; ☎ 87 22 46; Rupertgasse 10; ☻ 10.30am-midnight Mon-Sat) The cavernous brew-pub of the Salzburger Weissbierbrauerei, this is the place to guzzle cloudy wheat beers beside shiny copper vats. Choose from the wood-floored pub, the industrial-style bar or the shady beer garden out the back.

Living Room (Map p270; ☎ 87 73 61; Imbergstrasse 2a; ☻ 10am-2am Sun-Thu, 10am-4am Fri & Sat) Hugging the banks of the Salzach, this avant-garde newcomer combines a lounge-style bar with a decked terrace. Sink into a wicker armchair to admire the illuminated fortress and listen to mellow grooves. Meals are also served (€8.90 to €11.80).

Baboon Bar (Map p270; ☎ 88 59 32; Imbergstrasse 11; ☻ 7pm-4am Mon-Sat) Look out for the funky monkey at this hip riverside bar, playing '70s and '80s classics and acid jazz. The garden is popular on warm summer evenings.

Augustiner Bräustübl (Map p269; ☎ 43 12 46; Augustinergasse 4-6; ☻ 3-11pm Mon-Fri, 2.30-11pm Sat & Sun) With swinging steins and pretzels a-plenty, this monk-run brewery proves that quaffing clerics can enjoy themselves. Fill your huge stone mug from the pump in the foyer, visit the snack stands and take a pew beneath the chestnut trees in the 1000-seat beer garden.

Bellini's (Map p270; ☎ 87 13 85; Mirabellplatz 4; ☻ 9am-1am Mon-Fri, 11am-1am Sat & Sun) This Italian job next to Mirabellgarten is a cool, lively bar with a cobbled terrace, great cocktails and tasty *tramezzini*.

StieglKeller (Map p270; ☎ 84 26 81; Festungsgasse 10; ☻ 11am-11pm) Beneath the fortress, this Munich-style beer hall (it shares the same architect as the Hofbräuhaus) has an enormous garden above the city's rooftops. Beer is cheapest from the self-service taps outside.

Shamrock (Map p270; ☎ 84 16 10; Rudolfskai 12; ☻ noon-2am Sun, 3pm-2am Mon, 3pm-3am Tue & Wed, 3pm-4am Thu, noon-4am Fri & Sat) This spit-and-sawdust Irish pub screens big sport events. There's live music daily from 9pm and Guinness on tap.

O'Malley's (Map p270; ☎ 84 92 65; Rudolfskai 16; ☻ 6pm-2am Mon-Thu & Sun, 6pm-4am Fri & Sat) Shamrock's more laid-back twin is run by the same people and centres on a bar built from the timber of a 300-year-old Irish church.

ARGEkultur (Map p269; ☎ 84 87 84-0; www.argekultur .at; Josef-Preis-Allee 16; ☻ 9.30am-1am Mon-Fri, 6pm-1am Sat) Students and arty types hang out at this alterative haunt, which is a bar, a bistro and a small-scale performing arts venue rolled into one. Expect an eclectic line-up of concerts and parties.

May Day Bar (Map p267; ☎ 21 97www.hangar-7.com; ☻ 5.30pm-2am Sun-Thu, 5.30pm-3am Fri & Sat) After-dinner drinks are served at this bar in the hi-tech Hangar-7 complex, where Flying Bulls aircraft zip around the glasses and virtual bar staff interact with guests.

Entertainment

CLASSICAL MUSIC & MUSICALS

Schloss Mirabell's baroque Marble Hall (p270) sets the scene for **Schlosskonzerte** (☎ 84 85 86; www.salzburger-schlosskonzerte.at; tickets €8-31), Mozart recitals given by international soloists and chamber musicians.

The **Mozarteum** (Map p270; ☎ 87 31 54; Schwarz-strasse 26-28; tickets €15-60) stages the works of Mozart and other classical composers. More light-hearted are the **Mozart dinner concerts** (☎ 84 12 68-0; tickets €45; ☻ dinner) held by candle-light and starring performers dressed in period costume at Stiftskeller St Peter (p277). **Mozartconcerts** (www.mozartfestival.at), some with dinner, are also held at the Festung Hohensalzburg (p271).

If you're lucky enough to be in Salzburg during the Festspiele, try to get tickets for concerts, operas and plays at the **Festspielhaus** (Map p270; ☎ 84 45-579; Hofstallgasse 1), which is built into the sheer sides of the Mönchsberg.

If the above options sound too highbrow, the **Sound of Music Show** (☎ 82 66 17; with/without dinner €45/29; ☻ nightly May-Oct) at the Sternbräu (p277) might appeal. You'll feast on Maria's favourite things as performers bash out much-loved hits from the musical.

ROCK & JAZZ

Rockhouse (Map p267; ☎ 88 49 14; www.rockhouse.at, in German; Schallmooser Hauptstrasse 46; admission €10-20; ☻ 6pm-2am Mon-Sat) Playing to a young crowd, the Rockhouse is Salzburg's premier venue for rock and pop bands – check the website for details of what's on. There's also a tunnel-shaped bar that has DJs (usually free) and live bands.

Szene (Map p270; ☎ 84 34 48; www.szene-salzburg.net; Anton-Neumayr-Platz 2; tickets €10-45) Next to Republic, this venue hosts everything from DJs to cutting-edge dance productions and jam sessions. Visit the website for details of the line-up.

For live jazz, check out **Jazzit** (Map p269; ☎ 87 68 91; www.jazzit.at, in German; Elisabethstrasse 11), which stages regular gigs, or **Urbankeller** (Map p267; ☎ 87 08 94; Schallmooser Hauptstrasse 50; ☻ 5pm-1am), host to live jazz, blues, rock and funk.

THEATRE & CINEMA

Das Kino (Map p270; ☎ 87 31 00; www.daskino.at, in German; Giselakai 11; tickets €8) Independent and art-house films are screened in their original language at this small cinema. It's also a good place to pick up fliers for clubs and happenings around town. The Latin American Film Festival takes place here in March.

Landestheater (Map p270; ☎ 87 15 12-0; www .theater.co.at, in German; Schwarzstrasse 22; tickets €5-42) This leading performing-arts venue offers a varied programme of musicals, ballets, plays and operas (mostly in German).

Salzburger Marionettentheater (Map p270; ☎ 87 24 06-0; www.marionetten.at; Schwarzstrasse 24; tickets €18-35; ☻ May-Sep, Christmas, Easter & Mozart Week in Jan) Who says puppetry is just for kids? This traditional marionette theatre stages a repertoire of well-known operas – from *Bastien and Bastienne* to *The Magic Flute* – in a gorgeous baroque auditorium. The talented puppeteers (see boxed text, below) perform with grace

---

VOICES: GRETL AICHER, SALZBURGER MARIONETTENTHEATER

Tension is mounting behind the scenes at the Salzburger Marionettentheater (above): puppeteers take their positions, the music strikes up and the curtain rises on Mozart's *Marriage of Figaro*. The granddaughter of the theatre founder, Gretl Aicher, is there; her silhouetted hands fluttering as marionettes glide gracefully across the stage. She grew up with the theatre and has been puppeteering since she was 15. After the performance, she takes time out to answer a few questions:

How did the theatre rise from its humble beginnings? My grandfather was a sculptor and started the marionette theatre in a gym in 1913. He gave it to my father as a wedding present in 1926, who developed techniques and expanded the repertoire to include Mozart operas, fairy tales and, of course, the much-loved *Salzburger Kasperl* [an impish character like Punch]. We've been touring worldwide since 1932.

What is the fascination of performing with marionettes? Puppetry is perfecting the art of illusion. We try to make the marionettes lifelike with natural movements and the effect upon audiences is hypnotic. Each one is like a magical instrument that unleashes hidden emotions and desires. After a while, the technique becomes second nature and you just slip into the characters – they are my alter ego.

Which effects are achievable with marionettes that aren't possible on a 'human' stage? I love the fact you can make marionettes fly, take them apart, even swap their heads. These are tricks that actors can only achieve with complex special effects.

Why is Mozart's music such an inspiration to you? I can't name any composer that can breathe such life into marionettes as Mozart. His operas are joyful, playful, indescribable. They are the perfect companion for puppeteers.

How do you feel about the new Sound of Music production? Excited! It's challenging new territory for us, as it will be the first time we've ever staged a musical. It debuts in Salzburg in May 2008 and, from the look of things, is set to be an evocative and fascinating production.

TOP TEMPLES OF KITSCH

- **Miracle's Wax Museum** (Map p270; Getreidegasse 7) is the place to sniff out Mozart eau de toilette (€15), pocket a pair of yodeller's lederhosen (€13) or snap up a gorgeous Sissi bust (€10) to grace your mantelpiece.

- **Residenzplatz** (Map p270) brims with high-quality kitsch – is it to be that sexy feathered alpine hat (€19.90), the stylish edelweiss neckerchief (€5) or child prodigy, Mozart, captured forever in a snow globe (€5.50)?

- **Gifts & Things** (Map p270; Judengasse 6) isn't cheap, but who can resist the gem-encrusted Fabergé egg playing The Blue Danube (€65) or the won't-stop-whistling marmot (€8)?

- **Candela** (Map p270; Getreidegasse 24) is a must if you've always wanted a metallic German Christmas pickle (€3.50 to €10) to hang on your tree. Glittering papayas and gaudy carrots complete your festive fruit-and-veg collection.

- **Perfect** (Map p270; Universitätsplatz 4) has the solution to carry your kitsch home. Whatever your favourite pet – poodle, Pekinese or Siamese puss – this boutique has a bejewelled purse (€12) or bag (€40) to suit.

---

and gusto to create the illusion of life-sized performers on a miniature stage.

Shopping

You can souvenir-shop for everything from tight-fitting dirndls to cuckoo clocks in the *Altstadt*, particularly on bustling Getreidegasse and Judengasse, but should be prepared to pay over the odds – this is firmly tourist territory. Design divas with bulging bank balances head for boutique-lined Linzer Gasse and Griesgasse.

Salzkontor (Map p270; Waagplatz 6) The shelves in this tiny shop are stocked with mineral-rich Salzkammergut salt, ranging from herby concoctions to bath crystals scented with lavender and citrus.

Kaslöchl (Map p270; ☎ 84 41 00; Hagenauerplatz 2) There's no room to swing a cat in Salzburg's smallest cheese shop. Squeeze in to buy delicious organic, locally sourced cheeses such as creamy Vorarlberger or fresh cheese with basil.

Stiftsbäckerei St Peter (Map p270; Mühlenhof; 10am-5pm Mon-Fri, 10am-noon Sat) Right next to the monastery, this 900-year-old bakery still bakes tasty loaves in a wood-fired oven.

Drechslerei Lackner (Map p270; ☎ 84 23 85; Badergasse 2) The hand-carved nutcrackers, nativity figurines and filigree Christmas stars are the real deal in this traditional craft shop.

Fürst (Map p270; ☎ 84 37 59; Getreidegasse 47) The *Mozartkugeln* (Mozart balls) at this speciality chocolate shop are based on Paul Fürst's original 1890 recipe. The chocolate-coated nougat and marzipan treats cost €0.90 per mouthful.

Easter in Salzburg (Map p270; ☎ 84 17 94; Judengasse 13) It's impossible to pass this shop without gawping: an incredible 150,000 real, hand-painted eggs are spread over two glittering floors. Prices range from €2 for a modestly painted hen's egg to €146 for an ostrich egg bearing a portrait of Mozart.

Christmas in Salzburg (Map p270; ☎ 84 67 84; Judengasse 10) Just opposite Easter in Salzburg, this five-floor shop puts Santa's grotto to shame. Here, gold cherubs, stockings and delicate baubles replace the eggs. Just, for goodness' sake, don't trip…

Getting There & Away

AIR

Salzburg airport (Map p267; ☎ 85 80-0; www.salzburg -airport.com), half an hour by bus from the city centre, has regular scheduled flights to destinations all over Austria and Europe. Low-cost flights from the UK are provided by **Ryanair** (☎ 0900 210 240; www.ryanair.com). Other airlines flying into Salzburg include **British Airways** (☎ 0179 567 567; www.britishairways.com) and **KLM** (☎ 858 09 69; www.kl m.com).

BUS

Buses depart from just outside the *Hauptbahnhof* (Map p269) on Südtiroler Platz, where timetables are displayed. Bus information and tickets are available from the information points on the main concourse.

Hourly buses leave for the Salzkammergut between 6.30am and 8pm – destinations include Bad Ischl (€8.70, 1¾ hours), Mondsee

(€5.40, 50 minutes), St Wolfgang (€7.90, 1¾ hours) and St Gilgen (€5.20, 50 minutes). All prices are for one-way trips. Return tickets include travel on the local city-bus network. For information on bus travel further afield and an online timetable see www.postbus.at.

CAR & MOTORCYCLE

Three motorways converge on Salzburg to form a loop around the city: the A1 from Linz, Vienna and the east; the A8/E52 from Munich and the west; and the A10/E55 from Villach and the south. The quickest way to Tyrol is to take the road to Bad Reichenhall in Germany and continue to Lofer (Hwy 312) and St Johann in Tyrol.

TRAIN

Salzburg is well served by InterCity (IC) and EuroCity (EC) services. For train information call ☎ 05-1717 (8am to 8pm daily), or visit the office in the *Hauptbahnhof*. Tickets (no commission) and train information are also available from **Salzburger Landesreisebüro** (Map p270; ☎ 87 34 03; Schwarzstrasse 11).

Fast trains leave from the *Hauptbahnhof* hourly for Vienna's Westbahnhof (€43.40, 3½ hours), travelling via Linz (€19.90, 1½ hours). The two-hourly express service to Klagenfurt (€31.70, 3¼ hours) runs via Villach.

The quickest way to Innsbruck is by the 'corridor' train through Germany; trains depart at least every two hours (€33.80, two hours) and stop at Kufstein. Trains to Munich take about two hours and run every 30 to 60 minutes (€27); some of these continue to Karlsruhe via Stuttgart.

If you hop on the train in Salzburg you can also hop off in Berlin (€119, eight hours), Budapest (€70.60, seven hours), Prague (€55.40, seven hours), Rome (€90, 10½ hours) or Venice (€50, 6½ hours).

Getting Around
TO/FROM THE AIRPORT

Salzburg airport is less than 4km west of the city centre at Innsbrucker Bundesstrasse 95. Bus 2 (€1.80, 25 minutes) departs from outside the terminal roughly every 10 minutes and terminates at the *Hauptbahnhof*. This service operates from 5.30am to 11pm and doesn't go via the old town, so you'll have to take a local bus from the *Hauptbahnhof* once you arrive, or walk (15 to 20 minutes).

A taxi between the airport and the centre costs about €15.

BICYCLE

Salzburg has an excellent cycling network and hiring your own set of wheels is a carbon-neutral, hassle-free way of exploring the city and its surrounds. Next to the *Hauptbahnhof*, **Top Bike** (☎ 06272-46 56; www.topbike.at; Südtiroler Platz 1; ◷ 10am-5pm Apr-Oct, 9am-5pm Jul & Aug) rents bikes for around €15 per day (half-price for kids). The Salzburg Card (see p268) offers a 20% discount off these rates.

BUS

Bus drivers sell single (€1.80), 24-hour (adult/child €4.20/2.10) and weekly tickets (€11.70). Single tickets bought in advance from *Tabak* (tobacconist) shops are cheaper (€1.60 each) and are sold in units of five. Children under six years travel free.

Bus routes are shown at bus stops and on some city maps; buses 1 and 4 start from the *Hauptbahnhof* and skirt the pedestrian-only old town.

BUS TAXI

'Bus taxis' operate from 11.30pm to 1.30am (3am on weekends) on fixed routes, dropping off and picking up along the way, for a cost of €3.50. Ferdinand-Hanusch-Platz is the departure point for suburban routes on the left bank, and Theatergasse for routes to the right bank.

CAR & MOTORCYCLE

Parking places are limited and much of the old town is only accessible by foot, so it may be better to avoid taking your car in – there are three park-and-ride points to the west, north and south of the city. The largest car park in the centre is the Altstadt Garage under the Mönchsberg. Expect to pay around €14 per day; some restaurants in the centre will stamp your ticket for a reduction. Rates are lower on streets with automatic ticket machines (blue zones); a three-hour maximum applies (€3 or €0.50 for 30 minutes) 9am to 7pm on weekdays.

Car rental offices include:

Avis (Map p269; ☎ 87 72 78; Ferdinand-Porsche-Strasse 7)

Europcar (Map p267; ☎ 87 16 16; Gniglerstrasse 12)

Hertz (Map p269; ☎ 87 66 74; Ferdinand-Porsche-Strasse 7)

FIACRE

A *Fiacre* (horse-drawn carriage) for up to four people costs €33 for 25 minutes. The drivers line up on Residenzplatz. Not all speak English, so don't expect a guided tour.

TAXI

Taxi fares start at €3 plus around €2 per kilometre. To book a radio taxi, call ☎ 81 11 or ☎ 17 15. There's a huge taxi rank outside the main train station.

AROUND SALZBURG

HELLBRUNN

An archbishop with a wicked sense of humour, Markus Sittikus built the yellow-painted **Schloss Hellbrunn** (Map p267; ☎ 82 03 72-0; www.hellbrunn.at; Fürstenweg 37; adult/child/family €8.50/3.80/21.50; ⏰ 9am-4.30pm Apr & Oct, 9am-5.30pm May & Jun, 9am-10pm Jul & Aug) in the 17th century as a pleasure palace and an escape vault from his functions at Residenz. The Italianate villa became a wild retreat for rulers of state who flocked here to eat, drink and generally be merry. It was a Garden of Eden to all who beheld its exotic fauna, citrus trees and trick fountains – designed to sober up quaffing clerics without dampening their spirits. Domenico Gisberti, poet to the court of Munich, once penned: 'I see the epitome of Venice in these waters, Rome reduced to a brief outline.'

Today, Hellbrunn attracts the giggling tourist masses in summer; most are here for the fabulously eccentric Wasserspiele (trick fountains). Be prepared to get *very* wet as you wander past stone lions, cherubs and statues that drench you with water when you least expect it. For a right good soaking, step inside the mother-of-pearl Neptune Grotto or gaze up to admire the 200 limewood figurines at the water-driven Mechanical Theatre. Tours run every 30 minutes. To lose the crowds, take a stroll along the broad oak-lined avenues in the glorious Schloss gardens; these are open year-round till dusk.

Getting There & Away

Hellbrunn is 4km from Salzburg. Bus 25 stops directly outside the Schloss every half-hour (€1.70) – city passes are valid. Catch the bus from the *Hauptbahnhof* or Rudolfskai in the old town.

UNTERSBERG

Rising above Salzburg, 1853m-high **Untersberg** (Map p265) affords a tremendous vista of the surrounding Alps. In winter, skiers swoosh down the 7.5km piste, while in summer the mountain is a magnet for hikers, rock climbers and paragliders. A cable car to the top (up/down/return €11/9.50/18) runs every half-hour year-round except for two weeks in April and six weeks from 1 November. Take bus 25 or 16 from Salzburg *Hauptbahnhof* to St Leonhard to the valley station.

GAISBERG

Follow the road that snakes up to **Gaisberg** peak (Map p265; 1287m) and you'll find there's a tremendous panorama of Salzburg and the Salzkammergut from the 5km Gaisberg Rundwanderweg, which follows a balcony trail. Unless you have your own transport, the only way up is to take bus 151 (€2.60 return, 30 minutes), departing four or five times a day in summer from Mirabellplatz (Map p270). From November to March the bus only goes as far as Zistelalpe, about 1.5km short of the summit.

HALLEIN

☎ 06245 / pop 18,900 / elev 460m

Often eclipsed by its big brother, Salzburg, Hallein (Map p265) has industrial outskirts that belie its well-preserved medieval core: a warren of narrow streets and inner courtyards peppered with art workshops, boho cafés and pastel-hued town houses. Tie that with a strong Celtic heritage and must-see salt mine and you're looking at a place that merits at least a day of your time.

Orientation & Information

The train station is east of the Salzach River: walk ahead, bear left and turn right to cross the river for the town centre (five minutes). The post office is opposite the train station. The **tourist office** (☎ 853 94; www.hallein .com; Mauttorpromenade 6; ⏰ 8.30am-5.30pm Mon-Fri) is on the narrow Pernerinsel island adjoining the Stadtbrücke.

Sights
KELTENMUSEUM

Recently brought bang up to date with an all-glass façade overlooking the Salzach, the **Keltenmuseum** (Celtic Museum; ☎ 807 83; Pflegerplatz 5; adult/child €6/2.50; ⏰ 9am-5pm) runs chronologically through the region's heritage in a series of beautiful vaulted rooms. It begins with a fine collection of Celtic artefacts including Asterix-style helmets, an impressively reconstructed chariot and a selection of bronze brooches, pendants and buckles. The 1st floor traces the history of salt extraction in Hallein, featuring high points such as a miniature slide and the mummified Mannes im Salz (man in salt) unearthed in 1577. There is a pamphlet with English explanations (€2.50).

SALZWELTEN SALZBURG

Austria's biggest show-mine, **Salzwelten Salzburg** (☎ 06132-200 2400; www.salzwelten.at Ramsaustrasse 3; adult/child/family; €16.50/9.90//34.70; ⊗ 9am-5pm Apr-Oct, 10am-3pm Nov-Mar) pays tribute to the salt that filled Salzburg's coffers during its princely heyday. Visitors don an Oompa Loompa–style boiler suit to descend to the bowels of the earth and board a rickety train. The tour passes through a maze of claustrophobic passageways, over the border to Germany and down a 27m slide – don't break, lift your legs and ask the guide to add wax for extra speed! After crossing a salt lake on a wooden raft, a 42m slide brings you to the lowest point (210m underground) and back to good old Austria. Guided tours depart every half an hour. Bus 41 (€1.80, 12 minutes) runs from Hallein train station hourly on weekdays, less often at weekends.

KELTENBLITZ

Bad Dürrnberg's family-friendly summer toboggan run, **Keltenblitz** (☎ 851 05; Bad Dürrnberg; adult/child €8.80/6; ⊗ 11am-5pm Mon-Fri, 10.30am-5pm Sat & Sun May-Jun & Oct, 10am-6pm daily Jul-Sep) is ideal for those who want to pick up speed after visiting the show-mine. A chairlift whisks passengers to the top of Zinken mountain, where they board little wheeled bobsleds to race 2.2km downhill around hairpin bends. The thrill is over in a flash and affords fleeting views of the Salzach Valley.

Festivals & Events

First-rate musicians and artists draw crowds to the two-week **Halleiner Stadtfestwoche**, which takes place from June to July each year. The festival is one of the headliners on the summer events programme in Salzburgerland, with a line-up spanning everything from classical concerts to live jazz, theatre, comedy acts, readings and ex-

hibitions. For more details, see www.forum-hallein.at (in German).

Sleeping & Eating

Hallein can be visited on a day trip from Salzburg, but there are plenty of value-for-money places to stay if you'd rather base yourself here. The tourist office helps book private rooms.

Pension Sommerauer (☎ 800 30; www.pension-hallein.at; Tschusistrasse 71; s/d €37/57; Ⓟ Ⓡ) Housed in a 300-year-old farmhouse, the rustic rooms at this guesthouse are a bargain. There's a heated pool and conservatory, plus lots of kiddie stuff including a playroom, sandpit and swings.

Pension Hochdürrnberg (☎ 751 83; Rumpelgasse 14; d/tr €52/60; Ⓟ) Surrounded by meadows, this lovely farmhouse in Bad Dürrnberg offers countrified rooms decorated with warm pine and crisp white linen. The furry residents (rabbits, sheep and cows) keep children amused.

Hotel Auwirt (☎ 804 17; www.auwirt.com; Salzburgerstrasse 42; s/d €52/84; campsites per adult/child/tent €5.20/4/3.50; Ⓟ Ⓠ) The light-filled rooms at this three-star hotel are simple but comfy (ask for one with a balcony). It makes a great base for families with its tree-shaded garden and adventure playground. Freshly squeezed juice and homemade jam are served at breakfast.

Koi (☎ 741 08; Schantzplatz 2; lunch €6.90-7.90; ⊗ 9am-11pm Mon-Sat, 10am-6pm Sun) Buddha welcomes you to Hallein's hippest café. The design is industrial cool with Asian overtones – from chocolate-coloured leather benches to giraffe-print cushions. The menu tempts with fresh-from-the-wok noodles and crunchy beansprout salads, washed down with organic juices. There's a cool breeze to be had on the raised terrace by the stream.

Café Barock (☎ 806 86; Gollinger-Tor-Gasse 1; lunch €6.90; ⊗ lunch & dinner Mon-Sat) Tucked down an alleyway, this little bistro is bedecked with eye-catching modern art. When the sun's out, its cobbled square framed by tall town houses is a popular lunch spot. The chalked menu-board includes lots of pasta, focaccia and vegetarian options.

Stadtkrug Hallein (☎ 830 85; Bayrhamerplatz 10; lunch buffet €6.90, mains €7-10.50; ⊗ lunch & dinner Mon-Fri, dinner Sun) Tables fill quickly during the midday rush at this bustling, wood-beamed restaurant in the centre. If it's warm, pull up a chair beside the trickling fountain on the square to refuel with an enormous schnitzel or plate of goulash.

Getting There & Away

Hallein is 25 minutes south of Salzburg by bus or train with departures roughly every 30 minutes (€3.70). The main train station in Salzburg sells the Salz Erlebnis Ticket (€22), which covers the train to Hallein, a bus transfer and entry to the salt mine.

WERFEN

☎ 06468 / pop 3200 / elev 525m

For a village of small proportions, Werfen has some real stunners: the world's largest accessible ice caves, the soaring limestone turrets of the Tennengebirge and a medieval fortress lording it over the valley are just the tip of the iceberg. Little wonder, then, that this scenic setting is where the famous picnic took place in *The Sound of Music* – the hills here are definitely alive and kickin'.

Orientation & Information

The town hugs the northern bank of the Salzach River, five minutes' walk from the train station. The friendly **tourist office** (☎ 53 88; www.werfen.at; Markt 24; ☼ 9am-5pm Mon-Fri Sep-Jun, 9am-7pm Mon-Fri, 5-7pm Sat Jul & Aug) hands out information and maps.

Sights

BURG HOHENWERFEN

Location, location… On its fairy-tale perch above Werfen, **Burg Hohenwerfen** (☎ 76 03; adult/child/family €13/7/30; ☼ 9am-6pm Jul & Aug, 9am-5pm May, Jun & Sep, 9am-4.30pm Apr & Oct, closed Mon in Apr) has one to rival the best. Set against the backdrop of the glowering Tennengebirge range, the fortress was built in the 11th century to guard the valley and Salzach River below, but its current appearance dates to 1570. Highlights include the 16th-century belfry that commands far-reaching views over Werfen and the dungeons that display the usual nasties such as the iron maiden and thumb screw. The entry fee also covers the spectacular falconry show in the grounds (11am and 3pm), where falconers in medieval costume release eagles, owls, falcons and vultures to wheel in front of the ramparts. There is a commentary in English and German.

Both the fortress and the ice caves can be squeezed into a day trip from Salzburg if you start early; visit the caves first, and be at the fortress for the last falconry show. The stiff walk up from the village takes a brisk 20-minutes. For taxis, call ☎ 52 93.

EISRIESENWELT

Billed as the world's largest accessible ice caves, **Eisriesenwelt** (☎ 52 48; www.eisriesenwelt.at; adult/child €8/4, with cable car €17/8.50; ☼ 9am-4.30pm Jul & Aug, 9am-3.30pm May, Jun, Sep & Oct) is a glittering ice empire that spans 30,000 sq m and comprises 42km of narrow passages burrowing deep into the glacial heart of the mountains. It may feel warm outside, but temperatures plummet to subzero as soon as you enter the crevice in the cliffs; similar to the blast of cold air that hits you upon opening the freezer. Be sure to pack sturdy footwear and warm layers.

Taking a tour through these Narnia-like chambers of shimmering blue ice is an extraordinary experience. As you climb wooden steps and duck down pitch-black passages, with carbide lamps aglow and fingers frozen, otherworldly ice sculptures, columns, walls and lakes emerge from the shadows. Among these fantastical formations are Frigga, the polar bear, and Odin, the elephant, named after gods in Norse mythology. A high point is the 42m *Eispalast* (ice palace), where the frost crystals twinkle when a magnesium flare is held up to them. A womblike tunnel leads to a flight of 700 steps, which descends back to the entrance.

In summer, minibuses (single/return €2.80/5.60) operate every 20 minutes between Eisriesenstrasse in Werfen and the car park, which is a 15 to 20-minute amble from the bottom station of the cable car. The last bus departs at 7pm. Allow roughly three hours for the return trip (including tour). You can walk the whole route, but it's a challenging four-hour ascent, rising 1100m above the village. To discover the magnificent scenery that lies above the ground, consider hiking the tough but incredibly rewarding Tennengebirge Circuit (see p97), which starts just before the caves.

Sleeping & Eating

Most of Werfen's sleeping and eating options are lined up along the village's main street, Markt. The tourist office will make bookings for no commission

Camping Vierthaler (☎ 565 70; www.camping -vierthaler.at; Reitsam 8, Pfarrwerfen; campsites per adult/child/tent €4.40/1.70/4.80, bungalows d/tr/q €23/30/37; ☼ Apr-Sep) This lovely campsite on the bank of the Salzach River has a back-to-nature feel.

SALZBURG & SALZBURGER LAND

Facilities feature a snack bar and playground. Bungalows with kitchenettes, patios and barbecue areas are also available.

Weisses Rössl (☎ 52 68; Markt 39; s/d €30/50) This marshmallow-pink guesthouse in the centre is a good budget deal, offering basic but spacious rooms with sofas and cable TV. The rooftop terrace has amazing views of the fortress and Tennengebirge.

Pension Obauer (☎ 522 40; Markt 36; s/d €35/64; **P**) Not to be confused with the swish restaurant below, this place runs rings around most of Werfen's pensions. The rooms are immaculate with wooden floors, comfy beds and scatter rugs. The family runs the deli next door, so you'll sample their cheese and homemade sausages at breakfast.

Obauer (☎ 521 20; www.obauer.com; Markt 46; mains €24-48, set lunch/dinner €35/50; ☒ lunch & dinner) Karl and Rudi Obauer cook up a storm in this Michelin-starred restaurant. Everything here strikes the right chord, from the sleek design to the creative cuisine and locally sourced ingredients (most of the fruit and herbs are grown in the garden). Signature dishes include tender Werfen lamb, trout strudel and catfish with capers.

Getting There & Away

Werfen can be reached from Salzburg by Hwy 10. Trains from Salzburg (€7.10, 50 minutes) run approximately hourly.

SOUTHERN SALZBURG PROVINCE

Many of the blockbuster sights in Southern Salzburg Province are covered in the Hohe Tauern National Park Region chapter (p310), but the following places are definitely worth a look. If you're driving to Radstadt or Mauterndorf in the remote Lungau region, keep an eye out for the original Roman milestones that punctuate the Tauern Pass.

LIECHTENSTEINKLAMM

One of the deepest and longest ravines in the Alps, the **Liechtensteinklamm** (Liechtenstein Gorge; ☎ 06412-60 36; adult/child €3.50/2.20; ☒ 8am-6pm May-Sep, 9am-4pm Oct) is off the beaten track but well worth the detour. The jaw-dropping chasm was carved out during the last Ice Age and takes its name from Johann II, Prince of

Liechtenstein, who poured plenty of money into making the gorge accessible in the 19th century. Following raging waters flanked by vertical 300m-high cliffs, the footpath crosses bridges and passes through tunnels gouged into slate cliffs veined with white granite. The mossy boulders and crags glisten with spray from the water, which is at its most striking in the late afternoon when the sunlight turns it opal blue. The trail culminates at a spectacular 50m waterfall. Allow at least an hour to walk the gorge.

Buses operate frequently between Werfen and St Johann im Pongau (€2.80, 30 minutes), which is a 4km walk from the gorge. Free parking is available.

FILZMOOS

☎ 06453 / pop 1400 / elev 1055m

Dwarfed by the shimmering glaciers of the Dachstein massif and fringed by rolling pastures, Filzmoos is an unspoilt village that despite its growing appeal as a ski resort has managed to preserve its rural charm and family-friendly atmosphere. The centrally located **tourist office** (☎ 853 94; www.filzmoos.at; Filzmoos 50; ☒ 8.30am-5.30pm Mon-Fri) provides stacks of information on activities in the region and will help book accommodation.

Activities

In winter, Filzmoos is a top **ski resort** for novices, with gentle and uncrowded slopes that are easily accessed from the centre. Overshadowed by the distinctive peak of Bischofsmütze (2454m), shaped like a bishop's mitre, the village shares 32km of downhill slopes with its neighbour, Neuberg, and is crisscrossed with 50km of serene **winter walking** trails. The nursery slopes, floodlit **toboggan run** and central ski schools make it an ideal resort for families.

When the weather warms, Filzmoos morphs into prime **hiking** territory. Avid walkers keen to trek among the 2000m-high limestone pinnacles should consider tackling the two-day Gosaukamm Circuit (see p95). Equally popular summer activities include **Nordic walking** on marked trails in the surrounding hills and **mountain biking** the challenging and scenic Dachstein Tour (see p79).

Mountain bikes, skis, snowshoes, sledges and cross-country equipment are available for hire at **Intersport Flory** (☎ 82 82; www.flory.at; Filzmoos 103); prices are given online.

SALZBURG & SALZBURGER LAND

Sleeping & Eating

Filzmoos has a smattering of modestly priced chalets, private rooms and hotels, though in the high winter season you should expect rates to be roughly 50% higher that those quoted in the following reviews.

Jugendgästehaus Aumühle (☎ 82 46; Filzmoos 26; dm €24; P) Backing onto forest, this darkwood chalet is five-star 'roughing it' with spacious four-bed dorms, convenient access to the slopes, a common room and garden. It's five minutes' walk into town.

Landhaus Elisabeth (☎ 83 36; www.landhaus-elisa beth.com; Filzmoos 137; s/d €43/72; P 🖳) This inviting chalet offers snug rooms with balconies or verandas. The sauna, sunny garden and free bike hire are extra perks. Delicious cakes make mouths water and waistlines expand in the café.

our pick **Bio-Hotel Hammerhof** (☎ 82 45; www .hammerhof.at; Filzmoos 6; s/d €73/130; P 🖳) Set in a beautifully converted 400-year-old farmhouse, this ecofriendly hotel is a gem. The light-filled rooms are decorated with plenty of natural wood and country touches; some have balconies and tiled ovens. The restaurant cooks with home-grown organic produce. Unwind in a herbal bath at the beauty centre or saddle a horse to canter off into the hills (the owner, Matthias, is a riding instructor and arranges tours).

Fiakerwirt Mandlinghof (☎ 82 09; Filzmoos 23; mains €5.50-11; 🕑 lunch & dinner) This rambling farmhouse and beer garden serves hearty fare such as schnitzel and pork roast. Kids love the pet goats, ducks and ponies. In winter, horse-drawn sleighs depart from here (€14 to €17 per person).

Getting There & Away

Filzmoos is a 10km detour from the A10/E55 Tauern-Autobahn motorway. Several buses operate daily between Salzburg *Hauptbahnhof* and Filzmoos (€11.90, 1½ hours), but most require a change at Bischofshofen.

RADSTADT

☎ 06452 / pop 4800 / elev 856m

Radstadt has an attractively walled town centre, with round turrets and a **Stadtpfarrkirche** (town parish church) that is a potpourri of Gothic and Romanesque elements. Most people, however, come for the fantastic skiing and snowboarding in the region, which forms part of the huge Salzburger Sportwelt skiing area. Around 100 lifts provide access to 300km of pistes geared mostly towards intermediates and beginners, plus several snowboard parks and high-altitude cross-country trails. For information, contact the **Salzburger Sportwelt Tourist Office** (☎ 06457-29 29; www.sportwel t-amade.com).

The same mountains attract active types in summer, too, with more than 1000km of walking trails and opportunities for canyoning, climbing, white-water rafting and mountain biking.

Getting There & Away

Radstadt is on the route of two-hourly IC trains running between Innsbruck and Graz, both about three hours away. Zell am See (€13.10, 80 minutes) and Bruck an der Mur (€24.30, 2½ hours) are on this route. From Radstadt, Hwy 99 climbs to the dramatic Radstädter Tauern Pass (1739m), then over to Carinthia. Just to the west is the A10/E55, which avoids the high parts by going through a 6km tunnel.

MAUTERNDORF

☎ 06472 / pop 1685 / elev 1122m

The sleepy village of Mauterndorf is postcard-perfect Austria; its narrow streets are dotted with candy-coloured houses and fountains. While the surrounding high moors and exposed bluffs are set up for walking and skiing, its remote setting in the Lungau region detracts the masses. The centrepiece of the village is medieval **Burg Mauterndorf** (☎ 74 26; adult/child €8/5; 🕑 10am-6pm May-Oct). Dominating a rocky outcrop, this 13th-century castle was built by the archbishops of Salzburg on the site of a Roman fort. The castle now houses a regional museum and provides the backdrop for various cultural events. It is believed that in the Middle Ages the main road passed directly through the castle courtyard and tolls were extracted from road users.

Getting There & Away

Mauterndorf is on Hwy 99. Bus 780 runs from Radstadt to the Mauterndorf post office (€7.10, 50 minutes, three times daily).

Carinthia

Few regions in Europe match the rugged beauty of Carinthia, and you'll find that travelling through it is often a serpentine journey in valleys and natural conduits. Carinthia can also at times seem larger than life: the high peaks, the gouged valleys and the glistening lakes, not to forget the flamboyant show of opulence in the capital, Klagenfurt, and the several popular resorts around the best-known of its 1270 pristine mountain lakes. The most popular of these lakes, like the large Wörthersee, have waters warmed to a comfortable swimming temperature by thermal springs. In stark contrast, parts of Carinthia have a 'backwoods' feel that comes from its isolation, the presence of primary industries and its often conservative politics. Consistently 'red' Villach, an important crossroad, defies this description with dynamic development, and the people living in far-flung villages and towns themselves, though often conservative by nature, are also surprisingly open.

Carinthia's deep medieval heritage is celebrated in picturesque walled villages such as Friesach and Gmund, and impressive castles like the hilltop fortress of Hochosterwitz. Many of the towns and villages nestled in Carinthia's rolling hills hold an annual summer festival, with folk-music groups and bands of roving performers coming from neighbouring Italy and Slovenia to take part alongside locals. The province's proximity to Slovenia (the border between Austria and Slovenia has been redrawn several times over the centuries) means that many of the place names are of Slavic origin and Slavic surnames are common among the local inhabitants.

HIGHLIGHTS

- Hiking the spectacular Garnitzenklamm gorge and cycling through the mountainous wilds around **Hermagor** (p301)

- Visiting the innovative **Die Spur des Einhorns exhibition** (p301) in Friesach, Carinthia's prettiest medieval village

- Swimming the shores of the **Wörthersee** (p292) and enjoying a lakeside meal afterwards at **Restaurant Maria Loretto** (p294)

- Stopping over in lively **Villach** (p297) for skiing in winter, some splashy fun in summer in the nearby lakes, or hiking in the mountains

- Transporting yourself to the tranquil ambience of Tibet at the **Heinrich Harrer Museum** (p302) in Hüttenberg

- Admiring the views from the top of **Burg Hochosterwitz** (p304), a spectacular medieval castle

Friesach ★ ★ Hüttenberg
Millstättersee ★
★ Burg Hochosterwitz
Hermagor ★ Villach ★ ★ Klagenfurt
★ Wörthersee

| POPULATION: 560,300 | AREA: 9536 SQ KM | HIGHEST ELEVATION: GROSSGLOCKNER 3797M |

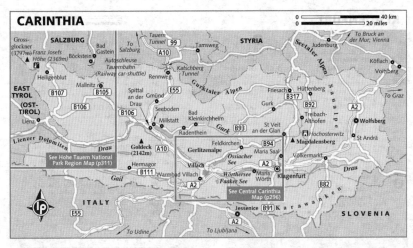

History

Carinthia (once called Carantania) belonged to Slovenian tribes until the 800s, when the Avars, an eastern tribe, invaded. The locals called upon the forces of the Bavarian monarchy to help them, leading to the gradual displacement of Slavic culture by a Germanic one. Carinthia became part of Austria in 1335.

The Slovenes attempted to reclaim the southern part of Carinthia after WWI, with a Yugoslav army crossing the border and occupying Klagenfurt, the provincial capital. On October 10 in 1920 the province was restored to Austria after a popular vote.

Climate

Carinthia gets more sunshine than elsewhere in Austria – in summer it can be blazingly hot, with lake water temperatures reaching 25°C to 28°C. The mild climate means winters are milder than elsewhere, too, leading to a shorter ski season (late December to March). Hiking is good all summer, but the more exposed trails are best done in autumn.

National Parks

Carinthia shares an area of outstanding natural beauty, the Hohe Tauern National Park (p310), with neighbouring Salzburg province and Tyrol.

Getting There & Around

Klagenfurt airport has cheap connections with the UK (www.ryanair.com) and Germany (www.tuifly.com), plus Austrian domestic flights (www.aua.com). Klagenfurt and Villach are the main hubs for trains from elsewhere in Europe.

Carinthia is divided into regional zones for public transport, with either single tickets or passes that are valid for 24 hours, seven days, 30 days or one year. Ticket clerks can advise, or contact **Kärntner Linien** (☎ 0463-5461821; www .kaerntner-linien.at) in Klagenfurt. Many of the lakes are served by boat services in summer.

The **Kärnten Card** (www.kaerntencard.co.at; 2-/5-week card €34/49) gives free/cheaper access to the province's major sights and 50% discounts on buses and trains. It's sold at hotels and tourist offices from mid-April to October.

KLAGENFURT

☎ 0463 / pop 92,400

Provincial and not an urban centre comparable with Graz or Vienna, Klagenfurt walks a very fine line between being Austria's boondocks capital and a playground for a partying set. For all this, it's an enjoyable, sunny city that offers easy access to some good swimming and water sports, and to lakeside villages on and around the beautiful Wörthersee. Several attractive medieval towns to the north are also within easy reach.

Ring roads today mark the site of the old city walls, pulled down in 1809 on the orders of Napoleon, while the city centre has attractive Renaissance courtyards, alleyways and arcades, many filled with smart boutiques and cafés.

CARINTHIA

CARINTHIA

KLAGENFURT

0 — 400 m
0 — 0.2 miles

INFORMATION
Café-bar G@tes...................................1 C4
Cheeta's...2 D4
Hauptbahnhof Post Office................3 C6
Kärntner Reisebüro............................4 B4
Main Post Office.................................5 B4
Tourist Office......................................6 B4

SIGHTS & ACTIVITIES
Dom (Cathedral)................................7 B5
Dragon Fountain.................................8 B4
Landesmuseum...................................9 C5
Landhaus...10 D4
Stadtgalerie (Main Building)...........11 D3
Stadtgalerie (Stadthaus).................12 C3
Stadthauptpfarrkirche St Egyd......13 D3

SLEEPING
Arcotel Moser Verdino.....................14 B4
Cityhotel Ratheiser...........................15 C4

Hotel Garni Blumenstöckl...............16 B5
Hotel Geyer.......................................17 C4
Hotel Liebetegger.............................18 C4
Hotel Palais Porcia...........................19 B4
Palais Hotel Landhaushof...............20 D4

EATING
Dolce Vita..21 D3
Market Stalls & Restaurants...........22 B5
Restaurant Arkadenhof..............(see 20)
Restaurant Salzamt....................(see 20)
Spar Supermarket.............................23 C5
Spar Supermarket.............................24 B4
Spar Supermarket.............................25 C6
Wirtshaus zum Heiligen
    Josef...26 B4
Zauberhütt'n......................................27 B4

DRINKING
Bierhaus zum Augustin....................28 D3
Checkpoint Charlie............................29 D4
Kamot...30 C4
Pankraz..31 C5

ENTERTAINMENT
Konzerthaus......................................32 C5
Stadttheater......................................33 C3

TRANSPORT
Bus Station..34 C6
City Bus Station.................................35 B4
Hertz...36 B6
Lend Ferry Departure Point............37 A5
Postbus Information.........................38 C6
STW Verkehrsbetriebe Office.........39 B4

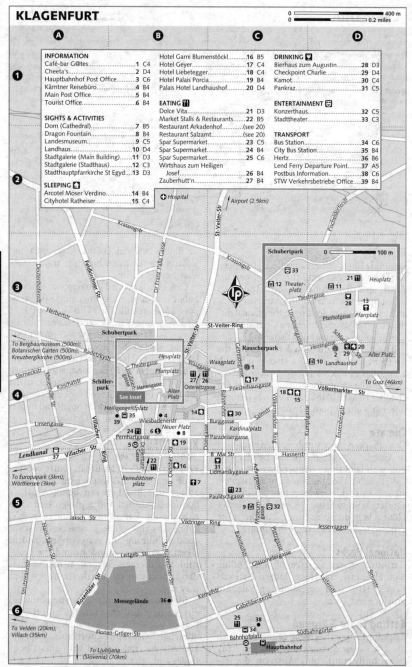

At the town's western limit is the wide green space of Europapark, home to a couple of children's attractions including the bizarre world-in-miniature of Minimundus.

Orientation

Klagenfurt lies 30km from Slovenia and 60km from Italy. The *Hauptbahnhof* (main train station; Map p290) is about 1km south of Neuer Platz, the centre of town. One block west of Neuer Platz is Heiligengeistplatz, the hub for local buses. Wörthersee is about 4km west of the city centre, with Europapark on its eastern shore.

Information

INTERNET ACCESS

Café-bar G@tes (Map p290; ☎ 50 97 77; gates@gates .at; Waagplatz 7; per 10 min €1; ☑ 9am-1am Mon-Fri, 5pm-1am Sat & Sun)

Cheeta's (Map p290; Herrengasse 7; €3 per 30 min; ☑ 2pm-2am) Dark and smoky, with games.

MEDICAL SERVICES

Hospital (Map p290; ☎ 538-0; St Veiter Strasse 47)

POST

Main Post Office (Map p290; Dr-Herrmann-Gasse 4; ☑ 7.30am-6pm Mon-Fri, 8am-noon Sat) One block west of Neuer Platz, with another branch by the station.

TOURIST INFORMATION

Tourist office (Map p290; ☎ 53 722 23; www.info .klagenfurt.at; Rathaus, Neuer Platz 1; ☑ 8am-6pm Mon-Fri, 10am-5pm Sat, 10am-1pm Sun) Sells Kärnten cards and books accommodation.

TRAVEL AGENCIES

Kärntner Reisebüro (Map p290; ☎ 56 400; www.krb .at; Neuer Platz 2; ☑ 9am-6pm Mon-Fri, 9am-noon Sat) Helpful and central travel service.

Sights & Activities

MUSEUMS & GALLERIES

If you've ever wondered what the fossilised head of an ice-age woolly rhinoceros looked like, a visit to **Landesmuseum Rudolfinum** (Map p290; ☎ 305 52; www.landesmuseum-ktn.at, in German; Museumgasse 2; adult/child & student/family €5/3/11.50; ☑ 10am-6pm Tue, Wed & Fri, 10am-8pm Thu, 10am-5pm Sat & Sun) will quell your idle speculation. The museum's *Lindwurmschädel* (dragon skull) was found in the 14th century and it even became the model for the head of Klagenfurt's central fountain. This museum also has lots

of Celtic armour and jewellery, and the multimedia 'Glocknerrama' – an acoustic and visual simulation that leads you to the peak of Austria's highest mountain.

Some excellent rolling art exhibitions are held in the **Stadtgalerie** (Map p290; ☎ 537 5532; www .stadtgalerie.net, in German; Theatergasse 4; adult/student/child €5/2.90/free; ☑ 10am-6pm Tue-Sun), which has a main venue on Theaterstrasse and a second nearby in the **Alpen-Adria-Galerie im Stadthaus** (☎ 537-5532; Theaterplatz 3; admission free; ☑ 10am-6pm Tue-Sun). Those in recent years have included works by Oskar Kokoschka and Californian pop-art maestro Mel Ramos.

The **Bergbaumuseum** (Mining Museum; off Map p290; ☎ 51 12 52; www.bergbaumuseum.at, in German; Prof-Dr.-Kahler-Platz 1; adult/child & student €5/3.20; ☑ 9am-6pm Apr-Oct) is a pleasant option for a rainy day. Exhibits including tools and drilling equipment are housed in tunnels that lead from the grounds of the botanical gardens deep into the hill. The locals took shelter here from Allied bombing during WWII.

Neuer Platz, Klagenfurt's central square, is dominated by the **Dragon Fountain** (Map p290), the emblem of the city. The blank-eyed, wriggling statue is modelled on the *Lindwurm* (dragon) of legend, said to have resided in a swamp here long ago, devouring cattle and virgins. The *Lindwurm* is depicted with the local hero who eventually clubbed it to death, wearing a scanty lion skin and sporting a truly terrifying moustache.

The provincial government headquarters, **Landhaus** (Map p290; ☎ 577 57-215; Landhaushof 1; ☑ 9am-5pm Apr-Oct), stands just to the west of Alter Platz. Go through the archway into the cobbled two-storey courtyard to truly admire the building's two steeples. The ceiling of the **Wappensaal** (interior chamber; adult/child €3/2) has a trompe l'oeil gallery painted by Carinthian artist Josef Ferdinand Fromiller (1693–1760), and depicting Carinthian landowners paying homage to Charles VI. Stand in the centre of the room for the best effect.

Alter Platz contains a number of historic buildings that provide a lovely backdrop for watching the world go by – best enjoyed from behind an ice cream or a glass of beer. Nearby is the **Stadthauptpfarrkirche St Egyd** (Pfarrplatz), with an ornate gold-leaf interior and some fine ceiling frescos. Its **Stadtpfarrturm** (tower; ☎ 537-2293; €1; ☑ 10am-5.30pm Mon-Fri, 10am-12.30pm Sat early Apr-early Oct) can be climbed for a good view of the city and surrounding countryside.

CARINTHIA

The **Dom** (cathedral; Domplatz 1), with its ornate marble pulpit and pink-and-white stuccoed ceiling, is another highlight.

At the far end of Radetzkystrasse is a rather limp **Botanischer Garten** (Botanical Garden; off Map p290; admission free; ⏰ 9am-6pm May-Sep, 9am-6pm Mon-Thu Oct-Apr). Adjoining the gardens is the **Kreuzberglkirche**, perched on a hillock with a set of very pretty mosaic stations of the cross on the path leading up to it.

EUROPAPARK VICINITY

The large, green expanse of Europapark and the *Strandbad* (beach) on the shores of Wörthersee are centres for splashy fun, particularly for kids. Boating and swimming are usually possible from May to September. Buses 10, 11, 12, 20, 21 and 22 from Heiligengeistplatz run to Minimundus, but usually only the 10, 11 and 12 continue the short distance to *Strandbad*.

Down near the Wörthersee, **Minimundus** (Map p292; ☎ 211 94-0; www.minimundus.at; Villacher Strasse 241; adult/student/child €12/8/7; ⏰ 9am-6pm Apr & Oct, 9am-7pm May, Jun & Sep, 9am-10pm Jul & Aug) has around 140 replicas of some of the world's architectural icons, downsized to a scale of 1:25. By lying on the ground with a camera, you can later impress your friends at parties with great snaps of the Taj Mahal, Eiffel Tower or Arc de Triomphe. Building materials are true to the original. The Sydney Opera House, Tower of London, Statue of Liberty and Schloss Neuschwanstein are also here. English guides to the less recognisable models –

such as Bad Ischl train station – are on sale for €4. There's a café and restaurant (normal size) on site.

Swimmers can dip a paw into the **Strand-bad** (Map p292; ☎ 0676-88 521 6331; www.stw.at/inhalt/Strandbaeder.htm; Metnitzstrand 2; day card adult/child €3.40/1.50, 1hr before closing €1.50/free; ⏰ 8am-8pm early May-late Sep), Klagenfurt's lakeside beach with cabins, restaurants and piers for basking. You can plough a circuit 100m offshore for 500m or so along the line of buoys and back. It's a decent swim of about 1km in warm waters in summer, and uncrowded. *Kästchen* (lockers large enough for day packs) in the *Strandbad* cost €1 plus €10 deposit and are located on the extreme right of the complex as you walk in.

There's also good swimming outside the buoys further south, past the Maria Loretto beach. A permanent nude bathing beach (marked FKK on the tourist office maps) is near Maria Loretto. Those lounge lizards for whom all this might sound a tad too strenuous will enjoy indulging in **paddle or electric boat** (per 30 minutes €2-6) escapades alongside the *Strandbad*.

Lounge lizards can also nip down the road to check out real-life role models at **Happ's Reptilienzoo** (Reptile Zoo; Map p292; ☎ 234 25; www.reptilienzoo.at, in German; Villacher Strasse 237; adult/student/child €9/8/5; ⏰ 8am-5pm winter, 8am-6pm summer); there are crocodiles plus all manner of creepers, crawlers and slitherers here for kids and adults to admire. Some signs are in English.

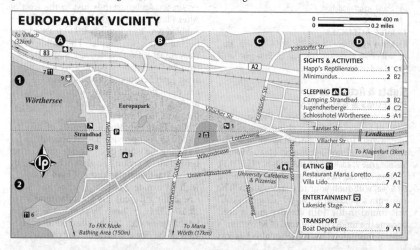

EUROPAPARK VICINITY

SIGHTS & ACTIVITIES
Happ's Reptilienzoo.................1 C1
Minimundus........................2 B2

SLEEPING 🏨 🏠
Camping Strandbad.................3 B2
Jugendherberge....................4 C2
Schlosshotel Wörthersee...........5 A1

EATING 🍴
Restaurant Maria Loretto..........6 A2
Villa Lido.........................7 A1

ENTERTAINMENT 🎭
Lakeside Stage....................8 A2

TRANSPORT
Boat Departures...................9 A1

WALKS

To take a walking tour, pick up the brochure in English from the tourist office. It has a map and detailed descriptions of monuments, historic buildings and hidden courtyards. Free guided tours depart from the tourist office at 10am during July and August.

Festivals & Events

Klagenfurter Stadtfest is a two-day music and theatre festival that takes place every year in early July. The **Wörthersee Festspiele** (Wörthersee Festival; ☎ 507355-0; www.woertherseefestspiele.com, in German; €45-70) happens every summer between late June and mid-August, with operas, ballets and pop concerts taking place on an offshore stage on the Wörthersee.

Sleeping

When you check into accommodation in Klagenfurt, ask for a *Gästekarte* (guest card), entitling you to discounts.

BUDGET

Camping Strandbad (Map p292; ☎ 211 69; www.tiscover .at/camping-klagenfurt, onsite caravan hire www.caravan -interland.nl; Metnitzstrand 5; site per person/tent €8/5; ☼ May-Sep; P ⛎). This shady camping ground gives free use of the *Strandbad* swimming complex. Caravans can also be rented here.

Jugendgästehaus Klagenfurt (Map p292; ☎ 23 00 20; www.oejhv.or.at; Neckheimgasse 6; dm/s/d €18.90/ 26.90/45.80; P ⛛) The modern HI hostel is near Europapark. To get there from the centre, take bus 10, 12 or 22 and get off at Jugendgästehaus or (depending on the bus route) Neckheimgasse.

Hotel Garni Blumenstöckl (Map p290; ☎ 577 93; www.blumenstoeckl.at; 10 Oktober Strasse 11; s €42-54, d €76-80) Rooms are arranged around a plant-filled courtyard in this two-star, family-run place in a 400-year-old building. The traditionally furnished ones aren't terribly grand, but a central position and very friendly owners make up for this.

Cityhotel Ratheiser (Map p290; ☎ 512 994; www .cityhotel-ratheiser.at, in German; Völkermarkter Strasse 10; s €53, d €72-75, ste €95-110; P) This quirky hotel has two extraordinary suites (8 and 10) with upstairs and downstairs sections joined by a spiral staircase. Bright and modern this hotel is not, but it has been in the same family for generations, and as a result it has some interesting connections with past people and events in Klagenfurt.

Schlosshotel Wörthersee (Map p292; ☎ 211 58-0; www.schloss-hotel.at; Villacher Strasse 338; s/d €48/76; P) There are a few of these in Austria – historic oddities that rise out of the landscape like Norman Bates' childhood house from the Hitchcock film *Psycho*. Rooms are definitely in need of a make-over, and if the sound of a night time freight train makes you wake in a sweat, it's not for you. It's packed with atmosphere, though, and all rooms except two singles face the lake.

Hotel Liebetegger (Map p290; ☎ 569 35; www.liebe tegger.com, in German; Völkermarkter Strasse 8; s/d €58/85; P ⛛) Though not an art hotel, the first two floors are decorated with original artwork in this three-star option. There are no designated non-smoker rooms, though.

MIDRANGE & TOP END

Hotel Geyer (Map p290; ☎ 578 86; www.hotelgeyer .com; Priesterhausgasse 5; s €55-75, d €80-106, tr €95-114; P ⛛) This three-star hotel offers some of the best value in town. Rooms are modern and comfortable, the breakfast room is tasteful and complemented by a summer patio. Although the walls can let through some sound from bathrooms and neighbours, it's still reasonably quiet.

Arcotel Moser Verdino (Map p290; ☎ 578 78; www .arcotel.at/moserverdino; Domgasse 2; s €74-162, d €108-240, ste €142-260, apt €172-280; ⛛) Prices in this excellent four-star hotel vary by demand, making it always worth a phone call, even if your budget is tight. What you get are high quality, modern rooms with flair, very helpful staff and a free stay for kids under 12.

Hotel Palais Porcia (Map p290; ☎ 51 15 90-0; www .hotel-palais-porcia.com; Neuer Platz 13; s €84-182, d €113-197, ste €197-349; P ⛛) This is a marvellously ornate and old-fashioned hotel on the 2nd floor of a historic building, right in the town centre. Expect lots of gilt, mirrors and red-velvet couches, with pink marble and gold taps in the bathrooms. It also has a private beach guests can use near its other hotel in Pörtschach.

Palais Hotel Landhaushof (Map p290; ☎ 59 09 59; www.landhaushof.at; Landhaushof 3; s €130, d €190-220, ste €380; ⛛) Klagenfurt's grandest hotel is housed in a converted Renaissance palace. Rooms range from elegant and traditional to kitsch and funky, with original baroque furniture given a new lease of life with new fabrics and colours. The restaurant, café and bar are a bonus, with an airy, glass-roomed atrium in

CARINTHIA

the main restaurant and café tables outside in the cobblestone courtyard.

Eating

Wörthersee Ätsch Petsch (Map p292; ☎ 220 440; mains €3-19; ♥ 4pm-late, closed Mon & Tue Sep-Apr, closed Mon May) At the Schlosshotel Wörthersee, this hip pub-like place serves grills, calamari, jacket potatoes and other tasty dishes. It's open until midnight (at least) on most nights

Zauberhutt'n (Map p290; ☎ 547 95; Osterwitzgasse 6; mains €5-17; ♥ lunch & dinner Mon-Fri, dinner Sat) The fried squid in a light garlic oil is a delight, but pasta, pizza and classic meat dishes all feature on the menu of this inexpensive, family-run restaurant. It's also the headquarters of the Magic Club of Klagenfurt (with a very unexpected visiting card).

Restaurant Arkadenhof ((Map p290; ☎ 590 959; Landhaushof 3; mains €7-20, 3-5 course evening menu €21-36 ♥ lunch & dinner Mon-Sat) This is the more formal of the two restaurants in the upmarket Palais Hotel Landhaushof with a menu of grills and steak flambéed in cognac, wok noodles, pasta dishes and classics like *Tafelspitz*.

Restaurant Salzamt (Map p290; breakfast buffet €15, mains €7-20; ♥ 7am-midnight) Next door to Arkadenhof is this smart bar and restaurant, which serves from the same menu.

our pick Restaurant Maria Loretto (Map p292; ☎ 244 65; Lorettoweg 54; mains €10-19; ♥ lunch & dinner, closed Jan & Feb) Situated on a headland above Wörthersee, this wonderful restaurant is easily reached by foot from the *Strandbad*. You might also hire a bicycle and make a day of it, perhaps taking a dip from reedy banks or the lakeside beach before or after the culinary deed. It does a very good trout and some flavoursome meat dishes, but it's the sheer character of the place that makes it a wonderful choice for food and casual drinks. Call ahead Mondays, when it's sometimes closed except from May to August.

Wirtshaus zum Heiligen Josef (Map p290; ☎ 500 807; Osterwitzgasse 7; mains €12-17; ♥ lunch & dinner Mon-Sat) This restaurant with outside tables serves excellent Austrian food, plus a few Italian vegetarian options such as risotto and gnocchi. There are daily soups and lunchtime specials and it has a very friendly English-speaking owner.

Villa Lido (Map p292; ☎ 21 07 02; Friedelstrand 1; mains €16-24.50, 3-4 course menu €32-39.50; ♥ lunch & dinner) A short walk along the lakeshore from Europapark, this classy and attractive lakeside restaurant has a café terrace on land and tables on a wooden jetty over the water (reserve for one of these). Its menu takes your taste buds through Italian saltimbocca, classic fish or red-meat dishes and pasta, and culminates in delicious sorbets. The upstairs lounge is open from 5pm till late.

Dolce Vita (Map p290; ☎ 554 99; Heuplatz 2; lunch menu €6-19; dinner mains €24-28, 6-10 course menu €58-90; ♥ lunch & dinner Mon-Fri) In a region strongly influenced by northern Italian cuisine, this restaurant is something of a local flagship. Inexpensive it is not, but it builds a seasonal menu mostly around fresh local produce and game, while also offering a lunchtime Venetian *Sarde in saor* (sardines in a marinade). Expect to pay about €14 for a pasta entree.

A fruit and vegetable market as well as a flower market (Map p290) comes to life on Benediktinerplatz on Thursday and Saturday mornings. There are several tiny restaurants in the market square and a set of food stalls inside, making it a very cheap and atmospheric place to pick up a lunch of sausages, stew or cheese.

Self-caterers can stock up at the Spar supermarkets on Dr-Hermann-Gasse (Map p290), Bahnhofstrasse (Map p290) or in the station itself.

Drinking

Winter nights in Klagenfurt are the liveliest as in summer many people decamp to the bars and nightclubs in the Wörthersee resorts of Pörtschach (p296) or Velden (p296). Herrengasse can be a bit of a teenage drinking dive, but there are alternatives.

Checkpoint Charlie (Map p290; ☎ 0650-221 20 20; Herrengasse 3; ♥ 9am-2am, closed Sun) This downbeat, low-life bar has an alternative feel and sometimes hosts live rock and blues outfits.

Café-bar G@tes (Map p290; ☎ 50 97 77; Waagplatz 1; ♥ 9am-1am Mon-Fri, 5pm-1am Sat & Sun) If you like Checkpoint Charlie, also try this place, which has a whacky edge.

Pankraz (Map p290; ☎ 516 675; 8 Mai Strasse 16; ♥ 9am-4am Mon-Sat, 1pm-1am Sun) Another good option for music lovers is this funkily decorated place, which sometimes features DJs and live music. There's a shop selling house and electronica CDs here, too.

Kamot (Map p290; ☎ 0676-562 56 55; Bahnhofstrasse 9; ♥ 7pm-2am) This jazz joint has a warm pub atmosphere and a bar where you can sit and chat into the late hours. It hosts some of the top national jazz names on the pub circuit, but it's a nice place for a drink anytime.

Bierhaus zum Augustin (Map p290; ☎ 51 39 92; Pfarrhofgasse 2; ☺ 11am-midnight Mon-Sat) Traditional in character, this place has an attractive, copper-plated bar and wooden floorboards. There's a cobbled courtyard at the back for cheap alfresco eating.

Entertainment

Entertainment options in Klagenfurt are somewhat limited, but you can catch plays, musicals and operas at the **Stadttheater** (Map p290; ☎ 540 64; www.stadttheater-klagenfurt.at, in German; Theaterplatz 4; tickets €4-64; ☺ box office 9am-1pm & 2-6pm Mon-Sat mid-Sep–mid-Jun), and the **Konzerthaus** (Map p290; ☎ 542 72; www.konzerthaus-klagenfurt.at, in German; Miesstaler Strasse 8) stages a mixed bag of opera and popular music. An events booklet from the tourist office is useful. In summer, the lakeside stage (Map p292) by the Europapark is a great experience.

Getting There & Away
AIR

Klagenfurt's **airport** (☎ 415 00-0; www.klagenfurt-air port.com; Flughafenstrasse 60-66) is 3km north of town. Ryanair connects Klagenfurt with London Stansted, TUIfly (Hapag-Lloyd Express) does a handful of northern German cities, and Austrian Arrows (Austrian Airlines) flies to Frankfurt am Main in Germany (p395).

BOAT

The departure point for boat cruises on the lake is a few hundred metres north of *Strandbad*. See p297 for information on time-tables and lakeside resorts.

BUS

Postbus services depart outside the *Hauptbahn-hof* (Map p290), where there's an **information office** (Map p290; ☎ 543 40; ☺ 7am-5pm Mon-Fri) with a timetable board outside. See p297 for infor-mation on buses going to lake resorts.

CAR & MOTORCYCLE

The A2/E66 between Villach and Graz skirts the north of Klagenfurt. Car rental offices:

Avis (☎ 559 38; Klagenfurt Airport)
Denzeldrive (☎ 5 01 05 41 40; Klagenfurt Airport)
Hertz (Map p290; ☎ 561 47; St Ruprechter Strasse 12)
LaudaMotion (☎ 0900 240 120; Klagenfurt Airport)

TRAIN

Frequent direct IC/EC (InterCity/EuroCity) trains run from Klagenfurt station to Vienna

(€44, four hours) and Salzburg (€31.70, 3¼ hours). Trains to Graz depart every one to two hours (€32, two to three hours); these go via Bruck an der Mur (€25, 2¼ hours). Trains to western Austria, Italy, Slovenia and Germany go via Villach (€7.60, 30 to 40 minutes, two to four per hour). See p300 for more information.

Getting Around
TO/FROM THE AIRPORT

To get to the airport, take bus 40 from the main train station or Heiligengeistplatz to Annabichl (€1.70, 25 minutes), then change to bus 45 (10 minutes). A taxi will cost about €6.

BICYCLE

In summer the tourist office works together with a local company hiring out **bicycles** (per 24 hr €10-19), which can also be picked up and dropped off at various points around the lake. The tourist office (p291) has a brochure with the points. Also see p297.

BOAT

A **motor ferry** (☎ 0664 34 25 788; one way adult/child €5/3) chugs along the Lendkanal between the centre of Klagenfurt, through Europapark and up to the shore of the Wörthersee (50 minutes, twice daily May to September).

BUS

Single bus tickets (which you buy from the driver) cost €1 for two or three stops or €1.70 for one hour. Drivers also sell 24-hour passes for €4, but these cost only €2.80 when pur-chased from the **STW Verkehrsbetriebe office** (Map p290; ☎ 521 542; Heiligengeistplatz 4; ☺ 7.30am-1.30pm Mon-Fri) near the city bus station. Validate your advance tickets after boarding.

TAXI

For taxi services in Klagenfurt, call ☎ 311 11 or ☎ 27 11. A taxi between the Wörthersee and the city costs about €9.

CENTRAL CARINTHIA

WÖRTHERSEE

Owing to its thermal springs, the picturesque Wörthersee is one of the warmer lakes in the region and among the best for swimming, frolicking on the lakeshore or whizzing

CARINTHIA

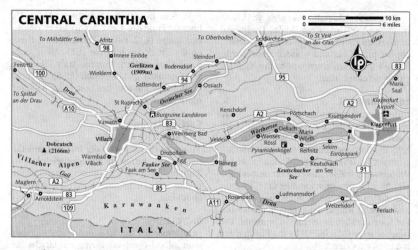

CENTRAL CARINTHIA

0 — 10 km
0 — 6 miles

across the waters in pursuit of sport. The average water temperature between June and September is 21°C. The lake stretches from west to east between Velden and Klagenfurt, and the long, thin shoreline provides unfolding vistas on a boat trip. The northern shore has the best transport access and is the busiest section. The website for lakeside towns is www.woerthersee.com.

Pörtschach
☎ 04272 / pop 2693
Tiny Pörtschach is the most exclusive of all Wörthersee resorts, with a distinctive tree-lined peninsula and a sumptuously curving bay on either side where society figures from Salzburg, Vienna and elsewhere spend time in villas and inhabit upmarket bars and restaurants.

Contact **Pörtschach Information** (☎ 04272-23 54; www.poertschach.at; Hauptstrasse 153; 8am-6pm Mon-Fri, 10am-6pm Sat, 10am-4pm Sun Jun-Aug, 8am-5pm Mon-Fri, 10am-2pm Sat May & Sep, 7.30am-4pm Mon-Thu, 7.30am-1pm Fri Oct-Apr) for information on (often expensive) hotels and its activities.

The cheapest rooms at the four-star **Seehotel Dr Jilly** (☎ 04272-2258; www.jilly.at, in German; Alfredweg 5-7; s €119-145, d €170-238; P ℝ) have no balconies, but at the top end you get lake views and a terrace in this quiet hotel situated on the lake with modern furnishing, wellness facilities and its own beach.

The most celebrated nightclub on the lake is **Fabrik** (☎ 0463-57 186 75; www.fabrik.at, in German; Saag 10; €17), in the tiny village of Saag between

Pörtschach and Velden. Shuttle buses run to here from both places.

Velden
☎ 04274 / pop 8577
Velden enjoys a reputation as the Wörthersee's top nightlife resort and is also the venue of various high-adrenaline sports events on summer weekends. It's a brash, lively place packed with a strange combination of young and beautiful people nursing cocktails and parties of old-age pensioners nibbling ice cream.

Veldener Tourismus (tourist office; ☎ 21 03-0; www.velden.at; Villacher Strasse 19; 8am-8pm Mon-Thu, 8am-10pm Fri & Sat, 9am-6pm Sun Jul & Aug, 8am-6pm Mon-Thu, 8am-8pm Fri & Sat, 9am-5pm Sun May, Jun, Sep & Oct, reduced hr Nov-Apr) can advise on accommodation and provide lists of events and bike hire locations.

Five kilometres south of Velden is Rosegg, with its **Tierpark** (animal park; ☎ 04274-523 57; www.rosegg.at; adult/child €6.50/3.60; 9am-6pm Jul & Aug, 9am-5pm Apr-Jun & Sep-Oct) and a **Schloss** (palace; ☎ 04274-30 09; www.rosegg.at; adult/child €5.50/3.30; 10am-6pm Tue-Sun May, Jun & Sep, daily Jul & Aug). Both of these are closed in winter.

Maria Wörth
☎ 04273 / pop 1254
Maria Wörth is a small resort on the southern shore dominated by two medieval churches. The larger **Pfarrkirche** combines Gothic, baroque and Romanesque elements, while the smaller 12th-century **Winterkirche** has some frescoes of the apostles.

On the hill southwest of Maria Wörth is the **Pyramidenkogel** (☎ 04273-2443; adult/child/family €6/3/16; ⏱ 10am-6pm Apr & Oct, 9am-7pm May & Sep, 9am-8pm Jun, 9am-9pm Jul & Aug), a hill topped by a rather avant-garde tower that provides fine views of Wörthersee and the surrounding mountain ranges. Further information is available from the Maria Wörth **tourist office** (☎ 04273-22400; www.maria-woerth.at; Seepromenade 5; ⏱ 8am-1pm & 2-6.30pm Mon-Fri, 10am-1pm & 2-5pm Sat & Sun Jul & Aug, 8am-12.30pm & 1.30-5.30pm Mon-Fri, 10am-12.30pm & 1.30-4.30pm Sat & Sun mid-May–Jun & early Sep, reduced hr rest of year).

Getting There & Around
BICYCLE
A circuit of the lake is about 50km, and enjoyable with an overnight stop. In summer a *Fahrrad Verleih* (rent-a-bike) scheme allows you to take a standard bicycle at one of many outlets round the lake and return it at any other (three hours/24 hours/one week/two weeks €6/10/40/70). Mountain bikes (€12/19/85/160) are also available. The tourist office in Klagenfurt is one convenient outlet. This and tourist offices around the lake can set you straight on others.

BOAT
STW (☎ 0463-211 55; schiffahrt@stw.at; St Veiter Strasse 31, Klagenfurt) runs motorboats and steamers on the lake from early May to early October. Boats call at both sides, stopping at Klagenfurt, Krumpendorf, Sekirn, Reifnitz, Maria Wörth, Pörtschach, Dellach, Weisses Rössl, Auen and Velden. They return by the same route, departing from Klagenfurt at least every two hours.

A **Tagesticket** (adult/child/family €10/6/28) is valid all day and allows as many stops as you like. Two-week tickets cost adult/child €28/17 (no family tickets). The longest trip (Klagenfurt–Velden) takes 1¾ hours on a steamer but motorboats are quicker.

BUS & TRAIN
Postbuses travel along both shores of the lake; for information call ☎ 0463-543 40. Three to four buses run between Villach and Klagenfurt weekdays and Saturday (€6.40, 1¼ hours), travelling along the northern shore. Two to three buses also run weekdays and Saturday along the southern lakeshore between Klagenfurt and Velden (€4.80, 40 minutes) via Maria Wörth.

Trains between Klagenfurt and Villach run along the northern shore of the lake (€7.60, 40 minutes). Regional trains from Klagenfurt stop at Krumpendorf (€2.90, seven minutes), Pörtschach (€4.40, 15 minutes) and Velden (€6, 20 minutes); express trains stop at only one or two of those stations.

CAR & MOTORCYCLE
The A2/E66 and Hwy 83, which runs closer to the shore, are on the northern side of the lake. On the southern side, the route is classified as a main road, but it's much smaller.

VILLACH
☎ 04242 / pop 58,300

Although there are more picturesque cities in the region, Villach is arguably the most dynamic, partly because it's an important transport hub for routes into Italy and Slovenia. It attracts an international bunch of visitors and is a very lively and liveable city. Consider using it as a base for exploring the nearby lakes, beaches and beauty spots.

Orientation & Information
The old town centre is south of the Drau River. The train and bus stations are north of the river. Villach is currently redeveloping its train station and Bahnhofstrasse area in a long-term upgrade. The area on the Drau is also being developed, so expect some temporary changes to locations we give here.
Café Nicolai (☎ 22 511; Nikolaigasse 16; per 10 mins €1; ⏱ 7am-9pm Mon-Fri, 7am-2pm Sat) Fast but expensive internet access.
Thalia (☎ 23 434 38; Hauptplatz 4) A large bookshop with guidebooks, hiking maps and some English-language books.
Tourist office (☎ 205-2900; www.villach.at; Rathausplatz 1; ⏱ 9am-6pm Mon-Fri, 9am-noon Sat Jul & Aug, 9am-12.30pm & 1.30-5pm Mon-Fri, 9am-noon Sat Apr-Jun, Sep & Oct, reduced hr rest of year) Helps with accommodation and maps. It's relocating to Bahnhofstrasse in 2008.

Sights
Pick up a copy of the tourist office's free walking booklet in English with descriptions of buildings and sights.

The monolithic **Stadtpfarrkirche St Jakob** (parish church of St Jakob; ☎ 205 3540; Oberer Kirchenplatz 8; ⏱ dawn-dusk) dominates the old town. The interior is interesting, but bring binoculars or a good zoom lens to really appreciate details of its frescoes. The far end of the nave has a stuccoed ceiling and a vast rococo altar in

CARINTHIA

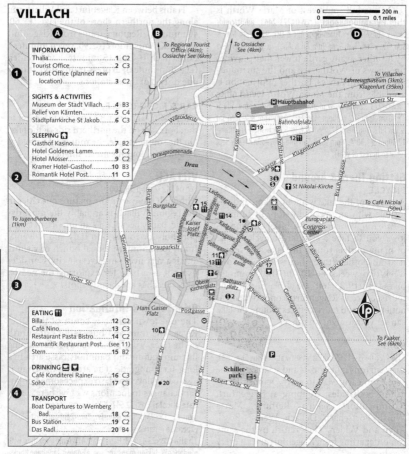

VILLACH

0 — 200 m
0 — 0.1 miles

INFORMATION
Thalia..................................1 C2
Tourist Office.....................2 C3
Tourist Office (planned new
  location)...........................3 C2

SIGHTS & ACTIVITIES
Museum der Stadt Villach......4 B3
Relief von Kärnten................5 C4
Stadtpfarrkirche St Jakob......6 C3

SLEEPING
Gasthof Kasino....................7 B2
Hotel Goldenes Lamm...........8 C2
Hotel Mosser.......................9 C2
Kramer Hotel-Gasthof..........10 B3
Romantik Hotel Post............11 C3

EATING
Billa..................................12 C2
Café Nino...........................13 C3
Restaurant Pasta Bistro........14 C3
Romantik Restaurant Post....(see 11)
Stern.................................15 B2

DRINKING
Café Konditerei Rainer.........16 C3
Soho.................................17 C3

TRANSPORT
Boat Departures to Wernberg
  Bad................................18 C2
Bus Station........................19 C2
Das Radl............................20 B4

To Regional Tourist Office (4km); Ossiacher See (6km)
To Ossiacher See (4km)
To Villacher Fahrzeugmuseum (3km); Klagenfurt (35km)
Zeidler von Goerz Str
Hauptbahnhof
Bahnhofplatz
Willroidersr.
Kassstrasse
Bahnhofstrasse
Klagenfurter Str
Draupromenade
Drau
Kaigasse
Brauhausgasse
St Nikolai-Kirche
To Café Nicolai (50m)
Lederergasse
Burgplatz
Ringmauergasse
Kaiser Josef Platz
Widmanngasse
Paradeisgasse
Rathausgasse
Hauptplatz
Völkendorfergasse
Kärntnergasse
Europaplatz Congress-Center
To Jugendherberge (1km)
Steinwenderstr.
Drauparkstr
Sellergasse
Leinigengasse
Freihausgasse
Fabrikstr
Flussgasse
Tiroler Str
Hans Gasser Platz
Oberer Kirchenplatz
Rathaus-platz
Postgasse
Gerbergasse
Klevenhüllergasse
To Faaker See (6km)
Italiener Str
10 Oktober Str
Schiller-park
Robert Stolz Str
Peraustr.
Hausergasse
Wittmanngasse
Schillerstr.

gold leaf, arrayed with fresh cream flowers, and its walls are studded with the ornate memorial plaques of the region's noble families. Each summer a pair of falcons nests in the **Stadtpfarrturm** (steeple; adult/child & student €2/1.20; 10am-4.30pm Mon-Sat May-Oct), and you can even follow their domestic life on a closed-circuit TV screen from the café across the street.

Relief Von Kärnten (relief map; ☎ 20 53 550; Peraustrasse; 10am-4.30pm Mon-Sat May-Oct) is a huge relief model of Carinthia housed in Schillerpark, south of the old town. It covers 182 sq metres and depicts the province at a scale of 1:10,000 (1:5000 vertically, to exaggerate the mountains).

Located 3km outside town, the **Villacher Fahrzeugmuseum** (☎ 25 530; Ferdinand-Wedenig-Strasse 9; adult/child €6.50/4.50; 9am-5pm mid-Jun–mid-Sep, 10am-noon & 2-4pm mid-Sep–May) focuses on icons of everyday motoring such as the Fiat Topolino, BMW Isetta and about 250 others. Take bus 5179 from the train station towards Zauchen.

Back in town, the **Museum der Stadt Villach** (☎ 20 53 500; Widmanngasse 38; adult/student €2.50/1.80; 10am-4.30pm Mon-Sat May-Oct) is a fairly unexciting museum covering local history, archaeology and medieval art.

Festivals & Events

On the first Saturday in August, the pedestrian centre is taken over by the **Kirchtag** (☎ 205 3211; www.villacherkirchtag.at, in German; tickets about €8), a folk-music festival featuring national and local musicians, as well as international acts from Italy, Latvia, Slovenia and elsewhere. There are plenty of costumes, food stalls and fireworks. Many events begin during the preceding week, culminating on the Saturday.

Sleeping

The tourist office can help with finding accommodation in town.

Jugendherberge (☎ 563 68; www.oejhv.or.at; Dinzlweg 34; dm/s/d €17.90/24.80/43.80) This HI hostel is about 1km west of the centre, off Sankt-Martiner-Weg. Rooms have their own shower and toilet from the corridor. Sauna facilities are on-site.

Gasthof Kasino (☎ 244 49; www.hotel-kasino.at; Kaiser Josef Platz 4; s/d €50/84; P 🖳) The corridors retain a rather dated look but the rooms themselves are quite modern and decorated in good taste at the centrally located Kasino. Although rooms are sizable, it's at the expense of the rather pokey bathrooms.

Kramer Hotel-Gasthof (☎ 249 53; www.hotel gasthofkramer.at; Italiener Strasse 14; s €45-75, d €83-132, tr €117-144; P) You'll find very good value among contemporary furnishings in rooms at this hotel just up the road from the Stadtpfarrkirche. They're spacious, have a comfortable feel and most are set away from the main street.

Hotel Goldenes Lamm (☎ 241 05; www.gold eneslamm.at; Hauptplatz 1; s/d/tr €63/100/126; P 🖳) With tatty corridors that definitely won't get your pulse zipping, this hotel has very uneven aesthetics throughout but a great location in the heart of town. Ask for something nice or check out a couple of rooms before choosing.

our pick Hotel Mosser (☎ 241 15; Bahnhofstrasse 9; s €55-68, d €85-150, ste €180-210, apt €140-190; P 🖳) Despite an unfortunate bomb-drop during WWII, this hotel retains genuine historic charm (look for the collection of old room keys in the cabinet downstairs). Some rooms have angled mirrors above the head boards for romantic interludes, and rooms and bathrooms here are very generous with space if the interlude turns to a wild escapade requiring room to move. You could probably even spend a good honeymoon or silver anniversary in some of the doubles.

Romantik Hotel Post (☎ 261 01-0; www.romantik -hotel.com; Hauptplatz 26; s €70-120, d 85-170, tr €175-190, ste €225-250; P 🖳) The corridors of this smart hotel offer a foretaste of its charms, with chandeliers and oriental rugs, but even some of the refurbished rooms don't quite pull off the act. The wooden furnishings have a light and breezy feel though, and there's a very good restaurant downstairs (below).

Eating & Drinking

Café Konditerei Rainer (☎ 243 77; Oberer Kirchenplatz 5; cakes €2.60; 🕙 7am-7pm Mon-Sat, 10am-7pm Sun) Villach's oldest café offers a sumptuous array of more than 50 different cakes, lunch snacks, a kid's play area, and in summer a screen with live pictures from the 'falcon cam' at the top of the church steeple (opposite).

Café Nino (☎ 24 802; Hauptplatz 28; mains €3-6; 🕙 7.30am-8pm Mon-Sat) Nino's is a friendly, buzzing café on the old town square, with plenty of tables outside and fresh calamari on the menu each Friday. It also serves great ice cream and extravagant coffees.

Romantik Restaurant Post (☎ 261 01-0; Hauptplatz 26; mains €5.90-16.50; 🕙 lunch & dinner Mon-Sat) The restaurant of the Romantik Hotel Post is decidedly more old-fashioned than most others, but it serves acclaimed regional specialities and has a cosy and intimate atmosphere. The midday meat or veg *Menü* (set menu) is good value and there's also a good selection of salads.

Stern (☎ 24 755; Kaiser Josef Platz 5; mains €9-13.50; 🕙 7am-midnight Mon-Thu, 7-2am Fri & Sat) This lounge and restaurant gets a clientele from the very young hanging out on the psychologist's couches and postmodern sofas during the day to a mixed crowd that comes here to feed on steak – its speciality (though Stern also does wok and salad dishes). The steaks are fine, but don't always live up to the lengthy check list you fill out to order one, and the chef certainly doesn't mess around with his meat when you tick 'well done'.

Restaurant Pasta Bistro (☎ 214 797; Kaiser Josef Platz 7; pasta €16, fish €10-16, salads €6.50-17.50; 🕙 lunch & dinner Mon-Fri, dinner Sat) This restaurant and vinothek set in a cosy, vaulted room offers an unusual menu of fish specialities alongside fresh, gourmet baguettes (as a main course) and a selection of salads and pastas (with about 16 different sauces). There are also a couple of meat and vegetarian dishes available.

Soho (☎ 0664-14 54 222; Freihausgasse 13; 🕙 9pm-late) Under the same management as Stern, this is Villach's fashionable bar-cum-club,

CARINTHIA

with a resident team of DJs and plenty of sponsored events during which you can dance to the beat.

The main area for bars extends from Hauptplatz to Kaiser-Joseph-Platz and north towards the river.

For self-caterers, there's a Billa supermarket opposite the train station, with various snack places close by.

Getting There & Around

Villach is situated on three Austrian ICE rail routes, which serve Salzburg (€28, 2½ hours, every two hours), Lienz (€18, 1½ hours, hourly) and Klagenfurt (€6.20, 30 to 40 minutes, two to four per hour). Direct services run to seemingly everywhere: Munich, Germany (€56, 4½ hours, four daily), Venice, Italy (€30, 3½ hours, three per day), Ljubljana (€17, 1¾ hours, four daily) and Bled (€11, one hour, six daily) in Slovenia, Zagreb (€33, 4½ hours, three daily) and Rijeka in Croatia (€33, 4¾ hours, once daily), and Belgrade, Yugoslavia (€73, 11½ hours, three daily).

Buses also radiate out from Villach; call ☎ 44410-1510 for Postbus information. The bus station is opposite the *Hauptbahnhof*. For information about bus services to the Wörthersee resorts, see p297.

Das Radl (☎ 269 54; www.das-radl.at, in German; Italiener Strasse 25; per day city bike/mountain bike €10/19) rents bikes in Villach and also from Bodendorf and Faak train stations on the Ossiaker and Faaker lakes respectively.

AROUND VILLACH
Faaker See & Ossiacher See

Villach is blessed with two major lakes nearby with low-key summer resorts. Both the **Faaker See**, situated 6km east of Villach and close to the Karawanken Range, and the **Ossiacher See**, 4km to the northeast, provide plenty of camping, boating and swimming opportunities. Above Annenheim and providing a backdrop to the Ossiacher See is **Gerlitzen** (1909m), a popular ski area. Expect to pay about €32 for a ski pass here. With its accessible pistes and decent nightlife, Villach is therefore quite a good winter stopover for skiing.

Browse through the region-wide accommodation brochure obtainable from the Villach tourist office, or contact the **regional tourist office** (☎ 04242-420 00; www.da-lacht-das-herz.at; Töbringer Strasse 1, Villach), for more on the lakes and skiing.

The local tourist offices at the specific resorts can also help out.

On the Ossiacher See, **boats** (☎ 04242 58071; www.schiffahrt.at/drau, in German) complete a crisscross circuit between St Andrä and Steindorf (adult/child €11.50/5.80, 2½ hours, approximately hourly from May to October). Boats run by the same company also navigate the Drau River from Villach Congress-Center to Wernberg Bad (one way adult/child €7/3.50, 45 minutes) via St Niklas an der Drau (about 2km northeast of the Faaker See) up to four times a day between late April and early October.

Regular train and Postbus services leave from the bus station and Villach train station, running along the northern shore of Ossiacher See via Annenheim (€1.70, 12 minutes) and Bodensdorf (€3.20, 20 minutes). Regular trains run to Faak am See (€3,20, 30 minutes) and frequent buses to Drobollach (€3.20, 20 minutes), both on the Faaker See.

You can also explore the region by bicycle. These can be hired in Villach if you ring ahead (see left), and at the Bodensdorf (Ossiacher See) and Faak (Faaker See) train stations; hotels and campsites in the region hire them out, too.

Burg Landskron

Situated between Villach and the Ossiacher See, the castle ruins of Burg Landskron are home to the impressive **Adler Flugschau** (falconry show; ☎ 04242-428 88; www.adlerflugschau.com; Burgruine Landskron, Schlossweg; adult/child €8/4; 🕙 11am, 2.30pm & 5.30pm Jul & Aug, 11am & 2.30pm Mon-Sat, 11am, 2.30pm & 4.30pm Sun May, Jun, Sep & Oct), a 40-minute spectacle featuring these birds of prey. **Affenberg** (Monkey Mountain; ☎ 04242-430375; adult/child €8/4; 🕙 9.30am-5.30pm, half-hourly Apr-Sep, hourly Oct), a monkey reserve, is also here.

Regular buses (€1.70, eight minutes) from alongside Villach's train station stop in St Andrä, below the castle.

Dreiländereck

Walkers and mountain bikers will find much to do in the **Dobratsch** (2166m) area, in the Villacher Alpen about 12km west of Villach. Just south of here, hiking trails go from the small town of Arnoldstein to the Dreiländereck – the point where Austria, Italy and Slovenia meet. At 1500m there's an **Alpine garden** (☎ 0664 91 42 953; adult/child €2.50/1; 🕙 9am-6pm Jun-early Sep) with flora from the southern Alps. To reach the garden, follow the Villacher Alpenstrasse from town. This is a toll road (€13 per car), but it's free from about November to mid-March, or free in summer with the Kärnten Card. It's closed to caravans. Dobratsch is popular with cross-country skiers.

Kowatsch (☎ 04242-442 39; www.kowatsch.at, in German) runs buses from Villach to Arnoldstein Monday to Saturday six times daily (€4, 30 minutes).

HERMAGOR

☎ 04282 / pop 7300

Situated about 50km west of Villach, Hermagor is popular as a base for skiing in the nearby Nassfeld ski pistes, where there are 110km of pistes (day pass €36) and also Nordic skiing trails and snowboarding runs; in summer it morphs into a low-key spot for hikers and mountain bikers. Hermagor is the starting point for hiking the spectacular Garnitzenklamm, a narrow gorge some 2.5km west of town (see p105).

Facilities such as banks, supermarkets and a post office are all central or near the tourist office.

The **tourist office** (☎ 2043; www.hermagor.com; Göseringlände 7; ⏰ 8.30am-6pm Mon-Fri, 8.30am-noon & 1-6pm Sat, 9am-noon Sun Jun-Aug, 8.30am-5pm Mon-Fri, 8.30am-noon Sat Sep-May) is about 400m west of the train station on the B111. It has well-informed staff with information on skiing, guided and unguided hiking, and mountain biking in the area.

The **Millennium-Express cable car** (adult/child €15/4 return) climbs 6km up to Nassfeld, making it Austria's longest. The valley station is in Tröpolach, 8km west of town along the B111 and then B90.

Hotel Bürgerbräu (☎ 250 85; www.buergerbrau.at; Gasserplatz 1; s/d €46/92) has clean, modern rooms and a helpful owner, free bicycle use for guests and facilities catering to skiers in winter – a free bus to the Millennium-Express picks you up here.

Getting There & Around

Every one to two hours trains run to Hermagor from Villach (€9.30, one hour), some continuing to Tröpolach (€2.90, 10 minutes) and complemented by a few buses each day (€1.70, eight minutes). **Bike Paradies** (☎ 2010; hermagor@bikeparadies.at; Obervellach 48), at the Rudolf service station 1km towards Villach on the B111, rents mountain/trek/child bicycles for €15/13/8 per day.

EASTERN CARINTHIA

Eastern Carinthia's prettiest medieval towns and most impressive castles lie north of Klagenfurt, on or close to Hwy 83 and the rail route between Klagenfurt and Bruck an der Mur, with mountain ranges on either side: the Seetaler Alpen and Saualpe to the east and the Gurktaler Alpen to the west.

FRIESACH

☎ 04268 / pop 5300

Once a key staging post on the Vienna–Venice trade route, Friesach is Carinthia's oldest town. The hills on either side of town bristle with ruined fortifications and the centre is surrounded by a moat (it's the only town in Austria that still has one) and a set of imposing, grey-stone walls. These have been tested to the fullest over the centuries, with successive invasions by the Bohemians, Hungarians, Turks and French before the town came under the wing of the Habsburgs in 1803.

Once a year Friesach's gates are locked, everyone in town dresses up in medieval costumes and Friesach re-enacts its history.

Orientation & Information

Picturesque Hauptplatz is a few minutes' walk from the train station along Bahnhofstrasse. Turn left on leaving the station. There's a bank with an ATM on the town square. The **tourist office** (☎ 43 00; www.friesach.at; Fürstenhofplatz 1; ⏰ 10am-4pm May-Sep, 8am-noon Mon-Fri Oct-Apr) is in the Spur des Einhorns exhibition complex.

Sights & Activities

Die Spur des Einhorns (☎ 43 00; www.friesach.at; Fürstenhofplatz 1; adult/student/child €5.50/3.50/2.50; ⏰ 10am-4pm May-Sep) is Friesach's main attraction, a contemporary and dreamlike art installation housed in a 15th-century bishop's palace and loosely based on the myths and stories of the medieval age in Europe. Music, voices and light effects accompany the visitor throughout a visit, from an 'enchanted forest' made of mirrors to the final resting place of the mighty sword, Excalibur. It's fascinating, beautiful and perfect for children and adults alike.

Ranged along the hills rising above Hauptplatz to the west are four ancient **fortifications**, all providing excellent views of the town and valley. The northernmost is Burg Geyersberg; the furthest south are the

CARINTHIA

Virgilienberg ruins. The middle two are the most easily visited from the town, with lovely views from **Peterskirche** (☎ 2272; ☿ 11am-5pm Tue-Sun May-Sep), accessible by paths ascending from the front of the Romanesque **Stadtpfarrkirche** (☎ 2272; ☿ dawn-dusk), dating from 927. Call or drop by the Pfarramt, next to the tourist office, to see Peterskirche outside these months.

Behind Peterskirche, Petersberg houses the small town **museum** (☎ 26 00; adult/child & student €3/1; ☿ dawn-dusk), with exhibits covering the town's medieval history and religious art. The Petersberg castle is also the site for open-air theatre performing anything from Shakespeare to Brecht in summer. Obtain details and tickets (prices ranging from about €10 to €20) from the tourist office.

Festivals & Events

The **Spectaculum** is held on the last Saturday in July: electric lights are extinguished and the town closed off and lit by torches and flares as jesters, princesses and armoured knights stroll around juggling, fire-eating and staging jousting tournaments and duels. Friesach reverts to the currency that made it famous, with medieval meals from street stalls being paid for with Friesach pennies. Contact the tourist office for event information.

Sleeping & Eating

Zum Goldenen Anker (☎ 23 13; www.goldeneranker.at.tf, in German; Bahnhofstrasse 3; s/d €26/52; **P**) This small *Gasthof* just off the main town square is the best deal in town. Some of the spick-and-span rooms have antique furniture and traditional ceramic stoves. Reception is in the restaurant next door.

Gasthof Weisser Wolf (☎ 22 63; astrid.david@weisser -wolf.at; Hauptplatz 8; s/d €32/64; **P**) This three-star guest house is cyclist friendly and, like the other two places mentioned, hires out bicycles to guests. Rooms here are clean and comfortable, some overlooking the square.

Metnitztalerhof (☎ 25 10-0; www.metnitztalerhof.at; Hauptplatz 11; s €53-62, d €88-106; **P** 💻) This pastel-pink edifice at the far end of the town square is the only four-star hotel in Friesach; rooms are modern and comfortable and have small balconies, but ask for one away from the restaurant exhaust fan. There's a sauna, Jacuzzi and steam room on site, plus a restaurant (mains €9 to €18.50) that serves Austrian and Carinthian dishes at lunch and dinner. There's a fine view of the square from the raised terrace.

Osteria (☎ 0664 99 33 822; €7.20-15; ☿ 11am-midnight Tue-Sat, 10am-9pm Sun) Downstairs from Gasthof Weisser Wolf, it serves pizza, pasta and traditional meat dishes.

Getting There & Away

Friesach is on the railway line between Vienna's Südbahnhof (€37, 3¾ hours) and Villach (€15, 1½ hours). Bruck an der Mur (€20, 1½ hours), St Veit (€6.40, 30 minutes) and Klagenfurt (€9.40, 40 to 60 minutes) are also on this route.

GURK

☎ 04266 / pop 1300

This small town (Krka in Slovenian), some 18km west of the Friesach–Klagenfurt road, is famous for its former **Dom** (cathedral; ☎ 82 36-12; Domplatz 11; ☿ closed during services), which was built between 1140 and 1200. With its harmonious pillared crypt, this is Austria's foremost church from the Romanesque epoch. Inside you will also find Gothic reticulated vaulting, and most of the church fittings are either baroque or rococo. The early-baroque high altar has 72 statues and 82 angel heads.

The frescoes in the **Bischofskapelle** (episcopal chapel; adult/child & student €3.70/3; ☿ guided tours 11.20pm, 2.20pm & 3.50pm), dating from around 1200, are all the more beautiful for the use of raw colours.

Getting There & Away

Go on a weekday if using public transport, when a morning train from Klagenfurt to Treibach-Althofen connects with a bus (€14, 1¼ hours). Direct buses also do the trip two to three times weekdays and Saturday from Klagenfurt (€11.30, 1¾ hours). With your own transport, take Hwy 93.

HÜTTENBERG

☎ 04263 / pop 1800

Step off the bus in the tiny mining village of Hüttenberg and you might be forgiven for thinking you've stumbled into Tibet: fluttering prayer flags rise up the cliff at the entrance to the town, and a giant painting of the Buddha gazes benevolently down on the populace. Hüttenberg is the birthplace of Austria's most famous explorer, Heinrich Harrer, who famously spent Seven Years in Tibet and was immortalised by Brad Pitt in film.

Outside the **Heinrich Harrer Museum** (☎ 8108; Bahnhofstrasse 12; adult/concession €7.50/4; ☿ 10am-5pm

Apr-Oct, till 6pm Jul & Aug) you can sip on a bowl of butter tea and listen to the rush of water through wooden prayer wheels, before going inside the beautiful stone and wood building to see the huge collection of objects and photographs Harrer brought back from his world travels. Opposite the museum is the Lingkor, a metal walkway built up the cliff face as an aid to prayer and meditation. The colourful prayer wheels made from oil drums are testament to Hüttenberg's history of being a site for heavy industry (this is an iron-ore mining area).

Getting There & Away

Three direct buses run to Hüttenberg weekdays from St Veit an der Glan, but only one is convenient on Saturday and none leave Sunday (€7.10, one hour). Two direct buses leave from Klagenfurt (€9.40, 1¼ hours); a few indirect bus services from both cities add to frequency Monday to Saturday. A train/bus connecting service works on weekdays via Treibach-Althofen (€13, one hour).

ST VEIT AN DER GLAN

☎ 04212 / pop 13,000

St Veit was historically important as the seat of the dukes of Carinthia from 1170 until 1518, when the dukes skipped down the road to Klagenfurt and the status of this town took an inelegant nosedive. These days it's a mildly interesting, mid-sized town that makes an agreeable base for explorations of the medieval towns and other attractions further north.

Orientation & Information

St Veit is near the junction of primary road routes to Villach (Hwy 94) and Klagenfurt (Hwy 83). To get to the pedestrian-only town centre from the *Hauptbahnhof*, walk left down Bahnhofstrasse for 600m and then go one block right.

The **tourist office** (☎ 288 806 911; www.stveit.car inthia.at, in German; Hauptplatz 23; ☷ 8am-8pm Mon-Sat, 9am-8pm Sun Jul-Sep; 8am-6pm Mon-Fri, 9am-noon Sat & Sun Oct-Jun) sells maps of the town for €1. There's also an information screen in the Rathaus.

Sight & Activities

The centrepiece of St Veit's Hauptplatz at No 1 is the **Rathaus**; its baroque stuccowork was applied in 1754 and features a double-headed eagle on the pediment. St Veit (the saint, not the town) stands between the eagle's wings. By walking through the Gothic vaulted passage you arrive at an arcaded courtyard bedecked with sgraffito (a mural or decoration in which the top layer is scratched off to reveal the original underneath).

Hauptplatz itself has a fountain at both ends and a central column erected in 1715 as a memorial to plague victims. The northeastern fountain, the **Schüsselbrunnen,** is surmounted by a bronze statue, created in 1566. This figure is the town mascot: its hand is raised as if in greeting, while a jet of water spits forth from its mouth. The southwestern fountain bears a statue of the local medieval poet, Walther von der Vogelweide.

For an antidote to the ubiquitous neoclassical architecture, have a look at the crazily tiled **Rogner Hotel Ernst Fuchs Palast** (below), a surrealist structure designed by mystical artist Ernst Fuchs.

The **Verkehrsmuseum** (Transport Museum; ☎ 5555-64; Hauptplatz 29; adult/child €3/free; ☷ 9am-noon & 2-6pm Apr-Jun, Sep & Oct, 9am-6pm Jul & Aug) is an unusual place appealing not only to railway freaks. It has lots of moving parts that whoosh and whistle, so the kids will get a kick out of it too, but its coup de grace is a simulator that allows you to drive a virtual locomotive between Maria Saal and Friesach. This is more difficult than it sounds. Don't forget to keep hitting the 'dead man's' pedal otherwise you'll be grinding to unscheduled stops while the attendant tells you rather unnervingly, 'Dead man, dead man!'

Sleeping

Gasthöf Sonnhof (☎ 2447; Völkermarkter Strasse 37; s/d €30/53; **P**) South of the rail tracks (15 minutes from the centre), the Sonnhof has light and modern, though slightly impersonal, rooms – some with a balcony.

Hotel Garni Mosser (☎ 3223; www.hotel-mosser .at, in German; Spitalgasse 6; s/d €35/64) This budget hotel is excellent value – the rooms are extremely comfortable, it's bang in the centre of town and there's a generous breakfast buffet.

Weisses Lamm (☎ 23 62; www.weisseslamm.at, in German; Unterer Platz 4-5; s €40, d €70-84; **P** ☐) This central, four-star place has rather poky rooms arranged around an atmospheric arcaded courtyard. There's also a sauna and a therapeutic massage service.

Rogner Hotel Ernst Fuchs Palast (☎ 4660-0; www.hotel-fuchspalast.at; Friesacher Strasse 1; s/d €82/130;

Ⓟ 🖥) If you're still shaking from the Transport Museum's simulator, Rogner will finish you off. Outside it is studded with blue and red glass tiles in fantastical and astrological designs. Inside, this surrealism trickles into the public areas, with fluted columns and jewel-like mosaics. That was where it ended when we visited, but it has new ownership, so hopefully the rather bland rooms will be spruced up soon.

Eating & Drinking

Suppenkasper (mains €7.50-14.50; ☯ lunch & dinner Mon-Sat) Downstairs at Hotel Garni Mosser, this place has simple and filling Austrian mainstays.

La Torre (☎ 39250; www.latorre.at; Grabenstrasse 39; mains €10-22, 6-course menu €58; ☯ lunch & dinner Tue-Sat) This magnificent Italian restaurant is set in one of the towers of the 14th-century town wall. As well as the smart, romantic interior there's a beautiful, walled garden and terrace and an Italian owner who exudes bonhomie. The calamari with inky spaghetti and peperoncino, washed down with wine, is a tasty lunchtime interlude.

The **restaurant** (mains €8.50-15, menus pizzas €6-10; ☯ lunch & dinner) at Weisses Lamm is a good place for cheap local eats, with several set-menu options. St Veit also has a couple of buzzing cafés in the centre, all catering to a mixed crowd.

Havanna (☎ 0676-84 34 89 100; Hauptplatz 29; ☯ 6pm-4am Tue-Sun) is a nightlife hub inside the Transport Museum building that kicks on till late.

Getting There & Away

St Veit is 33km south of Friesach and 20km north of Klagenfurt. Hourly express trains run to Villach (€9.30, 45 minutes), stopping at Friesach (€7.60, 25 minutes) and Klagenfurt (€4.40, 20 minutes). There are no left-luggage lockers at the station, but staff can usually help out.

Frequent Postbus services run to Klagenfurt, Maria Saal and Friesach.

BURG HOCHOSTERWITZ

This fairytale fortress (it claims to be the inspiration for the castle in *Sleeping Beauty*) drapes itself around the slopes of a hill, with 14 gate towers on the path up to the final bastion. These were built between 1570 and 1586 by Georg Khevenhüller, the then owner,

to protect against Turkish invasion. It certainly looks impregnable and the *Burgführer* information booklet (in English; €4) outlines the different challenges presented to attackers by each gate – some have spikes embedded in them, which could be dropped straight through unwary invaders passing underneath. The fortress is particularly imposing when viewed from the northeast – sit on the left of the train coming from Friesach.

The **castle** (☎ 04213-20 20; adult/child incl tour €7.50/4.50; ☯ 9am-5pm Apr & Oct, 9am-6pm May-Sep) has a museum featuring the suit of armour of one Burghauptmann Schenk, who measured 225cm at the tender age of 16. There's a small café serving sausages, soup, rolls and coffee at the top.

Getting There & Away

Regional trains on the St Veit–Friesach route stop at Launsdorf Hochosterwitz station, a 3km walk from the car park and the first gate, where a lift (€5) will take you directly to the castle.

MARIA SAAL

☎ 04223 / pop 3800

Maria Saal, a small town perched on a fortified hill 10km north of Klagenfurt, is famous for its pilgrimage church, whose twin spires can be seen for miles around. It is easily visited on an excursion from Klagenfurt or St Veit.

The **tourist office** (☎ 22 14-25; www.maria.saal .at; Am Platzl 7; ☯ 7.30am-4pm Mon-Fri) is just off Hauptplatz.

Sights & Activities

The **church** (☎ 22 14-12; Domplatz 1; ☯ dawn-dusk), sometimes known as the Wallfahrtskirche, was built in the early 15th century from volcanic stone, some of it filched from a nearby Roman ruin. Originally Gothic, it later received Romanesque and baroque modifications. The exterior south wall is embedded with relief panels and ancient gravestones – look for the Roman mail wagon carved into one of the stones and the weird frescoes of people growing out of bulbous flowers on the church ceiling (they represent the genealogy of Christ).

Getting There & Away

There are no left-luggage facilities in the small train station, but if you're just passing through on the way somewhere else, the ticket clerk might watch your bags. Regional trains stop hourly from St Veit (€4.40, nine minutes) and Klagenfurt (€2.90, nine minutes).

WESTERN CARINTHIA

Besides Hohe Tauern National Park (p310), the main attractions of Western Carinthia are Millstatt with its serene and pretty lake for swimming and boating, its abbey and famous music festival (p309), and Spittal an der Drau, with its stately Renaissance palace and pretty, floral park (right).

Both Millstatt and Spittal an der Drau are close to the primary road route north from Villach, the A10/E55 that leads to Salzburg. It has a special toll section (on top of the normal Autobahn toll) between Rennweg and a point north of the Tauern Tunnel (€9.50 for cars and motorbikes). Traffic jams are common.

GMÜND
☎ 04732 / pop 2600

Gmünd is an attractive 11th-century village with a walled centre and a 13th-century hill-top castle, **Alte Burg**. From 1480, Hungarians conducted a seven-year siege of the city and castle. They broke through and partially destroyed the castle; a fire in 1886, however, brought its ultimate demise. Today it's the setting for plays and musical events.

Of an entirely different era is the privately owned **Porsche Museum Helmut Pfeifhofer** (☎ 24 71; Riesertratte 4a; adult/child €7/3; 9am-6pm mid-May–mid-Oct, 10am-4pm mid-Oct–mid-Nov & late Dec–mid-May). A Porsche factory operated in Gmünd from 1944 to 1950 and the first car to bear that famous name (a 356) was handmade here. One of these models is on display (only 52 were built), together with about 15 other models and a couple of the wooden frames used in their construction. There's a film (in German) on Dr Porsche's life and work.

Gmünd has a range of inexpensive accommodation, including hotels with child-minding geared towards families with young children. Staff at the **tourist office** (☎ 22 22; www .familiental.com), in the *Rathaus* on Hauptplatz, can outline options.

Gasthof Kohlmayr (☎ 2149; www.gasthof-kohlmayr.at, in German; Hauptplatz 7; s/d €36/59; P) has cosy and affordable rooms in a 400-year-old building right in the heart of Gmünd and a restaurant (€6.50 to €13) serving tasty local fare.

Getting There & Away
Gmünd is not on a rail route; one to two hourly buses connect it with Spittal an der Drau (€4, 30 minutes) Monday to Saturday, but none runs on Sunday.

SPITTAL AN DER DRAU
☎ 04762 / pop 16,000

Spittal is an important economic and administrative centre in upper Carinthia. Its name comes from a 12th-century hospital and refuge that once succoured travellers on this site. Today it's a town with an impressive Italianate palace at its centre and a small, but attractive, park with splashing fountains and bright flowerbeds. To get into town from the station, walk straight up the road, then cut through the Stadtpark on your right.

Information
Post office (SüdTyrolerplatz 3; 8am-noon & 2-6pm Mon-Fri, 9-11am Sat) Near the train station. A second one is located off Tiroler Strasse.

Star (☎ 36 897; Tiroler Strasse 10; per 30min €1.50; 9.30am-9pm Mon-Sat, 11am-9pm Sun) Internet access and call shop. The Schloss Café (p307) also has access.

Tourist office (Kulturamt Spittal; ☎ 56 50 220; www .spittal-drau.at, in German; Burgplatz 1; 9am-8pm Mon-Fri, 9am-1pm Sat Jul & Aug, 9am-6pm Mon-Fri, 9am-noon Sat Sep-Jun) Round the side of Schloss Porcia.

Sights & Activities
SCHLOSS PORCIA
Boasting an eye-catching Renaissance edifice, **Schloss Porcia** (8am-8pm) was built between 1533 and 1597 by the fabulously named Duke of Salamanca. Inside, Italianate arcades run around a central courtyard used for summer **theatre performances** (☎ 42020-20; ksporcia@aon.at) and the top floors contain the enormous **Museum für Volkskultur** (Local Heritage Museum; ☎ 28 90; www.museum-spittal.com, in German; adult/child & student €5/2.50; 9am-6pm mid-April–Oct, 1-4pm Mon-Thu Nov–mid-Apr). Highlights are its 3-D projections, and one not to be missed has been developed in cooperation with the Hohe Tauern National Park: you sit at a joystick and navigate a virtual flight through the park, doing hair-raising climbs and dives between altitudes of 100m and 10,000m while changing the angle of flight. Another 3-D cinema projection takes you on a journey through Carinthia. The museum has a small brochure with information in English.

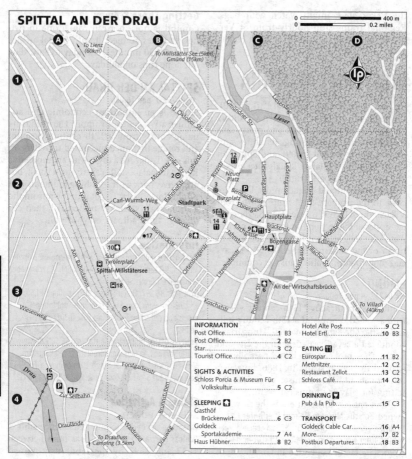

SPITTAL AN DER DRAU

INFORMATION		Hotel Alte Post..........................9 C2
Post Office.................................1 B3		Hotel Ertl...................................10 B3
Post Office.................................2 B2		
Star..3 C2		**EATING**
Tourist Office.............................4 C2		Eurospar....................................11 B2
		Mettnitzer..................................12 C2
SIGHTS & ACTIVITIES		Restaurant Zellot........................13 C2
Schloss Porcia & Museum Für		Schloss Café...............................14 C2
Volkskultur..............................5 C2		
		DRINKING
SLEEPING		Pub á la Pub...............................15 C3
Gasthöf		
Brückenwirt.............................6 C3		**TRANSPORT**
Goldeck		Goldeck Cable Car......................16 A4
Sportakademie.........................7 A4		More..17 B2
Haus Hübner............................8 B2		Postbus Departures.....................18 B3

GOLDECK

Spittal's nearest mountain, offering inspiring views, is **Goldeck** (2142m) to the southwest. In summertime, the peak can be reached by cable car (€10.50/15 one-way/return, 15 minutes) or by the Goldeckstrasse toll road (cars/motorbikes €12/6; reductions with *Gästekarte*). The road stops 260m short of the summit. In winter, the peak is the domain of skiers (lift pass adult/child €28/14). The cable car doesn't operate from mid-April to mid-June or from mid-September to mid-December.

Sleeping

Staff at the tourist office help with accommodation free of charge.

Draufluss Camping (☎ 24 66; www.drauwirt.com; Schwaig 10; site per adult/tent/car €4.70/3.70/3.50; ☯ mid-Apr–mid-Oct). This camping ground is about 3.5km from the town centre on the southern bank of the Drau River.

Jugendherberge (☎ 27 01; goldeck@jungehotels.at; s, d & dm per person €18, €26 half-board; ☯ Jul–mid-Sep & Christmas-Mar). The hostel is at the Goldeck mid-station (1650m), accessible only by cable car. Alpine skiing begins at the door.

Goldeck Sportakademie (☎ 0699-144 144 60; www.sportsacademy.at, in German; Zur Seilbahn 2; s, d & dm per person €22) This former youth hostel at the base of the Goldeck cable car has reinvented itself as a sports academy aimed at young skiers and snowboarders (there's ski hire and a ski school). It also has summer activities.

Gasthöf Brückenwirt (☎ /fax 2772; An der Wirtschaftsbrücke 2; s/d €30/60) Brückenwirt is a few minutes' walk east of the town centre, by the Lieser River. Most of the old-fashioned but comfortable rooms have a balcony and some have a view of the river. There's also a garden, a cheap restaurant and friendly staff.

Haus Hübner (☎ 2112; huebner.spittal@aon.at; Schillerstrasse 20; s €38, d €62-66, s apt €47, 2-4 person apt €62-74; **P**) This central, peaceful pension near Schloss Porcia has a lovely garden. The rooms are modern, clean and very comfortable, but some lack character. The minimum stay for apartments is five days.

Hotel Alte Post (☎ 22 17 0; www.tiscover.com/alte .post; Hauptplatz 13; s €43-55, d €86-110; **P**) Situated in the centre, this hotel caters to tour and ski groups, so it can fill up at times. Rooms are well appointed and comfortable, and a bonus is the ski room and transfers to the ski fields.

Hotel Ertl (☎ 204 80; info@hotel-ertl.at; Bahnhofstrasse 26; s/d €55/105; **P** **⊛**) Rooms are variable and some are in need of a makeover, but the standard is quite good and staff are very helpful at this three-star hotel close to the station (and convenient for day trips out of town). The pool is about 25m and outdoors.

Eating & Drinking

The tourist office has a good *Gastronomieführer* (Gastronomy Guide), with restaurants and bar listings (in German).

Schloss Café (☎ 47 07; Burgplatz 1; cakes €2.50, mains €3.50-8; ☽ 7.30am-8pm Mon-Sat, till midnight Jul & Aug; ▣) This bakery/café occupies one end of Schloss Porcia, with a terrace overlooking the fountains and greenery of the Stadtpark. It does a few light dishes, and for €2 per 30 minutes you get a laptop and can surf the internet at your table.

Restaurant Zellot (☎ 21 13; Hauptplatz 12; mains €6.60-20; ☽ lunch & dinner Tue-Sat) This is possibly the most important address in town: it's a funky and rather eccentric restaurant that does a good steak as well as Austrian staples. On top of that, it has the Glashaus bar and bistro (open 9am to 1am Monday to Saturday), and the Garage, a space for live acts and DJs that is decked out like a garage and whose features become even more intriguing after your second drink. It's open 9.30pm to 4am Friday and Saturday.

Mettnitzer (☎ 358 99; Neuerplatz 17; mains €9-21; ☽ lunch & dinner Wed-Sun) Zellot is a hard act to beat all round, but Mettnitzer – the finest

---

THE AUTOSCHLEUSE TAUERNBAHN

If you're driving to Bad Gastein from Spittal an der Drau, you'll need to use the *Autoschleuse Tauernbahn* (railway car-shuttle service) through the tunnel from Mallnitz to Böckstein. The fare for cars is €17 one way or €28 return (valid for two months). For motorcycles, the price is €10/20. For information, call ☎ 05 717. Departures are every 30 minutes in summer or 60 minutes in winter, with the last train departing at 10.25pm heading south, and 9.55pm going north. The journey takes 13 minutes.

---

eatery in town – does it from the purely gastronomic standpoint. It has a strong focus on steaks, and you can also get one of our favourites – a salad with beef strips (€8.90).

Just off Bahnhofstrasse is a Eurospar supermarket.

The main nightlife area is on Brückenstrasse and Bogengasse. It's a thin and eclectic line of lowlife bars and regular pubs. Occasionally stray dimwits from the local army barracks get tanked and aggro there, though. **Pub à la Pub** (☎ 33 445; Ponauer Strasse2; ☽ 7pm-2am) is one decent place to start.

Getting There & Away

Spittal-Millstättersee is an important rail junction: two-hourly IC/EC services run north to Bad Gastein (€9.90, 40 minutes), frequent regional services run west to Lienz (€11, one hour), and others to Villach (€7.60, 30 minutes, hourly), 37km to the southeast. The railway line north via Mallnitz-Obervellach clings spectacularly to the valley walls (sit on the left).

Postbuses leave from outside the train station to Gmünd (€4, 30 minutes, one to two hourly Monday to Saturday). Call ☎ 39 16 for schedule information.

For taxis, call ☎ 5580.

More (☎ 2555-0; service@more-der-spezialist.at; Bahnhofstrasse 11) rents city and mountain bikes for €9/45 per day/week. Get the tourist office's free city/regional map, which has paths marked.

MILLSTÄTTER SEE

Stretching out 12km and just 1.5km wide, the Millstätter See is second in size in Carinthia after the Wörthersee. It was gouged out during the Ice Age about 30,000 years ago, and today is studded with a handful of small towns. Millstatt on the north shore and Seeboden at the western end are the most important. Warm (about 22°C to 26°C in summer) and all but plugged at both ends, the lake lends itself to sailing, kayaking and open water swimming.

The central information office, **Infocenter Millstätter See** (☎ 04766-3700-0; www.millstaettersee .at; Thomas-Morgenstern-Platz 1; 🕑 9am-6pm), is situated in a new building in **Seeboden** with an unusual 'curtain' of water that parts as you enter. This symbolises 'touching the lake' (the curtain is tap water, though), a theme to bring people close to water (see boxed text, below). The Infocenter doubles as a call centre with English and Italian speaking staff, and there's a supermarket, café and ATM, as well as toilets, in or near the building.

Also in Seeboden (incidentally, the birthplace of ski-jumping ace Thomas Morgenstern), a few minutes' walk towards Hotel Steiner, is **Sportcamp Seeboden** (☎ 04762-816 69, 0664-993 1698; Seehofstrasse 23; 🕑 summer only), which rents mountain and city bikes (€13/52 per day/week), offers sailing courses and hires out windsurfing boards (€9 per hr), kayaks (€4 per hr) and sailing boats (€9 to €17 per hr).

The bus to Millstatt stops near the Infocenter in Seeboden (ask the driver to let you off there).

MILLSTATT
☎ 04766 / pop 3200

The genteel lakeside village of Millstatt lies 10km east of Spittal an der Drau on the northern shore. It got its name from Emperor Domition, an early Christian convert who tossed *mille statuae* (1000 heathen statues) into the lake.

A gaunt and crazed-looking sculpture of the emperor stands in the lake, portrayed in the act of consigning a Venus to a watery grave.

The town has three main parallel streets: the B98 (Kaiser-Franz-Joseph-Strasse) and square Georgsritterplatz, Marktplatz north (uphill) from this, and the beach road on the lake. Stiftgasse/Seemühlgasse, near Full House, connects all three.

The **tourist office** (☎ 20 23; www.millstaettersee .com; Marktplatz 8) inside the *Rathaus* can help with information on the town.

SIGHTS & ACTIVITIES

Apart from the lake itself, Millstatt's main attraction is its Romanesque **Benedictine abbey** (tours in German, adult/child €5/2.50; 🕑 tours 10.30am Wed & Fri, 10am Sat early Jun-Sep), founded in 1070. This pretty complex consists of the 11th-century abbey, a graveyard that invites a stroll, and foundation buildings south of the abbey, with lovely yards and arcades. If you walk downhill along Stiftsgasse from the abbey, you see on the left a 1000-year-old lime tree. Millstatt was no exception to the practice common during the Middle Ages of holding trials beneath a tree (often a lime tree) and using the same tree for hangings.

The **Stiftsmuseum** (Abbey Museum; ☎ 06246-750 35; Stiftsgasse 1; adult/child €2.50/1.50; 🕑 10am-noon & 2-6pm Jun-Sep) contains everything from documentation of the town's history to reliquaries and a geology collection.

Back on the lake, **Wassersport Strobl** (☎ 22 63; Seemühlgasse 56a) hires out sailing boats (€7 to €12 per hour) and electric boats (€10 to €12 per hour) as well as kayaks (€5 per hour).

East of Millstatt is **Bad Kleinkirchheim**, a spa resort and large winter skiing centre with 26 lifts and cable cars. Its **tourist office** (☎ 04240-82 12; www.badkleinkirchheim.at; Dorfstrasse 30) can help.

NOSHING ON A RAFT

Among the interesting tours and events on the Millstätter See, several are clustered around the idea of 'touching the lake' – designed to bring people close to the water. For example, you can have your own romantic dinner for two out on the water. A boat chugs you to a raft, the food is delivered in seven courses, and later it returns at some point to bring you back to digest it all – or file for divorce, as the case may be (this one costs €120 per person, including a romantic tour of the lake to prime the palate). If the kids get sick of watching from the shore while mum and dad bob about stuffing their faces, they can be placated with pirate hunts (€12) in costume and make-up, or mellowed out by the fascinating 'Massage of 1000 Hands', which is about meditating in water and capping it off with a cup of herbal tea. The helpful Infocenter Millstätter See (see above) can arrange the 1000 hands, the dinner and other goodies for you.

FESTIVALS & EVENTS

If two Carinthians meet, they start a choir, according to a local saying. If two Millstätters get together, they start a music festival, and one that's put this minute place firmly on the classical music map is the **Musikwochen Millstatt** (Millstatt music weeks; ☎ 2022-35; www.musikwochen.com, in German; tickets €13-35). It happens every year from May to September, with most performances taking place in the Abbey.

SLEEPING & EATING

The high season is June to September. It's advisable to check availability with tourist offices outside these months as some places go into winter hibernation. Most hotels and pensions are south of the B98. The cheapest are back from the lake.

our pick **Villa Verdin** (☎ 374 74; www.villaverdin.at, in German; Seestrasse 69; s €50-65, d €100-130; P 🖳) This converted 19th-century villa-hotel mixes contemporary design style with antiques and interesting junk to create a comfortable, informal yet stylish atmosphere. The rooms are all different, some with funky, red furniture and zebra-print accessories, some with Buddhas and Japanese screens. Several have enclosed verandas or balconies with views of the lake. It's gay friendly and there's also a retro beach café for daytime snacks and a low-key restaurant for evening meals.

Hotel See-Villa (☎ 21 02; www.see-villa-tacoli.com; Seestrasse 68; s €55-76, d €106-158, ste €156-181; P 🖳) Next door to Villa Verdin, this staid, old-fashioned hotel is a complete contrast: it's a handsome old building right on the lake, with a huge terrace restaurant, a private sauna and a swimming jetty. The rooms are wooden floored, creaky and quaint, with a variety of different styles and colour schemes, all very traditional. Its restaurant (mains €11 to €18) does a Greek salad at the low end, and a venison filet steak towards the top. It's open daily for lunch and dinner

Die Forelle (☎ 2050-0; www.hotel-forelle.at; Fischergasse 65; s €84.50, d €145-228; P 🖳 🖳) Some guests like its lakeside bar, others choose this large lakeside hotel for its wellness facilities, including whirlpool and various baths, fitness and chill-out rooms, plus a Hawaiian massage or cosmetic treatment. Rooms are well sized, the more expensive doubles have a balcony to the lake, and prices fall significantly in shoulder season or with special deals. Check out the website for details. Its mid-priced restaurant opens for lunch and dinner, and offers a reduced menu between meal times and half-board (€20 extra).

Bio-Hotel Alpenrose (☎ 2500; www.biohotel-alpenrose.at, in German; Obermillstatt 84; s €78-88, d €156-206; lunch buffet €5.50, 4-course evening meal €22; 🕑 1-5pm) This eco-hotel is 3km north of town in Obermillstatt and serves an organic lunch buffet and evening menu. It's open most of the year.

Pizzeria Peppino (mains €5.20-12; 🕑 4pm-midnight) is a good in-town eating option beyond hotel fare.

For pub entertainment, **Full House** (☎ 20 73; Kaiser-Franz-Josef-Strasse; 🕑 1pm-2am summer, 7pm-2am winter), near the Volksbank, is a nice hangout.

GETTING THERE & AWAY

Postbus services to Millstatt depart from outside Spittal train station (€3.20, 20 minutes, two hourly), with some continuing to Bad Kleinkirchheim (from Spittal €6.40, one hour). The road from Spittal gives good views of the lake – sit on the right.

Hohe Tauern National Park Region

Hohe Tauern National Park is no place for acrophobes: you're constantly on a high. This vast tract of mountainous terrain is Austria's largest nature reserve, and three is its magic number: almost 300 peaks towering 3000m create enormous ripples in the landscape. The park is carved up between Carinthia, Tyrol and Salzburgerland (which naturally stole the biggest slice of the strudel). The scenery invites applause: waterfalls gouge deep ravines, Pinzgauer cattle graze spongy pastures, vultures wheel in a china-blue sky and glaciers shimmer like diamonds in spiky tiaras. It is amazing.

The central vein is the precipitous Grossglockner Road, which twists like a ribbon through a crumpled white sheet at the foot of Grossglockner (3797m), the grandaddy of the Austrian Alps. Down south the Dolomites give you a toothy grin in Lienz, a Roman-rooted city with Italian pizzazz, while stepping west the Krimml Falls begin to thunder when the ice cracks. Further north it's a different picture, with life spiralling around the lake at Zell am See and Bad Gastein serving up a winning combination of ski and spa.

This is where Austria's wild things are, but it's no empty wilderness and the resident marmots, chamois and ibex share their playground with active types. The locals have been legging it up these peaks since the Stone Age, so it stands to reason that opportunities for serious hiking are plentiful. If you'd prefer to freewheel over hill and dale, tourist offices hand out maps of the cycling routes that crisscross the reserve. Up for an adventure? Nearly every village offers an array of pursuits for those keen to throw themselves down a cliff, along a river or off a mountain's edge. Tempted…?

HIGHLIGHTS

- Getting high on glacier views on the precipitous **Grossglockner Road** (p318)
- Bathing in radon-rich waters and basking in *belle époque* glory in **Bad Gastein** (p320)
- Kicking off your ski boots to chill in the igloo at **Kitzsteinhorn Glacier** (p314)
- Soaking in the misty spray of **Krimml Falls** (p317), Europe's highest waterfall at 380m
- Letting llamas lead the way through the dramatic Dolomites in **Lienz** (p323)

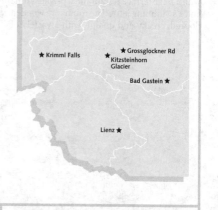

★ Krimml Falls
★ Grossglockner Rd
★ Kitzsteinhorn Glacier
Bad Gastein ★
Lienz ★

■ AREA: 1816 SQ KM   ■ HIGHEST ELEVATION: GROSSGLOCKNER 3797M

HOHE TAUERN NATIONAL PARK REGION

0 ____ 20 km
0 ____ 12 miles

To Innsbruck · Hopfgarten · Kitzbühel · Saalfelden · To Salzburg · Bischofshofen

TYROL · Saalbach · **311** · St Johann im Pongau

Kitzbüheler Alpen · Hinterglemm · Prielau · Thumersbach · Zell am See · *Zeller See* · Seespitz Strandbad · **311**

Thurn Pass · Schmittenhöhe (1965m) · **168** · Bruck · Täxenbach

Gerlos Pass · Neukirchen · Mittersill · *Salzach* · Kaprun · Fusch · **SALZBURG (SALZBURGER LAND)**

165 · Krimml · Gerlos · P *Hopfeldboden* · Kesselfall · *Wildpark Ferleiten* · Ferleiten · **167** · Bad Hofgastein

Krimml Falls · *Obersulzbachtal* · Kitzsteinhorn (3203m) · *Wasser-fallboden* · Grossglockner Rd · Kötschachtal

Felber Tauern Tunnel · *Mooser-boden* · Fuscher Törl (2428m) · Edelweiss Spitze (2577m) · Stubnerkogel (2246m) · Bad Gastein

Grossvenediger (3674m) · Matreier Tauernhaus · **108** · *Pasterze Glacier* · Hochtor · Böckstein · Graukogel (2492m)

Grossglockner (3797m) · Kaiser-Franz-Josefs-Höhe (2369m) · *Gletscher-strasse* · Guttal · Heiligenblut Toll · Sportgastein · Railway (car-shuttle) · *Autoschleuse Tauernbahn*

Hinterbichl · Matrei in Osttirol · Kals · **107** · Mallnitz

Isel · *Deferggen* · Grosskirchheim · Obervellach

St Jakob · *Schwarzach* · **106** · To Spittal-Millstättersee (30km)

EAST TYROL (OSTTIROL) · Winklern · *Möll*

ITALY · *Deferggengebirge* · Lienz · **CARINTHIA**

Sillian · *Drau* · **100** · *Lienzer Dolomiten* · Oberdrauburg · **100**

111 · Obertilliach · **110** · Kötschach

Karnische Alpen · *Gail*

History

The Austrian Alps once formed the boundary between the more-established southern Roman territories and their newer, less stable conquests to the north. The main trade route for pack animals ran along the pass at the end of the Tauern Valley, but few settlements were established due to the Romans' distrust of the treacherous climate (tales of malevolent, snowy spirits abounded) and difficult mountainous topography.

In 1971 the provinces of Carinthia, Salzburg and Tyrol agreed to the creation of a national park; regions were added in stages between 1981 and 1991 until it became Europe's largest national park. Today it's widely regarded as one of Europe's biggest conservation success stories, an example of an approach where the needs of the local population are addressed right from the start.

Information

All tourist offices in places bordering the park have maps of and information on Hohe Tauern. The *Experience in Nature* map (in English) shows information offices, overnight accommodation and tour ideas. You could also investigate the national park's website at www.hohetauern.at, listing the various provincial tourist offices responsible for the national park.

Climate

The national park has an Alpine climate with high rainfall, short summers and long winters with heavy snowfall. Avalanches are common in spring. Be aware that the sun is intense at high altitudes.

Dangers & Annoyances

Extremes of climate and terrain make parts of the park potentially dangerous for walkers and climbers. Always come prepared for abrupt changes in weather conditions and visibility, bring warm clothing and adequate maps, and consider taking a guide on more difficult routes. For more tips on staying safe in the mountains, see p86.

The number for emergency mountain rescue services is ☎ 140. Call ☎ 0512-291600 for weather information.

Getting There & Around

The main hubs for train services are Zell am See (for services to Salzburg and points north via St Johann im Pongau) and Lienz (for trains east and west into Tyrol and Carinthia).

The authorities are determined to limit the flow of traffic through the park, so most of the roads through it have toll sections and some are closed in winter. The main north–south road routes are Felber Tauern Rd, open year-round, and the Grossglockner Road (p318). The 5.5km-long Felber Tauern Tunnel is at the East Tyrol–Salzburg border: the toll is €10 for cars

and €8 for motorcycles. Buses on the Lienz–Kitzbühel route operate along this road.

Getting around by bus is made more attractive by special passes; such deals change periodically, so make inquiries upon arrival. Buying zonal day or week passes for provincial transport should work out significantly cheaper than buying single tickets.

ZELL AM SEE

☎ 06542 / pop 10,050 / elev 757m

Zell am See is Austria's Van Gogh – it lays on its colour thick. Taking the ice white canvas of the Hohe Tauern range, it suffuses it with a sapphire blue lake, emerald spruce forests, golden moors and the multicoloured sails of windsurfers. Step into the picture in summer and you're within easy reach of High Alpine walking trails, the Krimml Falls and the awe-inspiring Grossglockner Road. In winter, the scene shifts to downhill thrills in Zell am See and Kaprun, which together form the Europa Sports Region (p75). In both seasons, Zell am See's medieval centre serves up excellent dining and nightlife in its tangle of pedestrianised streets.

Orientation & Information

Almost adjacent to the main resort of Zell am See is the residential area of Schüttdorf,

---

HIKING & CLIMBING IN HOHE TAUERN NATIONAL PARK

Europe's biggest national park, Hohe Tauern is a mecca to hikers and climbers with its extraordinary landscape of verdant valleys, towering mountains, virgin forests and shimmering glaciers. The reserve has treks to suit every level of ability, from gentle day walks (see p102) to extreme expeditions to inaccessible peaks and ridges.

Freytag & Berndt produces nine 1:50,000 walking maps covering the national park and surrounding areas. If you plan to undertake major walking expeditions, you should plan your overnight stops in advance – some small-scale guesthouses provide food and accommodation, but they are widely scattered. Contact the regional or local tourist offices for accommodation lists.

Popular walking trails include the ascent of the **Grossvenediger** (3674m), a peak permanently coated with ice and snow and flanked by glaciers. The closest you can get by road is the **Matreier Tauernhaus Hotel** (1512m; ☎ 04875-88 11; www.matreier-tauernhaus.at; A-9971 Matrei in Osttirol) at the southern entrance to the Felber Tauern Tunnel. You can park here and within an hour's walk gain fine views of the mountain.

Anyone with mountain-climbing experience and a reasonable level of fitness can climb the mighty **Grossglockner** (3797m) via the 'ordinary' route, though guides are recommended. The main route for hikers begins from the **Adlersruhe (Eagles Rest) overnight hut** (☎ 04876-500), a four- to five-hour hike from Heiligenblut. From here, the route to the summit crosses ice and rocks, following a steel cable over a narrow snow ridge. The final ascent to the cross at the summit is relatively easy. It's essential to have the proper equipment (including maps, ropes and crampons) and to check weather conditions before setting out. For guides, contact the tourist offices in Heiligenblut or Kals, or ring the **mountain guides association** (☎ 04824-2700).

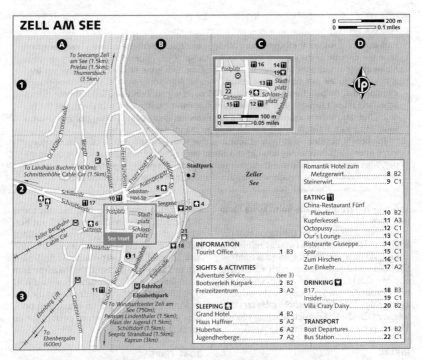

ZELL AM SEE

INFORMATION	
Tourist Office................................	1 B3

SIGHTS & ACTIVITIES	
Adventure Service.................	(see 3)
Bootsverleih Kurpark..............	2 B2
Freizeitzentrum........................	3 A2

SLEEPING	
Grand Hotel.............................	4 B2
Haus Haffner..........................	5 A2
Hubertus..................................	6 A2
Jugendherberge.......................	7 A2

Romantik Hotel zum	
Metzgerwirt........................	8 B2
Steinerwirt..............................	9 C1

EATING	
China-Restaurant Fünf	
Planeten..............................	10 B2
Kupferkessel............................	11 A3
Octopussy...............................	12 C1
Our's Lounge...........................	13 C1
Ristorante Giuseppe.................	14 C1
Spar..	15 C1
Zum Hirschen...........................	16 C1
Zur Einkehr..............................	17 A2

DRINKING	
B17...	18 B3
Insider......................................	19 C1
Villa Crazy Daisy......................	20 B2

TRANSPORT	
Boat Departures.......................	21 B2
Bus Station...............................	22 C1

which is generally cheaper for accommodation. Both are on the western shore of the Zeller See. You should ask for the handy *Gästekarte* (guest card) wherever you stay and show it for discounts on activities, sights and transport.

Tourist office (☎ 770-0; www.europasportregion .info; Brucker Bundesstrasse 1a; 🕑 9am-6pm Mon-Fri, 9am-noon, 2-6pm Sat, 10am-noon Sun mid-Dec–Feb & Jul-Aug). Staff at this office will help find rooms; there's also an accommodation board in the foyer with a free 24hr telephone.

Activities
SKIING
Zell am See has plenty to please powder freaks with 132km of downhill runs in its mountainous backyard, the Europa Sports Region. The terrain tends to be more tree-lined and scenic than hair-raising, but there are a couple of steep black pistes. The two must-ski biggies are **Schmittenhöhe** (1965m) and the glaciated **Kitzsteinhorn** (3203m); the latter also offers cross-country skiing, year-round glacier skiing on up to 13 pistes,

**HOHE TAUERN
NATIONAL PARK REGION**

LORD OF THE RINGOS

Zell am See has plenty of pedalos and rowing boats, but you might like to venture into the resort's wackier waters with a spin in the brand-new **BBQ-Donut** at Schmittenhöhe. From June to early October this giant Ringo (inflatable ring), complete with a charcoal grill in the centre and a shady parasol above to block the rays, floats leisurely across the summit's 2000m reservoir.

It's a deliciously different experience to glide across an Alpine lake with the aroma of steak filling your nostrils, an ice-cold beer on the side and 3000m-high peaks drifting into view. The Alps-meets-Australia experience costs €20 per person per hour for groups of up to five. Solo travellers keen to give the whole donut thing a go should turn up for the **Grilling & Chilling** picnic programme, which departs from the Schmittenhöhe cable car at 9.45am every Friday and costs €15.

ICE, ICE BABY

High above Zell am See, the Kitzsteinhorn Glacier is one place you're guaranteed a frosty reception since the opening of the subzero **Volvo XC Ice Camp**. If you're game for giving up your warm Alpine chalet in exchange for a hollowed-out ice cube, this igloo village 2500m above sea level is the place to live out your wildest Eskimo dreams. Frostbite? Forget it. These dome-shaped dwellings may be built from snow, but they feel positively cosy once you've blown out the tea lights and slipped beneath your thick reindeer-skin cover. Staying here isn't cheap at €147 per night, but rates include a fondue feast and few experiences can beat drinking *gluhwein* (mulled wine) at an ice bar before taking a starlit stroll on the glacier.

The benefit of being up so high, of course, is that you can be the first to carve up the slopes in the morning. Snowboarding fans can also attend free safety and freestyle workshops during the day. The camp is open from mid-December to April and overnighting is possible on Wednesdays and Saturdays. For more details, visit Zell am See tourist office or see www.icecamp.at.

---

and snowboarding at the **Volvo XC Ice Camp** (see above).

Combined lift passes for the region cost per adult/child €68.50/34 for a two-day minimum period; ski buses are free for ski-pass holders. Ski/boot rental prices are roughly €22/37 for one day. Cable cars (Ebenberg Lift and cityX-press) from Zell am See ascend to the ridge on either side of the **Schmittenhöhe cable car** (adult/child return €20.50/10.25), which reaches 1965m. These operate from December to April.

HIKING

The hiking around Zell am See is some of the finest in Austria; almost everywhere you tramp you're rewarded with splendid vistas of **Grossglockner** (3797m), standing like a shepherd guarding snow-white flocks. Snowfields often linger till early summer above 2000m, but when they melt the region becomes a trekking wonderland comprising 400km of trails that stretch from gentle ambles through flower-speckled pastures to the glacier trail at Kitzsteinhorn. For a taste of the dramatic scenery this region has to offer, consider walking the five- to six-hour **Pinzgauer Spaziergang** (p102), leading from Schmittenhöhe peak to Saalbach.

From June to mid-October, the tourist office arranges guided walks including mountain treks, picnic tours to a 2000m-high reservoir and, the perennial family favourite, llama expeditions. They also hand out a free *Wanderkarte* (walking map) to help plan your own route.

SWIMMING

When the weather warms, the chilly waters of the **Zeller See** can be tempting for a quick dip.

Lidos dotted around the lake include those at Seespitz, Thumersbach and Zell am See, which feature sunbathing lawns, solar-heated outdoor pools and splash areas for the little 'uns; all cost €5.60/3.50 per adult/child. Unless you're a fan of ice-bathing, the **Freizeitzentrum** (Leisure Centre; ☎ 785-0; Steinergasse 3-5; pool adult/child €7.90/5.70; ☼ 10am-10pm) is preferable to the lake in winter; it shelters a 25m swimming pool, plus a whirlpool and saunas perfect for an après-ski unwind.

BOAT TRIPS

A laid-back way to soak up the sights is to board a **boat tour** (☎ 789-0; adult/child €8.70/4.35; ☼ May-Oct) from Zell am See Esplanade for a 45-minute round trip of the lake. Boats also shuttle across the lake, occasionally stopping at **Seecamp Zell am See** (one-way/return €2.75/4.60). But if you'd prefer to row your own, a number of places along the promenade hire out rowing boats, pedalos and motorboats. Pick of the bunch is **Bootsverleih Kurpark** (☎ 0664-358 17 95; pedalo/motorboat per hr €10.50/13.50; ☼ 9am-10pm Apr-Oct), situated close to the Grand Hotel.

ADVENTURE SPORTS

A one-stop daredevil shop is **Adventure Service** (☎ 735 25; www.adventureservice.at; Steinergasse 9), which offers a long list of adrenaline-charged activities from tandem paragliding (€100) and white-water rafting (€44) to canyoning (€51 to €69), climbing (€41) and guided mountainbike tours (€22 to €29).

There's also plenty of high-speed action on the water, such as knuckle-whitening waterskiing or wakeboarding at **Strandbad Thumersbach** (☎ 0664-206 85 06; Pocherweg 28). The breeze that blows down from the mountains creates ideal conditions for windsurfing. To master the fine art of balancing on a board, slip on a wet suit and head for **Windsurfcenter Zell am See** (☎ 551 15; Seespitzstrasse 13; half-/full-day course €27/44).

Festivals & Events

Zell am See celebrates two summer festivals on the shores of its glistening lake. The first is held in mid-July and attracts a lively crowd with its line-up of fireworks, live music and sports events. The second, in early August, stages concerts and costumed parades. The **Zell Summer Night** festival runs from June to August and draws Dixie bands, street entertainers and improvised theatre to the town's cobbled streets and squares every Wednesday night.

Sleeping

Zell am See's best beds can fill up in a flash during high season, so it's wise to book ahead. Aside from the top-end hotels by the lake, there are loads of cheap-and-cheerful private rooms about town, which usually add 5% to 10% for stays of less than three nights; ask the tourist office for a list of such places. Expect winter prices to be roughly 50% higher than the summer rates quoted below.

BUDGET

Seecamp Zell am See (☎ 721 15; www.seecamp.at; Thumersbacherstrasse 34; campsites per adult/child €7.90/4.70; P) If waking up to views of Grossglockner appeals, camp out at this tree-shaded site on the lakeshore. Facilities include a shop, restaurant and kids club. Guided mountain-bike and hiking tours are available.

Haus der Jugend (☎ 571 85; www.hostel-zell.at, in German; Seespitzstrasse 13; 6/4/2-bed dm €17.50/19.50/21.50; P) For budget digs on the lake, head to this hostel with a waterfront terrace and prime vistas of the peaks. There's a windsurfing school and volleyball court a few paces away. The centre is a 15-minute stroll along the shore.

Jugendherberge (☎ 470 36; www.lbsh-zell.at, in German; Schmittenstrasse 27; dm €23.50; P 💻) Next to Haus Haffner, this place is a cut above your average HI hostel. The four-bed dorms are spotlessly clean and facilities include bike hire (per day €10), internet access, a gym and restaurant.

Haus Haffner (☎ 723 96-0; www.haffner.at; Schmittenstrasse 29; s €27, d €48, apt €60-73; P) Tucked down a quiet backstreet near the ski lift, this cheery guesthouse has spacious rooms and family apartments with rag rugs, kettles and chunky wood furniture (the owner is a cabinet maker!).

Pension Lindenthaler (☎ 572 21; Porscheallee 43; s/d €30/54; P 💻) This pension in Schüttdorf scores points for its chirpy staff, terrace and free internet access. The comfy rooms were recently revamped and painted in sunny shades. It's a 25-minute walk along the promenade into town.

Landhaus Buchner (☎ 720 62; www.landhausbuchner .at; Schmittenstrasse 57; s/d €39/58; P) The twittering birds in the forest behind Landhaus Buchner are likely to be your wake-up call at this quaint Alpine chalet. A short toddle from the lake, the light-filled rooms are a great deal. The party hut in the garden is a welcome bonus.

MIDRANGE & TOP END

Hubertus (☎ 724 27; www.hubertus-pension.at; Gartenstrasse 4; s/d €42/70; P 💻) Facing the ski lift, Hubertus has made other guesthouses green with envy since being awarded the Austrian Eco-Label. The three-star chalet uses 100% renewable energy (solar and wind power), serves local organic produce and fair-trade coffee at breakfast. The rooms are country style with laminate floors, crisp linen and floral drapes.

Steinerwirt (☎ 725 02; www.steinerwirt.com; Schlossplatz 1; s/d €55/110; P 💻) Steinerwirt has been around for donkey's years, but recently morphed into an arty boutique hotel. The light-filled rooms are defined by muted tones and untreated pinewood. Up in the attic, the Think Tank is a calm spot for early-morning meditation. The restaurant (open for both lunch and dinner) uses meat from Hohe Tauern pastures and fresh fish from the lake. Mains cost from €6 to €20.

Romantik Hotel zum Metzgerwirt (☎ 725 20; www.romantik-hotel.at; Sebastian-Hörl-Strasse 11; s €89-113, d €148-196, ste €199; P 💻 🔊) Creeping ivy envelops this little love nest dating to 1493. It's the small details that matter here: from the roaring fire in the lounge to the 300-year-old apple tree in the garden. Guests can bathe beneath the stars in the solar-heated outdoor pool or in a chocolate-filled bath in the spa.

Grand Hotel (☎ 788-0; www.grandhotel.cc; Esplanade 4-6; s/d/ste €113/226/328; P 💻 🔊) The *belle époque* beauty of Zell am See, this posh pad beside the lake has a private beach and waterfront spa that give it an exclusive air. The lobby is all chandeliers and sweeping staircases, while understated elegance sums up the rooms. Hundertwasser's *Österreich-Brunnen* (Austria Fountain) adds a splash of colour outside.

Eating

Zell am See has a number of decent restaurants; many at the plush hotels afford mesmeric views of the lake. The pedestrianised centre is a melting pot of Austrian and world flavours. Fish plucked fresh from the lake features on practically every menu.

Kupferkessel (☎ 727 68; Brucker Bundesstrasse 18; mains €6-23; 🕑 lunch & dinner Mon-Sat, dinner Sun) Once upon a time this wacky place was a petrol station. It has now been reincarnated as a family-friendly restaurant, filling tummies instead of tanks with mammoth steaks and cheap pasta dishes. There are plenty of curios to feast your eyes on – from mounted Vespas to portraits framed in toilet seats.

China-Restaurant Fünf Planeten (☎ 701 34; Loferer Bundesstrasse 3; lunch €5.50-5.90, mains €7-11; 🕑 lunch & dinner) Spicing up the centre is this Chinese den centred on a fish pond, where the midday crowds tuck into crispy spring rolls, beef with bean sprouts and huge plates of noodles.

Octopussy (☎ 470 42; Schlossplatz 2; mains €7-18.50; 🕑 dinner) There's very little that's Bond about this Octopussy, but the fishy menu certainly delivers with juicy crustaceans, spinach-stuffed octopus and grilled calamari. Retreat to the terrace on warm summer evenings.

Ebenbergalm (☎ 0664-351 2307; Schmitten 38, Ebenburg; mains €8-12; 🕑 lunch & dinner) Wild whiskered Günter and his (less hairy) sister, Gudrun, serve solid mountain fare at this little wooden hut near the top of the Ebenberg lift. Take a seat beside the tiled oven or on the panoramic terrace. You can walk up in around an hour or call for a lift (free pick-up from the town hotels).

ourpick Our's Lounge (☎ 772 44; Schlossplatz 5; mains €8-18; 🕑 10am-1am) Floor-to-ceiling glass walls, throne-like red velvet chairs and rotating exhibitions of modern art draw your attention to this sassy lounge bar. The vibe is young and the heated terrace jam-packed at weekends. The menu is a successful blend of Austrian and Mediterranean flavours – try the fresh scampi and vitamin-rich juices. There's free wi-fi for customers.

Zur Einkehr (☎ 723 63; Schmittenstrasse 12; mains €9.50-19; 🕑 lunch & dinner winter, dinner Mon-Sat summer) Near the slopes, this barn-style bistro is a local favourite. Sticky spare ribs and seafood lasagne

are polished off nicely with a pear schnapps (or three) at the crescent-shaped bar.

Ristorante Giuseppe (☎ 72 37 35; Kirchengasse 1; pizza €6-9.50, mains €10-22; 🕑 lunch & dinner) This upbeat bistro and café in the pedestrian-only centre hits the spot with Italian flavours. The antipasti and salads are tasty and the pizzas enormous. There's a pavement terrace and a rustic wood-panelled restaurant upstairs.

Zum Hirschen (☎ 774; Dreifaltigkeitsgasse 1; mains €14-25; 🕑 lunch & dinner) This smart restaurant creates an intimate mood with warm pine panelling, flickering candles and friendly yet discreet service. Signature dishes include Pinzgauer *Kasnocken* (cheese noodles) and crispy pork drenched in beer sauce.

Self-caterers can stock up on supplies at a number of supermarkets in the centre, including **Spar** (Brucker Bundesstrasse 4).

Drinking

Zell am See's nightlife gathers momentum in winter when ski bums descend on the town in droves. The following watering holes are also lively in summer high season.

B17 (☎ 474 24; Salzmannstrasse; 2; 🕑 5pm-2am Mon-Sat) This corrugated shack is stuck in a WWII time warp. The shell recreates a B17 bomber and is festooned with engines, army combats and fighter-plane pictures. The cheery barman mixes excellent fresh fruit cocktails and the measures are generous. Check out the heated roof terrace and free sweets in the loos.

Insider (☎ 739 69; Kreuzgasse 1; 🕑 7pm-4am) This groovy underground haunt with blood red walls and neon light panels lures a young crowd with its daily cocktail specials (the frozen daiquiris and lychee shots pack a punch). DJ Rudi spins mostly funk, and up-and-coming bands perform here three times a week.

Villa Crazy Daisy (☎ 725 26; Salzmannstrasse 8; 🕑 9pm-4am) The maddest cow in town, Daisy rocks in high season and is the place for full-on après-ski parties in winter. The raucous drinking hole occupies a rambling villa next to the Grand Hotel; head upstairs for live music, DJs and lots of slapstick fun.

Getting There & Away

Train destinations from Zell am See include Salzburg (€12.70, 1¾ hours, hourly), Kitzbühel (€9.90, 45 minutes, every two hours) and Innsbruck (€23.30, two hours, every two hours). You can hire bikes at any of the sports shops in town.

HOHE TAUERN NATIONAL PARK REGION

Buses leave from outside the *Bahnhof* (train station) and the bus station behind the post office. They run to various destinations, including Kaprun (€2.80, 20 minutes, hourly) and Krimml Falls (€8.70, 1½ hours, hourly). For details of buses to Lienz via Kaiser-Franz-Josefs-Höhe, see p318.

Zell am See is on Hwy 311 running north to Lofer, where it joins Hwy 312, which connects St Johann in Tyrol with Salzburg (passing through Germany). It's also just a few kilometres north of the east–west highway linking St Johann im Pongau with Tyrol (via the Gerlos Pass).

KRIMML

☎ 06564 / pop 890 / elev 1076m

Most people come to Krimml for the mountains, fresh air and pure water – all 380m of it. The mighty roar of the three-tier **Krimmler Wasserfälle** (Krimml Falls) echoes through the valley. Hung in mist, the brilliance of Europe's highest waterfall illuminates the deep-green pine forest like a spotlight in the dark. It's worthy of all the attention it gets, but spare a little time for Krimml's other charms – alpine pastures, vistas of Grossvenediger and the earthy authenticity of a village that hasn't yet let fame go to its pretty head.

Orientation & Information

The Krimml Falls are on the northwestern fringes of the national park, within the protected area. The village is about 500m north of the falls, on a side turning from Hwy 165. There are parking spaces (€4 per day) near the path to the falls, which branches to the right just before the toll booths for the Gerlos Pass road (see p318).

The **tourist office** (☎ 72 39; www.krimml.at; ☼ 8am-noon, 2.30-5.30pm Mon-Fri, 8.30-10.30am Sat) is in the village centre next to the white church. The post office is next door.

Sights & Activities

Near the entrance to the falls is **Wasserwunderwelt** (adult/child €7/3.50; ☎ 9.30am-5pm May-Oct), a water-related theme park with loads of hands-on activities for kids – from physics experiments to art installations and outdoor games where the aim is to get completely soaked.

Krimml's star attraction is, of course, the waterfall itself and the best way to get up close and feel the spray is to walk the **Wasserfallweg** trail (see Krimml Falls Loop, p104). The lower

levels are crawling with day-trippers in summer but the further you climb the quieter the path becomes. The **ticket & information offices** (☎ 201 13; adult/child €1.80/0.50, free Dec-Apr; ☼ ticket office 8am-6pm May-Nov, unattended Dec-Apr) are a few minutes' walk along the path.

Sleeping & Eating

Krimml is easily visited as a day trip from Zell am See. It's a shame to hurry, though, as this unspoilt village has some beautiful places in which to stay; many are set on a hillside overlooking the falls. The staff at Krimml tourist office can help arrange accommodation. Winter prices are roughly a third higher than those given here.

Hölzlahneralm (☎ 0664-402 68 78; www.hoelzlah ner.at; dm adult/child €18/12; ☼ May-Oct) High above the falls, this wood-shingled farmhouse is a superb budget choice. You'll need to do the legwork, but that makes the *Kaspressknödel* (dumpling in gooey Pinzgauer cheese) all the more welcome. The ecofriendly chalet generates its own electricity, uses natural spring water and has comfy bunks for weary walkers upstairs.

Hotel Klockerhaus (☎ 72 28; Wasserfallstrasse 10; www.klockerhaus.at; s/d €39/68; P ☢) This family-run hotel has a unique claim to fame: it nurtures the largest free-roaming guinea-pig colony in Salzburgerland. What you'll get is also more than just a hutch – neat and tidy rooms with balconies, views of the falls while you eat breakfast, an untreated pool and plenty to entertain the tots (a playground, goats and ubiquitous racing rodents).

ourpick Heimathaus Anton Wallner (☎ 71 17 67; Oberkrimml 8; apt €68-250) Way up there on Austria's most quirky list, this rickety chalet has heaps of charisma, with crooked beams and lantern-lit corridors that creak under the weight of their 400-year history. Owner Herbert has poured both love and labour into renovating the gorgeous apartments, where the horn-sledge beds (ask for the *Schlittenzimmer*) come with old-fashioned stripy nightcaps. The sign on the gate says: *Wanderer und andere lustige Leut wilkommen* (Walkers and other fun-loving folk welcome). If you fit either or both of these categories, come on in.

La Piazza (☎ 75 34; Oberkrimml 94; mains €6-12; ☼ dinner) After walking your socks off in the mountains, this central taverna fills the gap with its large helpings of spaghetti and pizzas from a wood-fired oven.

HOHE TAUERN NATIONAL PARK REGION

Getting There & Away

Buses run all year from Zell am See to Krimml (€8.70, 1½ hours, last return bus 5pm). The Krimml Falls path begins near the starting point of the *Tauernradweg* (cycle path) to Salzburg (175km) and Passau (325km).

GERLOS PASS

This High Alpine pass links the Zillertal (p346) in Tyrol to Krimml in Salzburgerland, zigzagging 12km through high moor and spruce forest and reaching an elevation of 1630m. The viewpoint above the turquoise *Stausee* (reservoir) is a great spot to pause for a picnic and tremendous views of the Alps. On the approach to Krimml near Schönmoosalm, there are also fine vistas of the Krimml Falls. The pass is open year-round and there is a toll: €7 for cars and €4 for motorcycles.

Buses make the trip between Krimml and Zell am Ziller (one-way including toll €8.70, 1½ hours) in Tyrol from 1 July to 30 September. By car, you can avoid using the toll road by following the (easy-to-miss) signs to Wald im Pinzgau, 6km north of Krimml.

GROSSGLOCKNER ROAD

Surely one of Europe's greatest drives, the snaking **Grossglockner Road** (Grossglockner Hochalpenstrasse; ☎ 065-46 650; toll per car/motorcycle €28/18; ☼ 6am-8pm May-15 Jun, 5pm-9.30pm 16 Jun-15 Sep, 6am-7.30pm 16 Sep-Oct) is a 1930s feat of engineering and a feast of perpendicular towers, ice blue glaciers and razor-sharp peaks. If the 43km highway doesn't take your breath away with its hairpin bends, the incredible views of Grossglockner ringed by snowy peaks should do the trick.

Linking Bruck in Salzburgerland to Heiligenblut in Carinthia, the former Roman trade route comprises 36 stomach-churning switchbacks, passing gemstone lakes, pine forest and high pastures streaked with waterfalls. As the hills are steep, the easiest way to tackle them is by car or motorbike. If you're fighting fit and fancy a challenge, however, a free and more carbon-neutral alternative is to get on your bike and pedal it. The going is pretty tough uphill but the downhill stretches are exhilarating.

Just before the start of the tour, you'll reach **Wildpark Ferleiten** (☎ 06546-220; www.wildpark-ferl eiten.at; adult/child €5.50/3; ☼ 8am-dusk May-Nov), a 15-hectare reserve home to 200 Alpine animals such as chamois, marmots and bears. Kids can let off steam in the playgrounds or on the mini-roller coasters.

Once through the tollgate, the road begins to climb steeply. Situated at 2260m is the **Alpine Nature Museum** (admission free; ☼ 9am-5pm), screening films on local flora and fauna. A little further along, a 2km side road (no coaches allowed) cuts a path through a wall of ice up to **Edelweiss Spitze** (2577m), the highest viewpoint on the route with a lookout tower affording 360-degree views of more than 30 peaks of 3000m. You can refuel with coffee and strudel on the terrace at the hut.

Soon you'll want your camera handy for **Fuscher Törl** (2428m), commanding superb vistas on both sides of the ridge, and the petrol blue lake at nearby **Fuscher Lacke** (2262m). Here there is a small exhibition that vividly documents the construction of the road; originally conceived as a way of beating the economic depression of the 1930s, it was built by 3000 men over the course of five years.

Hochtor (2504m) is the second-highest point on the pass, after which there is a steady descent to **Guttal** (1950m). Here the road splits: to the east lies Heiligenblut and the route to Lienz, while to the west is the 9km **Gletscherstrasse** (Glacier Road). Following the Gletscherstrasse, the initial views south to Heiligenblut are fantastic, yet soon your attention is drawn to the looming Grossglockner massif. The road features signs warning *Achtung Murmeltiere* (Beware of marmots); keep an eye out for burrowing rodents along the way.

The Gletscherstrasse emerges at **Kaiser-Franz-Josefs-Höhe** (2369m), where there is a visitor's centre with mountain-themed displays. It's a stupendous viewpoint from which to admire Austria's highest peak, Grossglockner, and the 9km **Pasterze Glacier**, a swirl of fissured ice that shimmers when the light hits it. Steps lead down to the edge of the glacier which, despite its majestic appearance, is receding at a disastrous rate because of global warming (it has shrunk to half its size over the past 150 years and is predicted to disappear entirely within 100 years). A popular walk taking in the glacier is Gamsgrubenweg, a trail that winds above the glacier and leads to a waterfall (allow roughly 1½ to two hours return).

Getting There & Away

Bus 5002 operates between Lienz and Heiligenblut nine times a day from Monday

---

WALK ON THE WILD SIDE

Anyone who wants to get out and stride through the Hohe Tauern National Park should consider signing up for one of the back-to-nature guided tours led by a team of well-informed rangers. From July to September, Hohe Tauern offers 36 hikes (11 are free with a guest card) that aim to get every last lovely drop out of the reserve. The broad spectrum covers everything from herb discovery trails to High Alpine hikes, around-the-glacier tours, gorge climbing, wildlife spotting (bring your binoculars), and early morning mountain photography courses. For the complete programme and price list, visit www.nationalpark.at.

---

to Friday (€7.10, one hour); services are less frequent at weekends. From 24 June to 23 September, four buses run from Monday to Friday and three at weekends between Heiligenblut and Kaiser-Franz-Josefs-Höhe (€3.90, 30 minutes). The buses connect neatly so that you can spend time in Heiligenblut and at Kaiser-Franz-Josefs-Höhe and still do the trip in one day. From 3 June to 23 September, bus 651 runs twice daily between Kaiser-Franz-Josefs-Höhe and Zell am See (€10.30, 1½ hours). Add an extra €2 per person to these fares to cover the toll.

HEILIGENBLUT
☎ 04824 / pop 1200 / elev 1301m

One of the single-most striking images on the Grossglockner Road is Heiligenblut, the needle-thin spire of its pilgrimage church framed by the glaciated summit of Grossglockner. The village's iconic scenery and easy access to the mountains draws skiers, hikers and (less-loveable) hordes of camera-toting tourists; stay overnight or get here early to avoid the crowds. The compact centre is lined with log chalets and, despite an overload of yodel-when-you-press-me kitsch, still retains some traditional charm.

Information
National park information office (☎ 27 00; www .hohetauern.at; 10am-5pm daily late May-early Oct, 3-6pm winter) In the Gästehaus Schober; has some museum exhibits. From 4pm to 5pm Monday to Friday someone from the Bergführerinformationsbüro (mountain guides office) gives advice on climbing and walking.

Tourist office (☎ 20 01 21; www.heiligenblut.at; 9am-6pm Mon-Fri, 9am-noon & 4-6pm Sat Jul-Aug, 9am-6pm Mon-Fri Dec-Apr, rest of the year 9am-noon & 2-6pm Mon-Fri, 9am-noon & 4-6pm Sat) On the main street, close to the Hotel Post bus stop. Books mountain guides.

Sights & Activities
Soaring skywards and clearly visible from the Gletscherstrasse, the **church** steeple of Heiligenblut demands attention. Steeped in legend, the 15th-century pilgrimage church shelters statues of saints and a fine late-Gothic altar. The tabernacle is purported to contain a tiny phial of Christ's blood – hence the name of the village (*Heiligenblut* means 'holy blood') – which was discovered in the possession of a saint named Briccius. He was buried in an avalanche on this spot more than a thousand years ago.

Heiligenblut's 55km of snow-sure slopes (geared towards beginners and intermediates) and a Bobo's Kids' Club make Heiligenblut a top choice for families. Most of the **skiing** takes place on Schareck (2604m) and Gjaidtroghöhe (2969m) peaks. A one-day local lift pass costs €34 and will also get you into other resorts in Carinthia and East Tyrol. In summer, **mountaineering** is a popular pursuit (see p312). Inquire at the tourist office for details of mountain-bike trails in the park.

Sleeping & Eating
Heiligenblut has a smattering of places to stay and eat, with most clustered around the village centre. Private rooms usually offer the best value and the tourist office can make bookings. Expect rates to increase 20% to 30% in winter.

Camping Grossglockner (☎ 20 48; Hadergasse 11; campsites per adult/child/car €6.90/3/2.50; P) Open year-round, this green and pleasant site on the outskirts of the village features a restaurant and affords prime vistas of Grossglockner.

Jugendherberge (☎ 22 59; www.oejhv.at; Hof 36; dm/r €18.40/26.40; reception 7-10am & 5-8pm; P) Near the church, this chalet-style HI hostel has light, spacious dorms and handy extras including ski storage and a common room. It's right next to the public swimming pool, sauna and climbing wall.

Hotel Senger (☎ 22 15; www.romantic.at; Hof 23; s/d €64/130; P) The colourful prayer flags fluttering at this farmhouse are a tribute to the Tibetan monks that stayed here during a visit to Austria. There is a real sense of being stuck in the mountains – think stone floors, open fireplaces and plenty of cosy nooks. All of the snug-as-a-bug rooms have balconies except room 24, which offers Grossglockner views instead.

Café Dorfstüberl (☎ 20 19; Hof 5; mains €7-12; ☖ lunch & dinner) Opening onto a tiny terrace, this smoky local den dishes up hearty, reasonably priced food. The *halbes Hendl* (half a roasted chicken) with a mound of potato salad goes down well.

Die Casa (☎ 20 28; Hof 9; mains €8-14; ☖ lunch & dinner) Step back to the 16th century at this alpine hut, where the walls are festooned with rams' heads, ploughs and leather boots. The first mountaineers to climb Grossglockner supped here, so expect wholesome fare (the grill platter and sander fillet are favourites). Retreat to the patio for stunning views.

Getting There & Away

As well as buses running to/from Kaiser-Franz-Josefs-Höhe from late June to September, there is a year-round service to/from Lienz (see p318).

BAD GASTEIN

☎ 06434 / pop 6100 / elev 1000m

Bad Gastein runs hot and cold: thermal waters gush from its hot springs and deep powder beckons skiers to the slopes of the Gasteiner Tal (Gastein Valley). A far cry from your chocolate-box Austrian ski resort, this grand old dame is spiritually somewhere between Brighton and St Moritz. The town exudes an air of 19th-century gentility with sublime *belle époque* villas, scintillating spas and higgledy-piggledy streets that afford glimpses of the Gasteiner Ache falls. The elixir of life? Take a deep breath and plunge into the radon-rich waters to find out…

Orientation & Information

Clinging precipitously to the valley slopes, Bad Gastein's winding streets are punctuated with scenic viewpoints. Tumbling through the centre in a series of waterfalls is the Gasteiner Ache. Its thundering waters can be heard throughout the valley. The *Bahnhof* is to the west of town and the central hub, Kongressplatz, down the hill to the east; make your way down near the Hotel Salzburger Hof.

Post office (Bahnhofplatz 9; ☖ 8am-noon & 2-5.30pm Mon-Fri, 8-10am Sat) Next to the train station.

Tourist office (☎ 06432-3393 560; www.gastein.com; Kaiser-Franz-Josef-Strasse 27; ☖ 8am-6pm Mon-Fri, 10am-4pm Sat & 10am-2pm Sun high season) To get here, go left from the train station exit and walk down the hill. Staff will find you accommodation free of charge. There's information on the national park in the foyer.

Sights

Bad Gastein still mirrors the grandeur of its 19th-century heyday, with *belle époque* villas and elegant hotels hugging its sheer cliffs. The best way to soak up the resort's ambience is by strolling its steep streets and manicured gardens.

Worth a peek on the way down to the waterfall is the **Gasteiner Museum** (☎ 34 88; 2nd fl, Haus Austria, Kongressplatz; adult/child €3/free; ☖ 10.30am-noon & 3.30-6pm, closed Nov & May). The collection is small but ambitious, spanning everything from minerals (including a 76kg-heavy rock crystal) to Stone Age artefacts, devilish *Krampus* (devil) costumes, vintage tourist posters and 19th-century oil paintings of Bad Gastein.

The nearby stone Wasserfallbrücke (waterfall bridge) is a great lookout point over the 341m-high **Gasteiner Ache** falls. Raging through the town and cascading into three brilliant turquoise pools, the waterfall has inspired painters and poets over the ages, and the negatively ionised air here is famed for its therapeutic benefits. The *Wasserfallweg* (waterfall trail) shadows the magnificent cataract.

Situated in the lower part of town, the late-Gothic **Nikolauskirche** (Bismarckstrasse) is a little gem of a church, tiled with wood shingles and built around a central pillar. Its interior is simple yet beautiful with an uneven flagstone floor, baroque altar and rudimentary frescoes that are fading with age. Look out for the statue of 16th-century physician Paracelsus outside.

Activities

Bad Gastein is famous for its **radon-laced waters**, which seep down from the mountains, heat up to temperatures of 44°C to 47°C around 2000m underground, then gush forth at 18 different springs in the area. Renowned since the Middle Ages for their healing properties, the thermal waters are said to repair human cells, alleviate rheumatism, boost potency and alleviate menopausal problems. Strauss and Sissi (Empress Elisabeth) both put the waters' benefits to the test; the empress was so impressed that she penned a poem beginning:

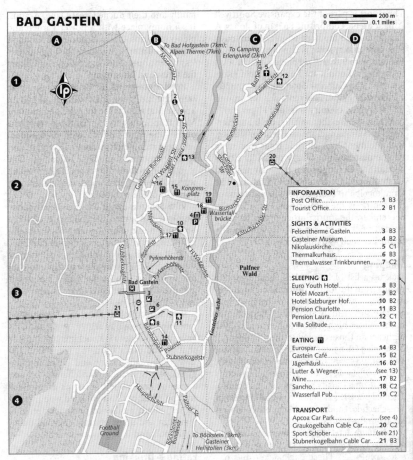

BAD GASTEIN

INFORMATION
Post Office.....................................1 B3
Tourist Office................................2 B1

SIGHTS & ACTIVITIES
Felsentherme Gastein...................3 B3
Gasteiner Museum........................4 B2
Nikolauskirche...............................5 C1
Thermalkurhaus.............................6 B3
Thermalwasser Trinkbrunnen....7 C2

SLEEPING
Euro Youth Hotel...........................8 B3
Hotel Mozart..................................9 B2
Hotel Salzburger Hof..................10 B2
Pension Charlotte........................11 B3
Pension Laura...............................12 C1
Villa Solitude...............................13 B2

EATING
Eurospar.......................................14 B3
Gastein Café................................15 B2
Jägerhäusl....................................16 B2
Lutter & Wegner..................(see 13)
Mine..17 B2
Sancho..18 C2
Wasserfall Pub.............................19 C2

TRANSPORT
Apcoa Car Park.......................(see 4)
Graukogelbahn Cable Car..........20 C2
Sport Schober.......................(see 21)
Stubnerkogelbahn Cable Car....21 B3

HOHE TAUERN NATIONAL PARK REGION

'Only sick bones I thought of bringing, where mystically your hot water springs…'

The product of 3000 years of geological forces, the radon is absorbed through the skin and retained in the body for nearly three hours. Most people take the cure by bathing in the radon-rich waters of the spa, but **vapour tunnels** burrowed deep in the rock and emitting radon gases are used for more intensive treatments. To sample the magical waters without splashing out, make the pilgrimage to **Thermalwasser Trinkbrunnen**. You can slurp or bottle the water for free at this fountain beside the Gasteiner Ache – two to six cups per day are recommended for glowing health.

A great glass elevator zooms from street level up to **Felsentherme Gastein** (☎ 222 30;

Bahnhofplatz 5; 3hr/day ticket adult €17.50/19.50, child €10/12; ☻ 9am-9pm Apr-Nov, 9am-10pm Dec-Mar), where you can take the rejuvenating waters. The spa shelters grottos, an adventure pool for kids and an outdoor thermal bath with pummelling massage jets, and superlative views of the mountains. Curative massages, radon baths and electrotherapy are available next door in the **Thermalkurhaus** (Bahnhofplatz 9; ☻ 8am-noon, 2-5pm Mon-Fri, 8am-nooon Sat).

In winter Bad Gastein's slopes and spas are a match made in heaven; a place where you can cruise challenging red runs before indulging in a little radon therapy. **Skiing** and **snowboarding** are centred on Stubnerkogel (2246m) and Graukogel (2492m), where the varied terrain is aimed mostly at intermediates.

The resort is part of the expansive Sportwelt Amadé arena, comprising 865km of slopes. A day ski pass in the high winter season costs €38. **Cross-country skiing** is also big news in Bad Gastein, with 90km of prepared *Loipe* (tracks) including a floodlit trail at Böckstein (3km south of Bad Gastein). **Sport Schober** (☎ 32 68-0; Stubnerkogel; ◷ 8am-6pm) rents skis for around €20 and cross-country sets for €11 per day.

When the weather warms, both Stubnerkogel and Graukogel are excellent for **walking**, with plenty of high-altitude trails traversing Alpine pastures and craggy peaks. The two-section Stubnerkogelbahn cable car near Bad Gastein's train station costs €15 return. The Graukogelbahn cable car, 300m northeast of the centre, is the same price. From June to September, the tourist office organises daily guided walks and can give tips on family favourites such as llama trekking.

Sleeping

Pick up a list of budget hostels and private rooms from the tourist office. Some of the resort's *belle époque* hotels feature their own spas and are surprisingly affordable. Expect rates in the winter high season to be roughly 30% higher than those quoted in these listings.

Camping Erlengrund (☎ 27 90; www.kurcamping -gastein.at; Erlengrundstrasse 6; campsites per adult/child/tent €7/4/7.50; P 💻 🍴) Close to a natural lake, this campsite offers shady pitches and, in summer, a heated pool. It's 2km north of Bad Gastein in Kötschachdorf and accessible by buses departing from the train station.

Euro Youth Hotel (☎ 233 00; www.euro-youth-hotel .at; Bahnhofsplatz 8; dm/s/d €16.45/25/40; ◷ closed Apr & Oct-Nov; P 💻) These backpacker digs occupy a rambling turn-of-the-century manor. The superb facilities include a restaurant, TV lounge and barbecue area. Ask the staff about adventure sports such as rafting and canyoning (costing about €38 per day) and bike hire (€10 per day). The hostel is 50m from the slopes and spa.

Pension Laura (☎ 27 04; Bismarckstrasse 20; s/d €24/42; P) Opposite Nikolauskirche, this pension's rooms teeter on the old-fashioned with loads of wood panelling and gingham, but they're cosy and good value. The restaurant downstairs has a gamey menu and walls smothered in stuffed animals.

Pension Charlotte (☎ 24 26; Paracelsusstrasse 6; s/d €25/50) Hidden down a side alley, this guesthouse is run by the super-friendly Weghofer

family and their docile Great Dane, Aramis. It's a homy place with a flower garden and plenty of curios – from handcarved *Krampus* masks to chattering budgies. The bright, spotless rooms open onto balconies overlooking the forest and mountains.

Hotel Mozart (☎ 268 60; www.hotelmozart.at; Kaiser-Franz-Josef-Strasse 25; s/d 46/82; P 💻) With a name that reflects the founder's passion for Mozart melodies, this smart three-star place pushes the right buttons with professional service, a radon-rich thermal bath and sunny, spacious rooms (some have balconies). The high-ceilinged breakfast room is glammed up with polished cherry wood, chandeliers and portraits of the virtuoso.

Villa Solitude (☎ 51 01; www.villasolitude.com; Kaiser-Franz-Josef-Strasse 16; ste €150-250; P 💻) The one-time home of an Austrian countess, this 19th-century villa shelters six suites crammed with oil paintings and antiques. The intimate salon downstairs is the place to slip into your role as lord or lady of the manor beside the grand piano. Lutter & Wegner is next door (see below).

Hotel Salzburger Hof (☎ 203 70; www.salzburgerhof .com; Grillparzerstrasse 1; s/d 103/176; P 💻 🍴) This *belle époque* beauty is knocking 100, but still charms the birds from the trees with her lemon-meringue façade and lavish interior. The lobby is swanky with chandeliers and a roaring fire, while the rooms are dressed with plush fabrics and polished wood. Other pluses include a galleried piano lounge, kids' play area and a spa offering thermal baths, whirlpools and indulgent treatments.

Eating & Drinking

Bad Gastein has a generous sprinkling of restaurants, cafés and snack bars; most line up along Kaiser-Franz-Josef-Strasse and offer appetising views of the thundering Gasteiner Ache.

Mine (☎ 301 41; Grillparzerstrasse 14; snacks €3-5.50; ◷ noon-1am summer, 9am-1pm winter) Crimson walls, cushion-filled nooks and wi-fi create a hip vibe at Mine – hands-down the best spot for a quick beer or bite to eat. The snacks are scrawled on a blackboard – try the delicious tortilla wraps.

Jägerhäusl (☎ 202 54; Kaiser-Franz-Josef-Strasse 9; mains €6.50-10; ◷ lunch & dinner) A zesty lemon-and-lime paint job and arched windows give this galleried villa an avant-garde twist. The menu is packed with Austrian staples such as tender beef and smoked trout, which are served on the maple tree-shaded terrace when the sun's out.

Gastein Café (☎ 50 97; Kaiser-Franz-Josef-Strasse 4; mains €6-14; ☒ lunch & dinner) Gastein Café is popular for its enormous terrace and smorgasbord of cuisines from Austria, Italy and virtually every other country under the sun. Dishes range from salmon-and-shrimp pizza to the humorously named *Pongauer Kasnocken* (a cheesy pasta dish).

Wasserfall Pub (☎ 54 70; Kaiser-Franz-Josef-Strasse 2; mains €6-14; ☒ lunch & dinner) The name makes no secret of the fact that this no-frills pub is right opposite the falls. There are a handful of tables outside where you can drink in the view over sizeable portions of pasta and schnitzel.

Sancho (☎ 217 62; Kaiser-Franz-Josef-Strasse 1; mains €12.50-18.50; ☒ dinner) Kitsch, colourful and as lively as a Mexican jumping bean, Sancho is a flamboyant affair decked out with dangling sombreros, stuffed cockatoos and Mayan murals. The jalapeno peppers and burritos are tasty, but the sizzling steaks are the stars of the show – thick, juicy and drenched in salsa.

Lutter & Wegner (☎ 510 11; Kaiser-Franz-Josef-Strasse 16; mains €15-24; ☒ lunch & dinner Fri-Sun, dinner Tue-Thu) The fairy-tale tower setting, fusion cuisine and terrace overlooking the Gasteiner Ache make this smart restaurant at Villa Solitude a top choice. Fine wines (choose from 180 bottles) accompany flavours such as porcini risotto and creole lamb curry.

Supermarkets in town include the **Eurospar** (☎ 60 01; Böcksteiner Bundesstrasse; ☒ 8am-7pm Mon-Thu, 8am-7.30pm Fri, 7.30am-5pm Sat) south of the train station.

Getting There & Away

IC express trains trundle through Bad Gastein's station every two hours, connecting the town to points north and south including Spittal-Millstättersee (€9.90, 40 minutes), Salzburg (€12.70, 1¾ hours) and Innsbruck (€30.20, three hours). When travelling north from Bad Gastein to Bad Hofgastein, sit on the right side of the train for the best views.

If you're driving south, you'll need to use the Autoschleuse Tauernbahn (railway car-shuttle service) through the tunnel that starts at Böckstein (€18 one-way).

AROUND BAD GASTEIN

Stepping three kilometres south of Bad Gastein, you reach the unassuming village of

Böckstein, whose medieval gold mine has been reinvented as a much-celebrated health centre, the **Gasteiner Heilstollen** (Gastein Healing Gallery; ☎ 375 30; www.gasteiner-heilstollen.com; ☒ mid-Jan–late Oct). Visitors board a small train at the Gasteiner Heilstollen that chugs 2km into the depths of Radhausberg mountain, where you absorb the healing radon vapours. The trial session costs €26, while the full three-week cure will set you back €513 (includes 10 entries to the tunnel).

Seven kilometres north of Bad Gastein is the sibling spa town of **Bad Hofgastein** (858m), where the big draw is the state-of-the-art **Alpen Therme** (☎ 06432-829 30; www.alpentherme.com; Senator-Wilhelm-Wilfling-Platz 1; adult/child €19.50/12; ☒ 9am-9pm Sat-Wed, 9am-11pm Thu, 9am-10pm Fri). This mammoth spa is split into six different worlds, where experiences stretch from relaxing in radon-rich thermal baths to racing down white-knuckle flumes. The sauna village comprises brine grottos, loft saunas, red-hot Finnish saunas and an ice-cold plunge pool. For some pampering, pop over to the beauty centre offering treatments such as goat's milk wraps and silky smooth hot-chocolate massages.

Bad Gastein, Bad Hofgastein and Böckstein are linked by both bus and rail. There are two access roads to the national park (with parking spaces at each road's terminus): the toll road (€4 per car – price included in the ski pass; see opposite) to Sportgastein; and the road that turns east just south of Bad Gastein and follows the Kötschachtal.

LIENZ

☎ 04852 / pop 13,000 / elev 673m

With the jagged Dolomites on its doorstep, Lienz dishes up Italian charm around its cobbled centre, where chirpy locals kick back with *gelato* (ice cream) in the palm-studded square. Just 40km north of Italy, this snippet of East Tyrol expertly blends big wilderness with cultural clout: the glacial Isel River, Roman treasures and a medieval castle brimming with art are all there for the savouring. But it's the mountains that really demand attention – austere beauties piercing the town's southern skyline and looking their best when the last of the sun makes their pinnacles blush.

Orientation

The town centre is within a 'V' formed by the junction of the rivers Isel and Drau. The pivotal Hauptplatz is directly in front of the train station; three other squares lead from it

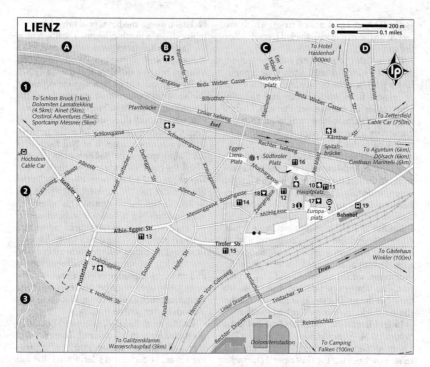

LIENZ

To Hotel Haidenhof (500m)
To Schloss Bruck (1km); Dolomiten Lamatrekking (4.5km); Ainet (5km); Osttirol Adventures (5km); Sportcamp Messner (5km)
To Zettersfeld Cable Car (750m)
Hochstein Cable Car
To Aguntum (6km); Dölsach (6km); Gasthaus Marinelli (6km)
To Gästehaus Winkler (100m)
To Galitzenklamm Wasserschaupfad (3km)
To Camping Falken (100m)
Dolomitenstadion

(Europaplatz, Südtiroler Platz and Bozener Platz). Hauptplatz has lots of parking in its *Kurzparkzone*, with a 90-minute limit during indicated hours.

Information

The Osttirol Card, available from the tourist office, gives free access to cable cars, pools and museums. It costs €35/17.50 per adult/child for eight days and is valid from June to September.

Library (☎ 639 72; Muchargasse 4; ✆ 9am-noon & 3-7pm Tue & Thur, 9am-1pm & 3-6pm Wed & Fri, 9am-noon Sat) Free internet access at four terminals.

Osttirol Werbung (☎ 653 33; www.osttirol.com) For information about the wider East Tyrol area. The office sends out information, but isn't set up for visits.

Post office (Bozener Platz 1; ✆ 7.30am-6.30pm Mon-Fri, 8-11am Sat) Opposite the train station.

Tourist office (☎ 652 65; www.lienz-tourismus.at; Europaplatz 1; ✆ 8am-6pm Mon-Fri, 9am-noon & 5-7pm Sat Jul–mid-Sep, 10-noon Sun Jul & Aug) Staff will help you find accommodation (even private rooms) free of charge.

Sights

STADTPFARRKIRCHE ST ANDRÄ

A Gothic gem just north of the Isel River, **Stadtpfarrkirche St Andrä** (St Andrew's church; ☎ 621 60; Pfarrgasse 4; ✆ daylight hr) is a quiet spot for contemplation. Peer inside the rib-vaulted interior to see 14th-century frescoes and a pair of tombstones sculpted in red Salzburg marble. Its hidden gem is the solemn **Kriegergedächtniskapelle** (war memorial chapel) sheltering Albin Egger-Lienz's eye-catching sculpture of Jesus in nought but a skimpy loin cloth, which scandalised the Vatican when it was unveiled to the public in 1925. To visit the chapel, pick up the key that hangs on the door at Pfarrgasse 13 (across the bridge facing the main entrance).

SCHLOSS BRUCK

Lienz's biggest stunner is this medieval fortress situated slightly west of town. Once the seat of the counts of Görtz, the hilltop castle now houses the **Heimatmuseum** (☎ 625 80; Schlossberg 1; adult/child €7/2.50; ☺ 10am-6pm Palm Sunday-1 Nov), which chronologically runs through Tyrol's heritage in its atmospheric rooms, displaying everything from oil paintings to Cold War memorabilia. The tower rotates exhibitions of avant-garde works and is worth climbing for exhilarating views over Lienz. The real highlight, however, is the sprawling gallery devoted to the emotive works of Albin Egger-Lienz (1868–1926), whose brushstrokes reveal recurring themes of toil, conflict and death. Among his masterpieces are the *Totentanz* (Dance of Death) and *Das Kreuz* (The Cross). When asked what he was working on shortly before he died in 1926, the artist bluntly replied '*Ich bin fertig*' (I have finished).

AGUNTUM

This **Roman archaeological site** (☎ 615 50; www .aguntum.info; Stribach 97; adult/child €5/3; ☺ 9.30am-4pm Apr–May & mid-Sep–Oct, 9.30am-6pm Jun–mid-Sep), with an ultramodern museum to boot, is unique in these parts. Excavations are still under way to piece together the jigsaw puzzle of this 2000-year-old *municipium*, which flourished as a centre of trade and commerce under Emperor Claudius. Take a stroll outside to glimpse the Roman spa, artisan quarter and a reconstructed villa. The glass-walled museum explores Lienz's Roman roots in greater depth, with interactive stuff for the kids (a virtual tour through Aguntum and dress-up costumes) and an exhibition featuring fun elements such as traditional Roman recipes. Sow's udder with sea urchins, anyone?

Activities

SKIING

The skiing in Lienz is geared mainly towards beginners and intermediates, with just a handful of knee-trembling black runs. Its downhill offer is not huge by Austrian standards, but the views of the rugged Dolomites are awesome. Most of the action takes place around **Zettersfeld**, where a cable car and five lifts whizz skiers up to slopes reaching between 1660m and 2278m. Slightly west of Lienz, **Hochstein** (2057m) is also popular for its groomed pistes; a free bus runs from the train station to the cable-car valley stations in summer and winter high seasons. One-day ski passes for both mountains cost €28.50 and the ski lifts run from 1 December to Easter, depending on snow. Multiday passes (eg two days for €70) cover all of East Tyrol's ski lifts (see www .topski.at, in German, for full ski-pass details). Several peaceful cross-country trails also crisscross the valley. Ski hire (from various outlets in town) starts at €20 per day, including boots, while cross-country equipment will set you back around €10.

WALKING

The tourist office can advise on the high-altitude trails that wriggle around the steely peaks of the Dolomites. For something more family-oriented, check out the **Galitzenklamm Wasserschaupfad** (☎ 0664-1567 457; adult/child €3/2; ☺ 9am-6pm Jul & Aug, 10am-5pm Jun & Sep, 10am-5pm Sat & Sun May & Oct, closed winter), a specially built walkway that clings to sheer cliffs above the gorge of the Drau. To get there, head for Leisach, 3km from Lienz.

You'd be forgiven for thinking you were in the Andes when on a trek with Karl-Peter, who runs **Dolomiten Lamatrekking** (☎ 680 87; www .dolomitenlama.at; Oberlienz 36; 2hr trek €30; ☺ year-round) and is a dab hand at getting those stubborn llamas to walk his way. The llamas obligingly lug the heavy packs, leaving walkers free to enjoy the stunning Hohe Tauern scenery. Tours take place come snow or shine and stretch from two-hour taster sessions to four-day uphill hikes.

The cable cars spring back to life for the summer season (June to September). The ride up to Hochstein costs €11 return, while Zettersfeld costs €10, or €17 including the chairlift to 2214m. Family and child fares are also available. If you're planning on making more than one trip, it makes sense to buy the Osttirol

Card. Both lifts are run by **Lienzer Bergbahnen** (☎ 639 75; Zettersfeldstrasse 38).

CYCLING

A network of mountain-bike trails radiates from Lienz, taking in the striking landscape of the Dolomites. Ask the tourist office for the map *Rad und Mountainbike Karte Osttirol*, which details cycling routes. **Probike Lienz** (☎ 735 36; Amlacherstrasse 1a; half-/full-day €13/18; ☽ 9am-noon & 2-6pm Mon-Fri, 9am-noon Sat) is the most central place to hire your own set of wheels.

ADVENTURE SPORTS

The foaming rivers, narrow gorges and pine forests of the Dolomites around Lienz are the perfect place for adrenaline-pumping sports such as white-water rafting, canyoning, rock climbing and kayaking. The following two companies, both based in the village of Ainet near Lienz, will set you up: **Osttirol Adventures** (☎ 0664-356 0450; www.osttirol -adventures.at) and **Sportcamp Messner** (☎ 0664-897 8259; www.raftcompany.at).

Festivals & Events

Lienz hosts the testosterone-fuelled **Dolomiten Mann** (www.dolomitenmann.com) in September, a Red Bull–sponsored iron-man competition billed as the world's toughest team challenge. Headlining the programme is the cross-country relay race, where teams of mountain-runners, paragliders, kayakers and mountain-bikers battle it out for the title. Lively open-air concerts and parties complement the line-up.

In late July, a free street festival takes the centre by storm, drawing top circus and theatre acts from around the world. Summer also welcomes a series of events celebrating Tyrolean culture, plus free concerts on Hauptplatz and in other squares (8pm on Wednesdays and Sundays June to September).

Sleeping

For a town of its size, Lienz has oodles of decent hotels, pensions and campsites. The tourist office will help you trawl through them and hands out a free brochure listing inexpensive private rooms; expect to pay around €15 to €20 per person per night. Wherever you stay, ask your host for the *Gästekarte* to receive discounts on local sights and transport.

BUDGET

Camping Falken (☎ 640 22; camping.falken@tirol.com; Eichholz 7; campsites per adult/child/tent €6.50/4/8.50; ☽ mid-Dec–late Oct; ℗ ▣) Pitch a tent beneath the apple trees at this camping ground 10 minutes' walk from the centre. The first-rate facilities include a minimarket, restaurant and playground, plus free access to Lienz swimming pools.

Gästehaus Masnata (☎ 655 36; Drahtzuggasse 4; d €38; ℗) Maria runs this little chalet with *Liebe* (love) and speaks good English. There's enough space to swing several well-fed moggies in the modern, balconied rooms. Rates don't include breakfast, but you can make a cuppa or snack in the kitchen. This place fills up quickly, so book ahead in high season.

Gästehaus Winkler (☎ 705 18; Roter Turmweg 5; s/d €19.50/39; ℗) Handy for the cycling and cross-country trails that are on its doorstep, this convivial pension on the town's southern fringes has eight comfy rooms. There's a well-kept garden, playground and ski storage room.

Goldener Stern (☎ 621 92; Schweizergasse 40; s/d €34/62; ℗ ✗) Framed by neat gardens, this 600-year-old guesthouse with bright, spacious rooms makes a great base for exploring Lienz. Breakfast is served in the pocket-sized courtyard in summer. Cheaper rooms with shared bathrooms are also available.

MIDRANGE & TOP END

Altstadthotel Eck (☎ 647 85; altstadthotel.eck@utanet .at; Hauptplatz 20; s/d €42/74) It's not quite as plush as its neighbour, Hotel Traube, but this hotel still exudes old-world charisma with its grandfather clock and wood-panelled corridors smothered in oil paintings. The good-value rooms have tea-making facilities. Guests can soak up Lienz views over brekkie in the conservatory.

Goldener Fisch (☎ 621 32; www.goldener-fisch.at; Kärntnerstrasse 9; s/d €45/88; ℗ ▣) The beer garden shaded by chestnut trees is a big draw at this family-run hotel. The Goldener Fisch offers contemporary rooms kitted out with mod cons such as wi-fi and satellite TV. Other pluses include the sauna and cosy restaurant (mains €5 to €17), which dishes up a mean *Tafelspitz* (boiled beef with apple and horseradish sauce).

our pick **Hotel Haidenhof** (☎ 624 40; www.haid enhof.at; Grafendorferstrasse 12; s/d €61/110; ℗ ▣) Perched above Lienz, this retreat oozes country charm. Fringed by pear and plum orchards, Haidenhof is where rustic farmhouse meets 21st-century chic. Rooms are understated yet elegant, with plenty of natural light and honey pine. After steaming in the sauna, the roof terrace is a fine place to curl up in a blanket and enjoy the vista of the Dolomites. In the South Tyrolean–style restaurant (mains €7 to €20), nearly everything that lands on your plate is home-grown: the herbs, the trout and even the apples in the strudel!

Hotel Traube (☎ 644 44; www.hoteltraube.at; Hauptplatz 14; s/d €82/124; **P ⌨ ☒**) This green-shuttered hotel on the main square has bags of charm; it catapults you back to the Biedermeier era with its high ceilings, polished antiques and wrought-iron balconies. The 6th-floor pool is a calm oasis overlooking Lienz's spires and the brooding Dolomites.

Eating

Italy is but a hop and skip away from Lienz and it shows: menus are often a double whammy of Tyrolean and Italian fare. When the sun shines, the Hauptplatz fills with the hum of chatter as locals spill from pavement cafés.

Hendl Ortner (☎ 623 91; Albin-Egger-Strasse 5; chickens €2.60; ☽ lunch & dinner, closed Jan-Apr) The tasty rotisserie *Hendl* (half-chickens) sprinkled with spices make this one of the best fast-food joints in town, but you're pretty stuffed if you don't like chicken.

Gasthaus Marinelli (☎ 682 08; Dölsach 78, Dölsach; mains €5-10; ☽ lunch & dinner Thu-Tue) Locals rave about the home-cooked local food at this tiny restaurant in the schnapps-making village of Dölsach, just outside Lienz. It's best to reserve in advance.

Pizzeria Da Franco (☎ 699 69; Ägidius-Pegger-Strasse; pizzas €6-9; ☽ lunch & dinner) This hole-in-the-wall pizzeria isn't plush, but the thin, crisp pizzas baked in a brick oven do Italy proud. Top that with cheery staff and pocket-pleasing prices and you're onto a winner.

Adlerstüberl Restaurant (☎ 625 50; Andrä-Kranz-Gasse 7; mains €7.50-13.50; ☽ lunch & dinner) Adlerstüberl is the grandaddy of Lienz, where grizzled locals put the world to rights over beer, humungous schnitzels and plates of piping goulash. Find a cosy nook in one of the vaulted rooms and join them.

Spice Tapas Bar (☎ 634 73; Südtirolerplatz 2; mixed tapas plate €8-10; ☽ dinner Wed-Mon) A slither of Seville in the Dolomites, this funky tapas bar has a menu full of the usual suspects (Serrano ham and chewy chorizo), plus a few wild cards such as kangaroo fillets and wild salmon in champagne froth. Grab a table outside to soak up the atmosphere.

La Taverna (☎ 647 85; Hauptplatz 14; mains €8.50-16; ☽ lunch & dinner, closed Mon) A staircase twists down to this wood-panelled taverna in the bowels of Hotel Traube. Chefs whip up Italian and Tyrolean flavours in the show kitchen (try the rocket tagliatelle). The resident Bacchus gives an indication of the mind-boggling wine list – there are 800 bottles to choose from.

For self-caterers, supermarkets include an **ADEG** (Hauptplatz 12) and a **Spar** (Tiroler Strasse 23).

Drinking

Lienz tempts the night-active with a pick' n'mix of relaxed drinking holes and quirky lounge bars; most places huddle around the pedestrianised square.

Petrocelli's (☎ 643 64-44; Hauptplatz 9; ☽ 8am-midnight) The bustling terrace on the square is the crowd-puller at this ice-cream parlour, which doubles as a trendy bar in the evenings. Tuned-in locals come to sip caipirinhas and indulge in people-watching.

Joy (Hauptplatz 9; ☎ 672 22; ☽ 10pm-4am Thu-Sat) Venture downstairs from Petrocelli's to Joy, a party haunt where DJs spin dance music till the wee hours.

s'Stöckl (☎ 640 70; Zwergergasse 2; ☽ 6pm-2am Mon-Fri, 8pm-2am Sat) There are no airs and graces about this spit-and-sawdust watering hole – a fine spot for Gösser brews and long chats at the bar. Cocktails are a bargain €3.50 during happy hour (8pm to 11pm).

our pick **Deep Blue** (☎ 644 440; Hauptplatz 14; ☽ 5pm-2am) Stepping down to this wacky lounge bar is like plunging to the bottom of the ocean. It houses the kind of aquarium (apparently it's Tyrol's biggest) that even Nemo would gladly sacrifice the sea for. Dangling fish and lanterns continue the aquatic theme. The cocktail-master also knows how to shake 'em (for something with a kick, try a Moscow Mule) but beware – one too many and you'll almost certainly see the room swim.

Getting There & Away

Regional transport in Tyrol comes under the wing of the **Verkehrsverbund Tirol** (VVT; www.vvt.at). For information on VVT transport tickets, valid for travel between Tyrol and East Tyrol, see p331.

BUS

Buses pull up in front of the train station, where the **Postbus information office** (☻ 8am-noon & 2-4pm Mon-Fri) is located. There are bus connections to the East Tyrol ski resorts of St Jakob, Sillian and Obertilliach, as well as northwards to the Hohe Tauern National Park. Buses to Kitzbühel (€13.20, 1½ hours) are quicker and more direct than the train, but they only go one to three times a day.

TRAIN

Most trains to the rest of Austria, including Salzburg (€30.20, 3½ hours), go east via Spittal-Millstättersee, where you usually have to change. The quickest and easiest route to Innsbruck (€20, 3¼ hours) is to go west via Sillian and Italy.

CAR & MOTORCYCLE

To head south, you must first divert west or east along Hwy 100, as the Dolomites are an impregnable barrier. For details of road routes to the north, see p312.

Tyrol

If you could bottle everything that sums up Austria surely Tyrol would be it: from the woodsy log chalets and wholesome food to the thigh-slapping tradition and alpine peaks rising like shark fins in a frothy white ocean. Few places can match it on a winter's day, with a big sky above, dazzling snow crunching underfoot and bracing mountain air filling your lungs. No wonder the locals are notoriously proud and independent. Who wouldn't be with all that?

There are plenty of reasons to fall for Tyrol: the people are down-to-earth, sincere and marvellously eccentric; the cities such as Innsbruck and Kufstein are gems (overshadowed by frosty mountains and complete with precipitous castles and medieval backstreets); the schnapps is potent; the powder deep; and the culture a happy marriage of old and new – shifting from rural farms and cobbled alleyways to Zen-like spas and crystalline edifices.

But it's the Alps that steal the show in a 'wow I'm in Austria' kind of way and nowhere else are they more prominent or accessible. Tyrol is a beauty with bumps and curves in all the right places, with resorts like Kitzbühel where you can find your ski legs, Mayrhofen where they'll turn to jelly on black runs, and St Anton where you can get legless in après-ski bars before wobbling down the valley. When sunshine spills across the green vales in summer, walks stretch from gentle strolls to week-long tramps over windswept passes where, with any luck, you might spot an eagle: Tyrol's most famous yet elusive high-flyer.

Tyrol's eastern region, Osttirol (East Tyrol), is cut off from the rest of the province by Salzburg and is covered in the Hohe Tauern National Park Region chapter (p323).

HIGHLIGHTS

- Strolling cobbled lanes to gaze upon the shimmering **Goldenes Dachl** (p337) in Innsbruck

- Quaking in your boots before hurtling down Austria's steepest slope, the **Harakiri** (p348) in Mayrhofen

- Rising above **Kufstein** (p354) in a rickety chairlift for awesome Wilder Kaiser views

- Revisiting the Neolithic world of Ötzi and soaking in Aqua Dome's flying saucers in the **Ötztal** (p356)

- Bopping in your snow boots to Europop with the après-ski crowd in **St Anton am Arlberg** (p362)

★ Kufstein

Innsbruck ★

St Anton
★ am Arlberg   Mayrhofen ★

Ötztal Valley ★

TYROL

| ▪ POPULATION: 685,000 | ▪ AREA: 10,626 SQ KM | ▪ HIGHEST ELEVATION: WILDSPITZE 3774M |

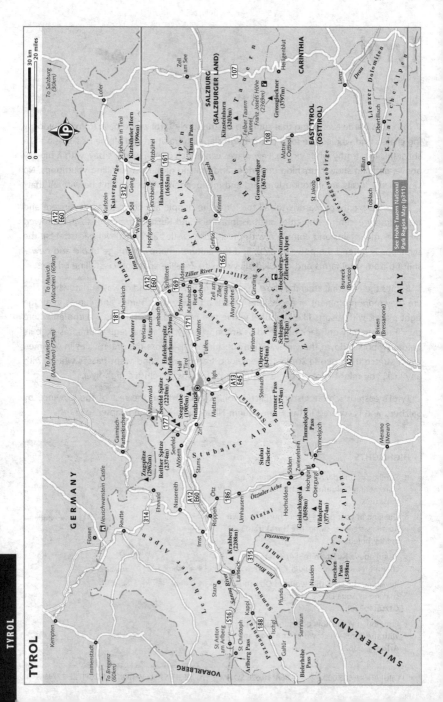

History

Despite its difficult alpine terrain, Tyrol has experienced influxes of tribes and travellers since the Iron Age, verified by the discovery of a 5500-year-old body of a man preserved in ice in the Ötztal Alps in 1991 (see boxed text, p357). The high Brenner Pass (1374m), crossing into Italy, allowed the region to develop as a north–south trade route early in its history.

Tyrol fell to the Habsburgs in 1363, but it wasn't until the rule of Emperor Maximilian I (r 1490–1519) that the province truly forged ahead. His soft spot for Innsbruck boosted the region's status and transformed the town into the administrative capital and a cultural centre. He also drew up the Landibell legislation in 1511 that passed the border defence over to the Tyroleans themselves, thus creating the celebrated *Schützen* (marksmen militia) which still exists today. When the last Tyrolean Habsburg, Archduke Sigmund Franz, died in 1665 the duchy of Tyrol was directly ruled from Vienna.

In 1703 the Bavarians attempted to capture Tyrol in the War of the Spanish Succession. In alliance with the French, they reached the Brenner Pass before being beaten back by the *Schützen*. But just a century later Tyrol passed into Bavarian hands under Napoleon. Bavarian rule of the province was short-lived and troublesome; in 1809 local innkeeper Andreas Hofer led a successful fight for independence, winning a famous victory at Bergisel (p336). The Habsburg monarchy unfortunately did not support his heroic stance and Tyrol was returned to Bavaria later that year. Hofer continued the struggle, and was shot by firing squad on Napoleon's orders on 20 February 1810.

The Treaty of St Germain (1919) dealt a further blow to the strong Tyrolean identity; prosperous South Tyrol was ceded to Italy and East Tyrol was isolated from the rest of the province.

A staunch ally of Mussolini, Hitler did not claim back South Tyrol when his troops invaded Austria in 1938. In the aftermath of WWII, Tyrol was divided into zones occupied by Allied forces until the country proclaimed its neutrality in 1955. Since then, Tyrol has enjoyed peace and prosperity: tourism (particularly the ski industry) has flourished and Innsbruck has twice hosted the Winter Olympics.

In 2008, all eyes are once again focused on the Tyrolean capital, as it gears up for the UEFA Euro Championships.

Climate

With almost 90% of Tyrol given over to mountains, the Alps rule much of the province's climate, with short summers, long cold winters and changeable weather. In the valleys the temperatures are surprisingly mild, helped no end by the *Föhn,* a warm south wind that sweeps down from the mountains.

Getting There & Away

Frequent international and national flights operate to Innsbruck. The main road and rail route in and out of Tyrol follows the Inntal (Inn River), with the east–west A12 autobahn cutting the province into almost equal halves, entering from Germany near Kufstein and exiting west of St Anton in Vorarlberg. The A13 connects Tyrol with Italy, crossing the Brenner Pass directly south of Innsbruck.

Getting Around

Regional transport comes under the wing of the **Verkehrsverbund Tirol** (☎ 0512-561 616; www .vvt.at; Innrain 25, Innsbruck; ☽ 8am-5pm Mon-Thu, 8am-noon Fri). Ticket prices depend on the number of zones you travel through; a single ticket costs €1.70 and it's €3.40 for a day pass. There are reductions for children, senior citizens and families. Tickets cover journeys on buses, trams and ÖBB (Austrian federal railway) trains.

Additionally, Tyrol is divided into 12 overlapping transport regions, which are individually covered by *Regio Ticket* (regional passes). A pass for individual regions costs €29/91.80 per week/month or €61/196.10 for all 12 regions. Innsbruck is an exception; see p343.

INNSBRUCK

☎ 0512 / pop 117,000

Tyrol's capital is a chameleon-like city: a place where you can spend the morning roaming medieval lanes and Habsburg palaces, and the afternoon ogling Zaha Hadid's spacey creations and sipping sundowners in riverside lounge bars. With its low-slung skyline, quietly confident air and the towering Alps as a backdrop, Innsbruck successfully blends past and present, urban and natural. Despite its prosperity and world-class museums, the city remains refreshingly unpretentious and friendly.

Suspended above the deep-green Inn River, the Alps are Innsbruck's monumental attractions: creeping up on street corners, reflecting in glass façades and sneaking into every snapshot. And this old man of the mountain still knows how to rock; home to Austria's third-largest student population, Innsbruck is a youthful city that pulsates in brewpubs, beer gardens and funky bars after dark. Providing you don't overindulge on the *Nachtleben* (nightlife), you'll have energy to whoosh down Nordpark's slopes or pick up supersonic speeds on Igls' bobsled run.

History

Innsbruck dates from 1180, when the little market settlement on the north bank of the Inn River spread to the south bank via a new bridge that gave the settlement its name – Ynsprugg.

In 1420 Innsbruck became the ducal seat of the Tyrolean Habsburgs, but it was under the reign of Emperor Maximilian I (r 1490–1519) that the city reached its zenith in power and prestige; many of the monuments, including the shimmering Goldenes Dachl (p337), are still visible today. Maximilian was not the only Habsburg to influence the city's architectural skyline: Archduke Ferdinand II reconstructed the Schloss Ambras (p335) and Empress Maria Theresia the Hofburg (p334).

Aside from the two world wars, Innsbruck has enjoyed a fairly peaceful existence over the centuries. More recently, its importance as a winter sports centre reached the international stage – it held the Winter Olympics in 1964 and 1976.

Orientation

Innsbruck sits in the Inn Valley, scenically squeezed between the northern Karwendel Alps and the southern Tuxer Vorberge mountains. Extensive mountain transport facilities radiating from the city provide superb walking and skiing opportunities. The centre is compact, with the *Hauptbahnhof* (main train station) just a 10-minute walk from the pedestrianed *Altstadt* (old town). The main artery in the *Altstadt*, Herzog-Friedrich-Strasse, connects with Maria-Theresien-Strasse, which is a major thoroughfare but is closed to private transport.

Information

BOOKSHOPS
The best source of international papers can be found at a handy newspaper stand on the corner of Riesengasse and Herzog-Friedrich-Strasse (Map p334).

Freytag & Berndt (Map p333; ☎ 572 430; Wilhelm-Greil-Strasse 15; ◷ 9am-1pm & 2-6pm Mon-Fri, 9am-noon Sat) Excellent source for maps and travel books.

Tyrolia (Map p334; ☎ 22 33-0; Maria-Theresien-Strasse 15) Stocks travel guidebooks and a decent selection of English literature.

Wagnerische Buchhandlung (Map p334; ☎ 595 05; Museumstrasse 4) University bookshop with a sizeable collection of English books.

INTERNET ACCESS
International Telephone Discount (Map p333; ☎ 562 921; Südtirolerplatz 1; per hr €2.50; ◷ 9am-11pm) Cheap phone calls as well.

Telesystem (Map p333; ☎ 931 093; Rathaus Galerien; ◷ 8am-6pm Mon-Fri, 8am-5pm Sat) Eight terminals with free internet access.

LAUNDRY
Bubble Point (☎ 56500-0750; soap & wash €4; ◷ 8am-10pm Mon-Fri, 8am-8pm Sat & Sun; ▣)
Andreas Hofer (Map p333; Andreas-Hofer-Strasse 37); Brixner (Map p333; Brixner Strasse 1) Self-service laundries with internet access for €6 per hour.

MEDICAL SERVICES
Landeskrankenhaus (Map p333; ☎ 50 40; Anichstrasse 35) The *Universitätklinik* (University Clinic) at the city's main hospital has emergency services.

MONEY
The *Hauptbahnhof* and Innsbruck Information have exchange facilities and *Bankomaten* (ATMs) are ubiquitous in the *Altstadt*.

POST
Main post office (Map p333; Maximilianstrasse 2; ◷ 7am-9pm Mon-Fri, 7am-3pm Sat, 10am-7.30pm Sun)
Post office (Map p333; Brunecker Strasse 1; ◷ 7am-5pm Mon-Fri) This second post office is handy to the *Hauptbahnhof*.

TOURIST INFORMATION
City Tourist Board (Map p334; ☎ 59 85-0; www .innsbruck.info; Burggraben 3; ◷ 8am-6pm Mon-Fri) Above Innsbruck Information, it mostly fields telephone inquiries.
Hauptbahnhof (Map p333; ☎ 583 766; ◷ 9am-7pm) Smaller office in the main train station.

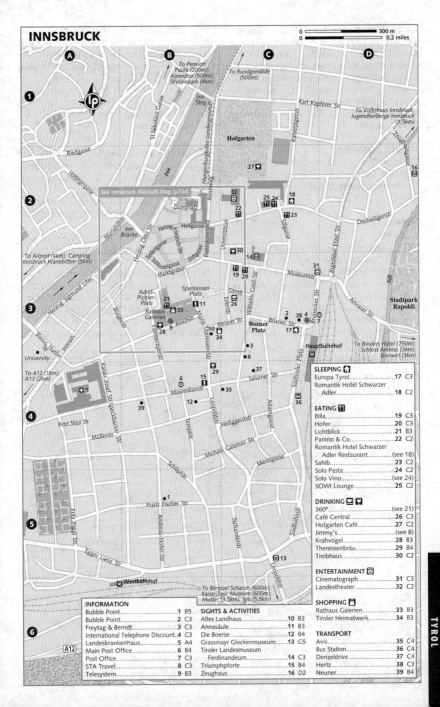

INNSBRUCK

0 — 300 m
0 — 0.2 miles

To Pension
Paula (200m);
Alpenzoo (500m);
Skylinepark (4km)

To Rundgemälde
(500m);

To Volkshaus Innsbruck;
Jugendherberge Innsbruck
(1.5km)

Hofgarten

See Innsbruck Aldstadt Map (p334)

To Airport (4km); Camping
Innsbruck Kranebitten (5km)

Stadtpark
Rapoldi

Bozner
Platz

Hauptbahnhof

To Binders Hotel (750m);
Schloss Ambras (3km);
Bierwirt (3km)

University

To A12 (1km);
A13 (2km)

To Bergisel Schanze (600m);
Kaiserjäger Museum (600m);
Mutter (3.5km); Igls (5.5km)

Westbahnhof

SLEEPING 🏠
Europa Tyrol...........................17 C3
Romantik Hotel Schwarzer
    Adler....................................18 C2

EATING 🍴
Billa.....................................19 C3
Hofer....................................20 C3
Lichtblick...............................21 B3
Panino & Co............................22 C2
Romantik Hotel Schwarzer
    Adler Restaurant...........(see 18)
Sahib....................................23 C2
Solo Pasta.............................24 C2
Solo Vino..........................(see 24)
SOWI Lounge..........................25 C2

DRINKING 🍷 🍸
360°..............................(see 21)
Café Central.........................26 C3
Hofgarten Café.......................27 C2
Jimmy's...........................(see 8)
Krahvogel...........................28 B3
Thereisienbräu.......................29 B4
Treibhaus............................30 C2

ENTERTAINMENT 🎭
Cinematograph.......................31 C3
Landestheater........................32 C2

SHOPPING 🛍
Rathaus Galerien.....................33 B3
Tiroler Heimatwerk...................34 B3

TRANSPORT
Avis.....................................35 C4
Bus Station............................36 C4
Denzeldrive............................37 C3
Hertz....................................38 C3
Neuner..................................39 B4

INFORMATION
Bubble Point................................1 B5
Bubble Point................................2 C3
Freytag & Berndt............................3 C3
International Telephone Discount.4 C3
Landeskrankenhaus.....................5 A4
Main Post Office...........................6 B4
Post Office....................................7 C3
STA Travel.....................................8 C3
Telesystem...................................9 B3

SIGHTS & ACTIVITIES
Altes Landhaus.............................10 B3
Annasäule.....................................11 B3
Die Boerse....................................12 B4
Grassmayr Glockenmuseum.........13 C5
Tiroler Landesmuseum
    Ferdinandeum............................14 C3
Triumphpforte...............................15 B3
Zeughaus......................................16 D2

TYROL

Innsbruck Information (Map p334; ☎ 53 56; www
.innsbruck.info; Burggraben 3; ⏰ 9am-6pm Apr-Oct,
8am-6pm Nov-Mar) Main tourist office with truckloads
of info on the city and surrounds, including skiing and
walking. Sells ski passes, public-transport tickets and city
maps (€1); will book accommodation (€3 commission); has
an attached ticketing service (open 9am to 6pm Monday to
Friday, and 9am to noon Saturday); and has internet access
(€1 for 10 minutes).

TRAVEL AGENCIES

STA Travel (Map p333; ☎ 588 997; innsbruck@statravel
.at; Wilhelm-Greil-Strasse 17; ⏰ 9am-6pm Mon-Fri)
Friendly student-focused travel agency with occasional
specials.

Sights
HOFBURG

Demanding attention with its lavish façade
and cupolas, the **Hofburg** (Imperial Palace; Map p334;
☎ 587 186; Rennweg 1; adult/student/child €5.50/4/1.10;
⏰ 9am-5pm) was one of Maria Theresia's favourites; though it's barely a rabbit hutch
when compared with her other home,
Schloss Schönbrunn in Vienna (p135). The
state apartments are a rococo feast, adorned

with gold swirls and chandeliers, but the
real eye-catcher is the 31m-long **Riesensaal**
(Giant's Hall). The hall is embellished with
frescoes and paintings of Maria Theresia
and her 16 children (including Marie
Antoinette), who look strangely identical –
maybe the artist was intent on avoiding
royal wrath arising from sibling rivalry in
the beauty stakes.

HOFKIRCHE & VOLKSKUNST MUSEUM

Both the following attractions are accessed
from Universitätstrasse 2, share the same
opening times and can be visited with a
combined ticket available from the **ticket office** (☎ 584 302; adult/child €6.50/3; ⏰ 9am-5pm Mon-
Sat, 10am-5pm Sun).

Opposite the Hofburg is the majestic
Hofkirche (Imperial Church; Map p334; adult/child €3/1.50),
which shelters the empty sarcophagus of
Emperor Maximilian I. Elaborately carved
from marble, the tomb is one of the finest
examples of German Renaissance sculpture.
The twin rows of 28 giant bronze figures
that flank the sarcophagus include Albrecht
Dürer's statue of the legendary King Arthur,

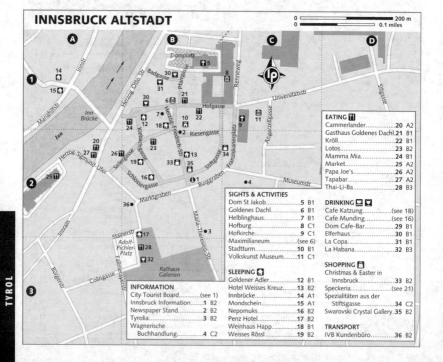

INNSBRUCK ALTSTADT

SIGHTS & ACTIVITIES	
Dom St Jakob	5 B1
Goldenes Dachl	6 B1
Helblinghaus	7 B1
Hofburg	8 C1
Hofkirche	9 C1
Maximilianeum	(see 6)
Stadtturm	10 B1
Volkskunst Museum	11 C1

SLEEPING	
Goldener Adler	12 B1
Hotel Weisses Kreuz	13 B2
Innbrücke	14 A1
Mondschein	15 A1
Nepomuks	16 B2
Penz Hotel	17 B2
Weinhaus Happ	18 B1
Weisses Rössl	19 B2

EATING	
Cammerlander	20 A2
Gasthaus Goldenes Dachl	21 B1
Kröll	22 B1
Lotos	23 B2
Mamma Mia	24 B1
Market	25 A2
Papa Joe's	26 A2
Tapabar	27 A2
Thai-Li-Ba	28 B3

DRINKING	
Cafe Katzung	(see 18)
Cafe Munding	(see 16)
Dom Cafe-Bar	29 B1
Elferhaus	30 B1
La Copa	31 B1
La Habana	32 B3

SHOPPING	
Christmas & Easter in Innsbruck	33 B2
Speckeria	(see 21)
Spezialitäten aus der Stiftsgasse	34 C2
Swarovski Crystal Gallery	35 B2

TRANSPORT	
IVB Kundenbüro	36 B2

INFORMATION	
City Tourist Board	(see 1)
Innsbruck Information	1 B2
Newspaper Stand	2 B2
Tyrolia	3 B2
Wagnerische Buchhandlung	4 C2

apparently Maximilian's biggest idol. Tyrolean hero Andreas Hofer (1767–1810) is also entombed in the church.

For an insight into Tyrolean craftwork, nip into the **Volkskunst Museum** (Folk Art Museum; Map p334; adult/child €5/1.50) next door. This rambling attic of a museum covers the entire spectrum of folk art, from handcarved sleighs and Christmas cribs to carnival masks and cow bells. On the 1st floor is the Gothic *Stube* (living room) complete with low-ceiling, wood panelling and antique tiled oven.

TIROLER LANDESMUSEUM FERDINANDEUM

A treasure-trove of Tyrolean history and art, this **museum** (Map p333; ☎ 594 89; www.tiroler-landes museum.at, in German; Museumstrasse 15; adult/child €8/4; ☯ 10am-6pm Jun-Sep, closed Mon Oct-May) showcases everything from Bronze Age finds to religious works and pewter creations. Highlights include brooding Dutch and Flemish masterpieces, Gothic altarpieces and famous paintings from the likes of Klimt and Kokoschka (see p52).

ZEUGHAUS

Emperor Maximilian's former arsenal, the **Zeughaus** (Map p333; ☎ 594 89-311; Zeughausgasse; adult/child €8/4; ☯ 10am-5pm Jun-Sep, closed Mon Oct-May) runs chronologically through Tyrol's cultural history. It kicks off with geological and mineral history, including the silver that made Hall and Schwaz medieval powerhouses, but mostly concentrates on Tyrol's much-loved historical figure, Andreas Hofer.

If you're a fan of Tyrolean music, check out the room housing over 100 CDs from the province's musical stars.

SCHLOSS AMBRAS

Perched dramatically above the centre, the city's biggest stunner is **Schloss Ambras** (off Map p333; ☎ 01-525 24-4802; Schlossstrasse 20; adult/student/family €4.50/3/6 Dec-Mar, €8/6/16 Apr-Oct, guided tours €2; ☯ 10am-5pm Dec-Jul, Sep & Oct, 10am-7pm Aug, closed Nov). Archduke Ferdinand II acquired the castle in 1564, the year he became ruler of Tyrol, and transformed it from a fortress into a palace. He was the mastermind behind the **Spanische Saal** (Spanish Hall), a 43m-long banquet hall with a wooden inlaid ceiling and Tyrolean nobles gazing from the walls. Also note the *grisaille* (grey relief) around the courtyard and the sunken bathtub where his beloved Philippine used to bathe.

Ferdinand instigated the magnificent Ambras Collection, encompassing three main elements. The **Rüstkammer** (Armour Collection) features intriguing pieces such as the armour for the archduke's second wedding – specially shaped to fit his protruding belly! – and the 2.60m suit created for giant Bartlmä Bon. The **Kunst und Wunderkammer** (Art and Wonders Collection) is crammed with fantastical objects, including a petrified shark, gravity-defying stilt shoes and the *Fangstuhl* – a chair designed to trap drunken guests at Ferdinand's raucous parties.

The **Portraitgalerie** features room upon room of Habsburg portraits. Portrait No 158 (Room 10) features a whiskered Charles VIII masquerading as a peasant while wearing a hat masquerading as an armchair. Maria Anna of Spain (No 126, Room 22) wins the prize for the most ludicrous hairstyle. When portraits of Habsburgs begin to pall, you can stroll or picnic in the extensive **castle gardens** (admission free; ☯ 6am-8pm), home to strutting peacocks.

Guided tours are available, but English tours must be reserved. Entry is cheaper in winter as some parts of the castle are closed. To get there take tram 6 or bus K.

GRASSMAYR GLOCKENMUSEUM

If you're heading for Bergisel, listen out for the bells at **Grassmayr Glockenmuseum** (Bell Museum; Map p333; ☎ 594 16-0; Leopoldstrasse 53; adult/child €4.50/2.50 ☯ 9am-5pm Mon-Fri), which explores 400 years of the Grassmayr family's bell-making tradition and exhibits some formidable Romanesque and Gothic examples. It's a hands-on kind of place where kids can watch the casting process and make loads of noise ringing bells to achieve different notes.

BERGISEL

Rising above Innsbruck like a celestial staircase is the glass-and-steel **Bergisel Schanze** (Bergisel ski jump; off Map p333; ☎ 589 259-0; www.bergisel.info; adult/child €8.30/4; ⏱ 9.30am-5pm). The brainchild of Iraqi architect, Zaha Hadid, the futuristic landmark was unveiled in 2002 and cost a whopping €15 million. From May to July, fans pile in to see athletes train, while preparations step up a gear in January for the biggest event on the ski jumping calendar, the *Vierschanzen-Tournee* (Four Hills Tournament).

It is 455 steps or a two-minute funicular ride to the top. From the 50m-high viewing platform, the panorama of the Nordkette range, Inn Valley and Innsbruck is breathtaking; though the cemetery at the bottom has undoubtedly made a few ski jumping pros quiver in their boots, not least plucky Brit Eddie 'the Eagle' Edwards, who broke his jaw and collarbone here in a spectacular missed jump.

Next to the stadium at the bottom, the **museum** is a small but fascinating hall of fame, crammed with black-and-white photos of death-defying daredevils that used to jump in leather shoes and without helmets.

Also worthwhile and included in the entry price is the nearby **Kaiserjäger Museum** (off Map p333; ☎ 582 312; Bergisel 1; ⏱ 9am-5pm Apr-Oct), the site of the famous battle in 1809 at which heroic Andreas Hofer defeated the Bavarians. On display are memorials to Tyrolean freedom fighters from this and other battles, and a handful of paintings from WWI by Albin Egger-Lienz.

ALPENZOO & AROUND

North of the centre, the **Alpenzoo** (off Map p333; ☎ 292 323; Weiherburggasse 37; adult/child €7/3.50; ⏱ 9am-6pm) is home to cuddly alpine animals including bears, chamois and ibex. To get there, walk up the hill from Rennweg or take bus W from the Marktplatz.

Almost directly south across the cold Inn River is the **Rundgemälde** (off Map p333; ☎ 584 434; Rennweg 39; adult/child €3/1.50; ⏱ 9am-5pm Apr-Oct), a 1000-sq-metre panorama painting depicting the Battle of Bergisel. The circular building that houses the painting also features an ex-

tremely evocative exhibition detailing epic overland trips by Austrian travel writer Max Reisch (1912–85) in the days before long-distance travel became so easy.

Activities

With 2000m peaks on its doorstep, Innsbruck is among Austria's top cities for indulging in outdoor pursuits and one of the few places in Europe where you can whiz from the city centre to the slopes in a matter of minutes. Aside from skiing and walking, rafting, mountain biking, paragliding and bobsledding (see boxed text, opposite) are all available to the daring. Also see the Outdoor Activities chapter (p74).

SKIING & SNOWBOARDING

Innsbruck is the gateway to an excellent ski arena that has hosted world-class competitions, such as the Winter Olympics in 1964 and 1976. The brand-new **Hungerburgbahn** (Map p333; www.nordpark.at) is great news for powder freaks. Designed by Zaha Hadid of Bergisel fame, the sleek cable railway looks like something out of a sci-fi film and links the Congress Centre to Hafelekar (2300m) in just 25 minutes.

At the top, snowboarding dudes can pick up speed on the half-pipe and practise jumps at the **Skylinepark** (off Map p333), while skiers can take their pick of runs which include several reds and one black. Heading south or west of Innsbruck, there is plenty of variety: Axamer Lizum, Patscherkofel, Kühtai, Rangger Köpfl, Glungezer, Schlick 2000 and Stubai Glacier. Most of the region's 270km of slopes are geared to intermediates.

A three-/seven-day Innsbruck Glacier Ski Pass to all areas costs €96/182 and all are connected by ski buses, free to anyone with the Innsbruck Card. Alternatively, the Innsbruck Super Ski Pass is available, covering the above ski areas plus Kitzbühel and Arlberg. Passes covering four out of six days cost €155.50; five out of six days costs €206.

Note that skiing is not only restricted to the winter months – the Stubai Glacier offers year-round skiing (p345).

WALKING

Crisscrossed with well-marked trails, the mountains surrounding Innsbruck are perfect for walking. The easiest way to reach any kind of altitude from the city is to hitch a ride on

COOL RUNNINGS

The fast and furious **Olympia Bobbahn** (Olympic bob run; ☎ 37 71 60; ☻ Tue & Thu Dec-Mar, Thu & Fri Jul-Sep) in Innsbruck-Igls was built especially for the 1976 Winter Olympics. Taking in 14 curves, a loop and a vertical drop of 124m, the bob run is 1.2km of pure hair-raising action. Thrill seekers can join a professional bobsled driver to give it a whirl; ice makes the run slippery smooth in winter, but it's also possible to race down in summer if you don't mind a bumpy ride. At €30 a pop, the minute of madness doesn't come cheap, but the buzz of whooshing down at speeds of 100km/h (miss a bend and you'll bounce like a pinball) is worth every cent. To reach Igls, take bus J from the Landesmuseum.

the Hungerburgbahn funicular to **Hafelekar**, where paths head off in all directions. You'll need a head for heights to tackle the **Klettersteig** (climbing trail); the ascent is not for the faint-hearted, traversing seven peaks and affording tremendous vistas of the Stubaier, Zillertaler and Ötztaler Alps. Fixed ropes ensure safety on the high alpine route that takes around seven hours to complete.

In summer, the funicular runs from 8.30am to 5.30pm and costs €10.80/18 one way/return to Seegrube and €11.50/19.10 to Hafelekar.

From June to October, Innsbruck Information arranges daily hiking tours with a professional mountain guide, free to those with a Club Innsbruck Card and suitable for those eight years and older. Pop into the tourist office to register and browse the programme, which includes highlights such as sunrise walks to Rangger Köpfl and lantern-lit strolls.

ADVENTURE SPORTS
Die Boerse (Map p333; ☎ 581 742; Leopoldstrasse 4; ☻ 9am-7pm Mon-Fri, 9am-5pm Sat) rents skis, snowboards and mountain bikes (€14 to €30 per day), and offers a free pick-up service from the airport, *Hauptbahnhof* or your hotel. For adrenaline-based thrills, check out the activities at **Inntour** (www.inntour.com) at the same address. This is the place to come if you want to white-water raft down the Inn River, bungee jump from the 192m Europabrücke (Europe Bridge) or ski on the Stubai Glacier.

Walking Tour
Innsbruck is a compact, walkable city and this 1½-hour amble covers the blockbuster sights.

Kick off your tour by gazing up at the baroque façades along Herzog-Friedrich-Strasse; most of these buildings were built in the 15th and 16th centuries and still ooze medieval charm. Particularly outstanding is

the 18th-century **Helblinghaus (1)**, with its fussy rococo ornamentation.

Almost directly opposite is the **Goldenes Dachl (2**; Golden Roof), the gem of Innsbruck's rich architectural collection. Its 2657 gilded copper tiles shimmer atop a Gothic oriel window; Emperor Maximilian used to observe street performers from the 2nd-floor balcony, which has a series of scenes depicted in relief (including the emperor himself with his two wives). Note the balustrade on the 1st floor, which bears eight coats of arms. Inside the building is a small but intriguing museum retelling the history of Maximilian, the **Maximilianeum**

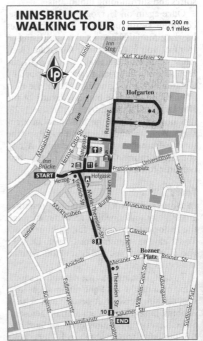

INNSBRUCK WALKING TOUR

(☎ 581 111; Herzog-Friedrich-Strasse 15; adult/child €4/2; ☺ 10am-5pm May-Sep, closed Mon Oct-Apr).

From the Goldenes Dachl, turn left up Pfarrgasse and then head towards Domplatz and **Dom St Jakob** (**3**; St James' Cathedral; Domplatz; ☺ 7.30am-9.30pm Mon-Sat, 8am-7.30pm Sun), where over-the-top baroque is everywhere to be admired. The Asam brothers from Munich completed much of the sumptuous art and stucco work, though the Madonna above the high altar is by the German painter Lukas Cranach the Elder.

Not far northeast of St Jakob is the **Hofgarten** (**4**), a peaceful pocket of greenery with manicured lawns, a palm house and a wonderful Indian Bean Tree.

From the park, follow Rennweg to the **Hofburg** (**5**; p334), Innsbruck's imperial palace, before nipping down Hofgasse for strudel and zingy juices at **Kröll** (**6**), and back onto Herzog-Friedrich-Strasse

Turn left and bear south, stopping at the 51m-high **Stadtturm** (**7**; city tower; ☎ 561 15 00; Herzog-Friedrich-Strasse 21; adult/child €2.50/1; ☺ 10am-8pm Jun-Sep, 10am-5pm Oct-May); climb its 148 steps for 360-degree views of the city's rooftops, spires and surrounding mountains.

Once again on Herzog-Friedrich-Strasse, continue south until the street becomes bustling Maria-Theresien-Strasse. Rising in front of you is the slender **Annasäule** (**8**; St Anne's Column), erected in 1706 to mark the repulsing of a Bavarian attack and topped by a statue of the Virgin Mary. After the next intersection, the fine baroque façade of the **Altes Landhaus (9)** sails into view; built in 1728, it is now the seat of the provincial government. Walk another 200m and you'll spy the marble **Triumphpforte** (**10**; Triumphal Arch), commemorating the marriage of the then emperor-to-be Leopold II.

Tours

Innsbruck Information (p334) organise guided city walks, which meander through the historical city centre for an hour or so. Tours leave at 11am and 2pm May to October and over Christmas, and cost €8 (€5 with an Innsbruck Card).

To capture more than the *Altstadt* in a tour, jump on a bright-red **Sightseer** (www.sightseer.at) bus, running between Alpenzoo and Schloss Ambras. Buses depart from Maria-Theresien-Strasse every 30 minutes between 9am and 5.30pm May to October, and every hour

from 10am to 6pm November to April. A day pass costs €8.80/6.20 for adults/children. Innsbruck Information sells tickets.

Festivals & Events

For three decades Innsbruck has been celebrating the **Festival of Early Music** (Festwochen der Alten Musik; ☎ 571 032; www.altemusik.at), a series of baroque concerts staged in July and August at venues such as Schloss Ambras (p334), the Landestheater (p342) and Dom St Jakob (left).

Other big bashes in this city include the **Innsbruck Summer Dance Festival** (www.tanzsommer .at, in German), held in June and July; **Easter Celebrations**, which include concerts, markets and processions; and the ever-popular **Advent Christmas Markets**, which spring to life in mid-November and run until 24 December.

Sleeping

Most of Innsbruck's budget digs, guesthouses and boutique hotels cluster in the *Altstadt* within staggering distance of the star attractions and bars. Aside from the options below, Innsbruck and the villages of Igls and Mutters offer private rooms that cost between €20 and €40; Innsbruck Information (p334) can make the bookings for you.

BUDGET

Camping Innsbruck Kranebitten (off Map p333; ☎ 284 180; www.campinginnsbruck.com; Kranebitter Allee 214; campsites per adult/child/car/tent €5.40/3.50/3.40/3.40; ☺ Apr-Oct; **P**) West of town and flanked by mountains, this tree-shaded campsite is far enough from Innsbruck to have a rural feel, but close enough to make reaching the centre a doddle. There's an onsite restaurant and playground.

Jugendherberge Innsbruck (off Map p333; ☎ 346 179; www.jugendherberge-innsbruck.at; Reichenauerstrasse 147; 6-/4-bed dm €15.50/18, s/d €33/50; **P** 🖳) It may not be a pretty face, but don't be put off by this hostel's '70s façade. Dorms are clean and comfy and the excellent amenities include a kitchen, laundry, TV room and bike rental. It's 2km northeast of the *Altstadt*; bus O from Museumstrasse pulls up outside.

Volkshaus Innsbruck (off Map p333; ☎ 395 882; www.volkshaus.at; Radetzkystrasse 47; dm €16.10-21.60) Overlooking sports fields, this HI hostel doesn't have as many facilities as the city's other hostels, but the rooms are decent and staff welcoming. Take bus R from

---

DEVIL IN DISGUISE

The goat-horned and hairy *Krampus* runs riot through the village of Igls each year on 5th December, the eve of St Nicholas. But if ol' St Nick is the goodie, the mean and menacing *Krampus* is definitely the baddie; instead of dishing out sweets, this devilish character in a shaggy costume and grotesquely carved mask is out there to scare kids silly – growling and cracking his whip as he flits through the streets in the Krampuslaufen parade.

As if one weren't enough, around 70 ghoulish *Krampusse* turn out to menace anyone who dares cross their path (the smaller, the better...). The little 'uns get to let out all that pre-Christmas excitement screaming at the top of their lungs and the grown-ups see the event as a village-wide excuse for a booze-up, so everyone is happy. By nightfall, it's not unusual to see *Krampus* slurring after one too many schnapps; after all, the devil is allowed to misbehave and leave the good-guy stuff to Santa.

---

the *Hauptbahnhof*. It's 2km northeast of the *Altstadt*.

our pick **Nepomuks** (Map p334; ☎ 584 118; Kiebachgasse 16; www.nepomuks.at; dm/d €21/52) Could this be backpacker heaven? Nepomuks comes pretty darn close. The smiley sisters that run these central digs welcome you with homy extras like free cocoa in the kitchen. The high-ceilinged dorms have bags of charm with little touches from pot plants to books and CD players. Wake up to a delicious breakfast in Café Munding (p342) next door with homemade bread, jam, pastries and freshly roasted coffee.

Pension Paula (off Map p333; ☎ 292 262; www.pension paula.at; Weiherburggasse 15; s/d €36/58; P) Perched above Innsbruck in the quiet St Nikolaus district, this family-run pension occupies an alpine chalet and has super-clean, homely rooms (most with balcony). It's up the hill towards the zoo and has great vistas across the city.

MIDRANGE

Innbrücke (Map p334; ☎ 281 934; www.gasthofinn bruecke.at; Innstrasse 1; s/d €39/67; P) This 15th-century townhouse is Tyrol's answer to Fawlty Towers with rather dated rooms, eccentric staff and an old-fashioned air. But you can't argue with the price and superb riverfront location.

Binders Hotel (Map p333; ☎ 334 36; www.binders .at; Dr Glatzstrasse 20; s €59-130 d €78-150; P 💻 🖵) Just east of the *Altstadt*, a nondescript exterior hides this sleeping beauty with wi-fi and loads of snazzy art features. The individually designed rooms range from Smartie shades to all-white with teak floors; the spacious loft suite has a trampoline-sized waterbed. Spa access costs €9.

Hotel Weisses Kreuz (Map p334; ☎ 594 79; www .weisseskreuz.at; Herzog-Friedrich-Strasse 31; s/d €62/108; P 🖵) Beneath the arcades, this atmospheric *Altstadt* hotel has played host to guests for 500 years, including a 13-year-old Mozart. Creaking stairs pass a trickling fountain up to the antique-filled reception. The spotless rooms are country-style with chunky pinewood and floral trimmings.

Weinhaus Happ (Map p334; ☎ 582 980; www.wein haus-happ.at; Herzog-Friedrich-Strasse 14; s/d €72/88; P) Happ exudes old-world atmosphere. The '70s-style rooms could do with a lick of paint, but its plus points are many: prime views of the Goldenes Dachl, a cavernous wine cellar and a rustic restaurant (mains €9.50 to €22.50).

Mondschein (Map p334; ☎ 227 84; www.mondschein .at; Mariahilfstrasse 6; s €75-95, d €115-140; P) The moon beams down as you enter this riverside hotel, housed in a 15th-century fisherman's hut. Rooms painted in blues and sunny yellows give way to Swarovski crystal-studded bathrooms glittering like a night sky.

Bierwirt (off Map p333; ☎ 342 143; www.bierwirt .com; Bichlweg 2; s/d €80/123; P 🖵) In a tranquil enclave 10 minutes' walk from Schloss Ambras, this chalet-style hotel has a country feel and comes complete with a wood-panelled restaurant and mosaic-tiled spa. Three of the spotless rooms are fully wheelchair accessible.

Weisses Rössl (Map p334; ☎ 583 057; www.roessl.at; Kiebachgasse 8; s/d €90/130; 🖵) An antique rocking horse greets you at this 600-year-old guesthouse. The vaulted entrance leads up to spacious rooms recently revamped with blonde wood, fresh hues and crisp white linen. The owner is a keen hunter, so it's no surprise that the restaurant (mains €7 to €18) has a meaty menu.

TYROL

TOP END

Goldener Adler (Map p334; ☎ 571 111; www.goldener adler.com; Herzog-Friedrich-Strasse 6; s/d €87/128; P) Since opening in 1390, the grand Goldener Adler has welcomed kings, queens and Salzburg's two biggest exports: Mozart and Mrs Von Trapp. Rooms are elegant with gold drapes and squeaky-clean marble bathrooms.

Romantik Hotel Schwarzer Adler (Map p333; ☎ 587 109; www.deradler.com; Kaiserjägerstrasse 2; s €103-162, d €145-220, ste €260-480; P 🖳 🐾) Calling all loved-up honeymooners…This romantic boutique hotel is arguably the top dog in town, particularly if your bank balance stretches to a spin in the white limo featured in Madonna's *Material Girl*. The fabulously OTT suites glitter with Swarovski crystals; the black-and-gold one is where Versace once snoozed in a solid marble bed! The spa is stunning with crystal fountains and Qigong treatments.

The Penz Hotel (Map p334; ☎ 575 657; www.thepenz .com, in German; Adolf-Pichler-Platz 3; s €135-190, d €180-240; P) Behind a sheer wall of glass, the Penz is a contemporary design hotel next to the Rathaus Galerien. The minimalist rooms in muted hues are glammed up with iridescent screens, flat-screen TVs and shiny chrome fittings. At breakfast, a whole table is piled high with exotic fruits.

Europa Tyrol (Map p333; ☎ 59 31; www.europatyrol .com; Südtiroler Platz 2; s €145-185, d €204-264, ste €324-424; P 🖳) Facing the *Hauptbahnhof*, this five-star hotel's marble lobby gleams as though elves spent the entire night polishing it. The Biedermeier rooms are decorated with stripy wallpaper and ruby-red carpets. Mick Jagger and Her Majesty Queen Elizabeth II top the list of famous past guests.

Eating

Innsbruck's *Altstadt* is crammed with restaurants, trattorias and pavement cafés, dishing up everything from steaming plates of Tyrolean *Gröstl* (potatoes and bacon topped with a fried egg) to fiery curries and cheap snack-bar grub. There are gourmet haunts if you want them, but eating out here needn't bust the budget.

RESTAURANTS

Mamma Mia (Map p334; ☎ 562 902; Kiebachgasse 2; mains €5-8; lunch & dinner) This no-frills Italian bistro has a great buzz, alongside huge pizzas, fresh salads and healthy pasta dishes. The sunny terrace is a favourite spot in summer.

Lichtblick (Map p333; ☎ 566 550; Rathaus Galerien; lunch €6.50-12, set menu €32-42; lunch & dinner Mon-Sat) Elegant simplicity sums up Lichtblick on the 7th floor of the Rathaus Galerien. The panoramic views over Innsbruck through glass walls are as appetising as flavours like duck breast on artichokes and nectarines.

Lotos (Map p334; ☎ 578 663; Seilergasse 5; lunch buffet Mon-Fri €7, mains about €9; lunch & dinner Mon-Sat) You'll need both chopsticks to tackle the generous portions of chop suey and *Verrücktes Huhn* (crazy chicken) at this Chinese haunt, tucked down an *Altstadt* alleyway.

Solo Pasta (Map p333; ☎ 587 206; Universitätsstrasse 15b; mains €7-18; 10am-1am Tue-Sat) This high-ceilinged spaghetteria draws a young crowd with its hip vibe and yummy pasta. Next door, Solo Vino has a more upmarket feel with Italian wines, antipasti and fresh fish on the menu.

Gasthaus Goldenes Dachl (Map p334; ☎ 58 93 70; Hofgasse 1; mains €7-18; lunch & dinner) Near the Goldenes Dachl, this snug tavern uses locally sourced produce to rustle up classic Tyrolean fare – try tender veal with sauerkraut or hearty lamb stew and dumplings.

Sahib (Map p333; ☎ 571 468; Sillgasse 3; mains €8-17; lunch & dinner) The aroma of Indian spices wafting from Sahib's humble doorway should tempt you in for scrummy tandoori and vegetarian dishes.

Tapabar (Map p334; ☎ 586 398; Innrain 2; mixed tapas €8.40-12.60; 8.30am-1am) Popular for its chilled vibe and late-night nibbles, this riverside Spanish bar is the place to order a plate of tasty tapas and a glass of Rioja. Catch free flamenco concerts every second Wednesday.

Cammerlander (Map p334; ☎ 586 398; Innrain 2; mains €8-17; 9am-1am) Tapabar's twin, this buzzy restaurant has a huge terrace on the banks of the Inn. The menu is a mixed bag of Austrian and world flavours, from schnitzel to chilli.

Thai-Li-Ba (Map p333; ☎ 567 888; Rathaus Galerien; mains €10-20; lunch & dinner Mon-Sat) Thai chefs cook up a storm in the show kitchen at this open-plan restaurant with pillar-box red walls and teak floors. The noodle and curry dishes are garnished with delicate orchids.

Papa Joe's (Map p334; ☎ 583 046; Seilergasse 12; mains €11-16; 4pm-1am Sun-Wed, 4pm-2am Thu-Sat) Toucans, waterfalls, palms, sharks…you name it, Papa Joe's is a snippet of Mexico. This wacky party haunt has a menu packed with jumbo steaks and jambalaya, and a Caribbean bar for after-dinner caipirnhas.

Romantik Hotel Schwarzer Adler Restaurant
(Map p333; ☎ 587 109; Kaiserjägerstrasse 2; mains €12-20;
☿ lunch & dinner Mon-Sat) Zebra stripes and cow
prints give this wood-panelled restaurant a
groovy twist. Expect seasonal flavours, atten-
tive service and eye-catching presentation.

QUICK EATS
Kröll (Map p334; ☎ 574 347; Hofgasse 6; snacks €2-3;
☿ 6am-midnight) Forget plain old apple, this hole-
in-the-wall café has plenty of strudel varieties,
including rhubarb, poppy, feta and plum. The
fresh juices pack a vitamin punch.

Panino & Co (Map p333; Universitätsstrasse 3; paninis €3;
☿ 9am-6.30pm Mon-Fri) Blink and you'll miss this
Italian deli, where you can create your own
panini with Parma ham, cheese and olives. It's
a good place to stock up on picnic supplies and
the cheery owner makes a mean espresso.

SOWI Lounge (Map p333; ☎ 507 799-5; Universitätsstrasse 15; 2-course menu €4-5; ☿ lunch Mon-Fri)
Brimming with students, this *Mensa* (university restaurant) has quick, cheap menus
and outdoor seating on a grassy quarter.

SELF-CATERING
Pick up groceries at the large indoor food
and flower **market** (Map p334; Herzog-Sigmund-Ufer;
☿ 7am-6.30pm Mon-Fri, 7am-1pm Sat) by the river in
Markthalle, or at Billa (Map p333) and Hofer
(Map p333) supermarkets, close together
on Museumstrasse.

Drinking
BARS
Innsbruck's healthy student population keeps
the bar and clubbing scene upbeat. Aside from
the gaggle of bars in and around the *Altstadt*,
numerous drinking dens huddle beneath the
railway arches on Ingenieur-Etzel-Strasse, an
area known as the Viaduktbögen.

Treibhaus (Map p333; ☎ 572 000; www.treibhaus.at,
in German; Angerzellgasse 8; ☿ 10am-1am) This cultural complex draws a boho crowd with its
big terrace, regular DJs and live music (salsa
libre Monday, jam session Tuesday, alternative Wednesday). In August, it hosts an
open-air cinema.

360° (Map p333; ☎ 0664-84 06 570; Rathaus Galerien;
☿ 10am-1am Mon-Sat) Clean lines, cream leather
and lounge music create a relaxed mood in
this sphere-shaped bar beside Lichtblick. Grab
a cushion and drink in 360-degree views of
the city and Alps from the balcony skirting
the bar.

Hofgarten Café (Map p333; ☎ 588 871; Rennweg 6a;
☿ 11am-4am) DJ sessions and a tree-shaded
beer garden are crowd-pullers at this
trendy café-cum-bar set in the greenery of
Hofgarten. Sip cocktails beneath the stars
or gaze up at the star-studded ceiling in
the pavilion.

Krahvogel (Map p333; ☎ 580 149; Anichstrasse 12;
☿ 10am-2am Mon-Sat, 5pm-1am Sun) A big black
crow guards the bar at this industrial-
style pub. It doesn't make much noise, but
the punters do after one too many Mind
Sweeper cocktails. There are regular live
bands and big-screen sports.

Elferhaus (Map p334; ☎ 582 875; Herzog-Friedrich-
Strasse 11; ☿ 10am-2am) Eleven is the magic
number at Elferhaus, where you can
nurse a beer beside Gothic gargoyles at
the bar or take a church-like pew to hear
live rock bands play. The haunt attracts a
20-something crowd that spills out onto
Herzog-Friedrich-Strasse.

La Copa (Map p334; Badgasse 4-6; ☿ 6pm-3am Mon-
Thu, 6pm-4am Fri & Sat) Every Thursday, flamenco
fans squeeze into this vaulted bodega to see
José Márquez and amigos. Guitars, tapas and
copious amounts of sangria keep the tone
strictly Spanish. Even Mr lightning footwork
himself, Paco Peña, has performed here.

La Habana (Map p334; ☎ 570 888; Rathaus Galerien;
☿ 8am-1am Mon-Sat) Che Guevara and Fidel
Castro grace the walls of this so-smooth
Cuban bar. Join the locals to sip cuba libres
and puff fat cigars.

Dom Cafe-Bar (Map p334; ☎ 238 551; Pfarrgasse 3;
☿ 11am-2am Jun-Sep, 5pm-2am Oct-May) Flickering
candles, vaulted ceilings and an HMV gramo-
phone set the scene in this Gothic-style bar.
Sink into a squishy sofa for a glass of red
or a hot *Waldbeerpunsch* (wild berry punch)
in winter.

Theresienbräu (Map p333; ☎ 587 580; Maria-
Theresien-Strasse 53; ☿ 10am-1am Mon-Wed, 10am-2am
Thu-Sat, 10am-midnight Sun) Copper vats gleam
and rock plays at this lively microbrewery,
which opens onto a garden seating 120 beer
guzzlers and pretzel munchers. The ceiling is
studded with 10,000 dried roses.

Jimmy's (Map p333; ☎ 57 04 73; Wilhelm-Greil-Strasse
19; ☿ 6pm-1.30am Mon-Thu, 8pm-2.30am Fri & Sat)
Buddha enlightens this party-hearty bar in
a courtyard near STA. Vodka shots are the
tipples of choice and the music is a blend of
hip-hop and funk.

TYROL

CAFÉS

Café Katzung (Map p334; ☎ 586 183; Herzog-Friedrich-Strasse 16; snacks €4-8; ☒ 8am-midnight Mon-Sat, 9am-midnight Sun) Expect lounge music, a lively vibe and the best hot chocolate in town at this cool café. Menu favourites include all-day breakfasts and warming carrot-mango soup.

Café Central (Map p333; ☎ 59 20; Gilmstrasse 5; coffee €2-4; ☒ 7.30am-11pm) The piano tinkles and newspapers rustle in this Viennese-style coffee house with chandeliers, high ceilings and naughty-but-very-nice cakes.

Café Munding (Map p334; ☎ 584 118; Kiebachgasse 16; |coffee €2-4; ☒ 8am-8pm) Modern art gives this 200-year-old café a contemporary kick. As well as whipping up delicious cakes – try the *Mundingzopf* – the family roast their own coffee and make preserves with fruit freshly picked from local farms.

Entertainment

Innsbruck Information (p334) produces a helpful monthly guide to the city's key events and exhibitions; it's mostly in German but is easy to navigate. The city has its own symphony orchestra that performs regularly in various venues. Schloss Ambras hosts a series of classical concerts in summer.

Landestheater (Map p333; ☎ 520 744; www .landestheater.at, in German; Rennweg 2; tickets €3-38; ☒ ticket office 8.30am-8.30pm Mon-Sat, 5.30-8.30pm Sun) Tyrol's seminal theatre stages year-round performances ranging from opera and ballet to drama and comedy.

Cinemas around town offer a special deal on Monday, when all seats are sold at the cheapest rate. For independent films shown in their original language head to **Cinematograph** (Map p333; ☎ 578 500; www.cinematograph.at, in German; Museumstrasse 31; tickets €6-8).

Shopping

Maria-Theresien-Strasse, the narrow cobblestone streets of the *Altstadt* and the Rathaus Galerien provide a quick shopping fix; here you can spend on handmade Tyrolean crafts, glitzy crystal jewellery and tasty local specialities.

Spezialitäten aus der Stiftsgasse (Map p334; ☎ 576 580; Stiftsgasse 3; ☒ 9.30am-6.30pm Mon-Fri, 9am-3pm Sat) An Aladdin's cave of homemade goodies, this vine-clad shop stocks honeys, oils, preserves and – if something more potent appeals – 600 types of liqueur.

Tiroler Heimatwerk (Map p333; ☎ 582 320; Meraner Strasse 2; ☒ 9am-6pm Mon-Fri, 9am-noon Sat) If you're looking for high-quality crafts, this place sells everything from *Dirndl* to hand-carved nativity figurines, stained glass and Tyrolean puppets.

Speckeria (Map p334; ☎ 562 068; Hofgasse 3; ☒ 9am-7pm) Carnivores are in their element at this vaulted deli in the *Altstadt*, where the shelves are stacked with smoked ham, sausage and *Hirschschinken* (venison ham).

Christmas & Easter in Innsbruck (Map p334; ☎ 579 580; Herzog-Friedrich-Strasse 30; ☒ 9am-7pm Mon-Sat, 9am-6pm Sun) This marvellously kitsch shop brims with spangly decorations, painted eggs, crib figurines and nutcrackers.

Swarovski Crystal Gallery (Map p334; ☎ 573 100; Herzog-Friedrich-Strasse 39; ☒ 8am-6.30pm Mon-Sat, 8am-6pm Sun Apr-Oct, 8am-6pm Mon-Fri, 8am-5pm Sat & Sun Nov-Mar) Part of the sparkling Swarovski empire, there's no room for clumsy shoppers in this gallery crammed with crystal trinkets and jewels.

Rathaus Galerien (Map p333; Maria-Theresien-Strasse 18; ☒ 9am-7pm Mon-Fri, 9am-5pm Sat) High-street shops, boutiques and cafés line this glass-roofed mall.

Getting There & Away

AIR

Innsbruck's **airport** (off Map p333; ☎ 225 25-0; www .innsbruck-airport.com; Fürstenweg 180), 4km to the west of the city centre, caters to a handful of national (Vienna and Graz) and international flights (London, Amsterdam, Antwerp, Bern, Frankfurt and Hannover), handled mostly by Austrian Airlines, BA, Lufthansa and Welcome Air.

BUS

The bus station (Map p333) is at the southern end of the *Hauptbahnhof*; its ticket office is located within the station.

CAR & MOTORCYCLE

The A12 and the parallel Hwy 171 are the main roads heading west and east. Highway 177, to the west of Innsbruck, continues north to Germany and Munich. The A13 is a toll road (€8) running south through the Brenner Pass to Italy. En route you'll cross the 192m Europabrücke (Europe Bridge), spanning the Sill River. Toll-free Hwy 182 follows the same route, passing under the bridge.

TRAIN

The *Hauptbahnhof* is Innsbruck's most convenient station, though some local trains also pull up at the Westbahnhof (actually to the south) and at Hötting (to the west).

Fast trains daily depart every two hours for Bregenz (€28, 2¾ hours) and Salzburg (€33.80, two hours). From Innsbruck to the Arlberg, the best views are on the right-hand side of the train. Two-hourly express trains serve Munich (€33.80, two hours) and Verona (€40, 3½ hours). Direct services to Kitzbühel also run every two hours (€13.20, one hour) while six daily trains head for Lienz (€20, three to five hours); some pass through Italy while others take the long way round via Salzburgerland.

Getting Around

TO/FROM THE AIRPORT

The airport is served by bus F. Buses depart every 15 or 20 minutes from Maria-Theresien-Strasse (€1.70); taxis charge about €8 to €10 for the same trip.

CAR & BICYCLE

Most of central Innsbruck has restricted parking, indicated by a blue line. You can park within these areas for a maximum of 1½ or three hours during set times (approximately shop hours). The charge is €0.50/1/1.50 for 30/60/90 minutes; tickets are available from pavement dispensers. Parking garages (such as the one under the *Altstadt*) will set you back about €15 per day.

Innsbruck's major car rental agencies and bike hire shops:

Avis (Map p333; ☎ 571 754; Salurner Strasse 15;
⊙ 7.30am-6pm Mon-Fri, 8am-1pm Sat)

Denzeldrive (Map p333; ☎ 582 060; Salurner Strasse 8;
⊙ 8am-6pm Mon-Fri)

Hertz (Map p333; ☎ 580 901; Südtiroler Platz 1;
⊙ 7.30am-6pm Mon-Fri, 8am-1pm Sat)

Neuner (Map p333; ☎ 561 501; Maximilianstrasse 23;
⊙ 9am-6pm Mon-Fri, 9am-noon Sat) Rents mountain bikes for €16/20 per half/full day.

PUBLIC TRANSPORT

Single tickets on buses and trams cost €1.60 (from the driver; valid upon issue), but if you plan to use the city's public transport frequently you're better off buying a 24-hour ticket (€3.40). Weekly and monthly tickets are also available (€10.70 and €36.20, respectively). Tickets bought in advance, which are available from *Tabak* (tobacconist) shops,

Information Innsbruck (p334) and the **IVB Kundenbüro** (Map p334; ☎ 53 07-500; Stainerstrasse 2; ⊙ 7.30am-6pm Mon-Fri), must be stamped in the machines at the start of the journey.

TAXI

For a taxi call ☎ 0800 222 22 55 or 53 11.

AROUND INNSBRUCK

HALL IN TIROL

☎ 05223 / pop 12,000

Nestled beneath the Alps, just 9km east of Innsbruck, Hall is caught in a medieval time-warp: slim townhouses and cobblestoned lanes lit by lanterns reveal that not an awful lot has changed since the 15th century when this small town grew fat on the riches of salt and silver. If you're in town for the *Weinherbst* festival in September, watch as the water in the Wilden Mannes fountain miraculously turns to wine…

Information

Staff at the **tourist office** (☎ 455 44; www.regionhall .at, in German; Wallpachgasse 5; ⊙ 8.30am-6pm Mon-Fri, 9am-5pm Sat) can point you in the direction of the town's attractions. They also organise daily **guided tours** (adult/child €6/3.50; ⊙ 10am Apr-Sep).

Sights & Activities

All streets lead to the Oberer Stadtplatz. Bordering this square is the 15th-century **Rathaus**, with its distinctive courtyard, complete with crenated edges and mosaic crests. Directly across the square, the spire of the 13th-century **Pfarrkirche** (parish church; admission free; ⊙ daylight hr) rises skywards. The highlight is the **Waldaufkapelle**, home to Florian Waldauf's grisly collection of 45 skulls and 12 bones, picked from the remains of minor saints. Each rests on embroidered cushions, capped with veils and elaborate headdresses, reminiscent of spiked haloes; the whole effect is both repulsive and enthralling.

A few paces away is the **Damenstift**, a convent founded in 1557 and graced by a baroque tower; unfortunately the convent's church is often locked. Not far from the Damenstift is the small **Bergbau Museum** (Fürstengasse; adult/child €3.50/2; ⊙ tours 11.30am Apr-Sep), which delves into the town's history of salt mining and can only be visited on a tour.

Stepping south of the medieval centre, you reach the ivy-clad **Burg Hasegg** (☎ 442 45;

Burg Hasegg 6; adult/child €4/3; ⊙ 10am-5pm Tue-Sun Apr-Oct, 10am-5pm Tue-Sat Nov-Mar), where a spiral staircase coils up to the 5th floor for far-reaching views over Hall. The castle had a 300-year career as a mint for silver *Thalers* (coins, the root of the modern word 'dollar'), and this history is unravelled in the **Münze Hall** (☎ 585 5165; Burg Hasegg 6; adult/child €6/4; ⊙ 10am-5pm Tue-Sun Apr-Oct, 10am-5pm Tue-Sat Nov-Mar), displaying water-driven and hammer-striking techniques. Audio guides are included in the price and kids can mint their own coin.

Sleeping & Eating

Gasthof Badl (☎ 567 84; Innbrücke 4; s/d €41/68; P) A short dash across the Inn River, this gem of a guesthouse has immaculate rooms (most with river view) and a tavern that knocks up a great strudel. Little 'uns will love the playground and docile St Bernard, Max. Rent a bike here to pedal along the banks to Innsbruck.

Parkhotel (☎ 537 69; www.parkhotel-hall.com; Thurn-feldgasse 1; s/d €92/146; P ⊡) It's a surprise to find such an avant-garde design statement in little Hall. This cylindrical hotel's curvaceous glass-walled rooms are decorated in earthy hues and feature free internet access and stunning mountain views.

Wurstkultur (☎ 527 45; Krippgasse 8; sausages €2-4; ⊙ 11.30am-2.30pm & 4.30-9pm Tue-Fri, 11.30am-2.30pm Sat) This hole-in-the-wall place excels in *Würstl* (sausages). The arm-long list includes paprika, curry and vegetarian bangers. Picking mustard to slather on them is also an adventure – try the beer, honey and orange varieties.

Getting There & Away

Hwy 171 goes almost through the town centre, unlike the A12/E45, which is over the Inn River to the south. The train station is about 1km southwest of the centre; it is on the main Innsbruck–Wörgl train line, but only regional trains stop here. Buses take longer but they stop in the town centre. From Innsbruck (€2.80, 30 minutes), buses leave every 15 minutes.

WATTENS

The quaint village of Wattens has one claim to fame: it's the glittering heart of the Swarovski crystal empire. This unique brand of bling certainly reels in the tourists and **Swarovski Kristallwelten** (Swarovski Crystal Worlds; ☎ 05224-510 80; Kristallweltenstrasse 1; adult/child €8/free; ⊙ 9am-6pm)

tops the list of Austria's most-visited attractions. Call them kitsch or classy, there is no doubting the popularity of these crystals, displayed in all their glory at this fantastical playground. A giant's head spewing water into a pond greets you in the park. Inside you'll find Alexander McQueen's crystal tree, zebras drifting past on ruby slippers in a twinkling theatre, and the world's biggest crystal, weighing in at 62kg. Terence Conran's shop by the exit is where, depending on your budget, you can buy a bejewelled pen for €1.30 or splurge on a €14,800 crystal-studded iguana. Decisions, decisions…

Swarovski Kristallwelten is best visited by bus (€3.80, 20 minutes). Leaving every half-hour (fewer on Sundays) from Innsbruck's *Busbahnhof* (bus station) heading for Schwaz, they stop at Swarovski Kristallwelten.

SCHWAZ
☎ 05242 / pop 12,400

Schwaz wielded clout in the Middle Ages when its eyes shone brightly with silver. In the 15th century it was, believe it or not, Austria's second-largest city after Vienna. For a taste of that past glory, go underground to the show silver mine or take a wander through the winding streets of this laid-back little town.

Information

The helpful **tourist office** (☎ 632 40; www.silber regionkarwendel.at; Franz-Josef-Strasse 2; ⊙ 9am-6pm Mon-Fri, 9am-noon Sat May–mid-Oct; 9am-noon & 2-6pm Mon-Fri, 9am-noon Sat mid-Oct–Apr) provides information on sights and accommodation in Schwaz.

Sights & Activities

Schwaz' biggest draw is its labyrinth of cobbled streets in the medieval centre. Taking pride of place on pedestrianised Franz-Josef-Strasse, the Gothic **Pfarrkirche** (parish church; admission free; ⊙ daylight hr) immediately catches your eye with its steep roof bearing 14,000 copper tiles.

Not far south is the **Franziskanerkirche** (Gilm-strasse; admission free; ⊙ daylight hr), blending Gothic and baroque styles. The church cloisters next door are a calm spot; Gothic windows and unfinished frescoes line its inner courtyard.

It's worth peeking inside the **Haus der Völker** (Ethnography Museum; ☎ 660 90; St Martin; adult/child €6/4; ⊙ 10am-6pm), just north of town, which presents the rich collection of local photographer Gert Chesi. Curiosities on display include Nigerian masks, Burmese gongs and voodoo ceremonial tools.

You almost feel like breaking out into a rendition of Hi-Ho at **Silberbergwerk Schwaz** (Silver Mine; ☎ 723 72; Alte Landstrasse 3a; adult/student/child €15/10/8; ☼ 9am-5pm May-Sep, 10am-4pm Apr & Oct, 10am-4pm Wed-Sun Nov-Mar), as you board a mini-train and venture deep into the bowels of the silver mine for a 90-minute trundle through Schwaz's illustrious past. The mine is about 1.5km east of the centre.

Sleeping & Eating

Pension Clara (☎ 639 11; Winterstellergasse 20; s/d €28/52) A peaceful garden, mountain views and old-fashioned hospitality define this charming guesthouse, five minutes' stroll from the centre. The large, well-equipped rooms are real value for money.

Café Luce (☎ 653 60; Burggasse 1; lunch €4.50; mains €6-7; ☼ lunch & dinner) This lively café is a local favourite for cheap lunches and post-work drinks in the courtyard. The simple menu features various takes on pasta, bruschetta and salads.

Hellas (☎ 677 04; Burggasse 4; lunch €6; mains €7-18; ☼ lunch & dinner Tue-Sun) Hellas is a classy little Greek place with vaulted ceilings, exposed brick and bold colours. The terrace is quite something: waiters have to cross the road to get there and perform a balancing act to ensure your tasty moussaka doesn't land on someone's bonnet.

Getting There & Away

Only 18km east of Innsbruck, Schwaz is an easy day trip. The train to Schwaz (€5, 20 minutes) is the quickest option.

STUBAI GLACIER

It's a bizarre feeling to slip out of sandals and into skis at the height of summer, but that's precisely what draws people to the Stubai Glacier. Just 40km from Innsbruck, the glacier is a year-round skiing magnet with great snow, no trees to dodge and around 100km of pistes catering to all levels. Summer skiing is limited to between 2900m and 3300m. Walkers are attracted to the network of trails lower down in the valley; a good hiking map for the area is Kompass' *Stubaier Alpen Serleskamm* (scale 1:50,000). The Stubaital branches off from the Brenner Pass route (A13/E45) a little south of the Europabrücke and runs southwest.

Stubaitalbahn (STB) buses from Innsbruck journey to the foot of the glacier (one way/return €7.70/13.80, one hour) on an hourly basis; one-way tickets can be bought from the driver, return tickets need to be purchased in advance.

If you're based in Innsbruck and want to go skiing for the day on the glacier, consider the package tour offered by Innsbruck Information (p334). For €49.50, you'll receive a return bus journey, ski or snowboard rental and a ski pass.

SEEFELD

☎ 05212 / pop 3000

The pointy peaks are there, but Seefeld isn't just about the downhill rush. This alpine resort's first love is *Langlauf* (cross-country skiing) and there are 262km of groomed trails to prove it. When the white stuff turns to slush, locals limber up on the region's superb network of hiking trails or brave the chilly green waters of Wildsee.

The central **tourist office** (☎ 05-088 00; www .seefeld.at; Klosterstrasse 43; ☼ 8.30am-6pm Mon-Sat, 10am-noon Sun mid-Jul–mid-Sep, 8.30am-6pm Mon-Sat rest of year) has stacks of info on accommodation and outdoor activities.

Sights & Activities

A must-see if you believe in miracles is 15th-century **Pfarrkirche St Oswald** (admission free; ☼ daylight hr). It was here that Oswald Milser gobbled a wafer reserved for the clergy at Easter communion in 1384. After almost being swallowed up by the floor, the greedy layman repented, but the wafer was streaked with blood – not from foolish Oswald but from Christ, naturally. Climb the stairway to view the **Blutskapelle** (Chapel of the Holy Blood), which held the original wafer.

It's a short stroll south of the centre to **Wildsee**, a bottle-green, pine-fringed lake that anchors **Reither Moor** conservation area; a 45-minute trail rings the lake and you can stop off for a refreshing dip at the *Strandbad* (bathing area). For longer, more challenging walks, cable cars ascend nearby **Seefeld Spitze** (2220m) and **Reither Spitze** (2374m); consult the tourist office for more information or join one of its regular guided walks.

Seefeld's raison d'être is **cross-country skiing**. Prepared *Loipe* (trails) crisscross the plateau to **Mösern**, 5km away, where there are fine views of the Inn River and the peaks beyond.

Downhill skiing here is geared towards intermediates and beginners. Seefeld is linked to other ski resorts, including Ehrwald (p358), Reith and Garmisch-Partenkirchen in Germany, all of which are covered by the **Happy Ski Card** (3 days adult/child €88/53). The two main areas are Gschwandtkopf (1500m) and Rosshütte (1800m); the latter connects to higher lifts and slopes on the Karwendel range.

Sleeping & Eating

For a resort of its size, Seefeld has a substantial choice of accommodation. The main drag around Dorfplatz is more low-key than après-ski, with a smattering of restaurants and bars vying for custom. Private rooms offer the best value, but expect rates to be a third higher during the winter season.

Landhaus Seeblick (☎ 23 89; Innsbrucker Strasse 165; s/d €28/56) Landhaus Seeblick is prettily situated opposite Wildsee. The warm, welcoming rooms open onto balconies – perfect for lounging and enjoying those lake views.

Hotel Garni Dorothea (☎ 25 27; hotel.dorothea@ aon.at; Kirchwald 391; s/d €35/70; P 🖭) Sweeping vistas over Seefeld unfold as you trudge uphill to this three-star hotel. The rooms in natural colours are spacious and modern. After carving up the slopes, the indoor pool and sauna are just the ticket.

Gruggerhof (☎ 32 54; Leutascherstrasse 64; apt €45-83; P) This alpine chalet oozes charm, with a blooming garden in summer and easy access to the slopes in winter. Natural light pours into the spruced-up apartments that come complete with kitchenettes and balconies.

Putzi's (☎ 49 55; Bahnhofstrasse 33; snacks €3-8; 🕑 lunch & dinner) For a beer and bite to eat, Putzi's is a safe bet, churning out good-value schnitzels, pizzas and burgers.

Strandperle (☎ 24 36; Innsbrückerstrasse 500; mains €8-15; 🕑 lunch & dinner, closed Apr & Nov) Overlooking the calm waters of Wildsee, Strandperle is a funky granite-and-glass place. The menu delivers fresh flavours such as jumbo green mussels and alpine beef fillets. The decked terrace has the finest views of the Alps anywhere in Seefeld.

Restaurant Südtiroler Stube (☎ 504 46; Reitherspitzstrasse 17; mains €10-21; 🕑 lunch & dinner) This low-beamed South Tyrolean restaurant pips the competition with delicious specialities such as rosemary-infused rack of lamb and tender venison medallions.

Getting There & Away

Seefeld is 25km northwest of Innsbruck, just off the Germany-bound Hwy 177. The road follows the Inntal until it rises sharply near Zirl. The track starts climbing soon after departing Innsbruck, providing spectacular views across the whole valley, especially if you sit on the left of a bus (€4.50, 35 minutes, 13 daily). Trains run to Mittenwald (€3.80, 20 minutes) every two hours and Garmisch-Partenkirchen (€11.80, 55 minutes), both in Germany.

NORTHEASTERN TYROL

THE ZILLERTAL

Sandwiched between the Tuxer Voralpen and the Kitzbüheler Alpen, the Zillertal (Ziller Valley) epitomises picture-postcard Tyrol. A steam train chugs through the broad valley, passing fertile farmland and limestone spires, affording glimpsed vistas of snowy peaks and the meandering Ziller River. As well as skis or walking boots, this is one place you'll be glad you packed that extra pair of lederhosen. It's an extremely traditional place, where down-to-earth locals still tune into *Alpen Rock* (alpine rock) and celebrate their heritage with gusto.

Practically every resort has its own tourist office, but the main **tourist office** (☎ 05288-871 87; www.zillertal.at; 🕑 8.30am-noon & 1-5.30pm Mon-Fri, 8.30am-noon Sat) covering the whole valley is in Schlitters, 6km from Jenbach. It stocks plenty of information on outdoor activities, along with the *Zillertaler Gästezeitung* (partially in English) magazine.

Four camping grounds are situated in the valley and there is a year-round **HI hostel** (☎ 05288-620 10; www.hihostels.com/dba/hostel004079 .de.htm; Finsingerhof, Finsing 73; dm €17; P) at Uderns, 12km south of Jenbach. Most beds are in chalet-style pensions, private rooms, holiday apartments or farmhouses. Ask staff at the tourist offices for help in finding somewhere (they usually won't charge), as there are dozens of options in each resort. Wherever you stay, inquire about the resort's *Gästekarte* (guest card).

Note that many places close between seasons, usually early April to late June and early November to mid-December. This includes many of the hotels, restaurants and bars mentioned below.

Activities

Mayrhofen is a prime spot for serious **skiing**, but there is downhill and cross-country skiing elsewhere. The Zillertaler Superskipass covers all 150-odd lifts in the valley; it starts at €126 for the minimum four days, or €139.50 for four out of six days. Ski buses connect the resorts.

In summer, the alpine valley morphs into excellent **walking** territory. A famous network of trails is the Zillertaler Höhenstrasse in the Tuxer Voralpen, but paths also fan out from the resorts of Ried, Kaltenbach, Aschau, Zell and Ramsau. Mountain huts at elevations of around 1800m beckon weary hikers; the handy *Hütten-, Ausflugs- & Erlebnisführer* booklet (German only) lists all the huts in the valley. A detailed walking map covering the entire region is the Kompass *Zillertaler Alpen & Tuxer Voralpen* (scale 1:50,000). If you're planning on spending a week or more in the valley between June and October, the value-for-money **Zillertal Card** (6/9/12 days €39.80/54.80/68.80) covers public transport, one journey per day on any of the Zillertal cable cars and entry to swimming pools.

Other adrenaline-based activities include rafting, rock climbing, paragliding and cycling. The Ziller and its tributaries are also good for fishing, but permits are only valid for certain stretches.

Festivals & Events

From late September, the Zillertal celebrates the **Almabtrieb**, where cows are led down from the high pastures adorned with elaborate floral headdresses, garlands and tinkling bells. The parade takes place on the first Sunday in October in Zell am Ziller and on the first and second Saturdays in October in Mayrhofen. The locals see the event as an excuse for a bit of a party; merrymaking involves food markets, bands blasting out folk music and plenty of schnapps for farmers that want to drown their sorrows at the prospect of another harsh winter shovelling cow dung.

Getting There & Away

The Zillertal is serviced by a private train line, the **Zillertalbahn** (☎ 05244-606-0; www.zillertal bahn.at), which travels the 32km from Jenbach to Mayrhofen.

Those with a thirst for nostalgia can take a *Dampfzug* (steam train) along the valley; it runs twice daily year-round (10.47am and 3.16pm). It takes about 85 minutes to reach the last stop, Mayrhofen, and costs €10.70 one way to either Zell or Mayrhofen. If you just want to get from A to B, it's better to take the *Triebwagen* (train) or bus as it costs €5.90.

ZELL AM ZILLER

☎ 05282 / pop 1840

Scenically located at the foot of knife-edge Reichenspitze (3303m), Zell am Ziller is a former gold-mining centre. There's now less sparkle and more swoosh about this rural and deeply traditional little village, home to 160km of pistes and a thrilling 7.5km flood-lit toboggan run. Warm weather lures active types, who come to hike in the hills or pedal up the Gerlos Pass to Krimml in the Hohe Tauern National Park (p317).

Orientation & Information

The **tourist office** (☎ 22 81; www.zell.at; Dorfplatz 3a; ☑ 8.30am-12.30pm & 2.30-6pm Mon-Fri) near the train tracks is a mine of information on walking, skiing and adventure activities in the area. At the other end of Dorfplatz is the post office, with bus stops at the rear.

Sights & Activities

The slender spire of the pink-and-white **Pfarrkirche** (parish church; admission free; ☑ daily) rises above the village and is surrounded by a sea of filigree crosses. You can peek inside the church, but you do so at your own risk – a sign on the door issues a warning that it is *not* a museum!

Abenteuer Goldbergbau (☎ 48 20; www.goldschau bergwerk.com, in German; Hainzenberg 73; adult/child €10/5; ☑ 9am-5pm) is a two-hour tour of a gold mine 2km east of Zell on the Gerlos road. The entry price covers a cheese-making demonstration and a visit to the animal enclosure, where kids can come face-to-face with deer, emus and llamas.

Aside from trekking and skiing, the mountains around Zell are ideal for **paragliding**. Paragliding specialist **Fly Zillertal** (☎ 0664-87 25 913; www.fly-zillertal.com, in German; Freizeitpark Zell) offers piloted trips descending 500m to 2300m (€55 to €130). Several rival firms offer similar deals; ask for details at the tourist office.

Bicycles (half/full day €8/12) can be rented from the train station.

Festivals & Events

Wafting around on hot-air currents is not recommended after a bellyful of super-strong Gauderbier (reputedly over 10% alcohol) brewed specially for the **Gauderfest** (www.gauder fest.at, in German). The festival takes place on the first weekend in May, and participants show off long-established rural skills: playing music, dancing and drinking heavily. The lavish main procession (participants wear historical costumes) and wrestling take place on Sunday.

Sleeping & Eating

Zell is dotted with chalets offering accommodation, with many west of the river in Zellbergeben. Rates are around 30% higher in the winter season.

Camping Hofer (☎ 22 48; www.campinghofer .at; Gerlosstrasse 33; campsites per adult/child/tent €6.60/4.20/6.80, guesthouse s/d €21/42; P ⓢ) Full of happy campers, this tree-shaded site offers first-rate facilities including a playground, grill area and heated pool. If you don't fancy roughing it, check out the well-kept rooms in the guesthouse.

ourpick Enzianhof (☎ 22 87; www.enzianhof.eu, in German; Gerlosberg 23; s/d €23/40) High on a hill, this chocolate-box chalet is the place to slip under the skin of the Zillertal: the farmer makes his own gentian schnapps, smokes his own ham and will even give you a lift from the village (call ahead). Open year-round, the farmhouse is perfectly located for hiking and skiing. Kids love the resident potbellied pigs and donkey, Julius.

Gästehaus Brindlinger (☎ 26 71; brindlinger.zell@ aon.at; Gaudergasse 4; s/d €26/52; P) Tucked down a quiet lane, this chalet has bright rooms with plenty of pine, rag rugs and balconies affording mountain views. The sauna is popular after a day on the slopes and Mrs Brindlinger will let you borrow bikes free of charge.

Café Reiter im Park (☎ 22 89-0; Freizeitpark Zell; pizzas €7-10; ⓨ dinner) Reiter serves up enormous pizzas and après-ski during the ski season. In summer, the garden is a favourite spot to eat fresh mussels and enjoy a few drinks.

Self-caterers can head to the **Billa** (Bahnhofstrasse 3) supermarket

Getting There & Away

Normal trains to Mayrhofen (€2.20, 12 minutes) and Jenbach (€5.20, 45 minutes) are cheaper than the steam train. Zell am Ziller is the start of the Gerlos Pass route to the Krimml Falls; buses tackle the pass from July to September up to four times daily (€4.50, one to 1½ hours).

Trains to and from Innsbruck (€10.20, 1½ hours, hourly) require a change at Jenbach.

MAYRHOFEN

☎ 05285 / pop 3900

Mayrhofen can feel like a sleepy village in summer with its alpine dairies, glass-clear lakes and trails twisting high into the mountains. But it dances to a different tune in winter. The skiing at Ahorn and Penken is some of Austria's finest: a double whammy of cruising and kamikaze in the shadow of the frosted Zillertal Alps. And when it comes to après-ski, this resort can strut in its snow boots with the best of them in slick bars and an incredibly cool igloo.

Orientation & Information

The **tourist office** (☎ 676 00; www.mayrhofen.at; Europahaus; ⓨ 8am-7pm Mon-Fri, 9am-6pm Sat, 9am-noon Sun) stocks loads of information and maps on the resort; look for the comprehensive *Info von A–Z*; it's free and written in English. There is a handy topographic model of the surrounding Alps and a 24-hour accommodation board.

Sights

For a fly-on-the-wall tour of a working dairy, head to the **Erlebnis Sennerei** (☎ 639 06-0; Hollenzen 116; admission with/without tasting €10.90/5.80, under 12yr free; ⓨ 10-11.30am & 12.30-3pm, closed Nov–mid-Dec). A glass-walled walkway reveals cheese-making processes, stepping from copper vats full of creamy milk to cheese ripening in salt baths. The final products are huge wheels of Tilsiter, Bergkäse and Graukäse, a mouldy grey cheese that is virtually fat-free. The dairy leaves the best till last: the **restaurant** (mains €7-14; ⓨ 10am-6pm) where you can savour local cheese-rich specialities like *Graukasrahmsuppe* (Graukäse cream soup).

Activities

Mayrhofen's ski region offers some fearsome runs including the mogul-free **Harakiri**, Austria's steepest piste with a knee-trembling 78% gradient. Snowboarders, meanwhile, are in their element on the kickers, boxes and half-pipe at **Burton Park** in the Penken area. A local ski pass, valid for ski lifts on Ahorn and Penken-Horberg (157km of piste), costs €36 for one day. A welcome newcomer for skiers is the speedy **Ahorn** cable car, accommodating 160 passengers in each gondola.

The resort provides easy access to year-round skiing on the **Hintertux Glacier**. The Hintertuxer Gletscher cable car is an attraction in itself, gliding above sheer cliff faces and a spine of peaks to the tip of the ice-blue glacier. The sundeck at 3250m affords phenomenal views of the Tuxer Alps and, on clear days, Grossglockner, the Dolomites and Zugspitze. Day passes cost €36. From Christmas till early May a free bus shuttles skiers from Mayrhofen to the glacier (included in the ski pass).

From late May to mid-October, the tourist office organises regular **guided walks** (free with a guest card), which include night ambles, herb trails and mountain hikes. If you prefer to go it alone, it also produces a list (in English) of popular walks heading out of the village. A detailed map of the region is the Kompass *Mayrhofen-Tuxertal-Zillergrund* (scale 1:25,000). From the village itself two cable cars give walkers a great head start; one-way/return fares on both the Ahorn (1965m) and Penken (1800m) are €9.50/14.50 in summer.

Action Club Zillertal (☎ 629 77; www.action-club-zillertal.com; Hauptstrasse 458) is the place to go for adventure sports from hydrospeeding the raging waters of the Ziller River (€33) to canyoning (€24 to €79), paragliding (€80 to €160) and skydiving from Radfeld/Kundl (€190). Next door, **Ski School Mount Everest** (☎ 628 29; www.habeler.com; Hauptstrasse 458) is run by famous Austrian mountaineer, Peter Habeler (see boxed text, p89), who offers day tours in the Zillertal Alps including the ascent of the 3476m Olperer (€79).

The stunning alpine scenery and mountain passes around the Zillertal encourage cyclists to grab a bike and get pedalling. The routes zigzagging up to Ginzling and Hintertux can be tough going, but the views are exhilarating. Inquire at the tourist office about tours. Bicycles can be rented from the **train station** (half/full day €8/12) and **Hervis Sports** (☎ 640 45; Einfahrt Mitte 433; half/full day €8/12).

Festivals & Events

Mayrhofen's hottest event is **Snowbombing** in early April when the masses descend on the resort for a week-long knees-up. Some of the world's top boarders battle it out on the slopes, but many just come for the crazy après-ski. Expect 24-hour bars, club nights,

a top line-up of DJs and wild inebriation. More details and tickets are available at www.snowbombing.com.

Sleeping

The tourist office can help you trawl through the mountain of sleeping options in the village; rates are roughly 20% higher in winter.

Gästehaus Emberger (☎ 644 37; Neu-Burgstall 303; www.gaestehaus-emberger.at, in German; s/d €19/36 P) It's worth the 20-minute walk out of town to this hilltop guesthouse. Pinewood, rag rugs and flower-strewn balconies give the rooms a homy touch. Other draws are the panoramic vistas of the Alps, a small sauna and gym.

Kumbichlhof (☎ 624 58; www.kumbichlhof.com; Kumbichl 874; s/d €27/46; P) This family-run farmhouse is a great budget choice. The décor teeters on the old-fashioned, but rooms are immaculate and have own balconies.

Hotel Central Garni (☎ 623 17; Hauptstrasse 449; s/d €40/52; P) You'll feel as snug as a bug in this friendly hotel, run by the same family since the 1930s. The rooms are simple and clean, and open onto balconies overlooking the mountains.

Hotel Kramerwirt (☎ 67 00; www.kramerwirt.at; Am Marienbrunnen 346; s/d €89/154; P ⚲ ▢) Ablaze with geraniums in summer, this rambling 500-year-old chalet has corridors full of family heirlooms, spacious rooms and an outside whirlpool. Get your tongue in a twist at the restaurant (mains €8 to €21) asking for the tasty *Zillertaler Bauernschmaus* (farmers' platter with meat, dumplings and sauerkraut).

Eating

Mayrhofen dishes up everything from rustic chalets churning out cheese-heavy dishes to cheap-and-cheerful pizzerias.

Metzgerei Kröll (☎ 623 64; Scheulingstrasse 382; snacks €2.50-7; ⏱ 7.30am-12.30pm & 2.30-6pm Mon-Fri, 7am-noon Sat) This family-run butchery is famed for its unique *Schlegeis-Speck* ham, cured in a hut at 1800m for three months to achieve its aroma. There are a handful of tables where you can sample this speciality and the delicious homemade sausages.

China-Restaurant Singapore (☎ 639 12; Scheulingstrasse 371; mains €7-12; ⏱ lunch & dinner) A pot-bellied Buddha greets you at Singapore, which spices up the village with its tasty Asian fare. Fill up on Sichuan beef or shark fin soup before crossing the street for drinks in Scotland Yard.

Mamma Mia (☎ 67 68; Einfahrt Mitte 432; mains €7-9; ☺ lunch & dinner) Outside the plush Hotel Elisabeth, this vibrant pizzeria recreates Italy with its terracotta floor, bold colours and murals of Florence. The wood-fired pizzas and salads are unrivalled in Mayrhofen.

Wirtshaus zum Griena (☎ 67 67; Dorfhaus 768; mains €7-15; ☺ lunch & dinner Tue-Sun) Set in high pastures, this woodsy 400-year-old chalet is the kind of place where you pray for a snow blizzard, so you can huddle around the fire and tuck into *Schlutzkropf'n* (fresh pasta filled with cheese).

Supermarkets include a **Billa** (Am Marienplatz) and **Spar** (Hauptstrasse).

Drinking

our pick White Lounge (☎ 622 77; Ahorn; ☺ Dec-Apr) Kick your skis off and chill at this 2000m-high igloo bar, sculpted entirely from ice. Squeeze into the Eskimo-style haunt for frozen cocktails or catch rays on the lounges at the snow bar outside. Things heat up at Tuesday's igloo party when partygoers race (or roll) downhill on sledges.

Mo's (☎ 634 35; Hauptstrasse 417; ☺ noon-1am) This popular American-themed bar attracts a young crowd with its chirpy staff, moreish finger food (try the nachos and mozzarella sticks) and live music at weekends.

Scotland Yard (☎ 623 39; Scheulingstrasse 372; ☺ 7pm-late) A snippet of Old Blighty in rural Austria, Scotland Yard is a British pub with all the trimmings: Guinness, darts and a red phone box where expats can pour their hearts out to folk back home after a pint or three.

For more après-ski action, head to the Schirm Bar at the top of the Penken gondola, where fired-up skiers and boarders shake their booties after downing €1 shots. Equally loud and lively at the bottom is the **Ice Bar** (☎ 67 05; Hauptstrasse 470), where go-go polar bears (we kid you not!) lure you onto the dance floor. Both stay open until around 8pm.

Getting There & Away

By normal train, it's €5.90 each way to Jenbach (55 minutes).

GINZLING

☎ 05286 / pop 400

Arriving in Ginzling, an adorable little village 8km south of Mayrhofen, is like travelling 100 years back in time. Silent, rural and lacking any obvious tourist infrastructure, this place is pure escapism.

The **tourist office** (☎ 52 18; www.ginzling.at; ☺ 8am-noon & 1-5pm Mon-Fri) is well set up for walking enthusiasts keen to explore the nearby Hochgebirgs-Naturpark Zillertaler Alpen. The park is an untouched alpine wilderness with a smattering of huts. Skiing is almost nonexistent; touring for experienced skiers is the only option.

In former lives, **Gasthof Alt-Ginzling** (☎ 52 01; www.altginzling.at; s/d €28/56; P) was a stable and a wayside inn for smugglers travelling to Italy. Today the 18th-century farmhouse oozes history from every creaking floorboard. The low-ceilinged, pine-panelled rooms are supremely comfortable and the restaurant (mains €7 to €16) serves locally fished rainbow trout.

During winter, buses to Mayrhofen are free for those with ski passes; outside the ski season it costs €2.80. A winding road (toll €10) continues on from Ginzling up the valley to the **Schlegeisspeicher** (1782m) reservoir, the trailhead for the stunning Zillertal Circuit (p87).

ACHENSEE

North of Jenbach, flanked by wooded slopes and ringed with beaches, the turquoise Achensee is Tyrol's largest lake at 9km. The **Achenseebahn** (www.achenseebahn.at; one way/return €18/22), a private cogwheel steam train, trundles to the lake from Jenbach between May and October, connecting with two-hour **boat tours** (www.tirol-schiffahrt.at, in German; adult/child €13/6.50) of the lake. Far-reaching views over the lake and the surrounding mountains can be had from Erfurter (1831m), which is easily reached by the **Rofanseilbahn** (adult/child return €15/9; ☺ 8.30am-5pm) from Maurach.

KITZBÜHEL

☎ 05356 / pop 8500

Ask an Austrian to rattle off the top ski resorts in the country, and Kitzbühel will invariably make the grade. This resort has a winning formula: fine intermediate terrain and a few black runs to challenge veteran skiers. Kitz, as locals nickname it, rounds that off with a labyrinthine medieval centre and enough Porsches and Prada to rival St Moritz in the glamour stakes. It's a slalom playground, a magnet to the golf-club-toting rich and a postcard Tyrolean village.

Orientation & Information

The main train station is 1km north of the resort's hub, centred on Vorderstadt and Hinterstadt. The central **tourist office** (☎ 777; www.kitzbuehel.com; Hinterstadt 18; ☼ 8.30am-6pm Mon-Fri, 9am-6pm Sat, 10am-6pm Sun Jul-Sep & Christmas-Easter, 8.30am-6pm Mon-Fri, 9am-1pm Sat rest of year) has loads of info in English and a 24-hour accommodation board.

Banks and ATMs are everywhere and the **post office** (Josef-Pirchl-Strasse 11) is midway between the train station and tourist office. Internet access is available at **Kitz Video** (Schlossergasse 10; per hr €5; ☼ 10am-9pm Mon-Sat, 2-8pm Sun).

Sights

Kitzbühel's medieval core is a tangle of cobbled streets lined with gabled houses in candy colours. Perched above the town, the 15th-century **Pfarrkirche St Andreas** (☎ 666 59; Pfarrauweg 2; ☼ daylight hr) fuses Gothic and baroque elements. Next door the **Liebfrauenkirche** (Pfarrauweg 4; ☼ daylight hr) is a rococo church with a chunky 48m belfry and an interior adorned with gold swirls and frescoes.

Museum Kitzbühel (☎ 672 74; Hinterstadt 32; adult/child €5/2; ☼ 10am-6pm mid-Jun–mid-Sep, 10am-1pm & 3-6pm early-Dec–mid-Mar, 10am-1pm Tue-Sat rest of year) traces Kitzbühel's heritage from its humble Bronze Age beginnings to the present day. The big emphasis is on winter sports and the town's famous son, champion skier Toni Sailer.

Ride to Kitzbüheler Horn to wander the serene **Alpine Flower Garden** (admission free; ☼ daylight hr summer), nurturing alpine blooms like arnica, edelweiss and purple bellflowers. It's best reached by **Kitzbüheler Horn cable car** (adult/child €15/8.50), but drivers can also wind their way up to the top of the mountain (road toll per car/motorcycle €4/2, plus €1.50 per person).

For a cooling dip in summer, venture 3km northwest of the centre to Kitzbühel's natural swimming hole, the tree-flanked **Schwarzsee**. There are two beach complexes, each costing about €3.50 per day.

Activities

Along with the activities listed below, Kitzbühel gets pulses racing with scenic flights, skydiving, ballooning, golf, water sports and even bungee jumping. **Element 3** (☎ 0664-1000 580; www.element3.at; Winklernfeld 1) is a one-stop shop for adventure sports, including rafting, climbing, canyoning and paragliding.

SKIING

The Kitzbühel region offers exceptional skiing on 150km of pistes geared mostly towards intermediates and accessed by 53 lifts and cable cars. Extending northeast, the **Kitzbüheler Horn** is much loved by snowboarders for its half-pipe and kickers, while beginners flock here for gentle cruising on sunny slopes.

Spreading southwest, the **Hahnenkamm** (1668m) connects with some heart-stopping black runs in the **Pengelstein** (1938m) area. A great way to find your ski legs is to tackle the red-and-blue runs that make up the scenic **Ski Safari**, linking the Hahnenkamm to Jochberg. The alpine tour is marked by elephant signs and is a good introduction to the entire ski area.

One-day/three-day and weekly passes (Christmas to mid-March) cost €38.50/101/202 in high season and €33.50/88/175.50 at all other times. Passes cover lifts, cable cars and ski buses as far south as Thurn Pass. For real powder freaks, the Kitzbüheler Alpen Skipass is ideal; it spans the whole region (including 243 lifts; Kitzbühel, Schneewinkel, Wilder Kaiser-Brixental, Alpbach and Wildschönau) and costs €196 for six consecutive days.

WALKING

Walking is Kitzbühel's main summer activity; zillions of walking trails head off in all directions from the town. The tourist office caters to walker's demands too, handing out a comprehensive *Wanderwegeplan* (hiking plan) free of charge. If you'd prefer some company on the trails, it also organises free guided walks daily at 8.45am for *Gästekarte* holders (mid-May to mid-October).

A cable-car pass also covering local buses will set you back €37.60 for three days' travel within seven days, or €51.50 for six days in 10. Individual ascent tickets cost €15.50/8.60 for adults/children (discounts available with *Gästekarte*) on either Hahnenkamm or Kitzbüheler Horn, the descent is free. Of the two peaks, vista vultures consider the view superior from Kitzbüheler Horn: the jagged Kaisergebirge range dominates to the north, and beyond the Kitzbüheler Alps, Grossglockner and Grossvenediger are visible in the south.

CYCLING

For those with a thirst for challenging but rewarding mountain biking, there are over 30

TYROL

KITZBÜHEL

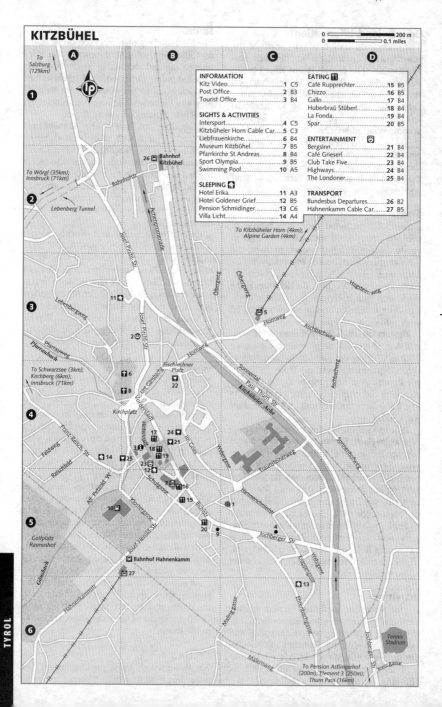

INFORMATION
Kitz Video	**1**	C5
Post Office	**2**	B3
Tourist Office	**3**	B4

SIGHTS & ACTIVITIES
Intersport	**4**	C5
Kitzbüheler Horn Cable Car	**5**	C3
Liebfrauenkirche	**6**	B4
Museum Kitzbühel	**7**	B5
Pfarrkirche St Andreas	**8**	B4
Sport Olympia	**9**	B5
Swimming Pool	**10**	A5

SLEEPING
Hotel Erika	**11**	A3
Hotel Goldener Grief	**12**	B5
Pension Schmidinger	**13**	C6
Villa Licht	**14**	A4

EATING
Café Rupprechter	**15**	B5
Chizzo	**16**	B5
Gallo	**17**	B4
Huberbräu Stüberl	**18**	B4
La Fonda	**19**	B4
Spar	**20**	B5

ENTERTAINMENT
Bergsinn	**21**	B4
Café Grieserl	**22**	B4
Club Take Five	**23**	B4
Highways	**24**	B4
The Londoner	**25**	B4

TRANSPORT
Bundesbus Departures	**26**	B2
Hahnenkamm Cable Car	**27**	B5

TYROL

cycle paths in, around and over the Kitzbühel area. All are marked on the *Mountainbiken und Radwandern* map available from the tourist office.

Bikes can be rented from **Intersport** (☎ 625 04; Jochbergerstrasse 7) and **Sport Olympia** (☎ 716 07; Bichlstrasse 26) for around €9 per day and can be transported free of charge on the Hornbahn, Hahnenkammbahn and Fleckalmbahn gondolas.

Festivals & Events

The legendary **Hahnenkamm** is the mother of all downhill races and one of the highlights of the FIS Alpine World Cup. Professional skiers from across the globe vie for the title in this notoriously tough race held in January. Late July sees tennis stars compete in the **Austrian Open** at the tennis stadium just off Jochberger Strasse.

Sleeping

Kitzbühel isn't the easiest place to find budget digs, but the *Gästekarte* (available from pensions and hotels) offers discounts to visitors and there are some good-value guesthouses outside of the centre. Expect a price hike of up to 50% during the high winter season.

Pension Schmidinger (☎ 631 34; Ehrenbachgasse 13; s/d €32/64; **P**) Five minutes from the main drag, this friendly pension has quiet, light-filled rooms with pine beds topped by fluffy duvets. The owners are clued up on skiing in Kitzbühel. Breakfast is a treat with local cheeses, hams and crusty bread.

Pension Astlingerhof (☎ 627 75; Bichlnweg 11; d €60; **P**) This wooden chalet has oodles of country charm with a mountain backdrop, home-grown produce and a garden where kids can run around. It's 15 minutes' walk from the centre.

Hotel Goldener Greif (☎ 643 11; www.hotel-goldener -greif.at; Hinterstadt 24; s/d €85/114; **P**) With its painted façade and walls festooned with hunting trophies, the Goldener Greif is a work of folk art. The cosy rooms are full of wood panelling, as is its rustic restaurant (mains €8 to €18).

Villa Licht (☎ 622 93; www.villa-licht.at, in German; Franz-Reich-Strasse 8; s/d €85/150; **P** 🖵 🐾) Surrounded by shady gardens, this green-shuttered Tyrolean chalet features recently revamped rooms in warm hues. A children's tree house, an outdoor pool and free wi-fi are other bonuses.

Hotel Erika (☎ 648 85; www.erika-kitz.at; Josef-Pirchl-Strasse 21; s/d €105/190; **P** 🐾) Turrets, towers and high ceilings define this Art Nouveau villa with luxurious rooms and polished service. The spa pampers with treatments from thalassotherapy to hay baths, and the manicured garden centres on a vine-clad pagoda and pond that are illuminated by night.

Eating

Aside from these options, the square is a safe bet for snacks and al-fresco dining. Many of the big hotels also have restaurants serving posh Austrian nosh.

Café Rupprechter (☎ 624 26; Josef-Herold-Strasse 3; 🕑 9am-7pm Mon-Sat, 10am-6pm Sun) Kitzbühel's best hazelnut ice cream, homemade strudel and pralines make the sweet-toothed locals squeal with pleasure at this family-run café.

Huberbräu Stüberl (☎ 656 77; Vorderstadt 18; mains €7-13; 🕑 8am-midnight Mon-Sat, 9am-midnight Sun) This vaulted tavern ditches the diet in favour of large portions of Austrian classics, such as schnitzel and liver dumplings, cooked to perfection.

Gallo (☎ 658 62; Vorderstadt 12; mains €7-16; 🕑 9am-midnight Tue-Sat, 2pm-midnight Sun) This trendy bistro-cum-bar jazzes up its minimalist interior with zebra stripes and mosaics. When the sun shines, diners spill out onto the terrace for antipasti, juicy steaks and wood-fired pizza.

La Fonda (☎ 736 73; Hinterstadt 13; mains €8-13; 🕑 dinner) Bedecked with sombreros, copper pans and colourful throws, this cave-like Mexican haunt rolls out favourites like fiery jalapeno peppers, nachos and enchiladas.

Chizzo (☎ 624 75; Josef-Herold-Strasse 2; mains €10-25; 🕑 lunch & dinner) A grandfather clock, white linen and fresh flowers create a refined ambience in Chizzo. The menu mixes Austrian and world flavours, from sander fillet on red wine risotto to Thai curry.

For self-caterers there's a **Spar supermarket** (Bichlstrasse 22).

Drinking & Entertainment

Kitzbühel rocks with fun-seeking skiers during the winter season. If you can muster up the energy after a day on the slopes, check out the following places.

The Londoner (☎ 714 28; Franz-Reisch-Strasse 4; 🕑 6pm-late Wed-Sat) This raucous British den has great beer, crazy events and plenty of slapstick fun.

Bergsinn (☎ 668 18; Vorderstadt 21; ☯ 9am-2am Mon-Sat, 11am-2am Sun) Pop art and sphere-shaped lights glam up this funky bar with a cocktail happy hour (8pm to 9pm) and free wi-fi access for customers.

Café Grieserl (☎ 727 52; Im Gries 6; ☯ 3pm-4am) There's Newcastle Brown Ale on tap at this barn-style watering hole with big-screen sports, live music and DJs at weekends.

Highways (☎ 753 50; Im Gries 19; ☯ 8pm-late) This wacky American-themed bar is the place to chill in a 1958 Buick, get bumper to bumper on the dance floor and munch a hot dog. When midnight strikes, the Jägermeister shots are €1 a pop. There are events nearly every night, from live bands on Fridays to electro on Saturdays.

Club Take Five (☎ 713 00; Hinterstadt 22; ☯ 10pm-late) Bright young things pack the dance floor at this see-and-be-seen club with a trio of bars and a VIP area. DJs pump out house, soul and funk.

Getting There & Away

Direct train services from Kitzbühel to Innsbruck (€13.20, one hour) run every two hours, while most trains to Salzburg require a change at Wörgl (€23.30, 2½ hours). For Kufstein (€8.30, one hour), change at Wörgl.

Getting to Lienz by train is tricky, as one or two changes are required (€34.80, four hours). Bus is a better option as it takes two hours (€13.20, twice daily). Heading south to Lienz, you pass through some marvellous scenery. Highway 108 (the Felber Tauern Tunnel) and Hwy 107 (the Grossglockner Road, which is closed in winter) both have toll sections; see p318.

KUFSTEIN

☎ 05372 / pop 16,000
In the 1970s, Karl Ganzer waxed lyrical about Kufstein in the hit song *Perle Tirols*. His yodelling melody may be cheesier than Camembert but the lyrics ring true: this town squatting beneath the towering limestone pinnacles of the Kaisergebirge and hugging the banks of the Inn River is indeed a gem. Little wonder control of the town was hotly contested by Tyrol and Bavaria through the ages until it finally became Austrian property in 1814.

Orientation & Information

Kufstein is the northernmost town in the Inntal, just 4km from Germany. The train station is on the west bank of river, a three-minute stroll from the main square, Stadtplatz. This is where you'll find the **tourist office** (☎ 622 07; www.kufstein.com; Unterer Stadtplatz 8; ☯ 8am-6pm Mon-Fri, 9am-1pm Sat). Staff will hunt down accommodation without charging commission. If you stay overnight, ask for the *Gästekarte*, which has different benefits in summer and winter.

Sights

The big draw in the centre is the gingerbready **Römerhofgasse**, a medieval lane that looks like a Disney film set with overhanging arches, lanterns and frescoed façades. Even the obligatory shops full of tourist kitsch detract little from this fairytale-like alleyway.

For an insight into Kufstein's turbulent past, head up to the clifftop **Festung Kufstein** (Kufstein Fortress; ☎ 602 350; Oberer Stadtplatz 6; adult/child summer €8.90/4.90, winter €8/4.40; ☯ 9am-5pm summer, 10am-4pm winter). The castle dates from 1205 (when Kufstein was part of Bavaria) and was a pivotal point of defence for both Bavaria and Tyrol during the struggles. The round **Kaiserturm** (Emperor's Tower) was added in 1522.

The lift to the top affords sweeping views over Kufstein and the surrounding peaks. Inside is the small but imaginatively presented **Heimatmuseum**, showcasing everything from Bronze Age urns to folk costumes and – drum roll please – Andreas Hofer's shoe. Below the Kaiserturm is the **Heldenorgel** (Heroes Organ) with 4307 pipes, 46 organ stops and a 100m gap between the keyboard and the tip of the pipes; the delay in the sounding of the notes makes playing it a tricky business. Catch recitals at noon and, in July and August, 5pm.

When the fortress is closed in the evening you can walk up the path in under 15 minutes and roam the ramparts and grounds free of charge. Dusk is also the best time to photograph the castle silhouetted against the mountains.

Activities

The **Kaisergebirge** range is a sheer wall of limestone to the east of Kufstein, rising to 2300m and stretching as far as St Johann in Tirol. It attracts walkers, mountaineers and skiers alike. The Kaisergebirge is actually two ranges, split by the east–west Kaisertal valley. The northern range is the Zahmer Kaiser (Tame Emperor) and the southern is the Wilder

Kaiser (Wild Emperor) – no medals for guessing which has the smoother slopes! Pick up a free *Wanderkarte* (walking map) from the tourist office.

A real blast from the past, the 1970s **chairlift** (one way/return €8/11; 9am-4pm May-Oct) to Wilder Kaiser has become a cult attraction. A sign says 'bouncing not permitted' and it soon becomes clear why: only itty-bitty bars prevent you from plummeting to the valley floor on this precipitous ride, which traverses ravines and cuts a path through dense forest home to deer and red squirrels. The magnificent Wilder Kaiser slides into view at the top station, which is the trailhead for the **Kaisergebirge Circuit** (see p89).

The tree-fringed **lakes** around Kufstein are best explored on foot or by bike; the closest are in the wooded area west of the Inn River, where there's a network of walking trails. Hechtsee, 3km to the northwest, and Stimmersee, 2.5km to the southwest, both have swimming areas that cost about €4. A free city bus goes to Hechtsee in summer during fine weather (ask at the tourist office).

Sleeping & Eating

Camping Maier (583 52; www.camping-maier.com, in German; Egerbach 54, Schwoich; campsites per adult/child/tent €4/2.70/6; P) Bordering woodland, this friendly campsite 5km south of Kufstein has tree-shaded pitches, plus a playground and outdoor pool to keep kids amused.

Gasthof-Pension Felsenkeller (627 84; www.felsenkeller.at, in German; Kienbergstrasse 35; s/d €38/72; P) In the foothills of the Kaisergebirge, this guesthouse is a calm haven hidden among tree-covered rocky crags. The country-style rooms are bright, spacious and have balconies. The cosy, wood-panelled restaurant serves freshly caught trout.

our pick Auracher Löchl (621 38; www.auracher-loechl.at; Römerhofgasse 3-5; s/d €56/98) Squeezed between Römerhofgasse and the Inn River, this hotel marries medieval charm with 21st-century comfort. The contemporary rooms are kitted out with chunky pinewood beds and flat-screen TVs (river or fortress views cost a little extra). Cross the footbridge to the low-beamed restaurant (mains €8 to €15), the one-time haunt of Andreas Hofer, where creaking floors and grinning badgers create a rustic feel. Enormous portions of Austrian classics like *Schweinshaxe* (basically half a pig) mean you'll roll out of the door fit to burst.

Inn-Café Hell (645 23; Unterer Stadtplatz 3; snacks & sweets €3-7; 8.30am-8pm summer, 9am-6pm winter) Facing the fast-flowing Inn, this central café opens onto a sunny terrace and whips up scrummy homemade strudel and walnut ice cream.

Batzenhäusl (624 33; Römerhofgasse 1; mains €7-14; lunch & dinner) Murals of merry wine-guzzlers reel you into Batzenhäusl, Tyrol's oldest wine tavern, which burrows into cliffs below the fortress. This eccentric, 500-year-old haunt is packed with curios from nativity scenes to 16th-century canon balls. The cuisine is seasonally inspired and the fluffy *Salzburger Nockerl* (Austrian soufflé) comes recommended.

Villa Masianco (636 33; Unterer Stadtplatz 18; mains €7-19; lunch & dinner) This sassy bistro on the square satisfies Kufstein's Italian cravings with risotto, fresh fish and tender veal fillets. Chandeliers, wooden floors and leather stools give the vaulted restaurant a modern kick. The chestnut tree-shaded terrace hums with life in summer.

Self caterers can stock up on supplies at the central **Spar** (Unterer Stadtplatz 27).

Getting There & Away

The hourly train to Kitzbühel (€8.30, one hour) requires a change at Wörgl. The easiest road route is also via Wörgl.

Kufstein is on the main Innsbruck–Salzburg train route; direct trains to Salzburg (€27.90, 1¼ hours) run every two hours; those to Innsbruck (€12.90, 45 to 70 minutes) are half-hourly, as some trains funnel down from Germany (Munich), which is on a direct line a little over an hour away. Buses leave from outside the train station.

SÖLL

 05333 / pop 3450

Söll is a well-known ski resort 10km south of Kufstein. Once a favourite of boozy, boisterous visitors in the 1980s, the resort has successfully reinvented itself and is now a family-oriented place with myriad outdoor activities in summer and winter.

The helpful staff at the **tourist office** (52 16; www.soell.com; Dorf 84; 8am-noon & 1.30-6pm Mon-Fri, 3-6pm Sat, 9am-noon Sun), in the centre of the village, provides information on activities and will help you find accommodation.

The highest skiing area overlooking the resort is Hohe Salve at 1828m, though Söll has also combined with neighbouring resorts Itter,

Hopfgarten, Kelchsau, Westendorf and Brixen to form the mammoth **Skiwelt** (www.skiwelt.at) area, comprising 250km of pistes. Passes are €35.50 for a day in the high season. Cross-country skiing is also a popular winter pastime, with trails running as far as St Johann in Tirol.

In summer, walkers are drawn to **Hohe Salve** (cable car one way/return €10/12). At the first stage of the cable car climbing the mountain is **Hexenwasser**, a walking trail dotted with fun family activities. Along the route are water obstacles, sundials, playgrounds, a working mill and bakery and an apiary. Throughout the summer you can see (and sample) bread, schnapps and cheese made the traditional way.

Getting There & Away

Söll is on Hwy 312 between Wörgl and St Johann in Tirol. It's not on a train line, but there are plenty of buses Monday to Saturday from Kufstein (€3.80, 50 minutes); only three run on Sunday.

WESTERN TYROL

STAMS
☎ 05263 / pop 1300

One of Tyrol's true architectural highlights is the ochre-and-white **Zisterzienstift** (Cistercian abbey; ☎ 62 42; Stiftshof 1; tours adult/child €4/2.50) in Stams, founded in 1273 by Elizabeth of Bavaria, the mother of Conradin, the last of the Hohenstaufens. Set in pristine grounds, the monumental façade stretches 80m and is easily recognised by its pair of silver cupolas at the front, which were added as a final flourish when the abbey was revamped in baroque style in the 17th century. The exuberant church interior is dominated by the high altar: the intertwining branches of this version of the 'tree of life' support 84 saintly figures surrounding an image of the Virgin. Near the entrance is the **Rose Grille**, an exquisite iron screen made in 1716. Crane your neck to admire the ceiling adorned with rich stuccowork, gold swirls and elaborate frescoes by Georg Wolker.

The abbey can only be visited by guided tour, from 9am to 11am and 1pm to 5pm (afternoon hours are shorter in May and from October to April). Tours leave every hour on the hour, except in July when they're available every half-hour. Marmalade and schnapps made on the premises can be bought from the **Kloster shop** (⊙ 9am-noon & 1-5pm).

Stams is on the train route between Innsbruck and Landeck, but only (frequent) regional trains stop here (€7, 35 minutes). Both the A12/E60 and Hwy 171 pass near the abbey.

THE ÖTZTAL
pop 12,000

The Ötztal (Ötz Valley) is a place of raw elemental forces: rugged mountains and wooded slopes, shimmering snowfields and blue glaciers shape this corner of Tyrol. Guarding the border to Italy, this is one of three river valleys running north from the **Ötztaler Alpen** to drain into the Inn River. Dwarfed by Tyrol's highest peak, **Wildspitze** (3774m), the region is a year-round magnet to skiers, hikers and mountaineers.

Most villages in the valley have supermarkets, banks, camping grounds and tourist offices. The latter can supply you with information on activities and accommodation; room rates are 30% to 50% higher in winter. If you're here in summer, ask about the **Ötztal Card** (7/10 days €56/74), which covers public transport, cable cars and numerous swimming pools in the valley.

Sights & Activities

After Ötz, the first village of any size along the valley is **Umhausen**, home to **Ötzi Dorf** (☎ 05255-500 22; adult/child €5.90/2.80; ⊙ 9.30am-5.30pm May-Oct), a fascinating open-air museum recreating the Neolithic world of Ötzi the ice man (see boxed text, opposite). A visit takes in traditional thatched huts, herb gardens, craft displays and enclosures where wild boar and oxen roam. From here, it's a pleasant 40-minute amble along a forest trail to Tyrol's longest waterfall, **Stuibenfall**, cascading 159m over slate cliffs and moss-covered boulders.

Just 10km down the valley is Längenfeld's futuristic spa, **Aqua Dome** (☎ 05253-64 00; www .aquadome.at; Oberlängenfeld 140; 3hr card adult/child Mon-Fri €14/7, Sat & Sun €16/9; ⊙ 9am-11pm). Set against the backdrop of the Ötztaler Alps, the focal point is its trio of flying saucer-shaped pools, where thermal waters gurgle and pummel you into a blissful state of relaxation. It's particularly spacey at night when a fluorescent pyramid illuminates the tubs; pick a jet to gaze up at the stars and summits.

The thermal baths anchor the **sauna** (€7; ⊙ 10am-11pm), a marvellously surreal experience for those who dare to bare. Abandon

---

ENTOMBED IN ICE

In September 1991 German hikers in the Ötztaler Alpen came across the body of a man preserved within the Similaun Glacier. Police and forensic scientists were summoned to the scene. The body had been found some 90m within Italy, but was appropriated by the Austrians and taken to Innsbruck University to be studied.

Experts initially decided it was about 500 years old. The ice man, nicknamed 'Ötzi' or 'Frozen Fritz', was thought to have been a soldier serving under Archduke Ferdinand. Carbon dating, however, revealed he was nearly 5400 years old, placing him in the late Stone Age and making him the oldest and best-preserved mummy in the world.

Ötzi became big news, more so because the state of preservation was remarkable; even the pores of the skin were visible. In addition, Ötzi had been found with 70 artefacts, including a copper axe, bow and arrows, charcoal and clothing. Physiologically he was found to be no different from modern humans. His face was reconstructed, right down to his dark hair and blue eyes. X-rays showed he had suffered from arthritis and frostbite, and his ribs had been broken.

For many years debate raged over how the Iceman met his end, but recent analysis has revealed Ötzi was involved in a violent struggle and died while trying to escape. Blood on his weapons and clothes were discovered to be from other persons, and an arrow wound to his back and knife gashes to his arms all pointed to a fight. His copper axe is still a matter of debate, however; while copper dating from the age of Ötzi has been found in other parts of Austria, Germany and Switzerland, it predates knowledge of the use of copper in the Ötztal area by 500 years.

Not everybody was worried about the finer points of his heritage, however. Several Austrian and Italian women contacted the university shortly after the discovery and requested that they be impregnated with Ötzi's frozen sperm, but the all-important part of his body was missing.

In 1998 Ötzi was relinquished to the Italians and became the centrepiece of a new museum in Bolzano.

---

modesty to swelter in barn-style saunas, hay rooms, honey-scented cabins and the vaulted *Dampf-Dom*, a steaming shrine where Gregorian chants play. For the ultimate chill-out, step inside the teeth-chattering ice chamber or the rain temple where you can choose to be drenched by a thunderstorm, a raging waterfall or fine morning mist.

Rolling 20km down the valley you hit **Sölden** (1377m), a ski resort with snow-sure slopes and pulsating nightlife. The resort's 150km of pistes include red and blue runs, glacier skiing at Rettenbach and Tiefenbach, plus the alpine rally on Big 3 – three summits over 3000m. The **tourist office** (☎ 05254-510-0; www.soelden.com, in German; Gemeindestrasse 4; ☼ 8am-6pm Mon-Sat, 9am-noon Sun) can arrange accommodation and has brochures on activities in the area. There are two ways to reach the surrounding rugged peaks from the village; a chairlift climbs to **Hochsölden** (2090m; one-way/return €5.50/7.50), while a cable car rises to **Gaislachkogel** (3058m; return €19.50) where there are sweeping views of the entire Ötztaler Alps. Ski passes are €41.50 for a day in the high season.

Further south is **Obergurgl** (1930m), the highest parish in Austria. It's another well-known ski resort popular with families, as pistes are mostly suitable for beginners and intermediates and continue right to the edge of the village. **Hohe Mut** (2659m) is a justly famous lookout, accessible by chairlift year-round. Obergurgl is actually at the head of the valley, but the road doubles back on itself and rises to **Hochgurgl** (2150m). Here the pistes are a little steeper and the views equally impressive. The Obergurgl **tourist office** (☎ 05256-6466; www.obergurgl.com, in German; Gurglerstrasse 18; ☼ 8am-6pm Mon-Fri, 8am-4pm Sat, 9.30am-noon Sun summer, 9am-5.30pm Mon-Sat, 9.30am-noon Sun winter) covers both resorts, as does one **ski pass** (day/week pass €41.50/228.50). A gondola provides easy access between Obergurgl's and Hochgurgl's pistes.

Just beyond Hochgurgl, where the road makes a sharp right-hand turn, is another viewing point, the **Windegg Belvedere** (2080m). The road continues into Italy over the **Timmelsjoch Pass** (2474m; car/motorbike €13/11) where it joins the course of the Timmelsbach River.

Getting There & Away

Arriving by train, get off at Ötztal Bahnhof, from where buses head south into the valley. In the summer and winter high seasons buses depart almost hourly (only every two hours in the low season) and go as far as Obergurgl (one way/return €8.30/16.60, 1½ hours). From mid-July to mid-September two morning buses continue as far as Timmelsjoch, on the Italian border, but a change is required at Obergurgl.

If you have your own wheels, you should be able to get at least as far as Hochgurgl all year, but the road beyond into Italy (via the Timmelsjoch Pass) is often blocked by snow in winter.

IMST
☎ 05412 / pop 9000
Beautifully situated in the wide Gurgltal (Gurgl Valley) and spreading towards a jagged range of peaks, Imst is one of the region's best-kept secrets. With its alpine-crisp air, undulating meadows and hidden ravines, this unassuming little town is a terrific base for silent uphill trudges. While skiers carve up the slopes in the nearby Ötztal, Haflinger horses graze on these hillsides – it's a taste of Tyrol before the tourists got there.

The **tourist office** (☎ 69 10-0; www.imst.at; Johannesplatz 4; ◷ 9am-6pm Mon-Fri, 9am-noon Sat) is highly informed on accommodation and activities in Imst and its surrounds; there's also free internet access.

Sights & Activities
Every four years, Imst plays host to a Shrovetide festival, the **Schemenlaufen** (ghost dance); the next takes place on 15 February 2009. The highlight is the vibrant parade of ghost-like characters, from hunchback *Hexen* (witches) to impish *Spritzer* that squirt water at spectators. To learn more about this age-old tradition, visit the **Fasnachthaus** (☎ 69 10; Streleweg 6; adult/child €4/1; ◷ 4-6pm Fri), which exhibits many of the handcarved ghost masks.

In summer, Imst is ideal for easy rambling with 350km of well-marked hiking trails heading off into the hills. A favourite among families is the three-hour loop that leads up the glacier-carved **Rosengartenschlucht** ravine to Hoch-Imst, where walkers can admire vistas of the Lechtaler Alps, bathe in a clear mountain lake and race downhill in a rickety roller coaster (see p91).

Sleeping & Eating
Imst has a sprinkling of good-value places to stay and eat. Drop into the tourist office for a list of private rooms, guesthouses and farms in the area.

HEAVY ROCK

Fans of rude rocks should make the pilgrimage to the bizarrely named **Erdpyramiden** (earth columns) in the little village of Roppen, 10 minutes from Imst. An hour's trudge along a narrow trail and past trickling waterfalls brings you to this collection of hoodoos – thin rock spires that suddenly pop up as you're wandering through the shady woods. Remnants of the last Ice Age and formed by erosion over centuries, these geological wonders assume various shapes and sizes. Among them are a couple of strikingly phallic monoliths that seem like ancient Austrian fertility symbols lost and long forgotten in this beautiful forest.

Camping Imst-West (☎ 662 93; Langgasse 62; campsites per adult/child/site €6/3/7.50) Perched above Imst, this friendly camping ground surrounded by pastures is a peaceful spot to pitch your tent. The first-rate facilities include a kiosk, snack bar and playground.

Gasthof Hirschen (☎ 69 01; www.hirschen-imst.at, in German; Thomas-Walch-Strasse 3; s/d €48/74; P 🖳 🖭) This central family-run guesthouse has comfy rooms, a swimming pool and free wi-fi. A plate of venison ragout is never far away in the wood-panelled restaurant (mains €10 to €18), where stag heads grace the walls.

Getting There & Away
The town is slightly to the north of the main east–west roads (the A12/E60 and Hwy 171), and is served by frequent buses and trains (from Innsbruck €10.20, one hour).

EHRWALD
☎ 05673 / pop 2550
The crowning glory of the small resort of Ehrwald is **Zugspitze** (2962m), marking the border between Austria and Germany. A speedy cable car (summer one way/return €21/32) sails to the crest, where there's a magnificent panorama of the main Tyrolean mountain ranges, as well as the Bavarian Alps and Mt Säntis in Switzerland. North of Zugspitze is Garmisch-Partenkirchen, Germany's most popular ski resort, which also offers access to the summit.

Ehrwald is linked with other resorts in Austria (including Seefeld) and Germany (including Garmisch-Partenkirchen) under the

Happy Ski Card (adult/child for the minimum 3 days €88/53). For information on accommodation and activities, contact the **tourist office** (☎ 05673-23 95; ehrwald@zugspitze.tirol.at; ☺ 8.30am-6pm Mon-Fri, 9am-6pm Sat) in the heart of the town. Staff will help find rooms free of charge.

Trains from Seefeld (€9.30, 1¼ hours) and Innsbruck (€16.30, two hours) to Ehrwald pass through Germany; you must change at Garmisch-Partenkirchen. Austrian train tickets are valid for the whole trip.

LANDECK

☎ 05442 / pop 7500

Sitting pretty above the fast-flowing Inn and Sanna Rivers, Landeck receives just a trickle of tourists. Yet it has an awful lot going for it: a clifftop medieval castle to act out Rapunzel fantasies, a precipitous gorge, and orchards in neighbouring Stanz that are perfect for summertime schnapps-guzzling. The Alps are the town's natural skyscrapers and provide a backdrop for high-altitude activities from skiing to hiking, cycling and white-water rafting.

Orientation & Information

Most of Landeck's restaurants and hotels cluster on Malserstrasse. Here you'll find the **tourist office** (☎ 656 00; www.tirolwest.at; Malserstrasse; ☺ 8.30am-noon & 2-6pm Mon-Fri, 8.30am-noon Sat), where the friendly staff will help book accommodation. If you're staying overnight in summer, pick up the Tirol West Card for free access to the major sights, outdoor pools and the bus network.

The train station is 1.5km to the east; to get into town walk left on leaving the station and stay on the same side of the river. Local buses also make the trip (one way €1.60).

Sights & Activities

Your gaze is drawn upward to the turrets and vine-clad towers of 13th-century **Schloss Landeck** (☎ 632 02; Schlossberg; adult/student €6.50/4; ☺ 10am-5pm Tue-Sun mid-May–Sep, 2-5pm Tue-Sun Oct). The 1st-floor museum showcases everything from Celtic figurines to handcarved *Krampus* masks. The castle is especially lovely at Christmas when the mechanised nativity scene is in full swing. For enviable views over Landeck and the Lechtaler Alps, climb the dizzying staircase to the tower.

Landeck attracts the odd skier or two to its 22km of gentle slopes (a day ski pass in high season costs €25), but is better known

for its excellent hiking trails. In summer, the **Venet cable car** (one way/return €10.20/12.20) zooms up to Krahberg (2208m), where there is a web of marked footpaths. The 280km Adlerweg trail (p86) also stops off in Landeck on its journey through Tyrol. The tourist office arranges guided walks, which are free with a Tirol West Card.

Adventurous types make for **Sport Camp Tirol** (☎ 646 36; www.sportcamptirol.at; Mühlkanal 1), offering activities from canyoning and paragliding to glacier tours, rock climbing and rafting on the Inn River. You can also rent **mountain bikes** (half/full day €18/22) here to head off on one of the tourist office's free GPS tours or tackle the downhill Inn Trail (p78).

A rollercoaster of water thrashes limestone cliffs at **Zammer Lochputz** (☎ 656 00; Hauptstrasse 53, Zams; adult/child €3.50/2.50; ☺ 9.30am-5.30pm May-Sep, 9.30am-4pm Oct), a fine specimen of a gorge just outside of Landeck. Cutting a path through pine forest, the trail passes viewpoints and some interesting rock formations – look out for the head of a bull and a nymph.

If the fresh air and activity have worked up a thirst, pop over to **Stanz** (4km away). Set on a sunny plateau dotted with apple and plum orchards, the village is home to 600 residents and a mind-boggling 65 schnapps distilleries. There are a number of rustic huts where you can kick back and taste the local firewater before rolling back down to the valley.

Sleeping & Eating

Hotel Sonne (☎ 625 19; www.hotel-sonne-landeck.at; Herzog-Friedrich-Strasse 10; s/d €28/56; P) It's hard to miss this dazzling canary-yellow hotel on the main drag. The décor is nondescript, but rooms are comfortable and reasonably priced.

Gasthof Greif (☎ 622 68; Marktplatz 6; s/d €34/56; P) Greif sits on a square above the main street just down from the castle. Its 1970s-style rooms are large and well kept, and its restaurant (mains €7 to €13) serves solid Tyrolean cuisine.

Tramserhof (☎ 622 46; www.tramserhof.at; in German; Tramserweg 51; s/d €62/104; P ≋) Nestled among trees, this lodge is a calm retreat 20 minutes' walk from the centre. The rooms are country-style with loads of natural light and warm pine. The spa shelters a whirlpool and sauna. Tuck into organic produce at breakfast.

Café Haag (☎ 623 28-0; Maisengasse 19; coffee & snacks €3-6; ☺ 8am-8pm Mon-Fri, 8am-7pm Sat, 10am-7pm

Sun) Locally picked plums are the key ingredient in this café's divine chocolates. Once you've sampled them, try the cakes – just the sugar kick needed for the uphill trudge to the castle.

Hotel Schrofenstein (☎ 623 95; Malserstrasse 31; mains €12-23; ☺ lunch & dinner) Schrofenstein's restaurant dishes up Austrian classics from veal goulash to spinach *Spätzle* (egg noodles) in wood-panelled surroundings. When the sun's out, pull up a chair on the chestnut tree-shaded terrace.

Getting There & Away

InterCity express trains operate hourly to Innsbruck (€11.90, 50 minutes) and every two hours to Bregenz (€19.90). Buses head in all directions, departing from outside the train station and/or from the bus station in the centre.

The A12/E60 into Vorarlberg passes by Landeck, burrowing into a tunnel as it approaches the town. Highway 315, the Inntal road, passes through the centre of town.

THE INNTAL
pop 11,250

Shadowing the turquoise Inn River, the Inntal (Inn Valley) extends for 230km within Tyrol. There are few major sights in this region but the scenery is beautiful, particularly around **Pfunds**, shifting from jagged pinnacles to gently rolling greenery. Many homes here are similar in design to those found in the Engadine in Grau-bünden, Switzerland, further up the Inn Valley.

South of Pfunds, you have the choice of routes. If you continue along the Inn you'll end up in Switzerland (infrequent buses). Alternatively, if you bear south to Nauders you'll soon reach South Tyrol (Italy) by way of the Reschen Pass (open year-round). Six buses daily run from Landeck to Nauders (€9.30, one hour), where it's possible to head on with public transport to Merano in Italy, but at least three changes are required.

THE PAZNAUNTAL
pop 5950

Grazing the Swiss border and running west of the Inntal, the **Paznauntal** (Paznaun Valley) is a dramatic landscape overshadowed by the glaciated peaks of the Silvretta range. The villages are low-key in summer, but the lull is broken in winter when a deep carpet of

snow draws skiers to party-hearty resorts like **Ischgl** (below).

The valley is undoubtedly one of Austria's best ski areas, despite (or because of) its relative isolation. The **Silvretta Ski Pass** (2-day pass adult/child €80/45.50) covers Ischgl, Galtür, Kappl and Samnaun, a duty-free area in Switzerland. Its summer equivalent (3-day pass adult/child €32.50/19.50) comprises cable cars, lifts, public transport over the Bielerhöhe Pass into Vorarlberg, and a number of swimming pools in Ischgl and Galtür.

Around 10km from Ischgl is the uncrowded resort of **Galtür**. This unspoilt village suffered a major disaster in February 1999 when an avalanche all but swept it away. A museum documenting the event has been built on the spot, the **Alpinarium Galtür** (☎ 05443-200 00; www .alpinarium.at, in German; adult/child €8/4; ☺ 10am-6pm Tue-Sun). Inside you'll find many poignant reminders of the devastation in the shape of photos, newspaper reports and some incredible video footage.

GETTING THERE & AWAY

Only a secondary road (Hwy 188) runs along the valley, crossing into Vorarlberg at Bielerhöhe Pass (p378), where there are excellent views. This pass (toll cars/motorcycles €11.50/10.50) is closed during winter and rejoins the main highway near Bludenz. Regular buses travel along the valley as far as Galtür (€7, 70 minutes) from Landeck.

Ischgl
☎ 05444 / pop 1500

When the first flakes fall, the alpine village of Ischgl becomes a quintessential powdersville with snow-sure slopes and a boisterous après-ski scene that gives St Anton am Arlberg a run for its money. The resort is a bizarre combination of rural meets raunchy; a place where log chalets and lap-dancing bars, folk music and techno coexist. Love it or lump it, this is no place for retiring wallflowers, especially during the season-closing Top of the Mountain Concert, which has welcomed a host of stars including Sting, Bon Jovi and Elton John in recent years.

ORIENTATION & INFORMATION

The **tourist office** (☎ 52 66-0; www.ischgl.com; ☺ 8am-6pm Mon-Fri, 9am-noon & 4-6pm Sat, 10am-noon Sun) stocks heaps of literature on hiking, biking and skiing in the area. Ischgl is compact and walkable, with most hotels, restaurants and bars huddling on Dorfstrasse, the main thoroughfare, which is just a short amble from the ski lifts.

ACTIVITIES

At the heart of the Silvretta Arena, Ischgl offers fabulous **skiing**, with ultramodern lifts and access to 230km of groomed slopes that are perfect for carving and cruising. The runs are mainly geared towards intermediates, but there are several black runs and off-piste opportunities to satisfy experts. The terrain is equally ideal for **snowboarding** with two half-pipes and a dedicated boarding park.

In winter, the 7km **toboggan track** (adult/child €10/4.50) offers a bumpy downhill dash through the snow from Idalp to Ischgl, which is particularly scenic when floodlit on Monday and Thursday nights.

There are few Austrian resorts that can match Ischgl for **mountain biking**. The mammoth Silvretta Mountain Bike Arena (p79) features 1000km of bikeable territory ranging from downhill tracks to circular trails and a technique park. Pick up a free map of the area at the tourist office. **Ischgl Bike** (☎ 52 62; www .ischgl-bike.at, in German; Ischgl 22) rents quality bikes for €23 per day.

Walking is another big draw in summer, ranging from gentle rambles alongside shimmering lakes to ambitious scrambling on the *Klettersteige* (fixed rope routes) at 2872m Greitspitz and 2929m Flimspitze. In total, the area comprises some 300km of trails interspersed with 18 mountain huts.

SLEEPING & EATING

The following accommodation is open year-round. Ischgl's best beds fill up quickly in winter, so booking ahead is recommended. Expect prices to be roughly double those quoted below in the high winter season. Aside from La Candela, the restaurants close in summer.

Designers from Laura Ashley to Philippe Starck have put their contemporary stamp on the rooms at boutiquey **Hotel Madlein** (☎ 52 26; Ischgl 144; www.ischglmadlein.com; s €127-210, d €150-280; P ⌨ ❄). A few paces from the ski lifts, this hip hotel lures with its Zen-style garden and slick cocktail bar. If you're seeking budget rather than blowout, centrally located **Eveline** (☎ 53 10; Ischgl 187; s/d €32/60; P) and **Vereina** (☎ 56 40; Ischgl 277; d €36; P) are

both cosy chalet-style pensions with a homy atmosphere and clean, comfy rooms.

There are loads of dining possibilities in the centre. A great choice for thin and crispy pizzas is **La Candela** (☎ 55 80; Ischgl 175; pizza €6-12; ❄ lunch & dinner) at Hotel Victoria. Housed in a dark-wood chalet, **Bauernküche Loba** (☎ 52 89; Ischgl 45; mains €8-17; ❄ dinner) rustles up huge portions of Tyrolean favourites like *Kasknödel* (cheese dumplings). The new kid on the slopes is the stone-and-glass **Alpenhaus Restaurant** (☎ 52 70; Idalp; mains €6-15; ❄ 9am-4pm) next to the Silvretta lift, with charcoal grill specialities and a fabulous sun terrace.

DRINKING

Ischgl's après-ski is so hot it's a wonder the snow doesn't melt: a cocktail of oompah-playing alpine barns, saucy go-go bars and chichi clubs shake the resort. The following places, except for the Golden Eagle Pub, only open in winter.

There's nothing like a little slope-side socialising to gear up for a big night out in Ischgl; lively après-ski haunts include **Kuhstall** (☎ 52 23; Ischgl 80; ❄ 3pm-midnight) and **Feuer & Eis** (☎ 59 18; ❄ 4-7pm), both offering an electric vibe, ear-splitting music and plenty of bopping in moonboots.

For a pint of Kilkenny, a laid-back vibe and ZZ Top at full blast, make for the **Golden Eagle Pub** (☎ 56 71; Ischgl 6; ❄ 8pm-2am). Even party diva Paris Hilton has been spotted slurping prosecco at the legendary **Pacha** (☎ 52 26; Hotel Madlein; ❄ 10pm-5am), which brims with beautiful people and sidles up to the Coyote Ugly lap-dancing bar. Another celebrity favourite is the wild **Trofana Arena** (☎ 600-700; Ischgl 334; ❄ 9pm-5am) with frequent live music, laser shows and scantily-clad go-go dancers.

GETTING THERE & AWAY

An efficient bus service operates between Landeck (€5.90, 55 minutes) and Ischgl hourly from Monday to Friday and every two hours at weekends.

ARLBERG REGION

The Arlberg region, shared by Vorarlberg and Tyrol, comprises several linked resorts and offers some of Austria's finest skiing. Heralded as the cradle of alpine skiing, St Anton am Arlberg is undoubtedly the best known and

TYROL

most popular resort. For other destinations in Arlberg, see p379.

The winter season is long, with snow reliable till about mid-April. Summer is less busy (and cheaper), though still popular with walkers. Even so, some of the restaurants, bars and discos that swing during the ski season are closed. Most others close between seasons, and open from late June to October. Many guesthouses and some hotels do likewise.

ST ANTON AM ARLBERG
☎ 05446 / pop 2600

In the beginning there was St Anton, a sleepy village in the rugged Arlberg. For centuries seasons were defined by the falling and melting of snow and the coming and going of cattle, until one day the locals beheld the virgin powder on their doorstep – and there was light! In 1901, the resort founded the first ski club in the Alps and downhill skiing was born. So if ever the ski bug is going to bite you, it will surely be here. Nestled at the foot of 2811m-high Valluga, St Anton am Arlberg is a cross between a ski bum's Shangri-La and Ibiza in fast-forward mode – the terrain is fierce and the nightlife hedonistic.

Orientation

St Anton is strung out along the northern bank of the Rosanna River. The modern train station is on the Rendl side, a few paces from the Dorfstrasse (pedestrian-only centre) and the ski lifts. A 10-minute stroll east is Nasserein, where novices can test out the nursery slopes. Further east still are the quieter slopes of St Jakob, easily accessed by the Nasserein gondola.

Information

The centrally located **tourist office** (☎ 226 90; www.stantonamarlberg.com; Arlberg Haus; ☒ 8am-6pm Mon-Fri, 9am-noon Sat & Sun summer, 8.30am-6pm Mon-Fri, 9am-6pm Sat, 9am-noon & 2-5pm Sun winter) has information on outdoor activities, maps and places to stay. There's an accommodation board and a free telephone outside.

The post office is near the Rosanna River, off the northern end of the pedestrian zone. **Mailbox** (Dorfstrasse 54; per hr €6; ☒ 8.30am-8.30pm winter, noon-5pm Mon-Fri summer) has internet access, but you can check emails for free in most ski shops.

Sights & Activities

The nostalgic **Ski & Heimat Museum** (☎ 24 75; Rudi-Matt-Weg 10; adult/child €3/1; ☒ 11am-5pm Tue-Sun Jul & Aug, 1-5pm Tue-Sun Sep-Jun) traces St Anton's tracks back to the good old days when skis were made of wood and men were as tough as hobnail boots.

St Anton is at the very pinnacle of Austria's alpine **skiing** and the spacey Galzigbahn gondola, launched in 2007, has further improved conditions. The terrain is vast and the skiing challenging, with exhilarating descents including the Kandahar run on Galzig and fantastic backcountry opportunities. Cable cars ascend to Valluga (2811m) from where experts can go off-piste all the way to Lech (with a ski guide only). For fledglings, there are nursery slopes on Gampen (1850m) and Kapall (2330m). Rendl is **snowboarding** territory with jumps, rails and a half-pipe. A single **ski pass** (1-/3-/7-day high-season pass €41.50/114/224, discounts at other times of the year) covers the whole Arlberg region. It is valid for 83 ski lifts, giving access to 276km of prepared pistes.

Adding to this enormous winter playground is the 4km-long **Rodelbahn** (toboggan run), where sledding fans can hurtle and bounce past snowy trees down to the valley; the track is floodlit every Tuesday and Thursday night. With glowing faces and frosty fingers, most sledders stop at the halfway hut, **Rodelalm** (mains €10-16), to warm up with schnapps and a big plate of *Schweinshaxe* (pork knuckles).

In summer, **walking** in the mountains is the most popular activity and the meadows full of wildflowers and grazing cattle are pure Heidi. During this time, a handful of **cable cars and lifts** (one way €4-18, return €5-20) rise up to the major peaks. If you're planning on going hiking, pick up a detailed booklet and map from the tourist office and consider purchasing a **Wanderpass** (7-day €30), providing unlimited access to all lifts, or a **St Anton Card** (€45), which offers the same benefits plus entrance to the town's indoor and outdoor swimming pool.

Cyclists are also catered for: the tourist office produces a small booklet (in German only) with a number of suggested trails in the area.

Sleeping

Budget beds are as rare as the yeti in St Anton, so it's worth booking ahead. Prices tend to drop the further you move from the centre; Nasserein and St Jakob are safe bets, just a

TYROL

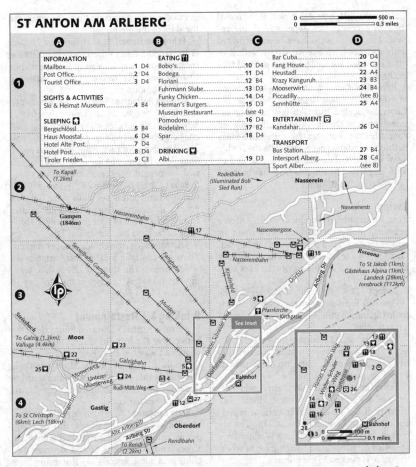

ST ANTON AM ARLBERG

INFORMATION		
Mailbox	1	D4
Post Office	2	D4
Tourist Office	3	D4
SIGHTS & ACTIVITIES		
Ski & Heimat Museum	4	B4
SLEEPING		
Bergschlössl	5	D4
Haus Moostal	6	D4
Hotel Alte Post	7	D4
Hotel Post	8	D4
Tiroler Frieden	9	C3

EATING		
Bobo's	10	D4
Bodega	11	D4
Floriani	12	B4
Fuhrmann Stube	13	D4
Funky Chicken	14	D4
Herman's Burgers	15	D3
Museum Restaurant	(see 4)	
Pomodoro	16	D4
Rodelalm	17	B2
Spar	18	D4
DRINKING		
Albi	19	D3

Bar Cuba	20	D4
Fang House	21	C3
Heustadl	22	A4
Krazy Kanguruh	23	B3
Mooserwirt	24	B4
Piccadilly	(see 8)	
Sennhütte	25	A4
ENTERTAINMENT		
Kandahar	26	D4
TRANSPORT		
Bus Station	27	B4
Intersport Alberg	28	C4
Sport Alber	(see 8)	

15- to 20-minute stroll away. There are hundreds of options in St Anton, but many of the smaller pensions only open in winter. The following places are open in summer (June to September) and winter (December to April). In the high winter season, rates can be as much as double as those given below.

Tiroler Frieden (☎ 22 47; tiroler.frieden@st-anton .at; Dorfstrasse 75; d €36; P) Backing onto the lower ski slopes, this quaint chalet is among St Anton's best budget digs. The no-frills rooms are old-style with heavy wood panelling and chintzy fabrics, but they're comfy and spotlessly clean.

Gästehaus Alpina (☎ 33 15; gaestehaus.alpina@ st-anton.at; Gsörerweg 26; s/d €23/40; P) This lovely wooden chalet in St Jakob is a 20-minute walk

from the centre. Opening onto balconies, the tidy rooms are kitted out with cable TV and broadband.

Haus Moostal (☎ 28 31; info@hausmoostal.at; Marktstrasse 14; s/d €29/52; P) You'll receive a warm welcome at this little gem of a guesthouse. Dressed in blonde wood furnishings, the bright rooms have squishy beds and wi-fi. There's a tiny sauna onsite.

Hotel Post (☎ 221 30; www.hotel-post.co.at; Walter-Schuler-Weg 2; s/d €62/114; P) This hotel's large, modern rooms are full of little extras such as bottled water, fruit and wi-fi. The meditation room, saunas and whirlpool are ideal for chilling out after a day on the slopes.

Bergschlössl (☎ 22 00; info@bergschloessl.at; Kandaharweg 13; s/d €69/125; P) Right next to the

Galzigbahn lift, you can't beat Berschlössl for easy access to the slopes and alpine appeal. The snug rooms have been decorated with a razor-sharp eye for detail, with fireplaces or tiled stoves and hand-painted tiles in the bathrooms.

Hotel Alte Post (☎ 54 46; www.hotel-alte-post .at, in German; Dorfstrasse 11; s/d €104/176; P ⚡ 💻) Centrally located, this 17th-century hotel exudes Tyrolean charm. Individually designed rooms feature four-star trimmings like fluffy bathrobes and internet access. The spa is a big draw with herbal saunas, a salt grotto and an arm-long list of treatments from hay baths to hot chocolate massages.

Eating

Because of the lopsidedness of St Anton's seasons, many restaurants only open in winter (high season times are given below). Quiet is not a word in St Anton's vocabulary and most places double as vibrant bars after dinner.

Bodega (☎ 427 88; Dorfstrasse 38; tapas €2.50-10; ☯ 3pm-1am) Tapas and *vino tinto* reel in crowds to this Spanish haunt, where live music creates a buzzy vibe.

Pomodoro (☎ 33 33; Dorfstrasse 5; mains €7-9; ☯ dinner) The homemade pasta and pizza at this lively bistro would make mamma proud. Prices are pocket-pleasing too.

Funky Chicken (☎ 302 01; Dorfstrasse 7; mains €7-11; ☯ 6pm-2am) St Anton's hottest chick, this livewire dishes up chicken in various guises, cheap beer and a pick'n'mix of DJs. The atmosphere is crazy, especially on Wednesday's so-called Swedish head-banging night when the place is packed to the gunnels.

Floriani (☎ 23 30; Alte Arlbergstrasse 13; mains €7-15; ☯ dinner Tue-Sun) This cheery family-run place rustles up a mix of Italian and Austrian grub

in wood-panelled surroundings; the pizzas are the stars of the menu.

Fuhrmann Stube (☎ 29 21; Dorfstrasse 74; mains €8-14; ☯ lunch & dinner) When snow blankets the rooftops, this cosy hideaway is a great spot to relax and tuck into a plate of steaming *Knödel* (dumplings).

Museum Restaurant (☎ 2475; Rudi-Matt-Weg 10; mains €15-25; ☯ dinner Tue-Sun) Under the Heimat Museum, this gorgeous Tyrolean restaurant cooks with locally sourced produce – you can even fish your own trout from the pond. Snuggle up by the open fire in winter or refresh with homemade ice cream in summer.

Bobo's (☎ 271 454; Dorfstrasse 60; ☯ 5pm-2am) Tex-Mex food and potent cocktails make Bobo's a perennial favourite. The party cranks up after fajitas and a fistful of nachos, with everything from karaoke to live bands and DJs.

Self-caterers have a choice of supermarkets. There's a centrally located **Spar** (Dorfstrasse 66), which houses the **Murr** (☎ 2202-0) deli, serving hot takeaway lunches from Monday to Saturday (€4 to €6).

Drinking & Entertainment

St Anton is Austria's Duracell Bunny: load the batteries in the form of several Jägermeister shots and watch it hop, bop and bounce off the walls till the wee hours. The après-ski is the wildest this side of the Alps and stamina is a prerequisite for completing (conscious) the infamous bar crawl.

Krazy Kanguruh (☎ 26 33; Mooserweg 19; ☯ 10am-8pm) Right next to the slopes, this drinking den is loud, fun and jam-packed after 5pm. Expect rounds of shots, an indoor snow machine and some serious ski stumbling back to the valley.

Bar Cuba (☎ 0664-6523 886; Dorfstrasse 33; ☯ 4pm-3am) This popular watering hole has big-screen

---

LOCAL'S FAVOURITE WATERING HOLES

Piccadilly (above) 'The live music is ideal for getting up on the bar to dance and the staff are super!' *Steffi, masseuse*

Funky Chicken (above) 'Because it's *the* craziest bar in St Anton. Cheap beer, lethal margaritas and insane staff – the perfect night out!' *Giles Dobson, student*

Heustadl (above) 'There's a very entertaining après-ski band where the waitresses are part of the show…' *Chris Ritson, powerline contractor*

Mooserwirt (above) 'You have to see this place to believe it – the lively crowd, DJs and lights make for a great après-ski experience. Bet your ski boots take you grooving…' *Jason, chalet worker*

Fang House (above) 'It's a good place to start your day with a coffee and finish it with a gluhwein. Great music, no *Schlager*! *Maggie Ritson, mum to be*

TYROL

sports, chirpy staff and aptly named cocktails like Cuban Cocaine and Sex on the Piste.

Albi (☎ 31 72; Dorfstrasse 78; ☒ 4pm-1am) If a spit-and-sawdust pub is what you're seeking, this place delivers with local characters at the bar and Guinness on tap.

Mooserwirt (☎ 35 88; Unterer Mooserweg 2; ☒ 11am-8pm) St Anton's undisputed king of après-ski, Mooserwirt claims to sell more beer per square metre than anywhere else in Austria. By teatime, the hilltop terrace heaves with swinging steins and Europop. The challenge is to make it down to St Anton in one piece, which begs the question: how can you ski when you're legless?

Sennhütte (☎ 20 48; ☒ 11am-8pm) This snug alpine chalet scores points for its sunny terrace, burning schnapps and frolicsome crowd. The one-man band Didi Diesel regularly takes the stage by storm.

Heustadl (☎ 302 97; ☒ 9.30am-7am) Just north of Sennhütte, this woodsy slopeside chalet is always packed to the rafters with a post-ski crowd craving beer and live music. Check out the bizarre legged bar stools.

Fang House (☎ 0676-4091 010; Nassereinerstrasse 6; ☒ 10am-10pm) When in Nasserein, nip into this cheery watering hole for a chat with Maggie and Chris. The house wine is Jägermeister, chilled at a glacial -18°C. One too many and skiers show their fangs. Ravenous skiers should look out for Herman's Burgers, a nearby hut-on-wheels operation where you can sink your teeth into a humungous burger for around €5.

Piccadilly (☎ 2213-276; Walter-Schuler-Weg 2; ☒ 9.30pm-4am) Locals call this place pick a willy

(the mind boggles), but to everyone else this very British pub is loud, crowded and the best place in town for live gigs.

Kandahar (☎ 302 60; Dorfstrasse 50; ☒ 7pm-6am) The décor at St Anton's premier clubbing venue is full of Eastern promise. First-rate DJs keep the dance floor packed till dawn.

Getting There & Away

St Anton is the easiest access point to the region. It's on the train route between Bregenz (€16.20, 1½ hours) and Innsbruck (€14.20; 1¼ hours), with fast trains every one or two hours. St Anton and St Christoph are close to the eastern entrance of the Arlberg Tunnel, the toll road connecting Vorarlberg and Tyrol. The tunnel toll is €8.50 for cars and mini-buses. You can avoid the toll by taking the B197, but no vehicles with trailers are allowed on this winding road.

Buses depart from stands southwest of the tourist office.

Getting Around

Free local buses go to outlying parts of the resort (such as St Jakob). Buses run to Lech and Zürs in Vorarlberg (one way €4.50); they are hourly (till about 6pm) in winter, reducing to four a day in summer. Taking a minibus taxi, which can be shared between up to eight people, is another option: the trip from St Anton to Lech costs €50.

Bicycles can be rented (half/full day €14/20) from **Sport Alber** (☎ 34 00; Dorfstrasse 15) and **Intersport Arlberg** (☎ 34 53; Dorfstrasse 1).

Vorarlberg

Vorarlberg is Austria's red hot chilli pepper – tiny but feisty. It squeezes in between Switzerland and Germany, and shakes its bootie with that ol' devil St Anton am Arlberg in Tyrol. It may have the smallest slice of the country's pie, but it's got the filling sussed: tranquil lakes, thundering rivers, forest-clad hills, snowy crags, castles and more cheese than you'll ever need for your crackers are all squashed into this western wedge.

Most people take a bite out of Bregenz first, the big daddy of the Bodensee (Lake Constance), where locals board yachts for a quick spin and skinny dip after work, gazing up at the giddy heights of the Pfänder to ponder on whether life can get much better. From here, the only way is up to the Bregenzerwald; wiggling through a mysterious land of rolling velvet hills, granite spires and villages choc-a-bloc with dairies. But up on those hills, it's not only the cheese that comes in cubes. Nudging up against woodsy farmhouses are the Bauhaus offspring: eco-friendly modernist houses that are revamping the landscape with straight edges, pale wood and glass walls. Stick-in-the-muds who once dissed them as overgrown Rubik's creations now stand corrected, as the province has become an architectural trailblazer with environmental credentials.

Vorarlberg also rocks in the outdoors department. To the south rise the 3000m-high giants of the Silvretta range, where a hike in the Alps affords vistas of the silver-white peak of Piz Buin. While further east, muddy boots are swapped for designer skis and salopettes in fashionable Lech and Zürs, where poseurs carve up the slopes, bask in five-star luxury and let their hair down with massive snowball fights.

HIGHLIGHTS

- Splashing in the Lake Constance and immersing yourself in modern art in **Bregenz** (p368)

- Pausing on the twisting road through the **Bregenzerwald** (p373) to nibble cheese in alpine dairies

- Swooshing down gentle slopes in **Montafon** (p378) to spy the iconic peak of Piz Buin

- Going back to the Middle Ages in the labyrinthine centre of **Feldkirch** (p374)

- Racing the filthy rich and famous on the pistes of **Lech** (p379)

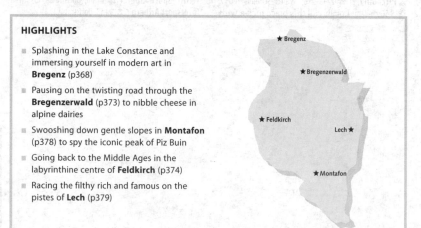

★ Bregenz
★ Bregenzerwald
★ Feldkirch
Lech ★
★ Montafon

■ POPULATION: 355,000   ■ AREA: 2601 SQ KM   ■ HIGHEST ELEVATION: PIZ BUIN 3312M

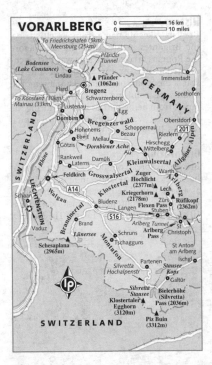

VORARLBERG

History

Vorarlberg has been inhabited since the early Stone Age but it wasn't until the arrival of the Celts in 400 BC, followed by the Romans in around 15 BC, that lasting settlements were maintained. Brigantium, the forerunner of Bregenz, was a stronghold of the Romans until around the 5th and 6th centuries, when the raiding Germanic Alemanni tribes increased their influence and effectively took over.

The province enjoyed a peaceful existence until the early 15th century, when it suffered substantial damage during the Appenzell War with the Swiss Confederation. Relations with its neighbour later improved to such an extent that in 1918 Vorarlberg declared independence from Austria and sought union with Switzerland. The move was blocked by the Allied powers in the post-war reorganisation of Europe; fears that an even-further reduced Austria would be easily assimilated into a recovering Germany were certainly founded. Today, Vorarlberg still looks first towards its westerly neighbours, and then to the Austrian capital, Vienna, 600km to the east.

Climate

Vorarlberg is a predominantly mountainous region with an Atlantic climate, plenty of snow in winter and an above average amount of precipitation (around 2000mm per year). Its weather can differ greatly from the east of Austria; quite often it can be sunny and warm in Vorarlberg and miserable in Vienna, or the other way around.

Language

Locals speak an Alemannic dialect of German which is closer to Schwyzerdütsch (Swiss-German) than to Hochdeutsch (standard German), a lingering legacy of the Germanic Alemanni tribes who settled in Vorarlberg, Switzerland and parts of southern Germany. This strong dialect is often quite hard for native German speakers to understand; the regional tourist office has even gone so far as to produce a *Voralbergisch für den Urlaub* (Vorarlberg dialect for the holiday) guide which translates common words and phrases into Hochdeutsch.

Getting There & Away

Vorarlberg has no international airport; the closest is Friedrichshafen in Germany. The province is connected by rail and A14 autobahn to the rest of Austria via the 14km Arlberg tunnel which runs under the Arlberg mountains. To the west, there are plenty of border crossings into Liechtenstein and Switzerland and the main access to Germany is the A14 heading north from Bregenz.

Bodensee ferries (p370) connect Bregenz to various towns and cities in Switzerland and Germany.

Getting Around

Vorarlberg is broken down into *Domino* (individual zones) which are in turn grouped into nine transport regions; a *Regio* travel pass covering one region costs €5.60/€13.60 for one day/week while a *Maximo* pass, costing €12.20/26.10, covers the entire province. Single *Domino* tickets cost €1.20 and a day pass €2.20 – these cover city transport in Bregenz, Dornbirn, Götzis, Feldkirch, Bludenz, Lech and Schruns/Tschagguns.

Children travel for half price and seniors, people with disabilities and students receive a 30% discount. Further information, including a handy timetable booklet, is available from the **Verkehrsverbund Vorarlberg** (☎ 05522-835

77, www.vmobil.at, in German; Herrengasse 12, Feldkirch; ⊗ 8am-noon & 1-5pm Mon-Fri).

BREGENZ

☎ 05574 / pop 27,000

The beauty of Bregenz is its ability to travel in space and time; it's a place where you can wake up to breakfast on the beach at Bodensee and within minutes survey the Austrian Alps from the 1064m-high Pfänder; roam the twisting cobblestone streets of the *Oberstadt* (upper town) then hit the crystalline waterfront for an avant-garde art fix; pedal through orchards hugging the shore and sample homegrown flavours in a boho café. From summertime playground to futuristic innovator, this city has a split personality. An instantly loveable one.

History

Bregenz takes its name from a Celtic tribe, the Brigantes, who settled the area before the Romans arrived. Bregenz was first documented as Brigancia in 802 and became the seat of the counts of the area. The city enjoyed a fairly peaceful life through the centuries (apart from being part of Bavaria during the Napoleonic Wars) and was crowned capital of Vorarlberg in the 20th century.

Orientation

Bregenz is spread out on the eastern shore of Bodensee with the Pfänder mountain (1064m) as a backdrop. The newer part of the city is near the waterfront, while its historical heart is 10 minutes' walk further inland. The *Bahnhof*

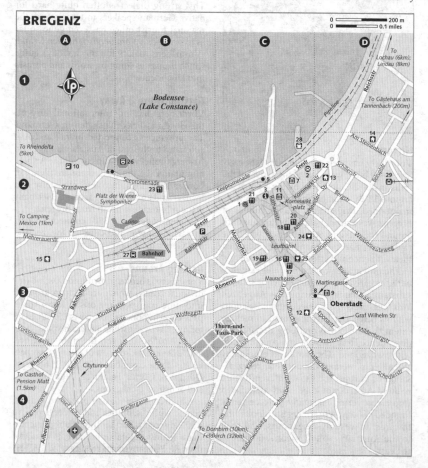

(train station) is a 10-minute amble east of the centre, the ferry terminal only a couple of minutes north across the railway tracks.

Information

Bregenz's new centre has a handful of banks and *Bankomat* (ATM) machines; the train station and post office also have a *Bankomat*. The tourist office has free internet access, and hands out a simple, free map of the city.

Cockpit-Café (☎ 0650-262 57 48; www.cockpit-cafe .com; Bahnhofstrasse 10; ☺ 8am-7pm Mon-Fri, 8am-6pm Sat) High-speed internet access, wi-fi, scanning and printing facilities.

Main post office (Seestrasse 5; ☺ 8am-7pm Mon-Fri, 8am-noon Sat)

Tourist office (☎ 49 59-0; www.bregenz.ws, in German; Rathausstrasse 35a; ☺ 8.30am-7pm Mon-Sat mid-Jul–mid-Aug, 8.30am-6pm Mon-Fri & 9am-noon Sat mid-Aug–early Sep, 9am-noon & 1-5pm Mon-Fri, 9am-noon Sat early Sep-Nov, 8.30am-6pm Mon-Fri, 9am-noon Sat Dec–mid-Jul) Information on the city and the surrounding area and can help with accommodation. Outside opening hours, brochures are stacked in front of the office.

Unfallkrankenhaus (☎ 4901; Josef Huter Strasse 12) Provincial hospital with emergency ward.

Sights

Set high above the lake is the **Oberstadt**, the oldest and most charming part of Bregenz with its maze of winding streets, candy-coloured houses and overgrown gardens. It is still guarded by defensive walls and the sturdy **Martinstor** (St Martin's Gate) festooned with a grotesque mummified shark. Not far past the gate is the bulbous, baroque **Martinsturm** (St Martin's Tower; ☎ 466 32; Martinsgasse; adult/child €1/0.50; ☺ 9am-6.30pm Tue-Sun Easter–mid-Oct), topped by the largest onion dome in central Europe. Take a peek at the 14th-century frescoes in the church on the ground floor before climbing up to the

small Vorarlberger Militärmuseum (military museum) for fine views over the town.

The new face of Bregenz is the **Unterstadt**, home to the **Vorarlberger Landesmuseum** (☎ 460 50; www.vlm.at, in German; Kornmarktplatz 1; adult/student €2/1; ☺ 9am-noon & 2-5pm Tue-Sun, daily during Bregenz Festival). This museum delves into the region's history, art and architecture with curiosities from Stone Age artefacts to a model Roman fort and an intricately carved *Tragorgel* (portable organ). The top floor showcases a superb collection of works by Swiss-born neoclassical artist Angelika Kauffmann (1741–1807).

Just across the way, the geometric **Kunsthaus** (☎ 485 94-0; www.kunsthaus-bregenz.at; Karl-Tizian-Platz; adult/concession €10/6; ☺ 10am-8pm) pops into view. With its soaring glass-and-steel exterior and concrete interior, this is a cube that would inspire Picasso to paint. Its cutting edge design is supposed to look like a lamp (use your imagination!). Flooded with natural light, the inside is stark, open-plan and perfect for rotating exhibitions of contemporary art.

Even if you can't bag tickets for the Bregenz Festival, the lakefront **Festspielhaus** (☎ 413-0; www.festspielhausbregenz.at; Platz der Wiener Symphoniker 1) is another must-see monolith. Blending concrete, tinted glass and clean lines, the striking edifice proves that creativity also comes in boxes. Jutting out onto the lake, the semi-circular Seebühne is where festival performances take place.

Activities

Everybody who arrives in Bregenz is bewitched by the **Bodensee**, Europe's third-largest lake, straddling Austria, Switzerland and Germany. In summer, the lake attracts **cycling** enthusiasts to the beautiful and blissfully flat trails lining its banks (see boxed text, p370). **Fahrradverleih Bregenz** (☎ 0650-541 3000;

BIKING BODENSEE

Perfectly suited for two-wheel adventures, the Lake Constance is ringed by the well-marked **Bodensee Radweg**. Itineraries, maps and distances are given online (www.bodensee-radweg .com). Depending on how fast you pedal, it takes around eight days to cover the entire 243km loop. Grab a bike in Bregenz and you'll soon be freewheeling through Austria, Germany and Switzerland, where landscapes change abruptly from willow-lined promenades to apple orchards, vineyards and half-moon bays framed against the backdrop of the Alps. High points of the cycling trail include:

- Refreshing with ice cream on **Lindau**'s palm-fringed promenade
- Watching bullet-shaped Zeppelins fly overhead in **Friedrichshafen**
- Steaming and (legally) skinny dipping at the lakefront spa at **Meersburg**
- Wandering narrow medieval streets in **Stein-am-Rhein**
- Exploring the monastic island of **Reichenau**, a Unesco World Heritage site
- Gazing up at the Münster's filigree spires in Roman-rooted **Konstanz**
- Sniffing beautiful blooms in the botanical gardens in **Mainau**
- Watching grey herons wade in the marshes at **Rheindelta** nature reserve

am Blumenmolo; 8am-9pm May-Sep) rents quality bikes for €16.50 per day.

Other activities on the lake include **sailing** and **diving** at Lochau, 5km north of town, and **swimming**. The best place for a quick dip or a barbecue is the **Pipeline**, a stretch of pebbly beach north of Bregenz so named for the large pipeline running parallel to the lake. If you fancy sunbathing and splashing around in the buff, there is a secluded naturist beach at Hard, 5km southwest of Bregenz. Alternatively, check out the open-air pools and volleyball court at the lakeside **Strandbad** (442 42; Strandweg; adult/child €3.50/2.80; 9am-8pm mid-May–Sep).

For those who would prefer to kick back and enjoy the view, there are numerous boat companies that ferry passengers across the lake from April to mid-October. **ÖBB-Bodenseeschifffahrt Bregenz** (428 68; www.boden seeschifffahrt.at, in German; Seestrasse 4) should be your first port of call for information on timetables and prices. Services to Konstanz peak at eight departures per day from early July to mid-September (one-way €12.40, 3¾ hours) and usually call in at Lindau, Friedrichshafen, Meersburg and Mainau.

Back on dry land, the **Pfänder** rises sharply above Bregenz and affords a breathtaking panorama of the lake and the pointy peaks of the Alps. A **cable car** (421 60-0; Steinbruchgasse 4; one-way adult/student/child €5.90/4.80/3, return €10.20/8.20/5.10; 8am-7pm) whizzes to the top.

At the summit, kids and fans of furry critters will love the **Wildpark**, a 30-minute circular trail bringing you close to deer, ibex and marmots in their near-to-natural habitat. There's also a **Greifvogelflugschau** (bird of prey show; adult/child €4.60/2.30; 11am & 2.30pm May-Sep), when feathered performers amaze with aerial feats.

Just 5km southwest of Bregenz lies the **Rheindelta** (05578-74478; Hard; www.rheindelta .com), where the River Rhine flows into the Bodensee. Comprising mossy marshes, reeds and mixed woodlands, this nature reserve is an unspoilt wilderness and a haven to more than 300 bird species including curlews, grey herons and rare black-tailed godwits.

Festivals & Events

The **Bregenz Festival**, running from late July to late August, is the city's premier cultural event. World-class operas, orchestral works and theatrical productions are performed on the Seebühne, a vast, open-air floating stage. Information and tickets (€26 to €125) are available from the **ticket centre** (407-6; www.bregenzerfestspiele.com; Postfach 311, A-6901 Bregenz) about nine months before the festival.

Sleeping

On the Austrian Monopoly board, two Bregenz streets (Römerstrasse and Rheinstrasse) occupy the most expensive property squares; this is reflected in the price of accommodation. Private rooms usually offer the best value (expect to pay around €30 per person).

If everything is fully booked, consider crossing the border to Lindau in Germany (8km away), where beds are plentiful and slightly cheaper. Lindau's **tourist office** (☎ 260 030; www.lindau.de; Ludwigstrasse 68; ☒ 9am-1pm & 2-7pm Mon-Fri, 2-7pm Sat & Sun May-Sep, 9am-1pm & 2-5pm Mon-Fri Oct-Apr) may be able to help.

Camping Mexico (☎ 732 60; www.camping-mexico .at; Hechtweg 4; campsites per adult/car/tent €5/4/4.50; ☒ May-Sep; **P**) It's hardly Acapulco, but this eco-labelled campsite by the lake is hot on environmental issues; it uses solar energy, recycles waste and serves locally sourced, organic food in the restaurant. The tree-shaded pitches are pleasant and the affable owners rent canoes from €25 per day.

Jugendgästehaus (☎ 428 67; www.jgh.at/bregenz; Mehrerauerstrasse 5; dm €19.20; **P** ▣) Housed in a former needle factory near the lake, this HI hostel now reels backpackers in with its spacious, super-clean dorms. The excellent facilities include a café, common room and restaurant.

Gästehaus am Tannenbach (☎ 441 74; Im Gehren 1; s/d €22/44; **P**) Just north of the centre, Tannenbach is a basic but homy guesthouse with well-kept, sizeable rooms and a pretty flower garden.

Gasthof Pension Matt (☎ 717 77; www.gasthofmatt .at; Wuhrbaumweg 36; s/d €45/90; **P**) This family-run guesthouse 20 minutes' walk from the centre is a real find. The serene rooms, painted in zesty lemon and lime shades, have cushy beds, squeaky-clean bathrooms and wifi. Enjoy breakfast on the leafy terrace.

Hotel Bodensee (☎ 423 00; www.hotel-bodensee.at; Kornmarktstrasse 22; s/d €66/120; **P**) The red-brick Hotel Bodensee is as central as they come. Its comfy rooms have an old-fashioned feel with warm tones and flouncy fabrics.

Hotel Germania (☎ 427 66-0; www.hotel-germania .at; Am Steinenbach 9; s/d €98/179; **P** ▣) On a quiet side street, this corporate hotel doesn't exactly ooze local character, but it has perks like a sauna, gym and wi-fi. Its contemporary rooms contrast chalk-white walls with parquet floors and bold prints.

ourpick **Deuring-Schlössle** (☎ 478 00; www .deuring-schloessle.at; Ehre-Guta-Platz 4; s €95-155, d €210-294; **P** ▣) Ivy creeps up the tower of this stunningly renovated castle in the *Oberstadt*. Rooms exude medieval charm with antiques and low beams, while marble bathrooms, de-

signer furnishings and wi-fi catapult you back to the 21st century. Pull up a chair beside the fire in the atmospheric restaurant (mains €20 to €30) to sample Heino Huber's cuisine using local organic ingredients like Bregenzerwald beef and Bodensee whitefish.

Eating

Many restaurants and cafés cluster along the lakefront or the narrow streets of the *Oberstadt*. In summer, little beats a picnic on the banks of the Bodensee; stock up on fresh bread, smoked fish, cheese and fruit at the **farmers' market** (Kornmarktplatz; ☒ 8am-1pm Tue & Fri).

ourpick **Cafesito** (Maurachgasse 6; bagels €3-4; ☒ 7.45am-7pm Mon-Fri, 9am-4.30pm Sat) Squeeze into this tiny café for the freshest bagels and smoothies in town. Lilac-yellow walls and modern art create a funky backdrop for a light lunch or cup of fair-trade coffee. Try the famous bikini bagel or chilli hot chocolate.

Pizzeria San Giuseppe (☎ 541 68; Bahnhofstrasse 2; mains €5-9; ☒ lunch & dinner) This great little place rolls out reasonably priced pizzas that are thin and crisp. On Friday and Saturday nights, San Giuseppe doubles as a popular bar.

Gösserbrau (☎ 424 67; Anton Schneider Strasse 1; mains €5-16; ☒ 9am-1am Mon-Thu, 9am-2am Fri & Sat) Gösserbrau is an optical illusion: one side is a wood-panelled tavern serving Austrian fare and the other an ubercool bar. Both have Gösserbrau brews on tap.

Bistro Duygu (☎ 544 55; Kirchstrasse 1; mains €6-8; ☒ 10am-1am Mon-Sat, noon-9pm Sun) Locals pile into this cheery Turkish place for late-night munchies such as lentil soup, falafels and honey-drenched baklava.

Viva Cantina (☎ 422 88; Seestrasse 7; mains €8-20 ☒ 5pm-3am Tue-Sun) Not only the chillis are lively at this Mexican cantina. The hip haunt doubles as a party place after shrimp fajitas and one too many tequilas. Retreat to the palm garden in summer.

Neubeck (☎ 436 09; Anton Schneider Strasse 5; lunch €9.50, mains €20-25; ☒ lunch & dinner Tue-Sat) Crisp white linen and red leather set the scene in this sleek bistro, opening onto a shady patio. Expect fusion cuisine, from scallops with ricotta-lemon ravioli to Thai crayfish curry. The two-course menu du jour is good value.

Wirtshaus am See (☎ 422 10; Seepromenade; mains €10-20; ☒ lunch & dinner) Loved-up couples grab a table on the lantern-lit terrace at this half-timbered villa overlooking the lake. Local specialities like Bodensee *sander filet* land on your plate.

The **GWL Shopping Centre** (Römerstrasse 2) has a Spar supermarket for self-caterers.

Drinking

A bunch of lively bars vie for your attention in Bregenz, including these favourites packed to the gunnels at weekends.

Wunderbar (☎ 477 58; Bahnhofstrasse 4; 10am-4am Mon-Sat, 2pm-1am Sun) Smooth funk plays in this boho bar with free internet access and neo-baroque touches from red velvet sofas to flickering candles. Browse the papers or sip cocktails beneath the cherubs.

Cuba (☎ 470 52; Bahnhofstrasse 9; 11am-4am Sat, 2pm-4am Sun) Glammed up with chandeliers and a sweeping staircase, this gallery-style bar attracts trendy types with Latin tunes and a top line-up of DJs.

KFL (☎ 439 71; Bergmannstrasse 6) KFL is the place to catch live jazz and jam sessions (many are free). Opening hours vary depending on the performance.

Wohnzimmer (Maurachgasse 3; 9pm-2am Wed-Sat) Clued-up locals head to this intimate den for everything from indie concerts to DJs spinning electro and punk.

Getting There & Around

Austrian Airlines fly to Altenrhein in Switzerland, the nearest airport. Friedrichshafen, in Germany, is the closest major airport served by a couple of no-frill airlines including Ryanair.

Four direct trains daily head for Munich (€39, 3½ hours) via Lindau, while trains for Konstanz (€45, 1½ to two hours) go via the Swiss shore of the lake and may be frequent, but require between one and four changes. There are four daily departures for Zürich (€30, 1¾ hours), all of which call in at St Gallen (€15, 45 minutes).

Nine trains daily depart for Innsbruck (€28, 2¾ hours), calling en route at Dornbirn (€2.30, 15 minutes), Feldkirch (€5.10, 30 minutes) and Bludenz (€10.90, one hour).

A daily bus service runs to Dornbirn (€2.30, 30 minutes) at least four times an hour; buses to Feldkirch (€5.10, two hours) depart twice hourly from Monday to Friday and hourly at weekends.

DORNBIRN & AROUND

Set against an alpine backdrop, **Dornbirn** is Vorarlberg's largest city. While its sights can't rival those in Bregenz, there's a refreshing lack of tourists. Wandering around the **Marktplatz**, you'll spot the crooked, 17th-century **Rotes Haus** (red house), which owes its beautiful blush to an unappetising mix of ox blood and bile. Next door, the slender Doric columns and free-standing Gothic belfry of **Pfarrkirche St Martin** catch your eye.

Dornbirn's biggest draw, though, are the creepy-crawlies at **Inatura** (☎ 05572-232 35; www.inatura.at; Jahngasse 9; adult/child/family €9.50/4.80/11.40; 10am-6pm). This hands-on museum is a great place for kids, who can pet (stuffed) foxes and handle (real) spiders, peer into bee and hornet nests, ogle at snakes and fish from behind glass and generally interact with nature. There's also a climbing wall and 3-D cinema.

Just 4km southeast of Dornbirn is the **Rappenlochschlucht** (Rappenloch Gorge), a dramatic ravine gouged out by the thundering Dornbirner Ache. Wooden walkways lead up to a viewpoint (10 minutes) and the turquoise Staufensee (30 minutes). If you're into gutsy motors, nip into the world's biggest **Rolls-Royce Museum** (☎ 05572-526 52; adult/child €8/4; 10am-6pm Apr-Oct, 10am-5pm Nov-Mar), situated at the bottom of the gorge. The hall of fame showcases royal Rollers that once belonged to the likes of Queen Elizabeth and George V.

Hohenems, 6km south of Dornbirn, was a haven for a large community of Jews in the 17th century. Their numbers dwindled in the 1860s, when Jews were eligible to live anywhere under Habsburg rule. Their legacy is explored in **Jüdisches Museum Hohenems** (☎ 739 89-0; Schweizer Strasse 5; adult/child €7/4; 10am-5pm Tue-Sun), housed in the Rosenthal villa. The Rosenthals built up a considerable textile business in the town, and part of their wealth – especially gorgeous period furniture – is on show, alongside photos, documents and religious artefacts from the long-defunct Jewish community. Huddled against a tree-lined hill just outside the town on the road to Götzis is the **Jewish cemetery**; get the key from the museum.

Getting There & Away

Dornbirn (€2.30, 15 minutes) and Hohenems (€3, 25 minutes) are on the Bregenz–Innsbruck railway line. Bus 47 departs from Dornbirn train station and passes by the Rappenloch Gorge (€1.60, 25 minutes, six daily).

VORARLBERG'S ARCHITECTURAL VISION

It's hard to believe that such a traditional province, with its cud-chewing cows, yellow cheese, stark mountains and wooden chalets, is among the most progressive places on the planet when it comes to architecture.

It all started back in the mid-1980s when a group of architects, constrained by the Austrian trade association of architects because of their ideas, split away from the pack and began calling themselves *Baukünstler* (building artists) rather than architects. They managed to gain support from the local authorities and create an environment where anything – as long as it was of high quality and cultivated craftsmanship – was possible.

Much of Vorarlberg's contemporary architecture is denoted by clean lines, sharp angles and plenty of glass and wood. And it's everywhere; private homes, bus stops, supermarkets and kindergartens all compete with hotels, restaurants and office buildings for your undivided attention. Arrive in a non-descript hamlet in the Bregenzerwald and you'll be confronted with not one but half a dozen architecturally sublime houses, or turn a corner in Bregenz or Dornbirn and out pops a building at the cutting edge of design.

Prominent buildings to look out for include Kunsthaus Bregenz (p369), Inatura Dornbirn (opposite), Dornbirn's Hotel Martinspark, Lauterach's Terminal V, Silvrettahaus (p378) and Lustenau's SIE-Zentrale. For more information, pick up a copy of *architektur land vorarlberg – zeitgenössische baukunst* (modern architecture) from the provincial tourist office; it's in both German and English and has a list of architecturally modern hotels.

BREGENZERWALD

In summer, the jangle of cow bells breaks the silence in the Bregenzerwald; in winter, it's the shuffle of snowshoes and swoosh of skis. Bregenz's glorious backyard is a finely woven tapestry of velvet-green pastures, pretty villages and limestone pinnacles. After filling your lungs with fresh air in the hills and stomach with cheese in alpine dairies, snug log chalets invite you to put your feet up by the fire and relax.

The **Bregenzerwald tourist office** (☎ 05512-23 65; www.bregenzerwald.at; Impulszentrum 1135, Egg; ⏰ 9am-5pm Mon-Fri, 8am-1pm weekends) provides details on the region's top attractions, including skiing (downhill and cross-country) and hiking. The **3 Täler Pass** (3-/7-day pass €93/178) covers the skiing regions of Bregenzwald, Grosses Walsertal and Lechtal. After working up an appetite on the slopes, you can dairy-hop your way along the *Käsestrasse* (see the boxed text, p374) that winds through the region.

Around 13km east of Dornbirn is the rural idyll of **Schwarzenberg** and its collection of chocolate-box chalets. The village springs to life from mid-May to September during the **Schubertiade** music festival. This celebration of Schubert's work is hugely popular, so book tickets months in advance from **Schubertiade GmbH** (☎ 05576-720 91; www.schubertiade.at; Schweizer Strasse 1, A-6845 Hohenems) and the local **tourist office** (☎ 05512-35 70; ⏰ 9am-noon & 2-5pm Mon-Fri,

10am-noon weekends during festival). The village is also home to the small but rewarding **Heimat Museum** (☎ 05512-29 88; adult/child €3/1; ⏰ 2-4pm Tue, Thu, Sat & Sun May-Sep, 2-4pm Tue & Sat Oct, 2-4pm during Schubertiade); this 300-year-old house displays regional arts and crafts and a handful of works by Angelika Kauffmann who had strong ties to the village.

Considering its size, Schwarzenberg has some wonderful places to sleep and eat. **Gasthof Hirschen** (☎ 05512-29 44; www.hirschenschwarzenberg.at; s/d €125/240; **P**) is an archetypal alpine chalet complete with crackling open fire, award-winning restaurant and antique-filled rooms. **Messnerstüble** (☎ 05512-20 02; Hof 19; mains €8-15; ⏰ lunch & dinner) serves a fine schnitzel alongside Swiss-inspired dishes like *Rösti* (fried potatoes) in a countrified chalet.

A zigzagging road links Schwarzenberg to **Bezau**. This village makes an excellent base for exploring the area, with plenty of accommodation and a rural atmosphere. The **tourist office** (☎ 05514-22 95; Platz 39; ☎ 9am-noon & 1.30-5.30pm Mon-Fri, 9am-noon Sat) provides information on walking, paragliding and skiing. In nearby **Bizau**, test-drive the thrilling **Sommerrodelbahn** (adult/child €9.50/6.80; ⏰ 9am-5pm Jun-Sep), a 1850m-long toboggan run comprising 80 hairpin bends. Further east, **Mellau** offers winter skiing and summer hiking; a **gondola** (summer one-way/return €6.80/9.40, winter day pass €29.50) rises to 1390m Alpe Rossstelle year-round.

The precipitous road continues east towards the Arlberg, passing through the peaceful villages of **Au** and **Schoppernau**. Halfway between the two is the **Diedamskopf cable car** (www.diedamskopf.at; one-way/return €10.50/14.30), which climbs to 2090m. From the summit, paragliders launch themselves into the air and walkers trundle back down the side of the mountain. Both places have tourist offices – see www.au-schoppernau.at for more details.

From Au, you have two choices: continue east to fashionable west Arlberg, or turn south and head for Bludenz. Scenically, both journeys are rewarding, passing through rugged alpine country on narrow, winding roads. About 9km along the southern route is **Damüls**, a high-alpine resort whose conical peaks attract skiers, walkers and tobogganers (the 3.5km sled run is floodlit twice weekly). Its **tourist office** (☎ 05510-62 00; 8.30am-noon & 1.30-6pm Mon-Fri) can help arrange accommodation. While you're here, climb up to the Gothic **Pfarrkirche** (admission free; daylight), with beautiful frescoes in good condition considering their age.

Getting There & Away

There are eight direct bus services daily to Bezau (€4.40, one hour) from Bregenz, but for most other destinations a change at Egg is required. A more direct travel option is from Dornbirn; Schwarzenberg (€3, 25 minutes), Bezau (€3.70, 50 minutes), Mellau (€4.40, one hour), Au (€5.80, 70 minutes) and Schoppernau (€5.80, 80 minutes) can all be reached a couple of times daily (times vary from season to season). For Damüls (€7.50, 1¾ hours), a change at Au is required.

FELDKIRCH

☎ 05522 / pop 29,300

Feldkirch whisks visitors back to the Middle Ages with its appealing jumble of gabled houses, chunky towers and cobbled streets that tumble down to the fast-flowing Ill River. While the town still has a firm grip on its medieval roots, a growing crop of avant-garde bars, kooky boutiques and pavement cafés give it a youthful twist.

Orientation & Information

The town centre is a few minutes' walk south of the train station (turn left upon exiting); here you'll find the helpful **tourist office** (☎ 734 67; www.feldkirch.at; Schlossergasse 8; 8.30am-noon & 1.30-5.30pm Mon-Fri, 9am-noon Sat), with lots of information and maps. The post office is opposite the train station.

Sights & Activities

Part of the pleasure in Feldkirch is strolling through its narrow alleyways dotted with half-timbered houses and arcades. Patrician houses and street cafés frame the town's main artery, the cobbled **Marktplatz**, which fills with the hum of chatter in summer.

Keep an eye out for the towers surviving from the old fortifications. These include the 40m-high **Katzenturm** (Hirschgraben), where Vorarlberg's biggest bell (weighing 7500kg) still tolls; the **Mühletor** (Mühletorplatz), also known as the Sautor, where the pig market was held in the Middle Ages; and the step-gabled **Churertor** (Heiligkreuzbrücke), once the gateway to the bridge that was used to transport salt across the Ill River to Switzerland.

Domkirche St Nikolaus (Schlossgraben; admission free; daylight) has a large, forbidding interior complemented by late-Gothic features and

---

PASS THE CHEESE

All those cows grazing on the Bregenzerwald's hillsides aren't there for nothing. Every year, their creamy silo-free milk goes into producing 4500 tons of cheese. The region's 40 cheeses include flavoursome Vorarlberger Bergkäse, nutty-sweet Emmentaler, walnutty Nussknacker and Weinkäse (ripened in red wine for three months). While you're here, try the cheesiest local speciality, *Käsknöpfle*, a take on gnocchi mixed with tangy Räskäse and topped with fried onions.

Serious fromage-ophiles should head for the Bregenzerwald **Käsestrasse** (Cheese Road), which zigzags past alpine dairy farms and independent artisans whose doors are open to hungry travellers. En route you can stop off at the Käsehaus in Andelsbuch to sample and buy cheese, the Sennschule Ingo Metzler in Egg to discover the secrets of cheesemaking, and the Bergkäserei in Schoppernau for a peek in the cheese cellar, tastings and free guided tours (5pm on Mondays). More details to help plan your dairy-hopping itinerary are available online at www.kaesestrasse.at.

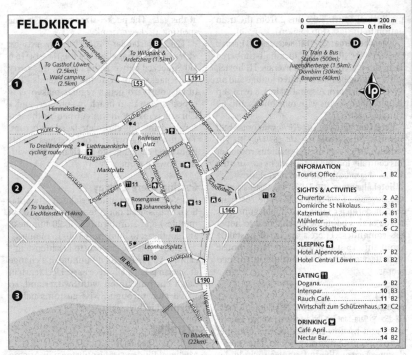

FELDKIRCH

INFORMATION	
Tourist Office..........................1	B2

SIGHTS & ACTIVITIES	
Churertor...............................2	A2
Domkirche St Nikolaus.........3	B1
Katzenturm............................4	B1
Mühletor................................5	B3
Schloss Schattenburg............6	C2

SLEEPING	
Hotel Alpenrose.....................7	B2
Hotel Central Löwen.............8	B2

EATING	
Dogana....................................9	B2
Interspar..............................10	B3
Rauch Café...........................11	B2
Wirtschaft zum Schützenhaus..12	C2

DRINKING	
Café April.............................13	B2
Nectar Bar...........................14	B2

vibrantly coloured stained glass. The painting on the side altar is by local boy Wolf Huber (1480–1539), a leading member of the Danube school.

Rising above the town, 13th-century **Schloss Schattenburg** is classic fairytale stuff with its red turrets and creeping vines. It's a steep climb up to the ramparts, but you'll be rewarded with far-reaching views over Feldkirch's rooftops. Once the seat of the counts of Montfort, it now houses a small **museum** (☎ 719 82; Burggasse 1; adult/child €3/1; ☑ 9am-noon & 1.30-6pm May-Oct, 1-4pm Jan-Apr, closed Nov & Dec) displaying religious art, costumes and weaponry.

Facing the castle across the town is **Ardetzenberg** (631m), a heavily forested hill. At its northern end is the **Wildpark** (☎ 741 05; admission free; ☑ daylight), with a woodland trail and animal-friendly enclosures home to alpine fauna such as marmots, ibex and wild boar.

The Feldkirch region is crisscrossed with cycling trails, including the 30km **Dreiländerweg** (Three Country Trail), taking in beautiful scenery in Austria, Switzerland and Liechtenstein. Pick up the free *Feldkircher Radwegkarte* map from the tourist office. Bike

hire is available at **Gasthof Löwen** (Kohlgasse 1) for €12 per day.

Festivals & Events

In late May, Feldkirch revisits the Middle Ages with troubadours, knights and nonstop feasting at the **Montfortmarkt**. The **Feldkirch Festival** in June draws classical music lovers to historic venues. Other festivals include the **Gauklerfestival** in July, an enormous street party welcoming jugglers, fire eaters and clowns. Mulled wine warms up subzero temperatures at December's **Weihnachtsmarkt** (Christmas market).

Sleeping

Feldkirch offers a small but characterful selection of accommodation, including a smattering of good-value private rooms outside the centre.

Waldcamping (☎ 76001-3190; www.waldcamping.at; Stadionstrasse 9; campsites per adult/car/tent €5.60/3.90/4.80; ☑ Apr-Oct; P ☑) Pine trees shade this quiet campsite. The first-rate facilities include a barbecue area, playground and free entry to the Waldbad pool with waterslides and a volleyball court. Take bus 2 from the train station to the last stop (3.5km).

Jugendherberge (☎ 731 81; Reichsstrasse 111; dm/s/d €15.50/25.50/39; P ⬚) Set in a half-timbered barn, this is a cut above the average HI hostel, with creaking beams, a vaulted lounge and an ivy-clad courtyard. A spiral staircase twists up to light-filled dorms with pine bunks. Bus 60 trundles past.

Hotel Central Löwen (☎ 720 70; www.central-hotel-loewen.at; Schlossgraben 13; s/d €89/120; P ⬚) Modern art cheers up the spacious rooms at this centrally located hotel. Guests can use the sauna, steam bath and pool next door.

Hotel Alpenrose (☎ 721 75; www.hotel-alpenrose.net; Rosengasse 4-6; s/d €71/122; ⬚) The rose garden, Biedermeier salon and bubblegum-pink façade of this boutique hotel appeal to hopeless romantics. There's an air of nostalgia about this 16th-century merchant's house with its wood-beamed, antique-furnished rooms.

Eating

Dogana (☎ 751 26-3; Neustadt 20; lunch €8.70, mains €18-25; ⏱ 9am-1am Tue-Thu, 9am-2am Fri & Sat) Earthy tones and mellow music give this gourmet haunt a contemporary kick. The menu changes seasonally, but staples include delicious salads (try the curried *kikeriki*) and value for money lunches.

Wirtschaft zum Schützenhaus (☎ 852 90; Göfiser Strasse 2; mains €10-14; ⏱ lunch & dinner Thu-Mon) *Schiessen und Geniessen* (shoot and enjoy) is the motto at this half-timbered tavern, where lederhosen-clad staff bring humungous schnitzels to the table. The tree-shaded beer garden has prime views of the castle and a pet corner with fluffy rodents to keep kids amused.

Rauch Café (☎ 763 55; Marktgasse 12-14; mains €17-23; ⏱ 9am-1am Mon-Sat, 10am-1am Sun) Rauch's buzzy terrace is packed when the sun shines. If you can stomach chilli first thing, try the 'how to cure the hangover' breakfast (€12.90). The menu is Mediterranean with flavours like wild garlic gnocchi. DJs spin house music here after dark.

For self-caterers, there is an **Interspar** (Leonhardsplatz) supermarket at the southern end of the town centre.

Drinking

Café April (☎ 827 13; Neustadt 39; ⏱ 9am-midnight Tue-Sat, 10am-2pm Sun) Wacky touches like upside-down watering cans grab your attention at this café. The pocket-sized terrace is a fine spot for a relaxed drink.

our pick Nectar Bar (☎ 829 902; www.nectar-bar.at; Marktplatz 1; ⏱ 4pm-2am Mon-Thu; 11am-4am Fri & Sat) Squeezed between the houses, this party place packs 'em in at the weekends. The inner courtyard gets a regular makeover – expect a Hawaiian beach in summer, and a Christmas market in winter when 'tis the season to drink hot chocolate laced with rum. The fun-loving owner Tobias stages events from iPod challenges to Mexican nights with free-flowing tequila.

Getting There & Away

Buses depart from outside Feldkirch's train station. Trains head north to Bregenz (€5.10, 30 minutes) and Dornbirn (€3.70, 20 minutes), and southeast to Bludenz (€3.70, 15 minutes).

Feldkirch is the gateway to Liechtenstein's capital, Vaduz (€2.20, 40 minutes); a change at Schaan is normally necessary. Liechtenstein has a customs union with Switzerland, so you'll pass through Swiss customs before entering Liechtenstein.

BLUDENZ

☎ 05552 / pop 14,000

Medieval Bludenz is the only town in Austria (and perhaps the world) that can lay claim to having purple cows; the Milka ones churned out from the Suchard chocolate factory. When you've managed to drag yourself away from the *Schokolade,* explore the sweet centre lined with cobblestone streets and arcaded passageways, the legacy of the town's heyday as the seat of the Habsburg governors from 1418 to 1806.

Orientation & Information

The town centre is on the northern bank of the Ill River. The **tourist office** (☎ 621 70; www.bludenz.at; Werdenbergerstrasse 42; ⏱ 8am-noon & 2-5.30pm Mon-Fri Sep-Jun, 8am-noon & 2-5.30pm Mon-Fri, 10am-noon Sat Jul & Aug) is five minutes' walk from the train station and has free internet access.

Across the road is the town's **post office** (Werdenbergerstrasse 37), and not far east is a small pedestrian-only shopping area.

Sights & Activities

One of Bludenz's best features can't even be seen. Almost anywhere you wander in the centre, the rich, enticing aroma of chocolate will fill your nostrils. The source of these

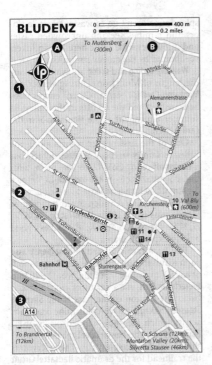

BLUDENZ

0 _____ 400 m
0 _____ 0.2 miles

To Muttersberg
(300m)

To Val
Blu
(600m)

Bahnhof

To Brandnertal
(12km)

To Schruns (12km);
Montafon Valley (20km);
Silvretta Stausee (46km)

INFORMATION	
Post Office	**1** A2
Tourist Office	**2** B2

SIGHTS & ACTIVITIES	
Brewery	**3** A2
Kletterhalle	**4** B2
St Laurentiuskirche	**5** B2
Stadtmuseum	**6** B2
Suchard Chocolate Factory Shop	**7** A2

SLEEPING	
Camping Seeberger	**8** A1
Landhaus Muther	**9** B1
Schlosshotel	**10** B2

EATING	
Altes Rathaus	**11** B2
Nova Bräu	**12** A2
Remise	**13** B3
Spar	**14** B2

boulders before tackling the real thing in the Alps.

About 1km north of the town centre, a **cable car** (☎ 627 52; Hinterplärsch; adult/child one-way €6.20/4, return €10.40/6.50; ☯ 9am-6pm Sun-Thu, 9am-10pm Fri & Sat May-Oct, 9.30am-5.30pm Sat-Thu, 9.30am-10.30pm Fri Nov-Apr) rises up to **Muttersberg** (1401m), the starting point for numerous hiking, Nordic walking and cycling trails. If you don't want to walk it, catch bus 1 from in front of the train station to the cable car station.

Bludenz is a good base for exploring the surrounding valleys. There are 15 **skiing** areas within a 30km radius and ski bus transport to/from Bludenz is sometimes included in the price of ski passes. **Walking** and **cycling** are other popular activities; the tourist office has thick booklets on summer and winter outdoor pursuits.

Sleeping

The tourist office can book accommodation. Private rooms usually offer the best value, even though a surcharge of around €3.50 per day applies for stays under three days.

Camping Seeberger (☎ 625 12; Obdorfweg 9; camp-sites per adult/tent €5.35/7.90; ⓟ) This leafy, well-kept campsite sits in the shadow of the Alps. Campers can relax in the whirlpool and sauna.

Landhaus Muther (☎ 657 04; Alemannenstrasse 4; s/d €35/70; ⓟ) Smothered in geraniums in summer, this homely chalet is fairly central. The rooms are old-style and simple, but fastidiously clean.

Val Blu (☎ 631 06; Haldenweg 2a; s/d €54/88; ⓟ ▣)There's not a single wood beam or checked curtain at this ultramodern spa hotel,

divine smells is the **Suchard chocolate factory**; unfortunately there are no guided tours but you can stock up on chocs at its **shop** (Fohrenburgstrasse 1; ☯ 9-11.30am & 1.30-4.30pm Mon-Thu, 9-11.30am & 1.30-4pm Fri). Chocolate also plays an important part in the children's **Milka Chocolate Festival** in mid-July, when 1000kg of the stuff is up for grabs in prizes. There's also music, games and plenty of kids too full of sugar to control.

To explore the other attractions, join a free **city tour** organised by the tourist office; departing at 10am on Thursday from mid-May till October. Affording snapshot views of the mountains, the **Kirchensteig** is a covered walkway that climbs up to the Gothic parish church, **St Laurentiuskirche** (Mutterstrasse; admission free; ☯ daylight), dominated by an octagonal, onion-domed spire. The **Stadtmuseum** (☎ 636 21; Kirchgasse 9; admission €1.50; ☯ 3-5pm Mon-Sat Jun-early Sep) houses a small display on folk art and prehistoric finds.

The Austrian Alpine Club's **Kletterhalle** (☎ 626 39; Untersteinstrasse 5; €6 plus €0.80 shoe hire; ☯ 9am-5pm Mon-Fri) is an excellent climbing hall where you can practise clambering up defined by glass walls and smooth contours. The functional, minimalist-style rooms feature wi-fi and flat-screen TVs.

Schlosshotel (☎ 630 16-0; www.schlosshotel.cc; Schlossplatz 5; s/d €80/130; P) Clinging to the cliffs above Bludenz, this smart hotel shelters modern rooms with balconies. There's a terrace for warm evenings and free mountain-bike hire for guests.

Eating

Remise (☎ 342 82; Am Raiffeisenplatz; lunch €7.90, mains €6-12; 10am-1am Mon-Fri, 9am-1am Sat) This laid-back café serves up an arty atmosphere and tasty snacks from salads and toasties to curries. The cultural venue next door regularly hosts exhibitions, film screenings and concerts.

Altes Rathaus (☎ 673 00; Rathausgasse 1a; mains €8-15; 10am-1am Mon-Sat) A sleek newcomer to Bludenz, this glass-fronted café on the main drag rustles up cheese-rich specialities, steaks and yummy cakes.

Nova Bräu (☎ 685 68; Werdenbergerstrasse 53; mains €8-16; 11am-2am Mon-Thu, 11am-4am Fri & Sat, 10am-3am Sun) Copper vats gleam at this cavernous brewpub, cranking out hearty fare like *Tafelspitz* (boiled beef) washed down with Fohrenburger beer (from the brewery opposite). At the front, Arche Nova bar is a ship complete with palms and fish lights; why a nautical theme in the Alps is anyone's guess!

In the pedestrian-only area in the town centre is the Kronenhaus department store, with a **Spar** (Werdenbergerstrasse 34) supermarket.

Getting There & Away

Bludenz is on the east–west InterCity (IC) express rail route, two hours from Innsbruck (€20.70, every two hours) and 45 minutes from Bregenz (€7.50, hourly). By regional train, Bregenz–Bludenz is 70 minutes (every 30 minutes).

The east–west A14 road passes just south of the Ill River and the town centre. Buses run down all five valleys around Bludenz.

MONTAFON

pop 15,540

Silent and unspoilt, the **Montafon** (www.montafon .at) was apparently Hemingway's favourite valley and is still a fine spot for a wee adventure. Running south from Bludenz, the vale is quilted green in summer, blanketed white in winter and silhouetted by the glaciated Silvretta range year-round. All that natural splendour doesn't go to waste: freestyle skiers and families seeking uncrowded pistes and a low-key vibe flock here, as do hikers spellbound by the craggy summits.

Walking, **cycling** and **skiing** are available along the length of Montafon. During winter, the **Montafon-Card** (3-/7-day pass €98/195) covers public transport and the 65 lifts in the valley; its summer equivalent is the **Montafon-Silvretta-Card** (€32/43).

One of the first proper resorts along the valley is family-friendly **Schruns**, which has a **tourist office** (☎ 05556-721 66; www.schruns-tschag guns.at; Silvrettastrasse 6; 8am-6pm Mon-Fri, 9am-noon & 4-6pm Sat, 10.30am-noon Sun mid-Jun–Sep, 8am-5pm Mon-Fri Oct–mid-Jun). A much-loved hangout of Hemingway in the 1920s, **Hotel Taube** (☎ 05556-723 84; Silvrettastrasse 1; s/d €30/96; P) makes a good base to explore the area.

The panoramic **Silvretta Hochalpenstrasse** soon winds its way under peaks rising to well over 2500m, before climbing over the 2036m **Bielerhöhe Pass** via a series of tight switchbacks. At the top of the pass is the **Silvretta Stausee** (2030m), an ice-cold alpine reservoir, across which the snow-capped peaks of **Piz Buin** (3312m) and **Klostertaler Egghorn** (3120m) shine brightly on a sunny day. The reservoir is the trailhead for the dramatic **Radsattel Circuit** (see p92).

A budget place to bed down at **Bielerhöhe** is the **Madlenerhaus** (☎ 05558-42 34; www.madlenerhaus .at; dm €8-10; Dec–mid-Jan, mid-Feb–Easter, mid-Jun–Oct). This DAV (German Alpine Club) alpine hut has comfy four- to 10-bed dorms and a **restaurant** (mains €5-12) serving solid Austrian fare. For more creature comfort, check into the architecturally innovative **Silvrettahaus** (☎ 05558-42 46; s/d €43/72; P) or homy **Piz Buin** (☎ 05558-42 31; www.pizbuin-silvretta.at, in German; s/d €40/72; mains €8-13; P). Both open from late May to early November and from Christmas to April.

Getting There & Away

There are plenty of daily trains from Bludenz to Schruns (€2.30, 20 minutes), from where up to five buses daily continue onto Partenen (€3, 35 minutes) at the base of the Silvretta pass. From mid-July to mid-October, eight buses daily climb from Partenen to the Silvretta Stausee (€2.30, 35 minutes). The Silvretta Hochalpenstrasse pass is controlled by a toll road, which costs €11.50/10.50 for cars/motorcycles.

WESTERN ARLBERG

☎ 05583

With its backbone of monochrome mountains and snow-sure slopes, the Arlberg region is one of Austria's top destinations for skiing. Though it straddles Vorarlberg and Tyrol, a single ski pass covers all of its resorts (see p362).

A picture-postcard village, **Lech** (1450m) is a magnet to royalty (Princess Diana used to ski here), film stars and poseurs who like to pretend to be such from behind Gucci shades. It's also making strides as an eco-friendly ski resort (see boxed text, p72) with photovoltaic energy operating its lifts and a biomass heating plant. The terrain is well suited to intermediates, with some advanced off-piste possibilities. A cable car scales Rüfikopf (2362m), but most of the lifts and runs are on the opposite side of the valley, on the Kriegerhorn (2178m) and Zuger Hochlicht (2377m). The central **tourist office** (☎ 21 61-0; www.lech-zuers.at; ⏰ 8am-6pm Mon-Sat) has bags of info on skiing and walking possibilities and an accommodation board. From July to September, it also arranges themed walks (free with the local *Gästekarte*) ranging from sunrise hikes to botanical strolls.

Six kilometres south lies **Zürs** (1716m), a smaller resort with its own **tourist office** (☎ 22 45; ⏰ 9am-noon & 2-5pm Mon-Fri). The cable car runs throughout the year, but in summer the resort has all the character of a dust bowl.

One kilometre south of Zürs is the **Flexen Pass** (1773m), after which the road splits: the western fork leads to **Stuben** (1407m), the eastern one to St Anton am Arlberg in Tyrol.

Sleeping

Almost every street in Lech and Zürs is lined with hotels (many five-star), but it's still worth booking ahead in winter. Cheaper options are private rooms and holiday apartments. Expect prices to be 30% to 50% higher than those quoted here in the winter high season. Any of the following are fine bets.

Pension Alwin (☎ 309 30; pension@alwin.at; No 309; s/d €31/62; P ▣) A bargain place close to the centre, this pinewood chalet features bright rooms with parquet floors. After a day on the slopes, the sauna is the perfect wind down.

Haus Nenning (☎ 24 08; nenning.lech@aon.at; No 149; s/d €32/64; P) This cheery chalet opposite Schlegelkopf lift has snug wood-panelled rooms and a garden. Bike rental and ski storage are available.

Pension Waldesruh (☎ 24 02; waldesruh@vol.at; No 144; s/d €36/66; P) Set back from the road, this quiet chalet offers neat and tidy rooms with balcony.

Eating

Many hotels have a fine, albeit slightly pricey, restaurant. Self-caterers can head to Spar on the main street. The following places are independent of a hotel:

Ambrosius Stüble (☎ 419 30; No 239; mains €7-16; ⏰ lunch & dinner) Kick back on the sunny terrace at this traditional tavern near Rüfikopf lift; the schnitzel and *Kaiserschmarrn* (shredded pancakes) come recommended.

Hûs Nr. 8 (☎ 33 22-0; No 8; mains €8-16; ⏰ lunch & dinner) *Raclette* and fondue are on the menu at this rustic chalet, with a small patio and playground.

Fux (☎ 22 25; Omesberg 587; mains €16-30; ⏰ lunch & dinner) Glass walls and gold Buddhas jazz up this slick restaurant. The cuisine has an Asian twist – think Wagyu beef carpaccio and yellowfin tuna. The head-spinning wine list has 1700 bottles to pick from.

Getting There & Away

Buses run between Lech and Zürs (€1.20, seven minutes); both resorts have connections to St Anton am Arlberg (see p365). For Bludenz (€5.80, 1½ hours) and beyond, a change in Langen is required. Note also that snow occasionally blocks the Flexen Pass in winter. In summer, Lech can also be approached from the north, via the turning at Warth (1494m).

Directory

CONTENTS

ACCOMMODATION

You'll find it all in Austria – from simple mountain huts to five-star hotels fit for kings. Tourist offices invariably keep lists and details, and some arrange bookings for a small fee, while others will help free of charge.

Most hotel rooms in Austria have their own shower, although some rock bottom digs do still have *Etagendousche* (corridor shower). It's wise to book ahead at all times (often a day or two is enough), but especially well in advance during the high seasons: July and August, at Christmas and Easter and between December and April in ski areas. Some places don't accept telephone reservations. Confirmed reservations in writing are binding on either side and compensation may be claimed if you do not take a reserved room or if a reserved room is unavailable.

In mountain resorts, high-season prices can be up to double the prices charged in the low season (May and November, which fall between the summer and winter seasons). In other towns, the difference may be 10% or less.

In some resorts (not often in cities) a *Gästekarte* (guest card) is issued to guests. This card may offer discounts on things such as cable cars and admission, so check with a tourist office if you're not offered one at your resort accommodation.

The listings in the accommodation sections of this guidebook are arranged from budget to midrange to top-end options. The general price range split is anything below €60 per double for budget options, from €60 to €130 per double for midrange, and top-end is anything above €130. Vienna is an exception to the rule: budget ends at €70, midrange accommodation falls between €70 and €200, and top-end choices go over and above €200. Unless otherwise noted, we quote high-season rates throughout this book.

Prices are for rooms with bathroom and, unless noted otherwise, include breakfast. Before setting out, consider logging on to the following sites for more information:

www.austria.info Austrian National Tourist Office website, with links to accommodation sites.

www.austrian-hotelreservation.at Regional listings of hotels, alpine huts and chalets and online booking service; also in English.

www.campsite.at Comprehensive website listing around 70% of campsites in Austria; in a number of languages.

www.tiscover.at Hotels, rooms, last-minute deals and holiday packages, alongside general tourist information on Austria.

Alpine Huts

There are over 530 of these huts in the Austrian Alps maintained by the Österreichischer Alpenverein (ÖAV; Austrian Alpine Club; p83) and the German Alpine Club (DAV). Huts are found at altitudes between 900m and 2700m and may be used by the general public.

PRACTICALITIES

- The metric system is used in Austria; decimals are indicated with commas and thousands with points (full stops).

- International newspapers are widely available in the larger cities; local big sellers include *Kronen Zeitung*, *Kurier* and *Der Standard*.

- Independent broadcaster ÖRF (Österreichischer Rundfunk; Austrian Broadcasting Corporation; www.orf.at) runs a total of 13 radio stations and twoU TV channels, ÖRF1 and ÖRF2. Programmes are generally dubbed rather than subtitled. Radio station FM4 (103.8 FM) has news in English from 6pm to 7pm.

- You can get prints of digital photos and burn DVDs at many photo outlets.

- Wi-fi is widely available and often free to use.

- Electric sockets have the two small round holes common throughout Central Europe (220V AC, 50Hz). North American (110V) appliances will need a transformer.

- Videos in Austria use the PAL image-registration system (similar in the UK and Australia), and are not compatible with the NTSC system used in the USA, Canada and Japan.

Meals or cooking facilities are often available. Bed prices for nonmembers are around €24 to €30 in a dorm or €12 to €18 for a mattress on the floor. Members of the ÖAV or affiliated clubs pay half-price and have priority. Contact the ÖAV or a local tourist office for lists of huts and to make bookings.

Camping

Austria has over 490 camping grounds that offer users a range of facilities such as washing machines, electricity connections, onsite shops and, occasionally, cooking facilities. Camping gas canisters are widely available. Campsites are often scenically situated in an out-of-the-way place by a river or lake – fine if you're exploring the countryside but inconvenient if you want to sightsee in a town. For this reason, and because of the extra gear required, camping is more viable if you have your own transport. Prices can be as low as €3 per person or tent and as high as €8.

A majority of the campsites close in the winter. If demand is low in spring and autumn, some campsites shut, even though their literature says they are open, so telephone ahead to check during these periods. In high season, campsites may be full unless you reserve and higher prices may apply.

Free camping in camper vans is allowed in autobahn rest areas and alongside other roads, as long as you're not causing an obstruction. It's illegal to camp in tents in these areas. Note that 'wild camping' in cities or protected areas is also illegal.

While in the country, pick up camping guides from the **Österreichischer Camping Club** (Austrian Camping Club; ☎ 01-713 6151; www.camping club.at, in German; Schubertring 1-3, A-1010 Vienna) and a *Camping Map Austria* from the Österreich Werbung (p391).

Private Rooms

Rooms in private houses are cheap (anything from €18 to €40 per double) and in most towns you will see *Privat Zimmer* (private room) or *Zimmer Frei* (room free) signs. Most hosts are friendly; the level of service though is lower than in hotels. On top of this, you will find *Bauernhof* (farmhouses) in rural areas, and even *Öko-Bauernhöfe* (organic farms). Regional tourist offices (p391) are good information sources for farm stays.

Hostels

Austria is dotted with *Jugendherberge* (youth hostels) or *Jugendgästehaus* (youth guesthouses). Facilities are often excellent: four- to six-bed dorms with shower/toilet are the norm in hostels, while many guesthouses have double rooms or family rooms; internet facilities and a restaurant or café are commonplace.

Austria has over 100 hostels affiliated with Hostelling International (HI), plus a smattering of privately owned hostels. HI hostels are run by two hostel organisations (either can provide information on all HI hostels): **Österreichischer Jugendherbergsverband** (ÖJHV; ☎ 533 53 53; www.oejhv.or.at; Schottenring 28; 🕙 9am-5pm Mon-Thu, 9am-3pm Fri)

DIRECTORY

Österreichischer Jugendherbergswerk (ÖJHW;
☎ 533 18 33; www.oejhw.at; Helferstorferstrasse 4;
🕙 9.30am-6pm Mon-Fri).

Gästekarten are always required, except in a
few private hostels. It's cheaper to become a
member in your home country than to join
when you get to Austria. Nonmembers pay a
surcharge of €3.50 per night for a *Gästekarte*,
but after six nights the guest card counts as
a full membership card. Most hostels accept
reservations by telephone or email and some
are part of the worldwide computer reservations system. Dorm prices range from €14 to
€19 per night.

Cheap dorm-style accommodation is sometimes available in ski resorts even if there is
no hostel. Look for the signs *Touristenlager*
or *Matratzenlager* (dorm); unfortunately,
such accommodation might only be offered
to pre-booked groups.

Hotels & Pensions

Pensions and hotels (often known as *Gäste-
häuse* or *Gasthöfe*) are rated from one to five
stars depending on the facilities they offer.
However, as the criteria are different you can't
assume that a three-star pension is equivalent to a three-star hotel. Pensions tend to
be smaller than hotels and usually provide a
more personal service, less standardised fix-
tures and fittings and larger rooms. Hotels
invariably offer more services, including bars,
restaurants and garage parking.

With very few exceptions, rooms in hotels
and pensions are clean and well-appointed;
expect to pay an absolute minimum of around
€35/45 for a single/double room. Internet
booking, weekend or multiple-night deals,
or simply asking, can often result in a cheaper
room. Credit cards are rarely accepted by
cheaper places. In theory, hotel prices are not
negotiable; in practice, you can often haggle
for a better rate in the low season or if you're
staying more than a few days.

In low-budget accommodation, a room
advertised as having a private shower may
mean that it has a shower cubicle rather than
a proper en suite bathroom.

Where there is a telephone in the room it's
usually direct-dial, but this will still be more
expensive than using a public telephone. TVs
are almost invariably hooked up to satellite or
cable. Better hotels will usually have the added
bonus of a minibar.

BOOK YOUR STAY ONLINE

For more accommodation reviews and recommendations by Lonely Planet authors,
check out the online booking service at
www.lonelyplanet.com/hotels. You'll find
the true, insider lowdown on the best places
to stay. Reviews are thorough and independent. Best of all, you can book online.

Meals are usually available, either for guests
only, or more often, in a public restaurant on
site. A pension that supplies breakfast only
is known as a *Frühstückspension;* the hotel
equivalent is *Hotel-Garni.* Other hotels and
pensions will offer the option of paying for
half board (where breakfast and one main
meal is provided) or even full board (where all
meals are provided). In budget places, breakfast is basic, usually consisting of only a drink,
bread rolls, butter, cheese spread and jam. As
you pay more, breakfast gets better: in two-
star places it's usually *Erweitert* ('extended' to
include more choices) and in places with three
stars or more it's usually buffet style. A typical
buffet will include cereals, juices and a selection of cold meats and cheeses – maybe even
(in top places) hot food such as scrambled
eggs, sausage and bacon. In five-star hotels
breakfast generally costs extra, but may be
included in special, lower weekend rates.

Rental Accommodation

Ferienwohnungen (self-catering holiday
apartments) are very common in Austrian
mountain resorts, though it is often necessary to book these well in advance. The best
idea is to contact a local tourist office for lists
and prices.

University Accommodation

Studentenheime (student residences) are available to tourists over university summer breaks
(from the beginning of July to around the
end of September). During university terms
the kitchen and dining room on each floor
are open, but when they're used as seasonal
hotels these useful facilities generally remain
locked. Rooms are perfectly OK but nothing
fancy; some have a private bathroom. Expect
single beds (though beds may be placed together in double rooms), a work desk and a
wardrobe. The widest selection is in Vienna,
but look for them also in Graz, Salzburg and

Innsbruck. Prices per person are likely to range from €20 to €35 per night and sometimes include breakfast.

ACTIVITIES

See the Outdoor Activities chapter (p74) for details on walking, skiing, cycling and other outdoor pursuits in Austria.

BUSINESS HOURS

Offices and government departments generally open from 8am to 3.30pm, 4pm or 5pm Monday to Friday. There are no real restrictions on shop opening hours but most open between 9am and 6pm Monday to Friday and until 1pm Saturday (until 5pm in larger cities).

Banking hours are from 8am or 9am until 3pm Monday to Friday, and there are extended hours to 5.30pm on Thursdays. Many of the smaller branches close from 12.30pm to 1.30pm for lunch. Most post offices open for business from 8am to noon and 2pm to 6pm Monday to Friday; some also open on Saturday from 8am to noon. Restaurants serve lunch between 11am and 3pm and dinner from 6pm to midnight, and often close in between. Hours for cafés vary considerably and are included in our listings. As a rule, however, a traditional café will open around 7.30am and shut at about 8pm; pubs and bars close anywhere between midnight and about 4am throughout the week.

CHILDREN

The infrastructure for travellers with kids is good and getting better, and children are welcome at tourist attractions, restaurants and hotels. Regional tourist offices have focused a lot on kids recently and now produce brochures aimed directly at families. Museums, parks and theatres often have programmes for children over the summer holiday periods and local councils occasionally put on special events and festivals for the little ones.

Log on to www.kinderhotels.at for information on child-friendly hotels throughout the country. For helpful travelling tips, pick up a copy of Lonely Planet's *Travel with Children* by Cathy Lanigan.

Practicalities

Facilities are definitely improving throughout the country but not in all directions. Some restaurants do have children's menus but may not have high chairs or nappy-changing facilities. In general, only mid-range to top-end hotels have cots and can arrange daycare.

In the bigger cities, breast-feeding in public won't cause eyelids to bat. Everything you need for babies, such as formula and disposable nappies, is widely available. Rental car companies can arrange safety seats. Newer public transport, such as trams and buses in Vienna, are easily accessible for buggies and prams, but the older models can prove a nightmare. Sundays, public holidays, and during the summer holidays, children under the age of 15 travel free on Vienna's transport system (with photo ID; children between six and 16 can travel half-price, and travel for kids up to the age of six is always free).

Sights & Activities

With its parks, playgrounds and great outdoors, Austria has plenty to keep the kids entertained. Vienna has two great kids' museums and loads of swimming locations; see p138) for more details. Outside the capital, Graz has the only museum directed at children, FriDa & FreD (p228). Its Schlossberg Cave Railway (p228) will also entertain the little tykes. Closer to the capital, shallow Neusiedler See (p193) is a perfect place to holiday with children. In Linz, Ars Electronica (p203) and the Pöstlingberg (p204) are fine attractions for the kids, as is the Minimundus miniature park (p292) in Klagenfurt. Once the kids are finished with Minimundus, the region's lakes are an enticing destination, as is Die Spur des Einhorns (p301) in Friesach. Austrians love their puppets; one of the best puppet places is the Marionettentheater (p280) in Salzburg.

Trips underground also keep the kids amused; the Erzberg mine (p242) in Styria and the salt mines (p249) of Salzkammergut are exciting places.

CLIMATE CHARTS

Austria lies within the Central European climatic zone, though the eastern part of the country has what is called a Continental Pannonian climate, characterised by hot summers and mild winters. To the west, the Alps tend to draw the clouds, though the alpine valleys often escape much of the downfall. The *Föhn*, a hot, dry wind that sweeps down from the mountains, mainly in early spring and autumn – can be rather uncomfortable

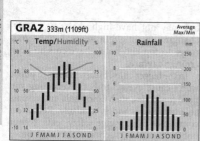

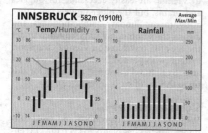

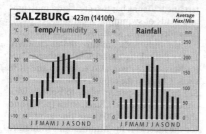

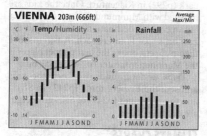

for some people and often has a bad reputation among Austrians.

The climate charts show average temperatures and rainfall in the larger cities, but these can vary wildly from year to year.

COURSES

Many places, including some of Austria's universities, offer German courses, and they can usually offer the option of accommodation for the duration. Two of the better known course providers in Vienna are:

Berlitz (Map pp120–1; ☎ 512 82 86; www.berlitz .at, in German; various locations; ☼ 8am-8pm Mon-Fri, 8am-12.30pm Sat) Offers private, intensive day and evening courses and has four offices in Vienna.

Inlingua Sprachschule (Map pp120–1; ☎ 512 22 25; www.inlingua.at; Neuer Markt 1, Vienna; ☼ 9am-6pm Mon-Fri) Courses run for a minimum of two weeks and can either be taken in the morning or some evenings. Classes are limited to six students and individual tuition is also available.

In Innsbruck, try the following:

Inlingua Innsbruck (☎ 562 031; www.inlingua-tirol .at; Südtirolerplatz 6) Year-round courses, usually in small groups.

Innsbruck University (☎ 587 233; www.uibk.ac.at /ihd; Innrain 52) Intensive courses in July and August.

Check the *Gelbe Seiten* (yellow pages) under *Sprachschulen* for more listings in other towns and cities.

CUSTOMS

Theoretically there is no restriction on what you can bring into Austria from other EU states. However, to ensure these remain for personal use, guideline limits are 800 cigarettes, 200 cigars, 1kg of tobacco, 10L of spirits, 90L of wine, 110L of beer and 20L of other alcoholic beverages. The same quantity can be taken out of Austria, as long as you are travelling to another EU country.

For duty-free purchases outside the EU, you may bring into Austria 200 cigarettes or 50 cigars or 250g of tobacco, plus 2L of wine and 1L of spirits. Items such as weapons, drugs (both legal and illegal), meat, certain plant materials and animal products are subject to stricter customs control.

DANGERS & ANNOYANCES

Austria is one of the safest countries to travel in and crime rates are low by international standards, but you should always be security conscious. Be wary of leaving valuables in hotel rooms; management will look after expensive items if you ask them, even in hostels. Don't leave valuables in cars, especially overnight. In general, let common sense prevail and don't make it easy for thieves by loosely carrying cameras and jewellery around.

In the event of theft or loss, get a police report – this will be necessary for you to claim on your travel insurance. Your consulate should be able to help replace documents if you're left in a desperate situation.

DISCOUNT CARDS

There are various discount cards available throughout Austria, covering either a region of a province or an entire province. Some are free and provide discounts at hotels and sights, while others must be purchased but may give you free entry to attractions and include public transport. Ask at your hotel or contact provincial tourist offices for details. Examples include the free Neusiedler See Card, and the Salzburg Card (from €23/11.50 adult/child) giving free entry to every sight in town and reduced entry to a further 27 attractions plus free public transport for the duration.

Senior Cards

In some cases senior travellers will be able to get discount admission to sights, but local proof is often required. It can't hurt to ask and show proof of age, though. The minimum qualifying age for Austrians is 65 for men and 60 for women.

Student & Youth Cards

International Student Identity Cards (ISIC) and Euro26 cards will get you discounts at most museums, galleries and theatres. You may even get a discount on air, bus and train tickets.

EMBASSIES & CONSULATES
Austrian Embassies & Consulates

The Austrian Foreign Ministry website (www.bmaa.gv.at) has a complete list of embassies and consulates. It's in German only, but is quite easy to navigate.

Australia (☎ 02-6295 1533; www.austriaemb.org.au; 12 Talbot St, Forrest, Canberra, ACT 2603)
Canada (☎ 613-789 1444; www.austro.org; 445 Wilbrod St, Ottawa, Ontario K1N 6M7)
Czech Republic (☎ 257 09 05 11; www.austria.cz; Viktora Huga 10, CZ-15115 Prague 5)
France (☎ 01-40 63 30 63; paris-ob@bmeia.gv.at; 6, Rue Fabert, F-75007 Paris)
Germany (☎ 030-202 87-0; www.oesterreichische-botschaft.de; Stauffenbergstrasse 1, D-10785 Berlin)
Hungary (☎ 01-479 70-10; www.austrian-embassy.hu; Benczúrutca 16, 1068 Budapest)
Ireland (☎ 01-269 45 77; dublin-ob@bmeia.gv.at; 15, Ailesbury Court Apt, 93, Ailesbury Rd, Dublin 4)
Italy (☎ 06-844 01 41; www.austria.it; Via Pergolesi 3, I-00198 Rome)

The Netherlands (☎ 070-324 54 70; den-haag-ob@bmeia.gv.at; van Alkemadelaan 342, 2597 AS Den Haag)
New Zealand (consulate only; ☎ 04-499 6393; austria@ihug.co.nz; Level 2, Willbank House, 57 Willis St, Wellington)
Slovakia (☎ 02-59 30 15 00; www.embassyaustria.sk; Venturska 10, SK-81101 Bratislava)
Slovenia (☎ 01-479 07 00; www.aussenministerium.at/laibach; Presernova cesta 23, SI-1000 Ljubljana)
UK (☎ 020-7344 3250; www.austria.org.uk; 18 Belgrave Mews West, London SW1X 8HU)
USA (☎ 202-895 6700; washington-ob@bmeia.gv.at; 3524 International Court NW, Washington, DC 20008)

Embassies & Consulates in Austria

All the embassies and consulates listed below are located in Vienna. For a complete listing of embassies and consulates, look in the Austrian telephone book under *Botschaften* (embassies) or *Konsulate* (consulates).

Australia (Map pp120-1; ☎ 506 74-0; www.australian-embassy.at; Mattiellistrasse 2-4)
Canada (Map pp120-1; ☎ 531 38-3000; www.kanada.at; Laurenzerberg 2)
Czech Republic (Map pp116-17; ☎ 899 581 11; www.mzv.cz/vienna; Penzingerstrasse 11-13)
France (Map pp120-1; ☎ 502 75 200; www.consulfrance-vienne.org; Wipplinger Strasse 24-26)
Germany (Map pp120-1; ☎ 711 54-0; www.wien.diplo.de/vertretung/wien; Metternichgasse 3)
Hungary (Map pp120-1; ☎ 537 80-300; kom@huembvie.at; Bankgasse 4-6)
Ireland (Map pp120-1; ☎ 715 42 46; vienna@dsa.ie; Rotenturmstrasse 16-18)
Italy (Map pp120-1; ☎ 713 56 71; www.ambvienna.esteri.it; Ungargasse 43)
The Netherlands (Map pp120-1; ☎ 01-589 39; www.mfa.nl/wen; 7th fl, Opernring 5)
New Zealand (consulate-general; Map pp120-1; ☎ 318 85 05; www.nzc.at; Salesianergasse 15/3)
Slovakia (Map pp114-15; ☎ 318 90 55; www.vienna.mfa.sk; Armbrustergasse 24)
Slovenia (Map pp120-1; ☎ 585 22 40; vdu@gov.si; Nibelungengasse 13)
Switzerland (Map pp116-17; ☎ 795 05-0; www.eda.admin.ch/wien; Prinz Eugen Strasse 7)
UK (Map pp116-17; ☎ 716 13-0; www.britishembassy.at; Jaurèsgasse 12)
USA (Map pp120-1; ☎ 313 39-0; www.usembassy.at; Boltzmanngasse 16)

FESTIVALS & EVENTS

Most festivals and cultural events are small-scale local affairs, so it's worth checking with local tourist offices or the Österreich Werbung (Austrian National Tourist Office;

ANTO; p391), which compiles a list of annual and one-off events taking place in Austria. The cycle of music festivals throughout the country is almost unceasing, and religious holidays provide an opportunity to stage colourful processions. **Corpus Christi** (the second Thursday after Whitsunday) brings carnivals, including some held on lakes in the Salzkammergut. **National Day** on 26 October inspires various events, often accompanied by much patriotic flag-waving.

More details of specific events are given in the text, but here's a selection of annual highlights throughout the country.

JANUARY

New Year concerts (1 January) The new year is welcomed throughout Austria with classical concerts. The Vienna Philharmonic's performance in the Staatsoper is the most celebrated.

Perchtenlaufen (5 to 6 January) Celebrated across much of western Austria, this festival promotes good fortune and a prosperous harvest for the forthcoming year. Locals dress as *Perchten* (spirits crowned with elaborate headdresses) and parade through the streets. Salzkammergut's equivalent is Glöckerlaufen.

FEBRUARY

Fasching (Shrovetide Carnival; 11 November to Shrove Tuesday) Austria's carnival season, which really only gets going at the end of January/beginning of February, when people parade around in fancy dress and party till the wee small hours. Look for *Fasching Krapfen* (a sweet bun filled with jam) during this time.

MARCH OR APRIL

Easter Easter is marked by a long-weekend or week-long holidays and family gatherings.

MAY

Maypole Day (1 May) Colourful, lively countrywide affairs accompanied by maypoles, plenty of alcohol and unabandoned merriment.

Wiener Festwochen (Vienna Festival Weeks; ☎ 589 22-22; www.festwochen.or.at) Wide-ranging programme of arts from around the world, from May to mid-June.

JUNE

Midsummer Night (21 June) A celebration of the summer solstice, with hilltop bonfires and partying through the night.

JULY & AUGUST

Music Festivals Classical, jazz and rock festivals take place throughout the country over summer.

OCTOBER

Cattle Roundup (early October) In the alpine areas the coming of autumn sees cattle herds coming down out of the mountains. The event is marked with various festivals.

Wine Harvest (all October) Styria, Burgenland and Lower Austria mark the grape harvest with bottle after bottle of wine and folk music.

NOVEMBER

Allerheiligen (All Saints' Day; 1 November) Austrians flock to cemeteries throughout the country to pay their respects to the dead.

St Martin's Day (11 November) The day of St Martin of Tours is marked with feasts of goose and wine.

DECEMBER

St Nicholas Day (5 to 6 December) More for the kids, this day sees St Nicholas drift from house to house handing out presents to good children. He is often accompanied by the *Krampus* (devil), who punishes the bad children (which never happens). In many places, this day is also marked by **Krampuslaufen**: young men dress up as demons in heavy wooden masks and run through the streets, terrorising villagers along the way.

Weihnacht (Christmas; 25 December) A quiet family affair, aside from the *Christkindlmärkte* (Christmas markets), which take place throughout the country from early December till the 24th.

FOOD

A full rundown on local cuisine, drinks, and our top eating experiences appears in the Food & Drink chapter (p59). As ballpark figures, budget mains are anything below €10, midrange from €10 up to €20, and top end anything above that.

GAY & LESBIAN TRAVELLERS

Vienna is reasonably tolerant towards gays and lesbians, more so than the rest of the country. Austria has received criticism in past years on its laws on homosexuality, but these days is close to European par. The age of consent for anyone – homosexual or heterosexual, man or woman – is 14, but if money's involved it's 18, and if one partner is 18 or older and the other between 14 and 16, additional youth-abuse laws swing into force. Police are not obliged to press charges if both partners are under 14, providing the age difference is less than two years.

The 'Gay & Lesbian Vienna' boxed text (p140) has specific listings of publications, organisations, hotels and bars for gays and lesbians. Online information (in German)

can be found at www.gayboy.at, www.rainbow
.or.at, www.gay.at and www.gayguide.at. The
Spartacus International Gay Guide, published
by Bruno Gmünder (Berlin), is a good international directory of gay entertainment
venues worldwide (mainly for men).

HOLIDAYS

Basically, everything shuts down on public
holidays. The only establishments open are
bars, cafés and restaurants and even some of
these refuse to open their doors. Museums
like to confuse things – some stay closed while
others are open and offer free admission. The
big school break is in July and August. This
is a time when most families go on holiday
so you'll find some places, like cities, a little
quieter and others, such as popular holiday
destinations, busier. Avoid ski breaks during much of February; school pupils have a
week off during that time and invariably the
ski slopes are full to overflowing with kids
and parents.

The public holidays in Austria are:

New Year's Day (Neujahr) 1 January
Epiphany (Heilige Drei Könige) 6 January
Easter Monday (Ostermontag)
Labour Day (Tag der Arbeit) 1 May
Whit Monday (Pfingstmontag) 6th Monday after Easter
Ascension Day (Christi Himmelfahrt) 6th Thursday after
Easter
Corpus Christi (Fronleichnam) 2nd Thursday after
Whitsunday
Assumption (Maria Himmelfahrt) 15 August
National Day (Nationalfeiertag) 26 October
All Saints' Day (Allerheiligen) 1 November
Immaculate Conception (Mariä Empfängnis) 8
December
Christmas Day (Christfest) 25 December
St Stephen's Day (Stephanitag) 26 December

INSURANCE

Organising a travel insurance policy to cover
theft, loss and medical problems is an essential part of planning for your trip. There is a
wide variety of policies available, so check
the fine print.

Some policies specifically exclude 'dangerous activities', which can include skiing,
motorcycling, rock climbing, canoeing and
even hiking. If you're planning on doing any
of these activities, be sure to choose a policy
that covers you.

You may prefer a policy that pays doctors
or hospitals directly rather than having to

pay on the spot and claim later. If you have
to claim later make sure you keep all documentation. Some policies ask you to call back
(reverse charges) to a centre in your home
country where an immediate assessment of
your problem is made.

Check that the policy covers ambulances
or an emergency flight home.

See p407 for more on health insurance.
For information on car rental insurance,
see p403.

INTERNET ACCESS

Wi-fi or network-cable access is available free
or with charges in many hotels. All top hotels
have plugs for connecting your laptop to the
internet, but as yet it's not possible to organise
an ISP in Austria for a short period (minimum
contracts run for 12 months) so you'll have to
arrange one from home. AOL's access number
in Vienna is ☎ 071-891 50 52, Compuserve's
☎ 071-891 51 61 and Eunet's ☎ 899 330.

Public internet access is well covered across
the country; for details of specific internet
cafés see individual destination chapters.
Prices are generally around €4 to €8 per hour.
If there are no cafés in town, it's worth checking with the local library; some have computer
terminals connected to the internet which
are often free to use. Remember to take some
form of ID with you.

LEGAL MATTERS

Austria offers the level of civil and legal
rights you would expect of any industrialised
Western nation. If you are arrested, the police
must inform you of your rights in a language
that you understand.

For information on the ages of sexual consent, see opposite.

In Austria, legal offences are divided into
two categories: *Gerichtsdelikt* (criminal) and
Verwaltungsübertretung (administrative).
If you are suspected of having committed a
criminal offence (such as assault or theft) you
can be detained for a maximum of 48 hours
before you are committed for trial. If you are
arrested for a less serious, administrative offence, such as being drunk and disorderly or
committing a breach of the peace, you will be
released within 24 hours.

Drunken driving is an administrative matter, even if you have an accident. However, if
someone is hurt in the accident it becomes a
criminal offence. Possession of a controlled

drug is usually a criminal offence. Possession of a large amount of dope (around 300g) or dealing (especially to children) could result in a five-year prison term. Prostitution is legal provided prostitutes are registered and have obtained a permit.

If you are arrested, you have the right to make one phone call to 'a person in your confidence' within Austria, and another to inform legal counsel. If you can't afford legal representation, you can apply to the judge in writing for legal aid.

Free advice is given on legal matters in some towns, for example during special sessions at Vienna's *Bezirksgerichte* (district courts). As a foreigner, your best bet when encountering legal problems is to contact your national consulate (see p385).

MAPS

Freytag & Berndt of Vienna offers the most comprehensive coverage of the country. It publishes good town maps (1:10,000 to 1:25,000 scale) and has a *Wanderkarte* series for walkers, mostly on a 1:50,000 scale. Motorists should consider buying its *Österreich Touring* road atlas; this covers Austria (1:150,000) and 48 Austrian towns. If this is too detailed then their *Österreich road map* (1:500,000) will suffice. Extremely detailed walking maps are produced by the ÖAV at a scale of 1:25,000. Kompass also has a range of excellent walking maps. The most detailed maps, however, are produced by the Bundesamt für Eich-und Vermessungswesen (BEV; Federal Office for Calibration and Measurement); their country-wide and regional maps are available in good bookshops and map stores.

Bikeline maps are recommended for those travelling round the country by bicycle; eight maps (1:100,000 or 1:75,000) cover the most popular areas for cycling and two delve into mountain biking in Carinthia and the Hohe Tauern National Park.

For getting around cities, maps provided by tourist offices, in conjunction with the maps in this book, are generally adequate. These are usually free, but where there's a charge you can probably make do with the hotel map instead.

MONEY

Like other members of the European Monetary Union (EMU), Austria's currency is the euro, which is divided into 100 cents.

There are coins for one, two, five, 10, 20 and 50 cents and for €1 and €2. Notes come in denominations of €5, €10, €20, €50, €100, €200 and €500. The Quick Reference on the inside front cover lists exchange rates.

ATMs

In Austria ATMs are known as *Bankomaten*. They are extremely common and are accessible till midnight, some are 24 hours. Even villages have at least one machine; look for the sign with blue and green horizontal stripes. ATMs are linked up internationally, have English instructions and are usually limited to daily withdrawals of €400 with credit and debit cards.

Check with your home bank before travelling for charges for using a *Bankomat;* there's usually no commission to pay at the Austrian end.

Cash

With the number of ATMs, the practice of carrying large amounts of cash around has become obsolete. It is, however, worth keeping a small amount in a safe place for emergencies.

Credit Cards

Visa, EuroCard and MasterCard are accepted a little more widely than American Express (Amex) and Diners Club, although a surprising number of shops and restaurants refuse to accept any credit cards at all. Upmarket shops, hotels and restaurants will accept cards, though. Train tickets can be bought by credit card in main stations. Credit cards allow you to get cash advances at most banks.

For lost or stolen credit cards, call the following:

Amex ☎ 0800 900 940
Diners Club ☎ 01-501 35 14
MasterCard ☎ 01-717 01 4500
Visa ☎ 01-711 11 770

Moneychangers

Banks are the best places to exchange cash, but it pays to shop around as exchange rates and commission charges can vary a little between them. Normally there is a minimum commission charge of €2 to €3.50, so try to exchange your money in large amounts to save on multiple charges. Banks at train stations often have longer hours, and *Wechselstuben* (money-exchange offices) – usually found in the centre of large cities or at train stations – even longer, but commissions are often high.

Taxes & Refunds

Mehrwertsteuer (MWST; value-added tax) in Austria is set at 20% for most goods. Prices are always displayed inclusive of all taxes.

All non-EU tourists are entitled to a refund of the MWST on single purchases over €75. To claim the tax, a U34 form or tax-free cheque and envelope must be completed by the shop at the time of purchase (show your passport), and then stamped by border officials when you leave the EU. To be eligible for a tax refund, goods must be taken out of the country within three months of the date of purchase. The airports at Vienna, Salzburg, Innsbruck, Linz and Graz have a counter for payment of instant refunds. There are also counters at major border crossings. The refund is best claimed as you leave the EU, otherwise you will have to track down an international refund office or claim by post from your home country.

Before making a purchase, ensure the shop has the required paperwork; some places display a 'Global Refund Tax Free Shopping' sticker. Also confirm the value of the refund; it's usually advertised as 13% (which is the refund of the 20% standard rate of value-added tax after various commissions have been taken), though it may vary for certain categories of goods.

Tipping

Tipping is a part of everyday life in Austria; in restaurants, bars and cafés and in taxis it's customary to give about 10%. Add the bill and the tip together and hand it over in one lump sum. It also doesn't hurt to tip hairdressers, hotel porters, cloak-room attendants, cleaning staff and tour guides one or two euros.

Travellers Cheques

All major travellers cheques are equally widely accepted, but you may want to use Amex, Visa or Thomas Cook because of their 'instant replacement' policies. A record of the cheque numbers and the initial purchase details is vital when it comes to replacing lost cheques. Without this, you may well find that 'instant' might take a very long time. You should also keep a record of which cheques you have cashed. Keep these details separate from the cheques.

American Express exchange services are run by Interchange Austria. A minimum commission of €5 is charged on Amex cheques in euros for amounts of €50 to €250, or 2% if the amount is above that. For non-Amex cheques it's €7/12 for €100/250. Amex cheques in US dollars are exchanged without charge. Banks typically charge €7 or more to exchange travellers cheques. Avoid changing a lot of low-value cheques as commission costs will be higher. Big hotels also change money, but rates are invariably poor. Look especially carefully at the commission rates charged by exchange booths; they can be quite reasonable or ridiculously high.

POST

Austria's postal service (www.post.at) is easy to use and reliable. *Postämter* (post offices) are commonplace, as are bright yellow post boxes. Stamps can also be bought at *Tabak* (tobacconist) shops. Sending a standard letter within Austria or Europe costs €0.55 and worldwide €1.25. The normal weight limit for *Briefsendung* (letter post) is 2kg; anything over this limit must be sent as a package. In Austria, mailing a 2kg package starts from €4.20. Sample prices for a 2kg package internationally are: Australia (€25), Canada & the USA (€18), and Germany & the UK (€14). Maximum weights range from 20 kg (including Italy, Canada) to 31.5 kg (including Austria, USA).

For post restante, address letters *Postlagernde Sendungen* rather than *Postlagernde Briefe* as the former is the preferred term in Austria. Mail can be sent care of any post office and is held for a month; a passport must be shown on collection.

SHOPPING

You could possibly base a whole trip around shopping – and leave broke. The items you'd be most likely to leave with are jewellery, glassware and crystalware, ceramics, pottery, woodcarvings, wrought-iron work and textiles. There are also many antique shops, especially in Vienna.

Designer fashion is on the move in Vienna, which, by a far cry, is Austria's best city for shopping. See the destination chapters for tips on shopping in large cities.

Don't overlook the many markets throughout the country; alongside local produce you may find some local folk-art gems.

For special reductions, look for *Aktion* (sales promotion) signs. Prices are fixed in shops, but it can't hurt to ask for 'a discount for cash' if you're making several purchases. Bargain hard in flea markets.

Top Viennese hotels have a free booklet entitled *Shopping in Vienna* that details all sorts of shopping outlets; there are similar booklets in other cities.

SOLO TRAVELLERS

There's no stigma attached to travelling solo in Austria. Most hostels, pensions and hotels have single rooms available and they're generally a little more than half the price of a double room.

Making contact with the locals is relatively easy in smaller towns and cities if you know a little German; without German, things are a little harder, but definitely not impossible. Many people speak good English, or at least enough to hold a conversation for an hour or two. In the bigger cities, pseudo-Irish and English pubs are havens for expats and Austrians keen on Guinness and a chat in English.

TELEPHONE

Austria's country code is ☎ 0043. **Telekom Austria** (☎ 0800-100 100; www.telekom.at, in German) is Austria's main telecommunications provider and maintains public telephones (particularly those inside or outside post offices) throughout the country. These take either

---

TELEPHONE NUMBERS EXPLAINED

Telephone numbers for the same town may not always have the same number of digits: some telephone numbers have an individual line, others a party line, and sometimes numbers are listed with an extension that you can dial direct. This is relevant for reading phone numbers listed in the telephone book. If, for example, you see the number 123 45 67 ... -0, the 0 signifies that the number has extensions. Whether you dial the 0 at the end or not, you will (with a few exceptions) get through to that subscriber's main telephone reception. If you know the extension number of the person you want to speak to, simply dial that instead of the 0 and you'll get straight through to them.

---

coins or phonecards and a minimum of 20 cents is required to make a local call. Every post office has a phone booth where both international and national calls can be made; rates are cheaper from 6pm to 8am Monday to Friday and on weekends. Another option is call centres, which have recently been introduced into the telecommunications arena. They offer competitive rates, especially for long-distance calls.

Free phone numbers start with ☎ 0800 or ☎ 0810 while numbers starting with ☎ 0900 are pay-per-minute. When calling Austria from overseas drop the zero in the area code; ie the number for Vienna's main tourist office is ☎ 0043 1 211 14-555. When calling a number from within the same town or city, dialling the town's code is not required; however, when placing a call to elsewhere in Austria (or from a mobile) the code needs to be used.

Directory assistance for numbers in Austria and the EU is available on ☎ 11 88 77.

International Calls

To direct-dial abroad, first telephone the overseas access code (00), then the appropriate country code, then the relevant area code (minus the initial 0 if there is one), and finally the subscriber number. International directory assistance is available on ☎ 0900 11 88 77.

Tariffs for making international calls depend on the zone. To reverse the charges (call collect), you have to call a free phone number to place the call. Some of the numbers are listed below (ask directory assistance for others):

Australia ☎ 0800-200 202
Ireland ☎ 0800-200 213
New Zealand ☎ 0800-200 222
South Africa ☎ 0800-200 230
UK ☎ 0800-200 209
USA (AT&T) ☎ 0800-200 288
USA (Sprint) ☎ 0800-200 236

Mobile Phones

Austria's *Handy* (mobile phone) network works on GSM 1800 and is compatible with GSM 900 phones but generally not with systems from the USA or Japan. *Handy* numbers start with 0699, 0676, 0664, 0660 and 0650. The major *Handy* networks – Drei, One, A-1 and T-Mobile – sell SIM cards with €10 worth of calls for €39. Telering, a smaller operator, has SIM cards for €30 with €30 worth of calls. Refill cards can be purchased from supermarkets and Trafik for €20 or €40. Before buying an Austrian SIM card, confirm that your phone is unlocked; check with your home network before leaving.

Reciprocal agreements with foreign providers do exist, but check with your own provider before leaving home for costs and availability. If your provider is European, www.roaming .gsmeurope.org will help you work out costs inside Austria.

You can rent mobile phones at **Tel-Rent** (☎ 01-700 733 340; rental incl phone & SIM card per day/ week €18/90, additional weeks €54), located in the arrivals hall at Schwechat Airport in Vienna. Delivery or pick-up within Vienna is available for €26.

Phonecards & Internet Calls

There's a wide range of local and international *Telefon-Wertkarte* (phonecards), which can save you money and help you avoid messing around with change. They are available from post offices, *Tabak* and train stations. Large internet cafés (p387) have Skype software on their terminals and headphones for internet telephony, but you'll need to register and put money on your account in order to make calls to landlines or mobile phones.

TIME

See the World Time Zones (p446-7) for Austria's position.

Note that in German *halb* is used to indicate the half-hour before the hour, hence *halb acht* means 7.30, not 8.30.

TOURIST INFORMATION
Local Tourist Offices

Any town or village that tourists are likely to visit will have a centrally situated tourist office and at least one of the staff will speak English. They go by various names – *Kurort*, *Fremdenverkehrsverband*, *Verkehrsamt*, *Kurverein*, *Tourismusbüro* or *Kurverwaltung* – but they can always be identified by a white 'i' on a green background.

Staff can answer inquiries, ranging from where and when to attend religious services for different denominations, to where to find vegetarian food. Most offices will have an accommodation-finding service, often free of charge. Maps are always available and usually free.

Some local tourist offices hold brochures on other localities, allowing you to stock up

on information in advance. If you're empty-handed and arrive somewhere too late in the day to get to the tourist office, try asking at the railway ticket office, as staff there often have hotel lists or city maps. The tourist office may have a rack of brochures hung outside the door, or there may be an accommodation board you can access even when the office is closed. Top hotels usually have a supply of useful brochures in the foyer.

In addition, each province has its own tourist board (see list below), though some of these are geared more to handling written or telephone inquiries than dealing with personal callers.

Burgenland Tourismus (☎ 02682-633 84-0; www .burgenland.info, in German; Schloss Esterházy, Eisenstadt; 🕓 8.30am-5pm Mon-Fri) A regional tourist office set up more for telephone and email requests.

Kärnten Information (☎ 0463-3000; www.kaernten .at; Casinoplatz 1; A-9220 Velden; 🕓 8am-6pm Mon-Fri) Carinthia's regional tourist office, with information on the *Kärnten Card*.

Niederösterreich Werbung (Map pp120-1; ☎ 01-536 10 6200; www.niederoesterreich.at; 🕓 8.30am-5pm Mon-Thu, 8.30am-4pm Fri) The official information office for Lower Austria. Ask about the *Niederösterreich-Karte*, a card that entitles you to discounts throughout the province. At the time of research, the office was moving to a new address in St Pölten. See the website or contact the St Pölten tourist office for new details.

Oberösterreich Tourismus (☎ 070-22 10 22; www .oberoesterreich.at; Freistädter Strasse 119, A-4041 Linz) The information office for Upper Austria has a very large selection of brochures which can be requested by mail.

Österreich Werbung (ANTO; ☎ 0810-10 18 18; www .austria.info) Austria's national tourist office; phone and email inquiries only.

Salzburger Land Tourismus (☎ 0662-668 8-0; www .salzburgerland.com, in German; Wiener Bundesstrasse 23, A-5300 Hallwang bei Salzburg) Like other regions, Salzburger Land also offers a discount card, the *Salzburgerland Card*.

Steirische Tourismus (☎ 0316-400 30; www.steier mark.com; St Peter Hauptstrasse 243, A-8042 Graz) Staff at this Styria information office are happy to send you piles of useful information on the province.

Tirol Info (☎ 0512-72 720; www.tirol.at; Maria-Theresien-Strasse 55, A-6010 Innsbruck) Tyrol's regional tourist office.

Vorarlberg Tourismus (☎ 05574-425 25-0; www .voralberg-tourism.at; Bahnstrasse 14, Tourismushaus, A-6901 Bregenz) Information office for Austria's most westerly province.

Tourist Offices Abroad

The Austrian National Tourist Office has branches in many countries. In most European countries, there are no drop-by visitor services and inquiries are handled centrally by multilingual staff in Vienna. ANTO offices can be reached from inside these countries at the following:

Australia (☎ 02-9299 3621; info@antosyd.org.au; 1st fl, 36 Carrington St, Sydney, NSW 2000)

Canada (☎ 0416-96 33 81; anto-tor@sympatico.ca; 2 Bloor Street West, Suite 400, Toronto, Ontario M4W 3E2)

Czech Republic (☎ 800 180 800; info@rakousko.com)

France (☎ 0811 60 10 60; vacances@austria.info)

Germany (☎ 01802 10 18 18; urlaub@austria.info)

Hungary (☎ 06 800 12726; informacio@austria.info)

Ireland (☎ 189 093 01 18; holiday@austria.info)

Italy (☎ 02-46 75 191; vacanze@austria.info)

Japan (☎ 03-358 222 33; oewtyo@austria.info; Kokusai Shin-akasaka Bldg; West Tower 2F, 6-1-20 Akasaka, Minato-ku, Tokyo 107-0052)

Spain (☎ 902 999 432; informacion@austria.info)

Switzerland (☎ 0842 10 18 18; ferien@austria.info or vacances@austria.info)

The Netherlands (☎ 0900 04 00 181; vakantie@austria.info)

UK (☎ 0845 101 18 18; holiday@austria.info)

USA (☎ 212 944-6880; travel@austria.info; 9th fl, 120 West 45th St, New York, NY 10036)

For other countries and representatives, contact the Austrian National Tourist Board for the complete list of addresses, or visit www.austria.info and use the country portal selector (top right).

TRAVELLERS WITH DISABILITIES

The situation in Austria for travellers with disabilities is improving but is still by no means plain sailing, especially outside Vienna. Ramps leading into buildings are common but aren't universal; most U-Bahn stations have wheelchair lifts but on buses and trams you'll usually be negotiating gaps and one or more steps.

For distance travel, ÖBB, the Austrian National Railways, has a section for people with disabilities on its website (www.oebb.at). Change to the English language option, then go to 'Personenverkehr and submenu 'Barrier-free travelling'. You can also get information and arrange your trip by calling ☎ 5-1717 (051717 inside Austria) 7am to 9pm. Press 5 after the recorded message, and 5 again for 'notification of trips of wheelchair users

or persons with other handicaps'. You must book at least three days in advance. No special service is available at unstaffed stations.

The detailed pamphlet, *Vienna for Visitors with Disabilities*, from Tourist Info Wien (p123), is available in German or English. In other cities, contact the tourist office directly for more information.

Some of the more expensive (four star or above, usually) hotels have facilities tailored to travellers with disabilities; cheaper hotels invariably don't.

Organisations

There is no national disabled organisation in Austria, but the regional tourist offices or any of the following can be contacted for more information:

Behinderten Selbsthilfe Gruppe (☎ 03332-65 405; www.bsgh.at; Presslgasse 5, 8320 Hartberg, Styria)

Bizeps (Map p122; ☎ 523 89 21; www.bizeps.at, in German; Kaiserstrasse 55/3/4a, Vienna)

Upper Austria tourist office (www.oberoesterreich .at/nohandicap, in German) Information on contacts, guides and wheelchair hire.

VISAS

Visas for stays of up to three months are not required for citizens of the EU, the European Economic Area (EEA), much of Eastern Europe, Israel, USA, Canada, the majority of Central and South American nations, Japan, Korea, Malaysia, Singapore, Australia or New Zealand. All other nationalities require a visa; the Ministry of Foreign Affairs website at www.bmaa.gv.at has a list of Austrian embassies where you can apply for one.

If you wish to stay longer you should simply leave the country and re-enter. For those nationalities that require a visa, extensions cannot be organised within Austria; you'll need to leave and reapply. EU nationals can stay indefinitely but are required by law to register with the local *Magistratisches Bezirksamt* (magistrate's office) if the stay exceeds 60 days.

Austria is part of the Schengen Agreement which includes all EU states (minus Britain and Ireland) and Switzerland. In practical terms this means a visa issued by one Schengen country is good for all the other member countries and a passport is not required to move from one to the other (a national identity card is required, though). Things are a little different for the 10 new EU-member states which joined in 2004; a passport is still required to move in and out of these countries, but check with your local embassy for more up-to-date information. Austrians are required to carry personal identification, and you too will need to be able to prove your identity.

Visa and passport requirements are subject to change, so always double-check before travelling. Lonely Planet's website, www.lonelyplanet.com has links to up-to-date visa information.

VOLUNTEERING

Voluntary work is a good way to meet people and do something for the country you're visiting. In Austria, maintaining hiking trails is popular, but other volunteer projects range from joining a performance group on social issues to repairing a school fence outside Vienna. Generally, there's something for everyone, young or senior, lasting anything from a week to 18 months or more.

The key to finding a volunteer position in Austria is to hook up with the networks in your home country and/or if you speak German, to approach an Austrian organisation directly. If you speak German, you can track down an organisation from the Austrian government website www.freiwilligenweb.at (in German).

Networks rely mostly on people using their websites to locate projects; go to Travel Tree (www.traveltree.co.uk), a portal for volunteers. International Voluntary Service Great Britain (IVS; www.ivs-gb.org.uk) uses this portal and is networked with the worldwide group Service Civil International. In Australia, International Volunteers for Peace (www.ivp.org.au) also uses this network. Volunteers for Peace (www.vfp.org) in the US is for US and Canadian citizens and has a difficult-to-find searchable Project Directory down the bottom of its website. The Canada-based Canadian Alliance for Development Initiatives and Projects (CADIP; www.cadip.org) is also open to US and Canadian citizens.

One European foundation with excellent programmes is the Bergwald Projekt, which offers volunteer work protecting and maintaining mountain forests in Austria, Germany and Switzerland. Generally, the Austrian programmes last one week. The contact is the **Oesterreichischer Alpenverein** (fax 0512-57 55 28; www.bergwaldprojekt.at, in German; Wilhelm-Greil-Strasse 15, 6010 Innsbruck).

WOMEN TRAVELLERS

In cities, Austrian women enjoy the same status and opportunity as men, although 'Stone Age' gender customs have survived in some conservative, rural parts of the country.

Women travellers should experience no special problems. Fortunately, physical attacks and verbal harassment are less common than in many other countries. However, normal caution should be exercised when travelling alone or in unfamiliar situations. Some Austrian trains have a special section for women travelling alone and a growing number of underground car parks have a section near the staffed ticketing office designated as a women-only parking space.

Cities usually have a *Frauenzentrum* (women's centre) and/or telephone helplines. In Vienna, for example, there is the Frauennotruf (☎ 01-71 719), an emergency, 24-hour hotline for reporting rape and sexual violence.

WORK

EU nationals can work in Austria without a work permit or residency permit, though as intending residents they need to register with the police (or the magistrate's office if in Vienna).

Non-EU nationals need both a work permit and a residency permit and will find it pretty hard to get either. Inquire (in German) about job possibilities via local labour offices; look under *Arbeitsmarktservice* in the White Pages for the closest office. Your employer in Austria needs to apply for your work permit. Applications for residency permits must be applied for via the Austrian embassy in your home country. A good website for foreign residents is www.wif.wien.at.

Teaching is a favourite of expats in the bigger cities; look under *Sprachschulen* (language schools) in the *Gelben Seiten* (phone book) for a list of schools. Ski resorts are another good place to look for work; there are often vacancies in snow clearing, chalet cleaning, restaurants and ski-equipment shops. Language skills are particularly crucial for any type of work in service industries. Your best chance of finding work is to start writing or asking around early – in summer for winter work and in winter for summer work. Some people do, however, get lucky by arriving right at the beginning of the season and asking around; tourist offices and ski shops should be able to point you in the direction of current vacancies.

In October, grape-pickers are usually required in the wine-growing regions.

Useful books for those searching for work abroad include *Working in Ski Resorts – Europe & North America* by Victoria Pybus, *Work Your Way Around the World* by Susan Griffith, and *The Au Pair and Nanny's Guide to Working Abroad* by Susan Griffith and Sharon Legg. All these titles are published in the UK by Vacation Work (www.vacationwork.co.uk).

Online jobs are listed on a number of websites, including:

www.ams.or.at Austria's labour office; in German.

www.jobfinder.at Directed towards professionals; in German.

www.jobpilot.at Comprehensive site with loads of professional jobs; in German.

www.studentenjob.com Specialises in student jobs; in German.

www.virtualvienna.net Aimed at expats, with a variety of jobs, including UN listings.

Transport

CONTENTS

GETTING THERE & AWAY

Austria is well connected to the rest of the world. Vienna and four of the country's regional capitals are served by no-frills airlines (plus regular airline services). Europe's extensive bus and train networks crisscross the country and there are major highways from Germany and Italy. It's also possible to enter Austria by boat from Hungary, Slovakia and Germany.

ENTERING THE COUNTRY

A valid passport is required when entering Austria. The only exception to this rule occurs when entering from another Schengen country (all EU states minus Britain and Ireland); in this case, only a national identity

---

> **THINGS CHANGE...**
>
> The information in this chapter is particularly vulnerable to change. Check directly with the airline or a travel agent to make sure you understand how a fare (and ticket you may buy) works and be aware of the security requirements for international travel. Shop carefully. The details given in this chapter should be regarded as pointers and are not a substitute for your own careful, up-to-date research.

---

card is required. Procedures at border crossings from other EU countries are relatively lax compared with procedures at airports, and provincial capital airports are stricter than those in Vienna. See p392 for more information.

AIR

Vienna is the main transport hub for Austria, but Graz, Linz, Klagenfurt, Salzburg and Innsbruck all receive international flights. Flights to these cities are often a cheaper option than those to the capital, as are flights to Airport Letisko (Bratislava Airport) which is only 60km east of Vienna in Slovakia. Bregenz has no airport; your best bet is to fly into Friedrichshafen in Germany or Altenrhein in Switzerland. With advance booking, no-frills airlines can be very cheap.

Seriously consider booking early over the Christmas and New Year period; prices tend to soar at this time.

Airports & Airlines

Austrian Airlines (code OS; ☎ 05 17 89; www.aua.com; Hegelgasse 21) is the national carrier and has the most extensive services to Vienna. It is a member of Star Alliance (www.staralliance.com).

See the Getting There & Away sections of individual chapters for airlines flying to/from Austria's international airports:

Airport Letisko Bratislava (BTS; ☎ 421 2 3303 33 53; www.airportbratislava.sk) Serves Slovakia's capital Bratislava and has good transport connections to Vienna.

Graz (GRZ; ☎ 0316-29 02-0; www.flughafen-graz.at, in German)

Innsbruck (INN; ☎ 0512-225 25-0; www.innsbruck -airport.com, in German)

Klagenfurt (KLU; ☎ 0463-41 500; www.klagenfurt -airport.com)

Linz (LNZ; ☎ 07221-600-0; www.flughafen-linz.at)

Salzburg (SZG; ☎ 0662-85800; www.salzburg-airport .com, in German)

Vienna (VIE; ☎ 01-7007 22233; www.vienna airport.com)

Tickets

Except for the no-frills carriers, airlines themselves rarely offer the cheapest deals direct; it can pay, however, to explore their websites. A good travel agent can give you advice as well as a cheap deal, though internet purchases will often be better than these.

You can book online directly with airlines or web-based companies selling flights; the following are good places to start:

Airbrokers (www.airbrokers.com) USA company specialising in cheap tickets.

Cheap Flights (www.cheapflights.com/www.cheapflights.co.uk) Very informative site with specials, airline information and flight searches, mainly from the USA and UK.

Expedia (www.expedia.com/www.expedia.co.uk) Online travel company listing major airlines; the earlier you book the better.

Flight Centre (www.flightcentre.co.uk) Respected operator handling direct flights, with sites for Australia, New Zealand, the UK, USA and Canada.

Hotwire (www.hotwire.com) Bookings from the USA only; some cheap last-minute deals.

Last Minute (www.lastminute.com) One of the better sites for last-minute deals, including hotels.

Orbitz (www.orbitz.com) Cheap deals when flying from the USA.

Price Line (www.priceline.com) Name-your-own-price USA site.

STA Travel (www.statravel.com) Popular for international student travel, but you don't necessarily have to be a student to take advantage of deals; website linked to worldwide STA sites.

Travel (www.travel.com.au/www.travel.co.nz) Reputable Australia and New Zealand online flight bookers.

Travelocity (www.travelocity.com) USA site that allows you to search fares to/from practically anywhere.

Australia & New Zealand

From this side of the globe, it's worth investigating round-the-world (RTW) tickets, as these may not be much more expensive than a straightforward return ticket. Check the travel agencies' advertisements in the Yellow Pages and the Saturday travel sections of the *Sydney Morning Herald*, the *Age* in Melbourne and the New Zealand *Herald*.

From Australia, Austrian Airlines/Lauda Air offers flights via Bangkok to Vienna (five times weekly from Melbourne and Sydney). As with flights coming from North America, there are plenty of connections via London and Frankfurt.

For the location of **STA Travel** branches call ☎ 1300 733 035 or visit www.statravel.com.au. **Flight Centre** (☎ 133 133; www.flightcentre.com.au) has offices throughout Australia. For online bookings, try www.travel.com.au. In New Zealand, both **Flight Centre** (☎ 0800 243 544; www.flightcentre.co.nz) and **STA Travel** (☎ 0508 782 872; www.statravel.co.nz) have branches throughout the country. The site www.travel.co.nz is recommended for online bookings.

AIRLINES FLYING TO AND FROM AUSTRIA

Aside from Austrian Airlines, the following airlines connect Austria to the rest of the world:

Air Berlin (AB; ☎ 0810-1025 73 800; www.airberlin.com; hub Köln Bonn Airport; Köln)

Air France (AF; ☎ 01-502 22-2400; www.airfrance.fr, in French; hub Roissy-Charles De Gaulle Airport, Paris)

Alitalia (AZ; ☎ 01-505 17 07; www.alitalia.com; hub Leonardo DaVinci International Airport, Rome)

British Airways (BA; ☎ 01-7956 7567; www.britishairways.com; hub Heathrow Airport, London)

Delta Air Lines (DL; ☎ 01-7956 7023; www.delta.com; hub Hartsfield-Jackson Airport, Atlanta)

German Wings (4U; ☎ 0820 240554; www.germanwings.com; hub Bonn Airport, Köln)

Flybe (BE; www.flybe.com; hub Exeter International Airport, Exeter)

InterSky (ISK; ☎ 05574-488 00; www.intersky.biz; hub Friedrichshafen Airport)

KLM (KL; ☎ 0900-359 556; www.klm.at; hub Schiphol Airport, Amsterdam)

Lauda Air (NG; ☎ 0820 320 321; www.laudaair.com; hub Vienna International Airport)

Lufthansa (LH; ☎ 0810-1025 80 80; www.lufthansa.com; hub Frankfurt Airport)

Niki (HG; ☎ 0820 737 800; www.flyniki.com; Vienna International Airport)

Ryanair (FR; ☎ 0900-210 240; www.ryanair.com; hub Stansted Airport, London)

Sky Europe (5P; ☎ 01-998 555 55; www.skyeurope.com; hub Airport Letisko Bratislava, Bratislava)

Styrian Spirit (Z2; ☎ 0508-051 212; www.styrianairways.com; hub Graz Airport)

Swiss International (LX; ☎ 0810-810 840; www.swiss.com; hub EuroAirport Schweiz, Basel)

Thomsonfly (BY; ☎ 019 289 598; www.thomsonfly.com; hub Luton Airport)

TuiFly (X3/HF; ☎ 01805 757510; www.tuifly.com; hub Hanover Airport)

Welcome Air (2W; ☎ 0512-295 296-300; www.welcomeair.com; hub Innsbruck Airport)

TRANSPORT

Continental Europe

Like spokes on a wheel, flights go from Vienna to all parts of Europe. Routes to the east are as well covered as those to the west, with Austrian Airlines flying regularly to Bucharest, Kiev, Moscow, St Petersburg, Vilnius, Warsaw and Yekaterinburg (among other destinations).

Austria's other international airports have connections to Belgium, Croatia, Greece, Germany, Italy, the Netherlands, Switzerland, Sweden, Spain and Turkey.

Recommended agencies include:

France Anyway (☎ 0892 893 892; www.anyway.fr); Last-minute (☎ 0892 705 000; www.lastminute.fr); Nouvelles Frontières (☎ 0825 000 747; www.nouvelles-frontieres .fr); OTU Voyages (www.otu.fr; specialises in student travel); Voyageurs du Monde (☎ 01 40 15 11 15; www.vdm.com)

Germany Expedia (www.expedia.de); Just Travel (☎ 089 747 3330; www.justtravel.de); Lastminute (☎ 01805 284 366; www.lastminute.de); STA Travel (☎ 01805 456 422; www.statravel.de; for travellers under the age of 26)

Italy CTS Viaggi (☎ 06 462 0431; www.cts.it, in Italian)

The Netherlands Airfair (☎ 020 620 5121; www.airfair .nl, in Dutch)

UK & Ireland

Discount air travel is big business in London. In addition to the travel sections of the major Sunday papers, check the travel classifieds in London's weekly *Time Out*, the *Evening Standard* and in the free online magazine *TNT* (www.tntmagazine.com).

Flybe connects Salzburg with Exeter and Southampton. Ryanair flies from London-Stansted to Klagenfurt and Salzburg. Austrian Airlines flies via London from Dublin to Vienna; Aer Lingus flies there direct, and British Airways flies Vienna, Innsbruck and Salzburg to London, as well as Salzburg to Manchester.

Some of the more reliable agents in London include:

Flight Centre (☎ 0870 890 8099; www.flightcentre .co.uk)

Flightbookers (☎ 0870 814 4001; www.ebookers .com)

North-South Travel (☎ 01245 608 291; www.north southtravel.co.uk) North-South Travel donates part of their profits to projects in the developing world.

Quest Travel (☎ 0870 442 3542; www.questtravel.com)

STA Travel (☎ 0870 160 0599; www.statravel.co.uk) For travellers under the age of 26.

Trailfinders (☎ 020-7938 3939; www.trailfinders.co.uk)

Travelbag (☎ 0870 890 1456; www.travelbag.co.uk)

USA & Canada

The North Atlantic is the world's busiest long-haul air corridor, and various newspapers contain ads placed by consolidators (discount travel agencies). San Francisco is the ticket-consolidator capital of the US, although some good deals can be found in Los Angeles, New York and other big cities.

All direct flights from the USA arrive in Vienna. Austrian Airlines has one daily scheduled flight from Washington DC and New York, and most days from Chicago. Passengers from other destinations in the USA fly with United Airlines or US Airways flights from gateway cities.

The following agencies are recommended for online bookings:

American Express travel site www.itn.net
Cheap Tickets www.cheaptickets.com
Expedia www.expedia.com
Lowest Fare www.lowestfare.com
Orbitz www.orbitz.com
STA Travel www.sta.com (for travellers under the age of 26)
Travelocity www.travelocity.com

In Canada, Austrian Airlines flies direct from Toronto daily; flights to or from elsewhere in Canada are with Air Canada. Austrian Airlines uses Lufthansa via Frankfurt am Main (Germany) for its daily Montreal connection. One recommended travel agent is **Travel CUTS** (☎ 800-667-2887; www.travelcuts.com), Canada's national student-travel agency.

LAND
Bus

Travelling by bus is a cheap but less comfortable way to cross Europe. It's easiest to book with **Eurolines** (www.eurolines.com; Vienna Map p0000-000; ☎ 798 29 00; www.eurolines.at; Erdbergstrasse 202; Graz ☎ 0316 67 11 55; Wiener Strassse 229), a consortium of coach companies with offices all over Europe.

While the bulk of Euroline buses pass through Vienna, its 14 stops in Austria include Graz, Linz, Salzburg, Klagenfurt and Innsbruck.

Eurolines runs buses to/from London (Victoria coach station) and Vienna (one way/return €84/156, 23 hours, five or seven days per week); anyone under 26 or over 60 gets a 10% discount on most fares and passes. For other destinations see www.eurolines.com.

Blaguss/Eurolines (see Colombus Reisen or Eurolines for contact details) has buses to Prague (one way/return €22/34, six hours, 8am and 5pm daily). **Columbus Reisen** (Map pp120-1; ☎ 534 11-123; Dr Karl Lueger Ring 8; ☺ 9am-6pm Mon-Fri, 9am-noon Sat) handles advance bookings.

For quick trips around Europe, both Eurolines and **Busabout** (☎ 020-7950 1661; www.busabout.com), a London-based firm, have bus passes. The **Eurolines Pass** is priced according to season. A 15-day pass costs UK£135 to £225 for adults, or 30 days for UK£205 to £299 (less for those under 26). It covers 35 cities across Europe (including Vienna and Salzburg).

Busabout offers two passes for travel around 50 European cities. It splits them into three different 'loops' which you can combine. From May to September the **Northern Loop** starts from Paris and includes Vienna, Salzburg and St Johann in Tyrol, as well as Prague and several German cities (one/two/three loops UK£289/489/599). Its **Flexipass** (UK£239 six cities, UK£29 per extra city) is another option.

Car & Motorcycle

Getting to Austria by road is simple as there are fast and well-maintained motorways through all surrounding countries. The first thing to do is turn on your headlights – day or night – or you will face a €15 fine.

There are numerous entry points into Austria by road from Germany, the Czech Republic, Slovakia, Hungary, Slovenia, Italy and Switzerland. Liechtenstein is so small that it has just one border crossing point, near Feldkirch in Austria. The presence of the Alps limits options for approaching Tyrol from the south (Switzerland and Italy). All main border-crossing points are open 24 hours; minor crossings are open from around 6am or 8am until 8pm or 10pm.

Proof of ownership of a private vehicle and a driver's licence should always be carried while driving. EU licences are accepted in Austria while all other nationalities require a German translation or an International Driving Permit (IDP). Third-party insurance is a minimum requirement in Europe and you'll need to carry proof of this in the form of a Green Card.

Carrying a warning triangle and first-aid kit in your vehicle is also compulsory in Austria. If you're a member of an automobile association, ask about free reciprocal benefits offered by affiliated organisations in Europe. For information on Austria's road rules and regulations, see p403.

Train

Austria benefits from its central location within Europe by having excellent rail connections to all important destinations. The *Thomas Cook European Timetable* gives all train schedules, supplements and reservations information. It is updated monthly and is available from Thomas Cook outlets. In the USA, call ☎ 800-367 7984.

Express trains can be identified by the symbols EC (EuroCity, serving international routes) or IC (InterCity, serving national routes). The French Train à Grande Vitesse (TGV) and the German InterCityExpress (ICE) trains are even faster. Extra charges can apply on fast trains and international trains, and it is a good idea (sometimes obligatory) to make seat reservations for peak times and on certain lines.

Overnight trips usually offer a choice between a *Liegewagen* (couchette) or a more expensive *Schlafwagen* (sleeping car). Long-distance trains have a dining car or snacks available.

Vienna is one of the main rail hubs in Central Europe; for details of the main train stations and the routes they serve, see p158. Elsewhere in Austria, Salzburg has express-train connections in the direction of Munich (€27, 1½ to two hours), Linz towards Prague (€41, five hours) and Regensburg (€45, two to 3½ hours), Graz towards Budapest (€43,

TRANSPORT

EUROPEAN RAIL PASSES

If you plan to travel widely in Europe, the following special tickets and rail passes may be worth pursuing. Some of these may have different names in different countries. For information on a range of rail passes, visit www.raileurope.com, www.raileurope.co.uk and www.railpassdirect.co.uk.

Eurail Pass

Only available to non-European residents, Eurail passes are valid for unlimited 1st-class travel on national railways and some private lines in much of Western Europe (the UK is not included) as well as Hungary and Romania. Passes come in 15- or 21-day lots (for US$656 or $852) or one-, two- or three-month lots (for US$1058, $1494 or $1843). The Eurail Flexi pass allows 10 or 15 days travel in two months and costs US$776 or $1020. Discounts on both are available for people travelling in groups and those under 26.

Eurail Select Pass

The Eurail Select Pass allows 1st-class travel for non-European residents in three, four or five bordering countries with a choice of five to 15 days over a two-month period. For Austria, that can include Germany, Hungary, Slovenia, Croatia, Italy and Switzerland (from US$417 to $921), but not Slovakia. The Eurail Select Pass Saver offers a cheaper deal for two or more people travelling together.

InterRail Pass

Only available to anyone who has lived in Europe for at least six months, this pass gives travellers unlimited travel for up to one month on most of the state railways of Western and Central Europe (except in their own country). A global pass offers 1st- and 2nd-class travel for five days within a 10-day period (€249/329), 10 days within 22 (€359/489), 22 continuous days (€469/629) or one month (€599/809). Discounts apply for those under 26. A country pass for Austria for three to eight days in one month is also available (€109-229) for 2nd class.

Regional Passes

Various regional passes for non-European residents combine 1st-class travel in Austria with one to three countries. These include the Austria–Czech Republic Pass (US$232), Austria–Croatia–Slovenia Pass (US$254), Austria–Hungary Pass (US$232) and the Austria–Switzerland Pass (US$358), all for four days in two months; the Austria–Germany Pass offers 1st- or 2nd-class (from US$312 to $560 for five to 10 days) travel. For most you can buy additional days, and group or youth prices are also available.

6½ to 7½ hours) and Ljubljana (€31, three to 3½ hours), Klagenfurt towards Ljubljana (€21, 2½ hours) and Venice (€35, four hours); and Innsbruck north to Munich (€44, two hours), south to Verona (€45, 3½ to 4½ hours) and west to Zürich (€47, 3¾ hours). Most of the services listed above depart at least every two to three hours daily (these prices may vary slightly depending on the type of train service).

In the UK, buy tickets through **Rail Europe** (☎ 08705-848 848; www.raileurope.co.uk). Travel by train from London involves taking the Eurostar to Paris (UK£59 to £309 return) and connecting to Vienna. All up, it takes about 16 hours.

For a 2nd-class one-way fare to/from Vienna expect to pay €180 from Paris (12 hours), €169 from Amsterdam (14 hours) and €47 from Prague (4½ hours).

RIVER

The Danube (Donau) is a traffic-free access route for arrivals and departures from Austria. Since the early 1990s the Danube has been connected to the Rhine by the River Main tributary and the Main-Danube canal in southern Germany. The MS *River Queen* does 13-day cruises along this route, from Amsterdam to Vienna, between May and September from around £2000. It departs monthly in each direction.

In Britain bookings can be made through **Noble Caledonia** (☎ 020-7752 0000; www.noble-caledonia .co.uk); it also makes bookings for the MS *Amadeus*, which takes seven days to get from Passau to Budapest. In the USA, you can book through **Uniworld** (☎ 1-800-733-7820, 1-818-382-2700 outside the US; www.uniworld.com), which handles this and many other Danube tours. For information on connections to Passau in Germany, see p208.

Heading east, boats travel to Bratislava (hydrofoil one way/return €27/54, 1¼ hours) three times daily from April to late October, plus Friday and Saturday evening from May to October. These Twin City Liner ships dock at the DDSG quay between Marienbrücke and Schwedenbrücke in Vienna (tickets are also sold there in summer; note that a new quay on the Danube Canal is in planning). A hydrofoil to Budapest (one way/return €89/109, 5½ hours) runs daily from mid-April to late October from the Handelskai office of the

company operating both services: **DDSG Blue Danube** (Map pp116-17; ☎ 588 80; www.ddsg-blue -danube.at; Handelskai 265; ⏰ 9am-5pm Mon-Fri, also 10am-4pm Sat & Sun Apr-Oct). Alternatively, bookings can be made through all Österreiches Verkehrsbüro offices (see p124 & p123).

GETTING AROUND

Transport systems in Austria are highly developed and generally very efficient, and reliable information is usually available in English. Individual bus and train *Fahrplan* (timetables) are readily available, as are helpful annual timetables.

Austria's main rail provider is the **Österreiche Bundesbahn** (ÖBB; Austrian Federal Railways; www.oebb.at), which has an extensive countrywide rail network. This is supplemented by a handful of private railways. Wherever trains don't run, a **Postbus** (www.postbus.at) usually does. Timetables and prices for many train and bus connections can be found online at www.oebb.at.

Most provinces have an integrated transport system offering day passes covering regional zones for both bus and train travel.

AIR

Flying in a country the size of Austria is not really necessary. Those who for special reasons do need to fly, though, will find a couple of airlines serving longer routes.

Airlines in Austria

Austrian Airlines (p395), and its subsidiaries Tyrolean Airways and Austrian Arrow offer several flights daily between Vienna and Graz, Innsbruck, Klagenfurt, Linz and Salzburg, and also flights between Graz and Linz, and Linz and Salzburg.

Welcome Air (p397) has flights from Innsbruck to Graz, along with a handful of international services.

BICYCLE

Cycling is a popular activity in Austria, and most regional tourist boards have brochures on cycling facilities and routes within their region. Separate bike tracks are common, not only in cities, but also in the country. The Danube cycling trail is something of a Holy Grail for cyclists, though there are many other excellent bike routes in the country. Most are close to lakes or rivers, where there are fewer hills to contend with. For more information on popular cycle routes, see the Outdoor Activities chapter (p77).

It's possible to take bicycles on any train with a bicycle symbol at the top of its timetable; these trains are either regional or *Eilzüge* (medium-fast trains). A transferable bicycle ticket valid on trains costs €2.90 per day, €7.50 per week and €22.50 per month. Sending a bike by courier as a *Bahnkurierpaket* costs €29 within Austria, arranged directly at the counter in the station. On some EC and IC trains you can accompany your bike (€6.80 for a day ticket). An international ticket for a bike costs €12 per day.

Hire

All large cities have at least one bike shop that doubles as a rental centre. In places where cycling is a popular pastime, such as the Wachau in Lower Austria and the Neusiedler See in Burgenland, almost all small towns have a rental shop and train stations have rental facilities. Rates vary from town to town, but expect to pay around €10 per day; see the destination chapters for specific details on bike hire.

BOAT

The Danube serves as a thoroughfare between Vienna and Lower and Upper Austria. Services are generally slow, scenic excursions rather than functional means of transport. For more information on boat travel in Vienna, see p158; for Lower Austria see p164; and for Upper Austria p208. Some of the country's larger lakes, such as Bodensee and Wörthersee, have boat services.

BUS

The *Postbus* (Post Bus) network is best considered a backup to the rail service, more useful for reaching out-of-the-way places and local destinations than for long-distance travel. Rail routes are sometimes duplicated by bus services, but buses really come into their own in the more inaccessible mountainous regions. Buses are fairly reliable, and usually depart from outside train stations. For remote travel, plan a day or two ahead and go on a weekday; services are reduced on Saturday, often nonexistent on Sunday.

For nationwide bus information, call ☎ 01-711 01 between 7am and 8pm, or log on to the websites www.oebb.at or www.postbus.at. Local bus stations or tourist offices usually stock free timetables for specific bus routes.

Costs

Bus fares are comparable to train fares; however, you can't buy a long-distance ticket and make stop-offs en route as you can on a train. Prices are listed throughout the destination chapters; here are a few sample one-way fares:

Destination	Cost	Duration (hr)
Graz–Klagenfurt	€14.70	2½
Kitzbühel–Lienz	€13.20	2
Salzburg–Bad Ischl	€8.70	1½
Salzburg–Zell am See	€13.30	2
Vienna–Mariazell	€23.30	3½

Reservations

It's possible to buy tickets in advance on some routes, but on others you can only buy tickets from the drivers. More often than not, though, there is no need to make reservations as most Austrians and tourists use the railway system.

CAR & MOTORCYCLE

Driving in Austria is a pleasure; roads are well maintained, signs are everywhere and rules are usually adhered to. The use of *Personenkraftwagen* (PKW) or *Auto* (cars) is often discouraged in city centres though, and it is a good idea to ditch your trusty chariot and rely on public transport.

The fastest roads around the country are the autobahns, identified on maps by national 'A' numbers or pan-European 'E' numbers (both are usually given in this book). These are subject to a general motorway tax. Their course is often shadowed by *Bundesstrassen* (alternative routes), which are as direct as the terrain will allow, sometimes using tunnels to maintain their straight lines. In the mountains, you can opt instead for smaller, slower roads that wind over mountain passes. These can add to your journey but the scenery often makes up for the extra time and kilometres. Some minor passes are blocked by snow from November to May. Carrying snow chains in winter is highly recommended and may be compulsory in some areas.

Cars can be transported by *Autoreisezüge* (motorail trains). Vienna is linked by a daily motorail service to Feldkirch (€95, 5½ hours), Innsbruck (€76, 4¾ hours), Lienz (€69, six hours), Salzburg (€40, 3½ hours) and Villach (€62, four hours), as is Graz to Feldkirch (€86, eight hours) and Villach to Feldkirch (€76, 7½ hours). Over 200 Austrian train stations offer Park and Ride facilities (free or cheap parking while you continue your journey by train). In rural areas, petrol stations may close on Sundays.

Motorcycling is a popular pastime in Austria, and many mountain passes play host to a multitude of riders over the summer months. Motorcyclists and their passengers must wear a helmet, and dipped lights must be used in daytime. As with cars, motorbikes should also carry a first-aid kit. The National Austrian Tourist Office can provide you with the *Austrian Classic Tour* brochure, which covers 3000km of the best roads for bikers in the country.

Automobile Associations

Two automobile associations serve Austria. Both provide free 24-hour breakdown service to members and have reciprocal agreements with motoring clubs in other countries; check with your local club before leaving. Both have offices throughout Austria, and it is possible to become a member, but you must join for a year, which costs €66.

If you're not entitled to free assistance, you'll incur a fee for call-outs which varies, depending on the time of day. The two associations are:

ARBÖ (Map pp116-17; 24-hour emergency assistance ☎ 123, 24-hour office 050 123 123; www.arboe.at; Mariahilfer Strasse 180; ◷ 8am-5.30pm Mon-Fri)
ÖAMTC (Map pp120-1; 24-hour emergency assistance ☎ 120, office 711 99-0; www.oeamtc.at; Schubertring 1-3; ◷ 8am-6pm Mon-Fri, 9am-1pm Sat)

Bring Your Own Vehicle

It is no problem to bring your own vehicle into Austria, as long as you have proof of ownership papers and third-party insurance. The car must also display a sticker on the rear indicating the country of origin.

Driving Licence

A licence should always be carried; see p398 for more information.

Road Distances (km)

	Bad Ischl	Bregenz	Bruck an der Mur	Eisenstadt	Graz	Innsbruck	Kitzbühel	Klagenfurt	Krems	Kufstein	Landeck	Lienz	Linz	Salzburg	St Pölten	Vienna	Villach	Wiener Neustadt
Bad Ischl	---																	
Bregenz	432	---																
Bruck an der Mur	170	577	---															
Eisenstadt	297	704	127	---														
Graz	193	600	54	175	---													
Innsbruck	239	193	384	511	407	---												
Kitzbühel	191	300	275	469	400	113	---											
Klagenfurt	245	510	145	298	133	322	264	---										
Krems	222	626	175	132	229	433	372	320	---									
Kufstein	161	271	331	460	356	78	37	286	355	---								
Landeck	316	117	461	588	484	77	186	394	510	155	---							
Lienz	232	424	266	393	277	178	94	144	432	142	248	---						
Linz	103	507	190	246	237	314	247	253	145	236	391	359	---					
Salzburg	58	374	228	362	264	181	129	223	257	103	180	180	138	---				
St Pölten	206	610	140	123	194	417	356	285	32	339	494	416	129	241	---			
Vienna	266	670	145	50	191	477	420	316	79	399	554	411	189	301	66	---		
Villach	250	486	178	335	170	287	226	37	353	251	370	109	330	188	318	353	---	
Wiener Neustadt	268	675	98	31	146	482	441	267	137	431	559	364	237	339	114	53	316	---

Fuel & Spare Parts

There is no problem finding fuel and car parts in Austria. *Tankstelle* (petrol stations) have diesel, *Benzin* (unleaded; 91 octane), Euro-Super (95 octane) and Super Plus (98 octane). Only a few have liquid gas and leaded petrol is no longer available in the country, but lead additives are available from most petrol stations.

Hire

The minimum age for hiring a car is 19 for small cars and 25 for prestige models, and a valid licence, issued at least a year ago, is required. If you plan to take the car across the border, especially into Eastern Europe, let the rental company know beforehand and double-check for any add-on fees.

For the lowest rates, organise car rental before departure. **Holiday Autos** (www.holidayautos.com) often offers very low rates and has offices or representatives in over 20 countries. By booking early, prices can be about 60% of those charged by the international companies.

Shop around to get the best deal; prices between the large multinational companies can vary wildly and local companies often undercut their bigger competitors. Expect rates for an economy-class car rental with insurance and unlimited kilometres over a three-day weekday to cost about €80 to €100 per day. This includes collision-damage waiver limiting liability to nothing or about €450, and insurance against theft of the vehicle. Drivers under 25 are usually required to pay €5 to €6 on top (more with Avis). Cheaper deals can be found on weekends or as special offers. All the multinational rental companies are present in Austria, plus LaudaMotion, a newcomer offering unusual cars. You should be able to make advance reservations online, or arrange something after arriving in Austria through one of the following companies:

Avis (☎ 01-1 5876241; www.avis.at)
Denzeldrive (☎ 01-740 20-0; www.denzeldrive.at, in German)
Europcar (☎ 01-866 1633; www.europcar.at)
Hertz (☎ 01-795 32; www.hertz.at)
LaudaMotion (☎ 0900 240 120; www.laudamotion .com, in German)
Sixt (☎ 1-5036616; www.sixt.at, in German)

Insurance

Third-party insurance is a minimum requirement in Austria. All companies offer Personal Accident Insurance (PAI) and Collision Damage Waiver (CDW) for an additional charge, although PAI may not be necessary if you or your passengers hold personal travel insurance.

Motorway Tax & Tunnel Tolls

A *Vignitte* (motorway tax) is imposed on all autobahn; charges for cars below 3.5 tonnes are €7.60 for 10 days, €21.80 for two months and €72.60 for one year. For motorbikes expect to pay €4.30 for 10 days, €10.90 for two months and €29 for one year. *Vignitte* can be purchased from motoring organisations, border crossings, petrol stations, post offices and *Tabak* shops.

Anything above 3.5 tonnes is charged per kilometre. The system uses a GO-Box, available from petrol stations along the autobahn for €5, which records the kilometres you travel via an electronic tolling system. A minimum of €45 must be loaded onto the box the first time, and €50 each time after that (maximum €500). Information on the system and prices can be found online at www.go-maut.at.

A toll is levied on some mountain roads and tunnels (*not* covered by the motorway tax). For a full list of toll roads, consult one of the automobile organisations mentioned on opposite.

Road Rules

The minimum driving age is 18, both for Austrians and foreigners. Like the rest of continental Europe, Austrians drive on the right-hand side of the road. Speed limits are 50km/h in built-up areas, 130km/h on autobahns and 100km/h on other roads. In some places, the speed on country roads is restricted to 70km/h. Priority is given to vehicles coming from the right, and Austrian road signs generally conform to recognised international standards. Wearing a crash helmet is compulsory for motorcyclists, and children under the age of 14 and/or shorter than 1.5m must have a special seat or restraint.

It is illegal to drive in Austria without your headlights on.

Austrian police have the authority to impose fines for various traffic offences. These can be paid on the spot (ask for a receipt) or within two weeks. The penalty for drink-driving – over 0.05% BAC (blood-alcohol concentration) – is a hefty on-the-spot fine and confiscation of your driving licence. Trams

TRANSPORT

are a common feature in Austrian cities; take care if you've never driven among them before. Trams always have priority. Vehicles should wait behind while trams slow down and stop for passengers.

Urban Parking

Most town centres have a designated *Kurzparkzone* (short-term parking zone), where on-street parking is limited to a maximum of 1½ or three hours (depending upon the place) between certain specified times. *Parkschein* (parking vouchers) for such zones can be purchased from *Tabak* shops or pavement dispensers and then displayed on the windscreen. Outside the specified time, parking in the *Kurzparkzone* is free.

HITCHING

Hitching is never entirely safe anywhere in the world and we don't recommend it. Travellers who decide to hitch should understand that they are taking a potentially serious risk. Those who choose to hitch will be safer if they travel in pairs and let someone know where they are planning to go. An alternative is to check notice boards at universities for people looking for passengers to share a trip.

LOCAL TRANSPORT

Austria's local transport infrastructure is excellent, inexpensive and safe. It runs from about 5am or 6am to midnight, though in smaller towns evening services may be patchy or finish for the night much earlier.

Tickets will generally cover all forms of public transport in a town or city. Passes and multi-trip tickets are available in advance from *Tabak* shops, pavement dispensers, and occasionally tourist offices. They usually need to be validated upon first use in the machine on buses or trams. In some towns drivers will sell single tickets, but rarely passes. Single tickets may be valid for one hour, 30 minutes, or a single journey, depending on the place, and cost about €1.70. If you're a senior, attending school in Austria, or travelling as a family, you may be eligible for reduced-price tickets in some towns.

You can usually buy excellent value one-day or 24-hour tickets which often only cost double the price of a single ticket. Weekly or three-day passes may be available too, as well as multi-trip tickets, which will work out cheaper than buying individual tickets for each journey.

Fines for travelling without a valid ticket easily outweigh the price it would have cost to buy one. Depending on the inspector, you could have real problems if you aren't carrying enough cash to pay the fine at the time you're caught.

Bus

Buses are the mainstay of local transport in Austria. Towns that require some form of public transport will at least have a local bus system; it will be well used, comprehensive and efficient.

Keep alert when you're about to get off a bus: if you haven't pressed the request button and there's nobody waiting at the bus stop, the driver will go right past it.

Metro

Vienna is the only city with a metro; see p160 for more details.

Taxi

On the whole, taxis are cheap, ubiquitous and safe. Stands are invariably located outside train stations and large hotels. Fares are metered and comprise two elements: a flat starting fee plus a charge per kilometre. A small tip is expected; add about 10% to the fare. Telephone numbers for taxi companies are given under Getting Around in the destination chapters.

Tram

Many of Austria's larger cities, such as Graz, Linz and Vienna, supplement their bus systems with convenient and environmentally friendly trams. Most towns have an integrated transport system, meaning you can switch between bus and tram routes on the same ticket.

TRAIN

Like much of Europe, Austria's train network is a dense web reaching the country's far-flung corners. The system is fast, efficient, frequent and well used. ÖBB (24-hr information ☎ 05 17 17; www.oebb.at) is the main operator, and is supplemented with a handful of private lines.

The German for train station is *Bahnhof* (abbreviated as *Bf*); the main train station is the *Hauptbahnhof* (abbreviated as *Hbf*). Some small rural stations are unstaffed and tickets cannot be bought there; these stations are indicated on timetables by a rectangle with a diagonal line through the middle. All

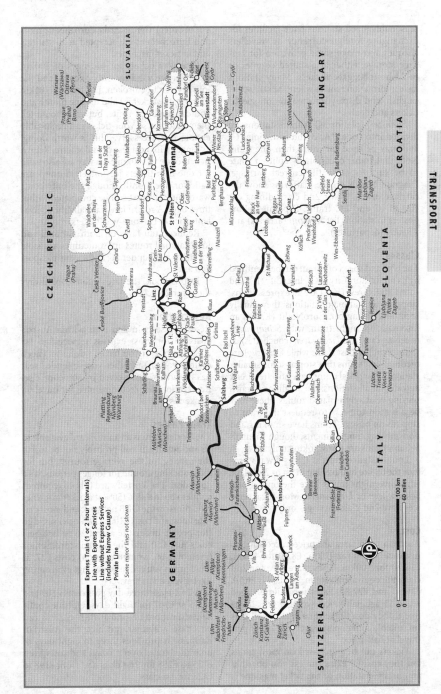

reasonably sized stations have facilities for exchanging foreign currency or travellers cheques and make some provision for luggage storage, either at a staffed counter or in 24-hour luggage lockers. Many stations have information centres where the staff speak English, and display information on special tickets and deals.

Bahnsteig (platforms) at train stations are divided into zones (A, B and sometimes C) and may be used for more than one train. Note that trains occasionally split en route so be sure to sit in the correct carriage. Diagram boards on the platforms show the carriage order (1st or 2nd class, dining car etc) of IC and EC trains. Separate yellow posters in stations list *Ankunft* (arrivals) and *Abfahrt* (departures).

Classes

The type and speed of a train can be identified by its prefix. EuroCity (EC), InterCity (IC) and InterCityExpress (ICE) are all express trains, stopping only at major stations; they usually include a dining car. EuroNight (EN) is an international night train, with *Schlafwagen* (sleeping cars) and *Liegewagen* (couchettes). D (*Schnellzug*) are fast trains while E (*Eilzug*) are medium-fast trains that stop at some smaller stations. Slow, local trains have no letter prefix and stop at all stations. On small local trains serving relatively isolated routes, there may be a button to press to request the train to stop (as on buses). Trains have smoking and nonsmoking compartments, though Vienna's S-Bahn trains are nonsmoking only.

Long-distance express trains always provide the choice of travelling in 1st or 2nd class, while overnight trains have the option of a *Schlafwagen* or *Liegewagen.* Most local services have 2nd-class carriages only.

Costs

Austrian train fares are priced according to distance: €1.90 for 10km, €8.30 for 50km, €16.20 for 100km. These fares are for 2nd class; the equivalent rate in 1st class is €6.70, €16.80 and €27.80. Fares for children aged six to 15 are half-price; younger kids travel free if they don't take up a seat. Small pets (in suitable containers) travel free; larger pets travel at half-price.

Tickets can be purchased on most trains but they cost €3 extra (unless you board at an unstaffed station or the ticket machine is

out of order). Credit cards, Eurocheque cards and Eurocheques are accepted at all stations and in ticket machines.

One-way tickets for journeys of 100km or under are valid for only one day and the journey can't be broken. For trips of 101km or more, the ticket is valid for one month and you can alight en route, but you should tell the conductor so your ticket can be suitably endorsed if necessary. This is worth doing, as longer trips cost less per kilometre. Return tickets of up to 100km each way are also valid for one day; tickets for longer journeys are valid for one month, though the initial outward journey must still be completed within three days. A return fare is usually the equivalent price of two one-way tickets.

Reduced rail fares on both national and international routes are sometimes available for those aged under 26; show your passport and ask.

In this book, the fares quoted are always those for 2nd class.

Reservations

Reserving seats in 2nd class within Austria costs €3 for most express services; in 1st class, it's free. If you haven't done so, check (before you sit) whether your intended seat has already been reserved by someone else. Reservations are recommended for travel on weekends.

Train Passes

The Vorteilscard is an annual card available to all and sundry. It will probably not be worth the money for the average tourist, but for those sticking around for longer periods, it's a good deal. The Vorteilscard (photo required) entitles you to a 45% (50% at a ticket machine) reduction on the ÖBB network and most private lines, and costs €100. The Vorteilscard 26 (for people under the age of 26 or families) costs just €20 and the Vorteilscard Senior (men over 65, women over 60) costs €27; at these prices you can make savings even during a relatively short stay.

A 2nd-class three-day pass costs €109 and peaks at €147 for eight days. Outside continental Europe, US and British citizens can purchase a similar product, the Austrian Railpass. It provides three to eight days of unlimited travel over 15 days and costs from €135 to €258 for 2nd class and from €198 to €328 for 1st class.

d idea to consult your
el health website before
s available:
gov.au/travel/
health.gc.ca
traveladvice/
l/

reciprocal arrangement
between their country
o need health insurance,
olicy that covers you for
ario, such as an accident
cy flight home. Find out
surance plan will make
providers or reimburse
health expenditures.

VACCINATIONS

ganisation (WHO) rec-
ellers should be covered
s, measles, mumps, ru-
l as hepatitis B regard-
n. Since most vaccines
nity until at last two
en, visit a physician at
leparture. See P410 for
cephalitis.

on **International** **Travel &**
revised annually and
er useful websites:
dvice on travel for the elderly.
.uk General travel advice

Information on women's

Travel health
ntry; updated daily

lers (currently called
nually updated leaf-
of Health in the UK
itish post office. It
nformation, ally
nded vaccines for

different countries, reciprocal health agreements and a European Health Insurance E111 application form. Lonely Planet's *Travel with Children* by Cathy Lanigan includes advice on travel health for younger children. Other recommended references include *Travellers' Health* by Dr Richard Dawood and *Travellers' Good Health Guide* by Ted Lankester.

IN TRANSIT

DEEP VEIN THROMBOSIS (DVT)
Blood clots may form in the legs during flights, chiefly because of prolonged immobility. The longer the flight, the greater the risk. The chief symptom of DVT is swelling or pain of the foot, ankle or calf, usually but not always on just one side. When a blood clot travels to the lungs, it may cause chest pain and breathing difficulties. Travellers with any of these symptoms should immediately seek medical attention.

To prevent the development of DVT on long flights you should walk about the cabin, contract the leg muscles while sitting, drink plenty of fluids and avoid alcohol and tobacco.

JET LAG & MOTION SICKNESS
To avoid jet lag (common when crossing more than five time zones) try to drink plenty of non-alcoholic fluids and eat light meals. Upon arrival, try to get exposure to natural sunlight and readjust your schedule (for meals, sleep and so on) as soon as possible.

Antihistamines such as dimenhydrinate (Dramamine) and meclizine (Antivert, Bonine) are usually the first choice for treating motion sickness. A herbal alternative is ginger.

IN AUSTRIA

AVAILABILITY & COST OF HEALTHCARE
Good healthcare is readily available and for minor self-limiting illnesses pharmacists can give valuable advice and sell over-the-counter medication. They can also advise when more specialised help is required and point you in the right direction. The standard of dental care is usually good; however, it is sensible to have a dental check-up before a long trip. For a forward, non-urgent appointment with a doctor might cost anything from €40 to

Health

CONTENTS

Travel health depends on your pre-departure preparations, your health care while travelling and how you handle any medical problems that develop. Major health worries are minimal in Austria; the population is very health-conscious, facilities are excellent, restaurants are highly sanitised and there are no major infectious diseases.

BEFORE YOU GO

Prevention is the key to staying healthy while abroad. A little planning before departure, particularly for pre-existing illnesses, will save trouble later. See your dentist before a long trip, carry a spare pair of contact lenses and glasses, and take your optical prescription with you. Bring medications in their original, clearly labelled, containers. A signed and dated letter from your physician describing your medical conditions and medications, including generic names, is also a good idea. If carrying syringes or needles, be sure to have a physician's letter documenting their medical necessity.

INSURANCE

If you're an EU citizen, a European Health Insurance Card (formerly an E111 form), available from health centres, covers you for most medical care. The cards will not cover you for non-emergencies or emergency repatriation home. Citizens from non-EU countries should

> It's usually a good idea to consult your government's travel health website before departure, if one is available:
> **Australia** www.dfat.gov.au/travel/
> **Canada** www.travelhealth.gc.ca
> **UK** www.doh.gov.uk/traveladvice/
> **US** www.cdc.gov/travel/

find out if there is a reciprocal arrangement for free medical care between their country and Austria. If you do need health insurance, make sure you get a policy that covers you for the worst possible scenario, such as an accident requiring an emergency flight home. Find out in advance if your insurance plan will make payments directly to providers or reimburse you later for overseas health expenditures.

RECOMMENDED VACCINATIONS

The World Health Organisation (WHO) recommends that all travellers should be covered for diphtheria, tetanus, measles, mumps, rubella and polio, as well as hepatitis B, regardless of their destination. Since most vaccines don't produce immunity until at least two weeks after they're given, visit a physician at least six weeks before departure. See p410 for advice on tickborne encephalitis.

ONLINE RESOURCES

The WHO's publication **International Travel & Health** (www.who.int/ith) is revised annually and is available online. Other useful websites:
www.ageconcern.org.uk Advice on travel for the elderly.
www.fitfortravel.scot.nhs.uk General travel advice for the layperson.
www.mariestopes.org.uk Information on women's health and contraception.
www.mdtravelhealth.com Travel health recommendations for every country; updated daily.

FURTHER READING

Health Advice for Travellers (currently called the 'T6' leaflet) is an annually updated leaflet by the Department of Health in the UK and available free in British post offices. It contains some general information, legally required and recommended vaccines for different countries, reciprocal health agreements and a European Health Insurance Card/E111 application form. Lonely Planet's *Travel with Children* by Cathy Lanigan includes advice on travel health for younger children. Other recommended references include *Traveller's Health* by Dr Richard Dawood and *Traveller's Good Health Guide* by Ted Lankester.

IN TRANSIT

DEEP VEIN THROMBOSIS (DVT)

Blood clots may form in the legs during plane flights, chiefly because of prolonged immobility. The longer the flight, the greater the risk. The chief symptom of DVT is swelling or pain of the foot, ankle or calf, usually but not always on just one side. When a blood clot travels to the lungs, it may cause chest pain and breathing difficulties. Travellers with any of these symptoms should immediately seek medical attention.

To prevent the development of DVT on long flights you should walk about the cabin, contract the leg muscles while sitting, drink plenty of fluids and avoid alcohol and tobacco.

JET LAG & MOTION SICKNESS

To avoid jet lag (common when crossing more than five time zones) try to drink plenty of non-alcoholic fluids and eat light meals. Upon arrival, try to get exposure to natural sunlight and readjust your schedule (for meals, sleep and so on) as soon as possible.

Antihistamines such as dimenhydrinate (Dramamine) and meclizine (Antivert, Bonine) are usually the first choice for treating motion sickness. A herbal alternative is ginger.

IN AUSTRIA

AVAILABILITY & COST OF HEALTHCARE

Good healthcare is readily available and for minor self-limiting illnesses pharmacists can give valuable advice and sell over-the-counter medication. They can also advise when more specialised help is required and point you in the right direction. The standard of dental care is usually good; however, it is sensible to have a dental check-up before a long trip. A straightforward, non-urgent appointment with a doctor might cost anything from €40 to €75.

Drugs, with or without prescription, must be paid for. *Apotheke* (pharmacies) handle all drugs, including aspirin.

ENVIRONMENTAL HAZARDS
Altitude sickness

Lack of oxygen at high altitudes (over 2500m) affects most people to some extent. The effect may be mild or severe and occurs because less oxygen reaches the muscles and the brain at high altitude, requiring the heart and lungs to compensate by working harder. Symptoms of Acute Mountain Sickness (AMS) usually develop during the first 24 hours at altitude but may be delayed up to three weeks. Mild symptoms include headache, lethargy, dizziness, difficulty sleeping and loss of appetite. AMS may become more severe without warning and can be fatal. Severe symptoms include breathlessness, a dry, irritative cough (which may progress to the production of pink, frothy sputum), severe headaches, lack of coordination and balance, confusion, irrational behaviour, vomiting, drowsiness and unconsciousness. There is no hard and fast rule as to what is too high: AMS has been fatal at 3000m, although 3500m to 4500m is the usual range.

Treat mild symptoms by resting at the same altitude until recovery, usually a day or two. Paracetamol or aspirin can be taken for headaches. If symptoms persist or become worse, however, *immediate descent is necessary*; even 500m can help. Drug treatments should never be used in order to avoid descent or to enable further ascent.

Diamox (acetazolamide) reduces the headache of AMS and helps the body acclimatise to the lack of oxygen. It is only available on prescription and those who are allergic to the sulphonamide antibiotics may also be allergic to Diamox.

Heatstroke

Heat exhaustion occurs following excessive fluid loss with inadequate replacement of fluids and salt. Symptoms include headache, dizziness and tiredness. Dehydration is already happening by the time you feel thirsty – aim to drink sufficient water to produce pale, diluted urine. To treat heat exhaustion, replace fluids with water and/or fruit juice, and cool the body with cold water and fans. Treat salt loss with salty fluids such as soup or Bovril, or add a little more table salt to foods than usual.

PREVENTING ACUTE MOUNTAIN SICKNESS

■ Ascend slowly – have frequent rest days, spending two to three nights at each rise of 1000m. If you reach a high altitude by trekking, acclimatisation takes place gradually and you are less likely to be affected than if you fly directly to high altitude.

■ It is always wise to sleep at a lower altitude than the greatest height reached during the day if possible. Also, once above 3000m, care should be taken not to increase the sleeping altitude by more than 300m per day.

■ Drink extra fluids. The mountain air is dry and cold and moisture is lost as you breathe. Evaporation of sweat may occur unnoticed and result in dehydration. A practical way to monitor hydration is by ensuring that urine is clear and plentiful.

■ Eat light, high-carbohydrate meals for more energy.

■ Avoid alcohol as it may increase the risk of dehydration.

■ Avoid sedatives.

■ Avoid tobacco.

In the UK, fact sheets are available from the **British Mountaineering Council** (177-179 Burton Rd, Manchester, M20 2BB).

Heatstroke is much more serious, resulting in irrational and hyperactive behaviour and eventually loss of consciousness and death. Rapid cooling by spraying the body with water and fanning is ideal. Emergency fluid and electrolyte replacement by intravenous drip is recommended.

Hypothermia

Proper preparation will reduce the risks of getting hypothermia. Even on a hot day in the mountains, the weather can change rapidly; carry waterproof garments, warm layers and inform others of your route.

Acute hypothermia follows a sudden drop of temperature over a short time. Chronic hypothermia is caused by a gradual loss of temperature over hours.

Hypothermia starts with shivering, loss of judgment and clumsiness. Unless re-warming occurs, the sufferer deteriorates into apathy, confusion and coma. Prevent further heat loss by seeking shelter, warm dry clothing, hot sweet drinks and shared bodily warmth.

Frostbite is caused by freezing and subsequent damage to bodily extremities. Seriousness is determined by wind chill, temperature and length of exposure. Frostbite starts as frostnip (white numb areas of skin) from which complete recovery is expected with re-warming. As frostbite develops the skin blisters and then becomes black. The loss of damaged tissue eventually occurs. Adequate clothing, staying dry,

keeping well hydrated and ensuring adequate calorie intake best prevent frostbite. Treatment involves rapid re-warming, avoiding re-freezing and rubbing the affected areas.

Insect Bites & Stings

Ticks, which are usually found below 1200m in undergrowth at the forest edge or beside walking tracks, can carry encephalitis (see p410).

Lyme disease (known as *Borreliose*) is a bacterial infection borne by ticks that can affect muscles, the skeleton and organs. It is easy to recognise in the early stage (a rash or red infection around the bite), and is treated with antibiotics. There is no vaccination against it.

Mosquitoes are found in Austria – they may not carry malaria but can cause irritation and infected bites. Use a DEET-based insect repellent.

Bees and wasps only cause real problems to those with a severe allergy (anaphylaxis). If you have a severe allergy to bee or wasp stings carry an 'epipen' or similar adrenaline injection.

Bed bugs lead to very itchy lumpy bites. Spraying the mattress with crawling-insect killer after changing bedding will get rid of them.

Scabies are tiny mites that live in the skin, particularly between the fingers. They cause an intensely itchy rash. Scabies is easily treated with lotion from a pharmacy; other

HEALTH

members of the household also need treating to avoid spreading scabies between asymptomatic carriers.

Snake Bites

Austria is home to several types of snake, which are more prevalent in the mountains. A couple can deliver a nasty, although not fatal, bite. Avoid getting bitten by wearing boots, socks and long trousers while hiking and do not stick your hand into holes or cracks. Half of those bitten by venomous snakes are not actually injected with poison (envenomed). If bitten by a snake, do not panic. Immobilise the bitten limb with a splint (eg a stick) and apply a bandage over the site with firm pressure, similar to a bandage over a sprain. Do not apply a tourniquet, or cut or suck the bite. Get the victim to medical help as soon as possible so that antivenin can be given if necessary.

Tickborne Encephalitis

Tickborne encephalitis (called FSME in Austria) is spread by tick bites. It is a serious infection of the brain and vaccination is highly advised for those in risk areas who are unable to avoid tick bites (such as campers, forestry workers and hikers or ramblers). Two doses of vaccine will give a year's protection, three doses up to three years'. The infection rate in Austria is low and declining (less than 100 cases in most years); this is kept down by comprehensive vaccination, especially in high-risk areas.

Distribution of tickborne encephalitis is uneven; the website www.zecken.at (in German; go to FSME then Verbreitungsgebiete Österreich) has excellent region-by-region maps on distribution that are useful for hikers. Local pharmacists always know whether FSME is a danger in their region and can advise if you're bitten.

Wearing long trousers tucked into walking boots or socks and using a DEET-based insect repellent is the best prevention against tick bites. If a tick is found attached, press down around the tick's head with tweezers, grab the tick as close as possible to the head and rotate continuously in an anticlockwise direction, without pulling, until the tick releases itself. (Chemist shops sell plastic tweezers especially for this purpose.) Avoid pulling the rear of the body as this may squeeze the tick's gut contents through the attached mouth parts into the skin, increasing the risk of infection and disease. Smearing chemicals on the tick will not make it let go and is not recommended.

TRAVELLING WITH CHILDREN

Anyone travelling with children should know how to treat minor ailments and when to seek medical treatment. Make sure the children are up to date with routine vaccinations, and discuss possible travel vaccines well before departure as some vaccines are not suitable for children under a year old.

In hot, moist climates, any wound or break in the skin is likely to let in infection. The area should be cleaned and kept dry.

Remember to avoid contaminated food and water. If your child has vomiting or diarrhoea, the lost fluid and salts must be replaced. It may be helpful to take rehydration powders for reconstituting with boiled water.

Children should be encouraged to avoid and mistrust any dogs or other mammals because of the risk of rabies and other diseases. Any bite, scratch or lick from a warm-blooded, furry animal should immediately be thoroughly cleaned. If there is any possibility that the animal is infected with rabies, immediate medical assistance should be sought.

WOMEN'S HEALTH

Emotional stress, exhaustion and travelling through different time zones can all contribute to an upset in the menstrual pattern. If using oral contraceptives, remember some antibiotics, diarrhoea and vomiting can stop the pill from working and lead to the risk of pregnancy – remember to take condoms with you just in case. Time zones, gastrointestinal upsets and antibiotics do not affect injectable contraception.

Travelling during pregnancy is usually possible but always consult your doctor before planning your trip. The most risky times for travel are during the first 12 weeks of pregnancy and after 30 weeks.

SEXUAL HEALTH

Emergency contraception is most effective if taken within 24 hours after unprotected sex. The **International Planned Parent Federation** (www.ippf.org) can advise about the availability of contraception in different countries. If emergency contraception is needed, head to the nearest healthcare centre or consult a doctor.

Condoms are readily available throughout Austria. When buying condoms, look for a European CE mark, which means it has been rigorously tested, and then keep them in a cool dry place or they may crack and perish.

Language

CONTENTS

The national language of Austria is German, though for a small country there are a surprising number of regional accents and dialects. This is due in part to the isolating influence of high mountain ranges, causing language to evolve differently in different communities. Austrians will probably tell you that even they have difficulty understanding the accents of compatriots from other regions; indeed, the dialect spoken in Vorarlberg is much closer to Swiss German (*Schwyzertütsch*) – a language all but incomprehensible to most non-Swiss – than it is to the standard High German (*Hochdeutsch*) dialect.

In some areas of the country, a significant minority may have a different first language to German. In Burgenland about 25,000 people speak Croatian, and in Carinthia about 20,000 people speak Slovene.

Fortunately for visitors, Austrians can switch from their dialect to High German whenever necessary, and many speak some English. Young people are usually quite fluent in English. As might be expected, English is more widely spoken in cities and tourist areas than in out-of-the-way rural districts. Staff at tourist and train information offices almost invariably speak English; hotel receptionists and restaurant waiters usually do as well, especially in the more upmarket establishments. As with any countries you visit, any attempt to communicate with the people in their native tongue will be appreciated, so some knowledge of German will definitely be an asset.

AUSTRIAN GERMAN

Though the grammar is the same as standard High German, there are also many words and expressions that are used only by Austrians. Some words are used throughout the country, others are only used in particular regions, although they'll probably be understood elsewhere. Most of them would not automatically be understood by non-Austrian German speakers. On the other hand, the 'standard' German equivalents would be understood by all Austrians.

Most of the greetings and farewells that we've included in the list of useful phrases are common only to Austria. *Servus* is an informal greeting, and can also be used when taking your leave. The word has been adopted as a motto by the Austrian national tourist office. *Grüss dich* or *Griassdi* (literally 'greet you') is also a familiar, informal greeting. It's especially used by people who don't want to bring God into the conversation (rather than *Grüss Gott* – 'greet God'). For 'goodbye', *Auf Wiederschauen* is the standard phrase; *Baba*, *Pfiati* or *Ciao* are less formal alternatives.

There are a number of ways to describe your lack of sobriety. If you're tipsy you can say *Ich bin beschwipst* or *Ich habe einen Schwips*. If you're definitely the worse for wear, the Viennese dialect expression is *I'hob an dulliö*. If you're very drunk, you could say *Ich bin zu*, though everyone will probably have figured that out already.

Some useful Austrian words are: *Blunzen* (black pudding); *Erdäpfel* (potato); *Faschiertes* (minced meat); *Gerstl* (money); *Karfiol* (cauliflower); *Maroni* (roasted chestnut); *Maut* (toll charge); *Müch* (milk); *Obers* (cream); *Paradeiser* (tomato); *Scherzl* (crust of bread); and *Stamperl* (glass for Schnapps). For more useful food-related words, see p65. To request the bill in a restaurant, simply say *Zahlen, bitte* (pay, please).

Words that are more specifically Viennese include:

Beisl	small tavern for food and drink
Bim	tram
Haberer	friend
Stiftl	glass (for wine)
Verdrahn	to sell

The words and phrases included in this language guide should help you through the most common travel situations. Those with the desire to delve further into the language should get a copy of Lonely Planet's *German Phrasebook*.

GRAMMAR

German grammar can be a nightmare for English speakers. Nouns come in three genders: masculine, feminine and neuter (m/f/n). The corresponding forms of the definite article ('the' in English) are *der, die* and *das*, with the universal plural form, *die*. Nouns and articles will alter according to complex grammatical rules relating to the noun's function within a phrase – known as 'case'. In German there are four cases: nominative, accusative, dative and genitive. We haven't allowed for all possible permutations of case in this language guide – it's simply too complex to cover here. However, bad German is better than no German at all, so even if you muddle your cases, you'll find that you'll still be understood – and your efforts will definitely be appreciated regardless.

If you've noticed that written German seems to be full of capital letters, the reason is that German nouns always begin with a capital letter.

PRONUNCIATION

It's not difficult to pronounce German because almost all sounds can be found in English. Follow the pronunciation guide and you'll have no trouble communicating.

Vowels

German	Pronunciation Guide	
a	a	as the 'u' in 'run'
	ah	as the 'a' in 'father'
ei	ai	as as in 'aisle'
ä	air	as in 'air', with no 'r' sound
oo	aw	as in 'saw'
e	ay	as in 'say'
	e	as in 'bed'
ie	ee	as in 'reef'
ö	er	as in 'her', with no 'r' sound
i	i	as in 'bit'
o	o	as in 'pot'
eu/äu	oy	as in 'toy'
u	oo	as in 'moon'
au	ow	as in 'how'
ü	ü	'ee' said with rounded lips
u	u	as in 'put'

Consonants

The only two tricky consonant sounds in German are **ch** and **r**. All other consonants are pronounced much the same as their English counterparts (except **sch**, which is always as the 'sh' in 'shoe').

The **ch** sound is generally like a hiss from the back of the throat, as in Scottish *loch*. When **ch** occurs after the vowels **e** and **i** it's more like a 'sh' sound, produced with the tongue more forward in the mouth. In this book we've simplified things by using the one symbol 'kh' for both sounds.

The **r** sound is different from English, and it isn't rolled like in Italian or Spanish. It's pronounced at the back of the throat, almost like saying a 'g' sound, but with some friction – a bit like gargling.

Word Stress

As a general rule, word stress in German falls mostly on the first syllable. In our pronunciation guides the stressed syllable is shown in italics.

ACCOMMODATION

Where's a ...?

Wo ist ...?	vaw ist ...
bed and breakfast	
eine Pension	ai·ne pahng·zyawn
camping ground	
ein Campingplatz	ain kem·ping·plats
guesthouse	
eine Pension	ai·ne pahng·zyawn
hotel	
ein Hotel	ain ho·tel
inn	
ein Gasthof	ain gast·hawf
room in a private home	
ein Privatzimmer	ain pri·vaht·tsi·mer
youth hostel	
eine Jugendherberge	ai·ne yoo·gent·her·ber·ge

MAKING A RESERVATION

(for phone and written requests)

To ...	An ...
From ...	Von ...
Date	Datum
I'd like to book ...	Ich möchte ... reservieren.
	(see the list under
	'Accommodation' for
	bed and room options)
in the name of ...	auf den Namen ...
from ... to ... (date)	Vom ... bis zum ...
credit card	Kreditkarte
number	Nummer
expiry date	gültig bis ... (valid until)
Please confirm	Bitte bestätigen Sie
availability and	Verfügbarkeit und Preis.
price.	

What's the address?
Wie ist die Adresse?
vee ist dee a·*dre*·se

I'd like to book a room, please.
Ich möchte bitte ein Zimmer reservieren.
ikh *merkh*·te *bi*·te ain *tsi*·mer re·zer·*vee*·ren

For (three) nights/weeks.
Für (drei) Nächte/Wochen.
für (drai) *nekh*·te/vo·khen

Do you have a ... room?
Haben Sie ein ...?   hah·ben zee ain ...
single
Einzelzimmer   ain·tsel·tsi·mer
double
Doppelzimmer mit   do·pel·tsi·mer mit
einem Doppelbett   ai·nem do·pel·bet
twin
Doppelzimmer mit zwei   do·pel·tsi·mer mit tsvai
Einzelbetten   ain·tsel·be·ten

How much is it per night/person?
Wie viel kostet es   vee feel *kos*·tet es
pro Nacht/Person?   praw nakht/per·*zawn*

May I see it?
Kann ich es sehen?   kan ikh es *zay*·en

Can I get another room?
Kann ich noch ein   kan ikh nokh ain
Zimmer bekommen?   *tsi*·mer be·*ko*·men

It's fine. I'll take it.
Es ist gut, ich nehme es.   es ist goot ikh *nay*·me es

I'm leaving now.
Ich reise jetzt ab.   ikh *rai*·ze yetst ap

CONVERSATION & ESSENTIALS

You should be aware that German uses polite and informal forms for 'you' (*Sie* and *du* respectively). When addressing people you don't know well you should always use the polite form (though younger people will be less inclined to expect it). In this language guide we use the polite form unless indicated by 'inf' (for 'informal') in brackets.

If you need to ask for assistance from a stranger, remember to always introduce your request with a simple *Entschuldigung* (Excuse me, ...).

Good day.
Grüss Gott. (pol)   grüs got
Hello.
Servus/Grüss Dich/   zer·vus/grüs dikh/
Griassdi. (inf)   gree·as·dee

Good ...   *Guten ...*   goo·ten ...
day   *Tag*   tahk
morning   *Morgen*   mor·gen
afternoon   *Tag*   tahk
evening   *Abend*   ah·bent

Goodbye.
Auf Wiedersehen.   owf vee·der·zay·en
Pfiati/Ciao. (inf)   pfya·tee/chau
See you later.
Bis später.   bis shpay·ter
Bye.
Tschüss/Tschau.   chüs/chow
How are you?
Wie geht es Ihnen? (pol)   vee gayt es ee·nen
Wie geht es dir? (inf)   vee gayt es deer
Fine. And you?
Danke, gut.   dang·ke goot
... and you?
Und Ihnen? (pol)   unt ee·nen
Und dir? (inf)   unt deer
What's your name?
Wie ist Ihr Name? (pol)   vee ist eer nah·me
Wie heisst du? (inf)   vee haist doo
My name is ...
Mein Name ist .../   main nah·me ist .../
Ich heisse ...   ikh hai·se ...

Yes.   *Ja.*   yah
No.   *Nein.*   nain
Please.   *Bitte.*   bi·te
Thank you   *Danke./*   dang·ke/
(very much).   *Vielen Dank.*   fee·len dangk
You're welcome.   *Bitte (sehr).*   bi·te (zair)

LANGUAGE

| Sorry. | Entschuldigung. | ent-shul-di-gung |
| Excuse me, ... | Entschuldigung. | ent-shul-di-gung |

(before asking for help or directions)

DIRECTIONS

Could you help me, please?
Können Sie mir bitte helfen?
ker-nen zee meer bi-te hel-fen

Where's (a bank)?
Wo ist (eine Bank)?
vaw ist (ai-ne bangk)

I'm looking for (the cathedral).
Ich suche (den Dom).
ikh zoo-khe (dayn dawm)

Which way's (a public toilet)?
In welcher Richtung ist (eine öffentliche toilette)?
in vel-kher rikh-tung ist (ai-ne er-fent-li-khe to-a-le-te)

How can I get there?
Wie kann ich da hinkommen?
vee kan ikh dah hin-ko-men

How far is it?
Wie weit ist es?
vee vait ist es

Can you show me (on the map)?
Können Sie es mir (auf der Karte) zeigen?
ker-nen zee es meer (owf dair kar-te) tsai-gen

SIGNS

Polizei	Police
Polizeiwache	Police Station
Eingang	Entrance
Ausgang	Exit
Offen	Open
Geschlossen	Closed
Kein Zutritt	No Entry
Rauchen Verboten	No Smoking
Verboten	Prohibited
Toiletten (WC)	Toilets
Herren	Men
Damen	Women

---

near	nahe	nah-e
far away	weit weg	vait vek
here	hier	heer
there	dort	dort
on the corner	an der Ecke	an dair e-ke
straight ahead	geradeaus	ge-rah-de-ows
opposite ...	gegenüber ...	gay-gen-ü-ber ...
next to ...	neben ...	nay-ben ...
behind ...	hinter ...	hin-ter ...
in front of ...	vor ...	fawr ...
north	Norden	nor-den
south	Süden	zü-den

| east | Osten | os-ten |
| west | Westen | ves-ten |

Turn ...
Biegen Sie ... ab.
bee-gen zee ... ap
left/right
links/rechts
lingks/rekhts
at the next corner
an der nächsten Ecke
an dair naykhs-ten e-ke
at the traffic lights
bei der Ampel
bai dair am-pel

EMERGENCIES

Help!
Hilfe!
hil-fe
It's an emergency!
Es ist ein Notfall!
es ist ain nawt-fal
Call the police!
Rufen Sie die Polizei!
roo-fen zee dee po-li-tsai
Call a doctor!
Rufen Sie einen Arzt!
roo-fen zee ai-nen artst
Call an ambulance!
Rufen Sie einen
roo-fen zee ai-nen
Krankenwagen!
krang-ken-vah-gen
Leave me alone!
Lassen Sie mich in Ruhe! la-sen zee mikh in roo-e
Go away!
Gehen Sie weg!
gay-en zee vek
I'm lost.
Ich habe mich verirrt.
ikh hah-be mikh fer-irt

HEALTH

Where's the nearest ...?
Wo ist der/die/das nächste ...? (m/f/n)
vaw ist dair/die/das naykhs-te ...
chemist
Apotheke (f)
a-po-tay-ke
dentist
Zahnarzt (m)
tsahn-artst
doctor
Arzt (m)
artst
hospital
Krankenhaus (n)
krang-ken-hows

I need a doctor.
Ich brauche einen Arzt.
ikh brow-khe ai-nen artst
Is there a (night) chemist nearby?
Gibt es in der Nähe eine (Nacht)Apotheke?
gipt es in dair nay-e ai-ne (nakht-)a-po-tay-ke
I'm sick.
Ich bin krank.
ikh bin krangk

It hurts here.
Es tut hier weh.
es toot heer *vay*
I've been vomiting.
Ich habe mich übergeben.
ikh *hah*·be mikh ü·ber·*gay*·ben
I have diarrhoea/fever/headache.
Ich habe Durchfall/Fieber/Kopfschmerzen.
ikh *hah*·be durkh·fal/*fee*·ber/*kopf*·shmer·tsen
(I think) I'm pregnant.
(Ich glaube,) Ich bin schwanger.
(ikh *glow*·be) ikh bin *shvang*·er

I'm allergic to ...
Ich bin allergisch gegen ... ikh bin a·*lair*·gish *gay*·gen ...
  antibiotics
  Antibiotika an·ti·bi·*aw*·ti·ka
  aspirin
  Aspirin as·pi·*reen*
  penicillin
  Penizillin pe·ni·tsi·*leen*

LANGUAGE DIFFICULTIES
Do you speak English?
Sprechen Sie Englisch?
shpre·khen zee *eng*·lish
Does anyone here speak English?
Spricht hier jemand Englisch?
shprikht heer *yay*·mant *eng*·lish
Do you understand (me)?
Verstehen Sie (mich)?
fer·*shtay*·en zee (mikh)
I (don't) understand.
Ich verstehe (nicht).
ikh fer·*shtay*·e (nikht)
How do you say ... in German?
Wie sagt man ... auf Deutsch?
vee zagt man ... owf doytsh

Could you please ...?
Könnten Sie ...? *kern*·ten zee ...
  speak more slowly
  bitte langsamer sprechen *bi*·te *lang*·za·mer *shpre*·khen
  repeat that
  das bitte wiederholen das *bi*·te vee·der·*haw*·len
  write it down
  das bitte aufschreiben das *bi*·te owf·shrai·ben

NUMBERS
0	*null*	nul
1	*ains*	aints
2	*zwei*	tsvai
3	*drei*	drai
4	*vier*	feer
5	*fünf*	fünf

6	*sechs*	zeks
7	*sieben*	*zee*·ben
8	*acht*	akht
9	*neun*	noyn
10	*zehn*	tsayn
11	*elf*	elf
12	*zwölf*	zverlf
13	*dreizehn*	*drai*·tsayn
14	*vierzehn*	*feer*·tsayn
15	*fünfzehn*	*fünf*·tsayn
16	*sechzehn*	*zeks*·tsayn
17	*siebzehn*	*zeep*·tsayn
18	*achtzehn*	*akh*·tsayn
19	*neunzehn*	*noyn*·tsayn
20	*zwanzig*	*tsvan*·tsikh
21	*einundzwanzig*	*ain*·unt·tsvan·tsikh
22	*zweiundzwanig*	*tsvai*·unt·tsvan·tsikh
30	*dreizig*	*drai*·tsikh
31	*einunddreizig*	*ain*·und·*drai*·tsikh
40	*vierzig*	*feer*·tsikh
50	*fünfzig*	*fünf*·tsikh
60	*sechzig*	*zekh*·tsikh
70	*siebzig*	*zeep*·tsikh
80	*achtzig*	*akh*·tsikh
90	*neunzig*	*noyn*·tsikh
100	*hundert*	*hun*·dert
1000	*tausend*	*tow*·sent
2000	*zwei tausend*	tsvai *tow*·sent

PAPERWORK
name	*Name*	*nah*·me
nationality	*Staatsan-*	*shtahts*·an-
	gehörigkeit	ge·*her*·rikh·kait
date of birth	*Geburtsdatum*	ge·*burts*·dah·tum
place of birth	*Geburtsort*	ge·*burts*·ort
sex/gender	*Sex*	seks
passport	*(Reise)Pass*	(*rai*·ze·)pahs
visa	*Visum*	*vee*·zum

QUESTION WORDS
Who?	*Wer?*	vair
What?	*Was?*	vas
Where?	*Wo?*	vo
When?	*Wann?*	van
How?	*Wie?*	vee
Why?	*Warum?*	va·*rum*
Which?	*Welcher?*	*vel*·kher
How much?	*Wie viel?*	vee feel
How many?	*Wie viele?*	vee *fee*·le

SHOPPING & SERVICES
I'm looking for ...
Ich suche ...
ikh *zoo*·khe ...

Where's the (nearest) ...?
Wo ist der/die/das (nächste) ...? (m/f/n)
vaw ist dair/dee/das (naykhs·te) ...

What time does it open/close?
Wann macht er/sie/es auf/zu? (m/f/n)
van makht air/zee/es owf/tsoo

Where can I buy ...?
Wo kann ich ... kaufen?
vaw kan ikh ... kow·fen

an ATM	*ein Geldautomat*	ain gelt·ow·to·maht
an exchange office	*eine Geldwechsel-stube*	ai·ne gelt·vek·sel·shtoo·be
a bank	*eine Bank*	ai·ne bangk
the ... embassy	*die ... Botschaft*	dee bot·shaft
the hospital	*das Krankenhaus*	das krang·ken·hows
the market	*der Markt*	dair markt
the police	*die Polizei*	dee po·li·tsai
the post office	*das Postamt*	das post·amt
a public phone	*ein öffentliches Telefon*	ain er·fent·li·khes te·le·fawn
a public toilet	*eine öffentliche Toilette*	ain er·fent·li·khe to·a·le·te

I'd like to buy ...
Ich möchte ... kaufen.
ikh merkh·te ... kow·fen

How much (is this)?
Wie viel (kostet das)?
vee feel (kos·tet das)

That's too much/expensive.
Das ist zu viel/teuer.
das ist tsoo feel/toy·er

Can you lower the price?
Können Sie mit dem Preis heruntergehen?
ker·nen zee mit dem prais he·run·ter·gay·en

Do you have something cheaper?
Haben Sie etwas Billigeres?
hah·ben zee et·vas bi·li·ge·res

I'm just looking.
Ich schaue mich nur um.
ikh show·e mikh noor um

Can you write down the price?
Können Sie den Preis aufschreiben?
ker·nen zee dayn prais owf·shrai·ben

Do you have any others?
Haben Sie noch andere?
hah·ben zee nokh an·de·re

Can I look at (it)?
Können Sie (ihn/sie/es) mir zeigen? (m/f/n)
ker·nen zee (een/zee/es) meer tsai·gen

more	*mehr*	mair
less	*weniger*	vay·ni·ger
smaller	*kleiner*	klai·ner·tee
bigger	*grosser*	gro·ser

Do you accept ...?
Nehmen Sie ...?   nay·men zee ...
  credit cards
  Kreditkarten   kre·deet·kar·ten
  travellers cheques
  Reisechecks   rai·ze·sheks

I'd like to ...
Ich möchte ...   ikh merkh·te ...
  change money (cash)
  Geld umtauschen   gelt um·tow·shen
  cash a cheque
  einen Scheck einlösen   ai·nen shek ain·ler·zen
  change some travellers cheques
  Reisechecks einlösen   rai·ze·sheks ain·ler·zen

I want to buy a phone card.
Ich möchte eine Telefonkarte kaufen.
ikh merkh·te ai·ne te·le·fawn·kar·te kow·fen

Where's the local Internet cafe?
Wo ist hier ein Internet-Café?
vaw ist heer ain in·ter·net·ka·fay

I'd like to ...
Ich möchte ...   ikh merkh·te ...
  get Internet access
  Internetzugang haben   in·ter·net·tsoo·gang hah·ben
  check my email
  meine E-Mails checken   mai·ne ee·mayls che·ken

TIME & DATES

What time is it?
Wie spät ist es?   vee shpayt ist es

It's (one) o'clock.
Es ist (ein) Uhr.   es ist (ain) oor

Twenty past one.
Zwanzig nach eins.   tsvan·tsikh nahkh ains

Half past one.
Halb zwei. ('half two')   halp tsvai

Quarter to one.
Viertel vor eins.   fir·tel fawr ains

am
  morgens/vormittags   mor·gens/fawr·mi·tahks

pm
  nachmittags/abends   nahkh·mi·tahks/ah·bents

now	*jetzt*	yetst
today	*heute*	hoy·te
tonight	*heute Abend*	hoy·te ah·bent
tomorrow	*morgen*	mor·gen
yesterday	*gestern*	ges·tern
morning	*Morgen*	mor·gen
afternoon	*Nachmittag*	nahkh·mi·tahk
evening	*Abend*	ah·bent

Monday	Montag	*mawn*-tahk
Tuesday	Dienstag	*deens*-tahk
Wednesday	Mittwoch	*mit*-vokh
Thursday	Donnerstag	*do*-ners-tahk
Friday	Freitag	*frai*-tahk
Saturday	Samstag	*zams*-tahk
Sunday	Sonntag	*zon*-tahk

January	Januar	*yan*-u-ahr
February	Februar	*fay*-bru-ahr
March	März	merts
April	April	a-*pril*
May	Mai	mai
June	Juni	*yoo*-ni
July	Juli	*yoo*-li
August	August	ow-*gust*
September	September	zep-*tem*-ber
October	Oktober	ok-*taw*-ber
November	November	no-*vem*-ber
December	Dezember	de-*tsem*-ber

TRANSPORT
Public Transport
What time does the ... leave?
Wann fährt ... ab?
van fairt ... ap

boat
das Boot — das bawt
bus
der Bus — dair bus
train
der Zug — dair tsook
tram
die Strassenbahn — dee *shtrah*-sen-bahn

What time's the ... bus?
Wann fährt der ... Bus?
van fairt dair ... bus

first
erste — *ers*-te
last
letzte — *lets*-te
next
nächste — *naykhs*-te

Where's the nearest metro station?
Wo ist der nächste U-Bahnhof?
vaw ist dair *naykhs*-te *oo*-bahn-hawf
Which bus goes to ...?
Welcher Bus fährt ...?
vel-kher bus fairt ...

A ... ticket to (Innsbruck).
Einen ... nach (Innsbruck).
ai-nen ... nahkh (*eens*-brook)

one-way
einfache Fahrkarte — *ain*-fa-khe *fahr*-kar-te
return
Rückfahrkarte — *rük*-fahr-kar-te
1st-class
Fahrkarte erster Klasse — *fahr*-kar-te *ers*-ter *kla*-se
2nd-class
Fahrkarte zweiter Klasse — *fahr*-kar-te *tsvai*-ter *kla*-se

The ... is cancelled.
... ist gestrichen. — ... ist ge-*shtri*-khen
The ... is delayed.
... hat Verspätung. — ... hat fer-*shpay*-tung
Is this seat free?
Ist dieser Platz frei? — ist *dee*-zer plats frai
Do I need to change trains?
Muss ich umsteigen? — mus ikh *um*-shtai-gen
Are you free? (taxi)
Sind Sie frei? — zint zee frai
How much is it to ...?
Was kostet es bis ...? — vas *kos*-tet es bis ...
Please take me to (this address).
Bitte bringen Sie mich — *bi*-te *bring*-en zee mikh
zu (dieser Adresse). — tsoo (*dee*-zer a-*dre*-se)

Private Transport
Where can I hire a ...?
Wo kann ich ... mieten?
vaw kan ikh ... *mee*-ten
I'd like to hire a/an ...
Ich möchte ... mieten.
ikh *merkh*-te ... *mee*-ten

automatic
ein Fahrzeug mit — ain *fahr*-tsoyk mit
Automatik — *ow*-to-*mah*-tik
bicycle
ein Fahrrad — ain *fahr*-raht
car
ein Auto — ain *ow*-to
4WD
ein Allradfahrzeug — ain *al*-raht-fahr-tsoyk
manual
ein Fahrzeug — ain *fahr*-tsoyk
mit Schaltung — mit *shal*-tung
motorbike
ein Motorrad — ain *maw*-tor-raht

How much is it per day/week?
Wie viel kostet es pro Tag/Woche?
vee feel *kos*-tet es praw tahk/*vo*-khe

petrol (gas)	Benzin	ben-*tseen*
diesel	Diesel	*dee*-zel
leaded	verbleites	fer-*blai*-tes
	Benzin	ben-*tseen*

ROAD SIGNS

Gefahr	Danger
Einfahrt Verboten	No Entry
Einbahnstrasse	One Way
Einfahrt	Entrance
Ausfahrt	Exit
Ausfahrt Freihalten	Keep Clear
Parkverbot	No Parking
Halteverbot	No Stopping
Mautstelle	Toll
Radweg	Cycle Path
Umleitung	Detour
Überholverbot	No Overtaking

LPG	Autogas	ow·to·gahs
regular	Normalbenzin	nor·mahl·ben·tseen
unleaded	bleifreies	blai·frai·es
	Benzin	ben·tseen

Where's a petrol station?
Wo ist eine Tankstelle?
vaw ist *ai*·ne *tangk*·shte·le

Does this road go to ...?
Führt diese Strasse nach ...?
fürt *dee*·ze *shtrah*·se nahkh ...

(How long) Can I park here?
(Wie lange) Kann ich hier parken?
(vee *lang*·e) kan ikh heer *par*·ken

Where do I pay?
Wo muss ich bezahlen?
vaw mus ikh be·*tsah*·len

I need a mechanic.
Ich brauche einen Mechaniker.
ikh *brow*·khe *ai*·nen me·*khah*·ni·ker

The car has broken down (at ...)
Ich habe (in ...) eine Panne mit meinem Auto.
ikh *hah*·be (in ...) *ai*·ne *pa*·ne mit *mai*·nem *ow*·to

I had an accident.
Ich hatte einen Unfall.
ikh *ha*·te *ai*·nen *un*·fal

The car/motorbike won't start.
Das Auto/Motorrad springt nicht an.
das *ow*·to/*maw*·tor·raht shpringkt nikht an

I have a flat tyre.
Ich habe eine Reifenpanne.
ikh *hah*·be *ai*·ne *rai*·fen·pa·ne

I've run out of petrol.
Ich habe kein Benzin mehr.
ikh *hah*·be kain ben·*tseen* mair

TRAVEL WITH CHILDREN

I need a/an ...
Ich brauche ...   ikh *brow*·khe ...

Is there a/an ...?
Gibt es ...?   gipt es ...

baby change room	
einen Wickelraum	*ai*·nen *vi*·kel·rowm
baby seat	
einen Babysitz	*ai*·nen *bay*·bi·zits
booster seat	
einen Kindersitz	*ai*·nen *kin*·der·zits
child-minding service	
einen Babysitter-Service	*ai*·nen *bay*·bi·si·ter·ser·vis
children's menu	
eine Kinderkarte	*ai*·ne *kin*·der·kar·te
(English-speaking) babysitter	
einen (englisch-	*ai*·nen (*eng*·lish-
sprachigen) Babysitter	shprah·khi·gen) *bay*·bi·si·ter
highchair	
einen Kinderstuhl	*ai*·nen *kin*·der·shtool
potty	
ein Kindertöpfchen	ain *kin*·der·terpf·khen
stroller	
einen Kinderwagen	*ai*·nen *kin*·der·vah·gen

Do you mind if I breastfeed here?
Kann ich meinem Kind hier die Brust geben?
kan ikh *mai*·nem kint heer dee brust *gay*·ben

Are children allowed?
Sind Kinder erlaubt?
zint *kin*·der er·*lowpt*

Also available from Lonely Planet:
German Phrasebook

Glossary

Abfahrt – departure (trains)
Altstadt – old city
Ankunft – arrival (trains)
ANTO – Austrian National Tourist Office
Apotheken – pharmacy
Auto – car
Autobahn – motorway

Bad – bath
Bahnhof – train station
Bahnsteig – train station platform
Bankomat – ATM; cash point
Bauernhof – farmhouse
Bauernmarkt – farmers market
Beisl – small tavern or restaurant
Benzin – unleaded petrol
Berg – hill or mountain
Bergbahn – cable car
Bezirk – district in a town or city
Bibliothek – library
Biedermeier period – 19th-century art movement in Germany and Austria
Botschaft – embassy
Brauerei – brewery
Briefmarken – stamps
Brunnen – fountain
Bundesbus – state bus; run by the railway (Bahnhbus) or the post office (Postbus)
Burg – castle/fortress
Buschenschank (Buschenschenken) – wine tavern(s)

Café Konditorei(en) – café/cake shop(s)
Christkindlmärkt – Christmas market

DAV – German Alpine Club
Dirndl – women's traditional dress
Donau – Danube
Dorf – village

EC – EuroCity; express train
EEA – European Economic Area; comprises European Union states plus Iceland, Liechtenstein and Norway
EN – EuroNight; international and domestic night train
EU – European Union

Fahrplan – timetable
Feiertag – public holiday
Ferienwohnung(en) – self-catering holiday apartment(s)
Festung – fortress

Fiaker – fiacre; small horse-drawn carriage
Flohmarkt – flea market
Flughafen – airport
Fluss – river
Föhn – hot, dry wind that sweeps down from the mountains, mainly in early spring and autumn
FPÖ – Freedom Party (politics)
Freizeitzentrum – sports and leisure centre
Friedhof – cemetery

Gästehaus – guesthouse; sometimes has a restaurant
Gästekarte – guest card; issued by hostels and resorts, used to obtain discounts
Gasthaus – inn or restaurant without accommodation
Gasthof – inn or restaurant; usually has accommodation
Gemeindeamt – local authority office

Hafen – harbour; port
Handy – mobile phone
Hauptbahnhof – main train station
Hauptpost – main post office
Hauptstadt – capital
Heuriger (Heurigen) – wine tavern(s)

IC – InterCity; express train

Jugendherberge/Jugendgästehaus – youth hostel

Kaffeehaus – coffee house
Kapelle – chapel
Kärnten – Carinthia (Austrian province)
Kino – cinema
Kirche – church
Klettern – rock climbing
Konsulat(e) – consulate(s)
Krankenhaus – hospital
Krügerl – glass holding 0.5L
Kunst – art
Kurzparkzone – short-term parking zone

Landesmuseum – provincial museum
Langlauf – cross-country skiing
Lieder – lyrical song
LKW – bus

Mahlzeit – Austrian salutation at the commencement of a meal
Markt – market
Maut – toll (or indicating a toll booth)
Mehrwertsteuer (MWST) – value-added tax

Melange – coffee
Mensa – university cafeteria
Mitfahrzentrale – hitching organisation
Münze – coins

ÖAMTC – national motoring organisation
ÖAV – Austrian Alpine Club
ÖBB – Austrian federal railway
Österreich – Austria
ÖVP – Austrian People's Party (politics)

Parkschein – parking voucher
Pension – B&B
Pfarrkirche – parish church
Pfiff – glass holding 0.125L
PKW – car
Platz – town or village square
Polizei – police
Postamt – post office
Postlagernde Briefe – poste restante
Privat Zimmer – private rooms (accommodation)

Rad – bicycle
radfahren – cycling
Radler – mixture of beer and lemonade
Rathaus – town hall
Reisebüro – travel agency

S-Bahn – suburban train system
SC – SuperCity; express train
Schloss – palace; castle
Secession movement – early 20th-century movement
in Vienna seeking to establish a more functional style in
architecture; led by Otto Wagner (1841–1918)
See – lake
sgraffito – mural or decoration in which the top layer
is scratched off to reveal the original colour/medium
underneath
Silvester – New Year's Eve

skifahren – skiing
Stadt – city
Stadtmuseum – city museum
Stadtpfarrkirch – see *Pfarrkirche*
Steiermark – Styria (Austrian province)
Stift – abbey
Stock – floor, in a multi-storied building
Strandbad – designated bathing area on a lake or river;
usually has an entry fee
Studentenheime – student residences
surfen – wind surfing

Tabak – tobacconist
Tagesteller/Tagesmenü – the set dish or meal of the
day in a restaurant; sometimes abbreviated as 'Menü'
Tal – valley
Telefon-Wertkarte – phonecard
Tirol – Tyrol
Tor – gate
Triebwagen – railcar

U-Bahn – urban underground rail system

Verein – club
Vienna Circle – group of philosophers centred on Vienna
University in the 1920s and 1930s
Vienna Group – avant-garde art/literary movement
formed in the 1950s

Wald – forest
wandern – walking/hiking
Wein – wine
Wien – Vienna
Wiener Gruppe – see *Vienna Group*
Wiener Kreis – see *Vienna Circle*
Würstel Stand – sausage stand

Zimmer frei – see *Privat Zimmer*
Zug – train

The Authors

ANTHONY HAYWOOD
Coordinating Author

Anthony was born in the port city of Fremantle, Western Australia, and pulled anchor early on to travel Europe and the US, mostly hitchhiking in those days. At that time Aberystwyth in Wales and Ealing in London were his wintering grounds. He later studied comparative literature in Perth and Russian at university in Melbourne. In the 1990s, fresh from a spell in post-Soviet, pre-anything Moscow, he moved to Germany. Today he works as a German-based writer and journalist and divides his time between Göttingen (Lower Saxony) and Berlin. Since a first encounter with Austria and the Austrians in the 1980s he's frequently returned to explore regions, swim lakes and annoy Viennese waiters.

For this edition, Anthony wrote the following chapters: Destination, Getting Started, Itineraries, History, The Culture, Food & Drink, Vienna, Lower Austria, Burgenland, Styria, The Salzkammergut, Carinthia, Directory, and Transport. He also contributed to the Walking in Austria chapter.

KERRY WALKER

After completing a languages degree, Kerry spent four years trotting the globe with a crazy German (her boyfriend, Andy). She vividly remembers her first encounter with *real* snow in the Tyrolean Alps, which sparked her love of Austria. Her memorable experiences writing this guide include star-trekking through a forest by night in Salzburger Land and waking up to the squeal of newborn piglets on a farm in Upper Austria. Born in Essex, Kerry's new home is the Black Forest, where she can be found hiking in the hills when not on her travels.

For this edition, Kerry wrote the following chapters: Environment, Outdoor Activities, Walking in Austria, Upper Austria, Salzburg & Salzburger Land, Hohe Tauern National Park Region, Tyrol and Vorarlberg.

Behind the Scenes

THIS BOOK

This 5th edition of Austria was coordinated by Anthony Haywood with assistance from co-author Kerry Walker. The Health chapter is based on original research by Dr Caroline Evans. The 4th edition was written by Neal Bedford and Gemma Pitcher. The first three editions were written by Mark Honan. This guidebook was commissioned in Lonely Planet's London office, and produced by the following:

Commissioning Editors Korina Miller, Fayette Fox
Coordinating Editors Rosie Nicholson, Dianne Schallmeiner
Coordinating Cartographer Jacqueline Nguyen
Coordinating Layout Designer Margaret Jung
Managing Editors Bruce Evans, Katie Lynch
Managing Cartographer David Connolly
Managing Layout Designer Adam McCrow
Assisting Editors Nigel Chin, Peter Cruttenden, Barbara Delissen, Shawn Low, Sally O'Brien, Susan Paterson, Diana Saad, Laura Stansfeld, Helen Yeates
Assisting Cartographers Alissa Baker, Anita Banh, Anna Clarkson, Csanad Csutoros, Mick Garrett, Peter Shields
Cover Designer Brendan Dempsey
Project Manager Rachel Imeson
Language Content Coordinator Quentin Frayne

Thanks to Katrina Browning, Andrea Dobbin, Janine Eberle, Jennifer Garrett, Imogen Hall, Lisa Knights, Celia Wood

THANKS
ANTHONY HAYWOOD

I'd like to thank predecessor authors Neal Bedford, Gemma Pitcher and Mark Honan – Neal especially for his good advice, even better party, and help with digs in Vienna. Big thanks to my commissioning editor Korina Miller and co-author Kerry Walker for their professionalism and good humour, and Mark Griffiths for mapping advice. The folks at MICA, especially Helge Hinteregger, provided lots of info and food for thought on music. Thanks also to Dr Stalzer from the Jüdisches Museum and to Peter Sigmund and colleagues from Marketing in the Donau-Niederösterreich Tourismus GmbH. Bernhard Schragl provided expert insight into the Toplitzsee. Many other people gave valuable assistance along the way. To name just a few: Frau Stuckstedde from Tourist Info Wien; Frau Geistberger in Bad Aussee; Johann Puchinger in Obertraun (especially for some useful tips on hiking trails); the people at Salzkammergut Touristik; Thomas Kalt in Villach; Corinna Moser in Spittal an der Drau; Thomas Möslinger in Bad Ischl; and Frau Hosp Gmunden. Last but not least, thanks to Sylvia for her support and to Freddie for biting me whenever I didn't move for a long period during write up.

SEND US YOUR FEEDBACK

We love to hear from travellers – your comments keep us on our toes and help make our books better. Our well-travelled team reads every word on what you loved or loathed about this book. Although we cannot reply individually to postal submissions, we always guarantee that your feedback goes straight to the appropriate authors, in time for the next edition. Each person who sends us information is thanked in the next edition – and the most useful submissions are rewarded with a free book.

To send us your updates – and find out about Lonely Planet events, newsletters and travel news – visit our award-winning website: **www.lonelyplanet.com/contact**.

Note: we may edit, reproduce and incorporate your comments in Lonely Planet products such as guidebooks, websites and digital products, so let us know if you don't want your comments reproduced or your name acknowledged. For a copy of our privacy policy visit www.lonelyplanet.com/privacy.

KERRY WALKER

Enormous thanks to my boyfriend, soul mate and travel companion Andy Christiani, who deserves a gold medal for his enthusiasm and support in researching this guide (and all those hours spent behind the wheel!). At Lonely Planet, special thanks to Korina Miller for entrusting me with this gig, Anthony Haywood for his advice and ideas, and Mark Griffiths for helping out with mapping issues. Sincere thanks to all the tourist professionals who made my life easier, particularly Dr Eduardo Santander and Rainer Ammann in Innsbruck; Maria Altendorfer in Salzburg; Doris Dengg in Mayrhofen; Isabella Staffner in Kufstein; and Ingrid Wohlfarter in Landeck. A great big thank you to the locals I met on the road who shared their fascinating stories: Gretl Aicher at Salzburger Marionettentheater; Sepp Holzer at Krameterhof; Peter Habeler in Mayrhofen; and Fritz Rath in Linz. Last but by no means least, thanks to the cool crowd in St Anton, especially Maggie and Chris Ritson, for their invaluable (and hilarious) tips on skiing and après-skiing.

OUR READERS

Many thanks to the travellers who used the last edition and wrote to us with helpful hints, useful advice and interesting anecdotes:

Savvas Apostolou, Adzura Azam, Emmanuelle de Mer, Julieanne & Stephen Dimitrios, Alzola Garrido, Paul M. Grant, Klaus Handler, Rachel Hewgill, Martin Hölzl, Andrew Hood, David M Hunt, Cheryl Johnston, Sat Kiwi, Stefan Lederer, Susanne Lenhart, Bob Morris, Paula New, Ralph Nicholls, Paul Ohashi, Debbie Porter, Jose Ramon, Katharina Schroeder, Simon Thomas, Kenneth Toyne, Mike van de Water, Richard Wade, Felix Widmer, Liz Wightwick, John Woods, Joseph Yeomans

ACKNOWLEDGMENTS

Many thanks to the following for the use of their content:

Globe on title page ©Mountain High Maps 1993 Digital Wisdom, Inc.

Internal photographs by Andy Christiani p8 (#1), p11 (#3 & #4), p14 (#2); Jamie Baker/Alamy p10 (#1); Jon Sparks/Alamy p10 (#2); Fantisek Staud/Alamy p12 (#1); Ribisl/Alamy p12 (#2); Jo Kirchherr p13 (#3); PBA/Alamy p13 (#4 & #5), p14 (#1). All other photographs by Lonely Planet Images, and by Jon Davison p5; Greg Elms p6 (#1); Mark Honan p6 (#2), p7 (#3); Witold Skrypczak p7 (#4); Martin Moos p8 (#2), p9 (#3 & #4), p15 (#3); Richard Nebesky p15 (#4); Gareth Mc Cormack p16.

Index

INDEX

INDEX

INDEX

GreenDex

Everyone's 'going green' these days and Austria is leading the way in many areas, from ecofriendly ski resorts to widespread recycling and organic farming. But how do you know which businesses are actually ecofriendly and which are simply jumping on the eco/sustainable bandwagon?

The following sights, activities, eating and accommodation choices have been selected by Lonely Planet authors because they demonstrate a commitment to sustainability. We've selected restaurants and hotels which serve up organic food or support local producers. Attractions are listed because they're involved in conservation or environmental education. For more tips about travelling sustainably in Austria, turn to the Getting Started chapter (p21).

If you think we've missed anywhere out, or if you disagree with our choices, email us at talk2us@lonelyplanet.com.au and set us straight for next time. For more information about sustainable tourism and Lonely Planet, see www.lonelyplanet.com/responsibletravel.

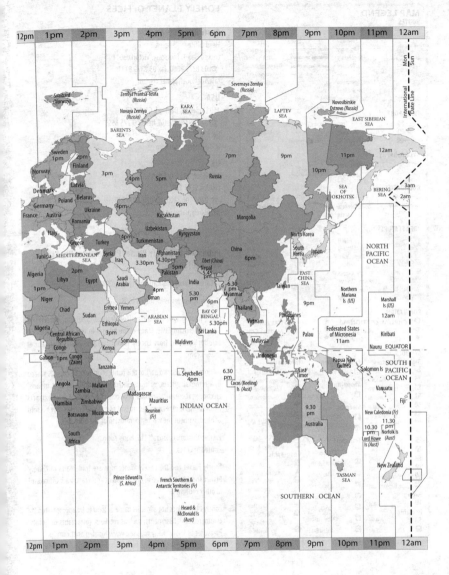

MAP LEGEND

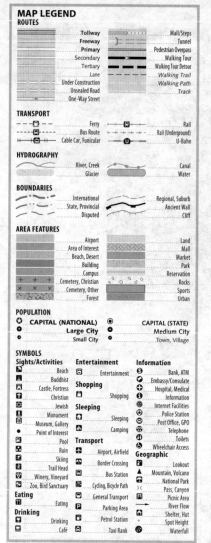

ROUTES
Tollway	Mall/Steps
Freeway	Tunnel
Primary	Pedestrian Overpass
Secondary	Walking Tour
Tertiary	Walking Tour Detour
Lane	Walking Trail
Under Construction	Walking Path
Unsealed Road	Track
One-Way Street	

TRANSPORT
Ferry	Rail
Bus Route	Rail (Underground)
Cable Car, Funicular	U-Bahn

HYDROGRAPHY
River, Creek	Canal
Glacier	Water

BOUNDARIES
International	Regional, Suburb
State, Provincial	Ancient Wall
Disputed	Cliff

AREA FEATURES
Airport	Land
Area of Interest	Mall
Beach, Desert	Market
Building	Park
Campus	Reservation
Cemetery, Christian	Rocks
Cemetery, Other	Sports
Forest	Urban

POPULATION
CAPITAL (NATIONAL)	CAPITAL (STATE)
Large City	Medium City
Small City	Town, Village

SYMBOLS

Sights/Activities
- Beach
- Buddhist
- Castle, Fortress
- Christian
- Jewish
- Monument
- Museum, Gallery
- Point of Interest
- Pool
- Ruin
- Skiing
- Trail Head
- Winery, Vineyard
- Zoo, Bird Sanctuary

Eating
- Eating

Drinking
- Drinking
- Café

Entertainment
- Entertainment

Shopping
- Shopping

Sleeping
- Sleeping
- Camping

Transport
- Airport, Airfield
- Border Crossing
- Bus Station
- Cycling, Bicycle Path
- General Transport
- Parking Area
- Petrol Station
- Taxi Rank

Information
- Bank, ATM
- Embassy/Consulate
- Hospital, Medical
- Information
- Internet Facilities
- Police Station
- Post Office, GPO
- Telephone
- Toilets
- Wheelchair Access

Geographic
- Lookout
- Mountain, Volcano
- National Park
- Pass, Canyon
- Picnic Area
- River Flow
- Shelter, Hut
- Spot Height
- Waterfall

LONELY PLANET OFFICES

Australia
Head Office
Locked Bag 1, Footscray, Victoria 3011
☎ 03 8379 8000, fax 03 8379 8111
talk2us@lonelyplanet.com.au

USA
150 Linden St, Oakland, CA 94607
☎ 510 893 8555, toll free 800 275 8555
fax 510 893 8572
info@lonelyplanet.com

UK
2nd Floor, 186 City Road,
London ECV1 2NT
☎ 020 7106 2100, fax 020 7106 2101
go@lonelyplanet.co.uk

Published by Lonely Planet Publications Pty Ltd
ABN 36 005 607 983

© Lonely Planet Publications Pty Ltd 2008

© photographers as indicated 2008

Cover photograph: Hot air balloon festival, Salzburg, Österreich, Schmid Reinhard/SIME. Many of the images in this guide are available for licensing from Lonely Planet Images: www.lonelyplanet images.com.

Printed through Colorcraft Ltd, Hong Kong.
Printed in China.